MONEY, CLASS, AND PARTY

An Economic Study of Civil War and Reconstruction

MONEY, CLASS, AND PARTY

*An Economic Study of Civil War
and Reconstruction*

By

ROBERT P. SHARKEY

BALTIMORE
THE JOHNS HOPKINS PRESS

Library of Congress Catalog Card Number 59-15423
This book was brought to publication with the
assistance of a grant from The Ford Foundation.
Originally Published, 1959
Second Printing, 1960
Third Printing, 1966
Johns Hopkins Paperbacks edition, 1967

TO MY MOTHER

TOMMY MCCOUN

FOREWORD

By C. Vann Woodward

Reading over Robert Sharkey's monograph again revives pleasant memories of seminars a decade or more ago at Johns Hopkins, where the key ideas of this work were developed in papers that he presented. Rereading it also raises some puzzling questions about pedagogy and research, about teachers and their craft, about students and what they learn, and about historical interpretation and how it develops.

For what Bob Sharkey was " taught," if that is the word, is not what he " learned," if his own teachings are the test. What he was taught about Reconstruction, at least for my part of the teaching, was something quite different. Nor was what I taught what I in turn had been taught at the feet of my first master in the subject. That was Professor Joseph Gregoire de Roulhac Hamilton of Chapel Hill, a worthy and charming representative of the Old South and an outstanding member of the old school, the Dunning School. But my teachings certainly *did* reflect the views of my second instructor in Reconstruction history—Howard Kennedy Beale.

Howard Beale's book *The Critical Year* was a sort of emancipation proclamation for young Southerners in the early 1930's. By that time it was clearly apparent that they could no longer continue to take refuge in the Dunning interpretation. Its demonology was dated, its racial bias unacceptable, its defensive stance embarrassing, and practically everyone under twenty-five agreed that it was old hat. The Marxians offered an alternative, and we experimented self-consciously with their vocabulary. But the freedmen did not make a very conventional proletariat, and there were always odds and ends left over that would not fit into the dialectic. Then came Howard Beale, a real Yankee of unimpeachable credentials, advanced views on race, and a crusading liberalism to boot.

In effect, what Beale told us was that we could have our cake and eat it, too. One could embrace an economic interpretation of Reconstruction without embracing dialectical materialism. One could renounce the Radicals and take high moral grounds in so doing. One could even endorse the professed moral aims of Radical Reconstruction and at the same time convict their advocates of hypocrisy. But most important of all, one could take the sting out of the century-old moral indictment of one's people by demonstrating the insincerity of their accusers. For Beale had shown the whole Radical crusade to be a mask to hide an essentially selfish, sectional, "business-industrialist" program that was harmful or indifferent to the mass of people North and South.

Charles Beard's unmasking of the members of the Federal Convention of 1787 never had the potent visceral appeal of Beale's unmasking of the Radicals, at least for Southerners. There were few, after all, who questioned that, all things considered, the Constitution of the United States was "a good thing." On the other hand there were quite a few, North and South, who entertained some unresolved doubts about Reconstruction. Moreover, as Sharkey points out, the Republican party was in rather low repute during the thirties, vulnerable to the suspicion of being friends of selfish business interests and indifferent to popular needs. With Beale for backing, one could now convict the party, at the moment of its highest moral and humanitarian pretensions, of covertly pursuing the traditional policy of serving selfish interests under the guise of humanitarian aims. In doing so it divided its opponents, who, though regrettably somewhat insensitive to the cause of the freedmen, were the true friends of the people.

This outlook was still viable in the intellectual community, at least during the early years of the Eisenhower Era. What Sharkey did to disturb the intellectual peace was to start picking away at the simplistic identification of the Republicans with the "business" community. He was not attempting moral rehabilitation or a whitewash. He simply pointed out how often "good" Republicans were divided over economic questions, especially money and tariff issues. Republicans were both inflationists and contradictions, both protectionists and free traders.

More annoying, he produced evidence of a positive correlation between the vote for populist-slanted monetary measures and the vote for radical reconstruction measures.

The seminar, teacher and students alike, resisted these disturbing complications in the interest of clarity and intellectual peace. Might not such a trend lead to complete revisionism? It might indeed, Sharkey admitted, and kept picking away at the foundations of order. In the end he had his way with the seminar, and other members, including Willie Lee Rose, James M. McPherson, Otto Olsen, and Tilden Edelstein, added their own contributions to the deterioration of peace and order in the field of Reconstruction history. Sharkey deserves credit, however, for priority in responsibility for the ensuing disorder.

What moral this brief chronicle has to teach about the mysteries of pedagogy and the obligations of teacher to student and vice versa would be difficult to adduce. It leaves me, at any rate, with more doubts to add to the numerous ones I already entertained about the orderliness of the processes of teaching and learning, the relative profit derived by teacher and student in the process, and the general tenability of the authoritarian posture on the part of the pedagogue.

New Haven, Connecticut
February, 1967

CONTENTS

MONEY, CLASS, AND PARTY

An Economic Study of Civil War and Reconstruction

PREFACE

Some years ago while a graduate student I made the discovery that Thaddeus Stevens had been a greenbacker. To my mind this fact did not conform at all well with the generally accepted notion of the " Second American Revolution." How could the leader of the Radical Republicans, that party which has long been associated with the triumph of business in America after the Civil War, possibly have been infected with the paper money heresy? The irritation and confusion were sufficiently great to induce further research into the politico-economic history of the Civil War and Reconstruction, and this volume is the final result. I am not so presumptuous as to feel that it is by any means the final word on a subject of great complexity. Its purpose will have been achieved if some light is thrown on more or less neglected aspects of the history of a most decisive decade in the molding of the American nation.

It is inevitable that many genuine debts are incurred in the writing of works of this nature. I wish to express particular gratitude to Professor C. Vann Woodward of The Johns Hopkins University under whose direction this work was completed and who has been a constant source of encouragement and intelligent criticism. Thanks are also due to Professor Charles A. Barker of the same institution who has made helpful suggestions. Two distinguished scholars provided help and encouragement at crucial stages of this work. To Professors Frederic C. Lane of Johns Hopkins and William B. Hesseltine of the University of Wisconsin my debts are extremely great.

The following academicians have read portions of this work, providing needed criticisms and helpful suggestions: Tom E. Davis of the University of Chicago; Francis C. Haber and Clifton K. Yearley of the University of Florida; Warren W. Hassler of the Pennsylvania State University; Lance Davis of Purdue University; Stuart Bruchey of the Michigan State University; Howard H. Quint of the University of Massachusetts; and Olin S. Pugh, Alfred G. Smith, Gustavus G. Williamson, Jr., Charles W. Coolidge, and Gordon Tullock of the University

1

of South Carolina. To all of these I should like to express my appreciation, at the same time acknowledging that they are in no way responsible for any errors of fact or interpretation which may appear. To my wife, Virginia Williams Sharkey, who has endured nobly in the tradition of those whose misfortune it is to be wedded to graduate students, my debt is obvious. Finally thanks are due to the Research Committee of the University of South Carolina for two summer grants which aided in the completion of this work.

ROBERT P. SHARKEY

University of South Carolina
Columbia, South Carolina
September 15, 1959

PREFACE TO THE PAPERBACK EDITION

Money, Class, and Party, which first appeared late in 1959, may, I think, be said to constitute another skirmish on what Bernard Weisberger has called "The Dark and Bloody Ground of Reconstruction Historiography." The past seven years have witnessed no abatement of the academic carnage. Important book-length treatments of the Reconstruction period have been published at the rate of one or two per year, and the number of significant articles has been quite considerable. An interest in Reconstruction historiography has been almost de rigueur for historians of the period. In this new preface I would therefore like to attempt a rather specialized historiographical task— namely, an assessment of the importance (or lack thereof) of the economic element in the various interpretations of the Reconstruction era.

Overall I think we can distinguish five different phases or schools of historical writing about the Reconstruction period. To be more precise, I should say there was a phase, followed by three schools of interpretation, followed by something that is yet too recent to be categorized as either a phase or a school. The various attitudes represented by the three schools are by no means mutually exclusive, and it is sometimes possible to find two or more of these different attitudes combined in the same work by a given historian. Of these three schools of thought it seems to me there are two that have provided us with interpretations of Reconstruction which are primarily economic.

The first phase of historical writing about Reconstruction lasted from the end of the Civil War until about the turn of the century. Perhaps it is too generous to categorize it as historical writing, for the books that were published were largely polemics and self-justifying memoirs. Of the latter variety there can be cited such works as James G. Blaine's *Twenty Years of Congress,* John Sherman's *Recollections,* and the chapters dealing with Reconstruction in the works of such Confederate notables as Jefferson Davis and Alexander H. Stephens. Many of these memoirs contain valuable material for the study of the period, but one would hardly go to them expecting a balanced and objective appraisal of the facts. Thus the years up until the turn of the century can conveniently be thought of as a phase in Reconstruction historiography, but it did not produce anything that today would be considered an interpretation.

The end of the nineteenth century marked the end of a phase of writing about Reconstruction. Thereafter I think we can profitably consider schools of interpretation which flourished during approximately the first six decades of the twentieth century.

The first and perhaps most lastingly influential of these schools was that associated with the name of William Archibald Dunning. In fairness it should be pointed out that much of the Dunning attitude is contained in the works of John W. Burgess, under whom Dunning studied at Columbia, and also in those of James Ford Rhodes and James Schouler. The attitude of the Dunning school emerged not only in the works of the master himself, *Essays on the Civil War and Reconstruction* and *Reconstruction: Political and Economic*, but also in the various monographs written by his students on Reconstruction in the Southern states. Howard Beale summed up the attitude of Dunning and his students when he wrote more than twenty-five years ago, " The emphasis of the Dunning school was upon the harm done to the South by Radical Reconstruction and upon the sordid political and economic motives behind Radicalism." In this view the South could have made a happy readjustment to changed conditions and to the Union had it not been for outside Radical interference. The Radicals thus emerge as chief villains. To Walter L. Fleming, a leading member of the Dunning school, Thaddeus Stevens is " vindictive and unscrupulous " while Charles Sumner is " unpractical, theoretical, and not troubled by constitutional scruples." The transformation of Andrew Johnson into a great statesman was a long, slow process, but its beginnings are seen in Dunning's *Reconstruction: Political and Economic*, where Johnson is given credit for " integrity of purpose, force of will, and rude intellectual force." Johnson does not emerge quite so well from the works of Fleming and James Ford Rhodes, but nonetheless the movement for his subsequent canonization has been fairly launched and reaches final fruition in the late twenties and early thirties with such works as the biographies by Lloyd Stryker and Robert Winston and Claude Bowers' polemic, *The Tragic Era.*

It is important to emphasize that the Dunning school did not produce an economic interpretation of Reconstruction. In Dunning's *Reconstruction: Political and Economic* economic events of the period are treated as they would be in any balanced history, but economic forces do not emerge as causal factors exerting great influence over the political complexion of Reconstruction. Indeed Dunning wrote in his *Essays on the Civil War and Reconstruction* that " The chief end of the Reconstruction Acts was purely political." This point of view was consistently held by all those historians who for purposes of analysis are considered a part of the Dunning school, from Walter L. Fleming to Claude Bowers and George Fort Milton.

The genesis of the second school of interpretation of Reconstruction can be rather precisely dated in 1927 with the appearance of Charles and Mary Beard's *Rise of American Civilization.* This is the work that contained the celebrated " Second American Revolution " thesis in which the Beards impressed their predilection for economic determinism upon the 1860's. Although the Beards were concerned largely with the meaning of the Civil War, their basic premises were independently utilized by Professor Howard Beale in his influential book, *The Critical Year*, for the purpose of explaining Reconstruction. Since the Beard-Beale interpretation of the Civil War and Reconstruction is dealt with critically and extensively in Chapter VII of the present work, it is only briefly summarized here.

In their treatment of the Civil War the Beards decidedly minimized the importance of battles and campaigns. Their emphasis was overwhelmingly on the economic results of the conflict. It was the " capitalists, laborers, and farmers of the North and West " who brought about the defeat of the Southern planting aristocracy and gained the spoils of victory. Disposing of the rather modest gains of the laborers and farmers in a few sentences, the Beards concerned themselves almost exclusively with the gains of capitalists, which they saw as the crucial issue. For the manufacturing entrepreneurs, war contracts, the enormous stimulus of inflation, and the erection of a highly protective tariff wall constituted gains of an enormous magnitude. For the bankers and the creditor class generally, the creation of a large national debt at high rates of interest and the establishment of a National Banking System endowed finance capitalists with a strength unknown in ante bellum days. The triumph of capitalism and the utter defeat of agrarian principles was thus the essence of the "Second American Revolution." In the accomplishment of this result the Beards saw the Republicans in Congress in the role of faithful agents for the capitalist class.

In *The Critical Year* Professor Beale applied the basic premises of the Beards' interpretation to the postwar period. Here again the important operative forces were economic. Political Reconstruction was mainly a facade that concealed the overwhelming determination of the capitalists to protect their hardwon gains. The chief danger arose from the likelihood of a renewed alliance between Southern planters and Western farmers, an alliance that might have been strong enough to subvert the structure of the new capitalist order. Realization of this danger steeled Radical determination to keep Southerners out of Congress and the South in a state of political limbo. Throughout his work Professor Beale was in accordance with the Beards in seeing the Republicans, especially the Radicals, as agents of "business" interests whose sound and fury over political Reconstruction was a mask to conceal their real interest in consolidating economic gains.[1]

This then was the Beard-Beale thesis, an essentially economic interpretation of Reconstruction. It is instructive to note that the Dunning interpretation of Reconstruction and the Beard-Beale interpretation were by no means antithetical, but that on the contrary they tended to reinforce and complement one another. In both interpretations the Radicals emerge as the villains. For the Dunningites the Radicals are abhorred because they were responsible for what were regarded as the horrors

---

[1] In his Foreword to the reprint of *The Critical Year* (New York, 1958) Professor Beale pointed out that his interpretation of the economic issues of Reconstruction had been completed three years before the *Rise of American Civilization* was published. It is thus apparent that Beale's assessment of economic forces was arrived at independently and owed nothing to the Beards. Nonetheless I feel that the two works appearing within the space of four years and utilizing the same basic premises reinforced and corroborated one another and that it is therefore valid to speak of the Beard-Beale interpretation.

and excesses of Reconstruction in the South. In the Beard-Beale interpretation the Radicals are regarded as equally reprehensible, for they emerge as a group of prating hypocrites whose fight for Negro suffrage is dictated by their concern for the necessity of maintaining economic hegemony for the capitalist class. Both schools are very high on Andrew Johnson. Indeed there are few finer tributes to Johnson than that contained in Beale's *The Critical Year*.

In accounting for the popularity and influence of what may be considered the hybrid Dunning-Beard-Beale view of Reconstruction, a few relevant factors must be borne in mind. In the first place the basic synthesis finally emerged in the thirties, a period when the Republican Party reached an all time low in popularity. It seemed altogether logical at such a time to project the attitudes of the Hoover administration backward in time and find that they were also shared by those arch-Radicals, Stevens, Wade, and Butler. After all, Republicans had always spoken for the vested interests, and Beale showed that this was as true in the 1860's as it was in the 1930's. Furthermore, economic interpretations had been considered quite sophisticated in historical circles ever since Beard had published his book on the Constitution. The " Second American Revolution " thesis also contained a delectable conspiracy facet, the idea that the Radicals had actually conspired deeply and darkly to carry out their heinous economic aims in a time of national crisis. As was the case with Beard's *An Economic Interpretation of the Constitution*, such a notion was too appetizing to resist. Finally, it was all too easy for Democratically (with a capital " D ") oriented historians with a distinct Southern bias to sympathize with Andrew Johnson, a noble representative of the Southern yeomanry who did battle not only with arrogant slaveholders but also with the Radical Republican representatives of the new industrial oligarchy. All of these factors, I think, contributed to the popularity of the Dunning-Beard-Beale synthetic view of Reconstruction, a synthesis well exemplified by James G. Randall's *Civil War and Reconstruction*, which incorporates the Dunning view of Radical vindictiveness with the Beard-Beale economic interpretation.

Another economic interpretation of the Civil War and Reconstruction is that of the Marxists. This interpretation also emerged in the 1930's and can be found in three books, two of which are strictly Marxist in origin and one which is a variant of Marxism. These are: the introduction by Richard Enmale [2] to the collection of letters and articles by Marx and Engels titled *The Civil War in the United States*; the work by James S. Allen again with an introduction by Richard Enmale called *Reconstruction: The Battle for Democracy*; and W. E. B. DuBois' book, *Black Reconstruction*. The first two works are strictly Marxist in outlook and the third is a variant, because while DuBois was a Marxist, he was also a Negro.

The points of similarity and difference between the Marxist view of the Civil War and Reconstruction and the other two schools of interpretation are both interesting and instructive. While there is a great deal of sympathy for and concurrence in the Beard-Beale economic interpretation, there is nothing but contempt for the Dunning school. In his introduction to Allen's book, Enmale typifies John W. Burgess as a " leading exponent of the Bourbon school " who " consciously endeavored at the turn of the century to rewrite the history of Reconstruction from a Southern viewpoint." Again he writes: " The main lines laid down by Burgess have found their most nauseating expression in *The Tragic Era* of Claude Bowers." Bowers' sins consist of being indifferent to Negroes, of vindicating Andrew Johnson, and of being very sympathetic to the fight of the ex-Confederates to preserve their old social order. Enmale finds an anti-Negro bias in the works of Dunning and his students and condemns James Ford Rhodes as a " Philistine " who takes the Southern point of view. DuBois in the concluding chapter to *Black Reconstruction*, which he calls " The Propaganda of History," takes the same point of view. He finds Burgess " frank and determined in his anti-Negro thought." Dunning he thinks more judicious but still basically anti-Negro. To DuBois, Dunning's students have been " one-sided and partisan to the last degree." The works of Milton and Winston are seen as failures in their attempt to vindicate Andrew Johnson. Bowers' *The Tragic Era* is categorized as " a classic example of historical propaganda of the cheaper sort." The Marxists are appalled at what treatment such Dunning school historians as Bowers

---

[2] Enmale—ENgels–MArx–LEnin.

and Milton have accorded the Radicals. DuBois writes: "The magnificent figures of Charles Sumner and Thaddeus Stevens have been besmirched almost beyond recognition."

In light of all this it is interesting to note the gentle and sympathetic treatment that is accorded the Beard-Beale thesis. Enmale asserts: "Although the Bourbon and the Philistine ignore the revolutionary implications of Reconstruction, the liberal bourgeois historian does not. In his *Rise of American Civilization*, Charles A. Beard, leading exponent of the school, recognizes that the revolution, released during the Civil War, continued during Reconstruction. The period completed the ruin of the former slave oligarchy and the triumph of the industrial bourgeoise. How the latter consolidated its position is shown in detail by Howard K. Beale in his *Critical Year: A Study of Andrew Johnson and Reconstruction*."

Though the Marxists go the first mile with what they term "the liberal bourgeois historians," they do not go the whole distance. Again Richard Enmale: "Yet, despite a promising beginning, liberal writers see only one side of the revolutionary picture. Failing to appreciate fully the class dynamics of historical development, they do not distinguish clearly between the various class forces at work. This leads them to ignore some of the most important revolutionary phenomena of Reconstruction. Not least is the part played by the freedman during the period. They accept uncritically the traditional role of the Negro people in the Reconstruction of the South. To Beard, '... the freedmen were in no way prepared to become an effective factor in the new order of society ... they were powerless in the hands of the governing group that directed the revolution and reconstruction from Washington. ...' Beale practically takes a similar view of the situation, a view strengthened by his belief that the Negro plantation hands were not only illiterate but ' had no conception of ... the meaning of terms like government, morality, suffrage, or even free labor.'" Enmale likes DuBois' treatment of the role of the Negro much better, but DuBois makes the mistake of seeing Reconstruction as a proletarian Marxian revolution whereas it was really a bourgeois revolution.

Just as Marx had much admiration for bourgeois capitalism and saw it as a necessary stage preceding proletarian revolution,

so the Marxists were willing to accept much of what they regarded as the Beardian bourgeois interpretation as a necessary
stage preceding the true Marxist interpretation of history.
Although both the Marxists and the Beard-Beale school saw
the meaning of the Civil War and Reconstruction in economic
terms, there is a difference in their treatment of the Radicals.
Beale saw Radical Reconstruction in the South as a smoke
screen behind which the Republicans consolidated economic
gains. To the Marxists who think of the Radicals as blameless
and progressive, there is no need for such a conspiracy concept.
Besides, no good Marxist would ever find it unusual for a
group to advance its own economic interests. Consequently
there is nothing shocking to Enmale or Allen in the fact that
the Radicals advocated their own economic interests *along with*
Negro suffrage. They are both consonant with advanced industrial capitalism. Thus to the Marxists, Stevens and Sumner
emerge not as conspirators but as progressive spokesmen of
bourgeois society.

While the Marxist view of the Civil War and Reconstruction
possesses a certain archaic interest, it never exercised much influence over the mainstream of historical writing. The Dunning-
Beard-Beale synthesis continued to hold sway over the minds
of the great majority of historians for more than a quarter of
a century. Only in recent years has this interpretation given
way to something too disparate and heterogeneous to be called
a " school " but which, because of its profound reaction to the
Dunning-Beard-Beale synthesis, has been termed " revisionism."
Though many " revisionist " studies were carried out in the
thirties, forties, and fifties, these dealt mostly with rather
specialized aspects of Reconstruction and were not sufficient
to crack the facade of the monolithic synthesis. Only in the
past eight or nine years has the revisionist tide become strong
enough to carry everything before it.

As Kenneth Stampp has noted, the revisionists have been a
heterogeneous group including in their ranks Negro historians,
disgruntled and skeptical Southerners, latter-day Northern abo-
litionists, and several foreign scholars. In recent years their
attitudes have been, I think, perceptibly affected by the social
and political climate of the 1960's of which the movement for
Negro equality has been such an important component.

The revisionist assault on the older synthesis has been carried out on at least three different levels. One level has involved the economic meaning of Reconstruction; the second has dealt primarily with the politics of the period with particular emphasis upon the role of Andrew Johnson; a third has concerned itself with the implementation of Radical Reconstruction in the South.

The Beard-Beale economic interpretation of the Civil War and Reconstruction was seriously questioned for the first time in 1959. In that year articles by Irwin Unger and Stanley Coben [3] showed the heterogeneous and conflicting nature of "business" attitudes toward such issues as the tariff and the currency. *Money, Class, and Party,* however, marked the first direct assault upon the "Second American Revolution" thesis. There is shown to be a great divergence of tangible interest and opinion among capitalists on such crucial economic issues as the tariff and contraction of the currency as well as upon the political issues of Reconstruction. The economic positions of farmers and workingmen are explored so as to throw new light upon their important roles in the Reconstruction drama. Far from being the faithful agents of some sort of monolithic "capitalist" interest, the Republican party is shown to be hopelessly divided on economic questions with the most Radical members tending in the direction of a high protectionist–soft money line.

In general the interpretation of motives and interests contained in the present work seems to have held up pretty well in the eight years since it appeared. It has, however, been subjected to criticism, notably in Irwin Unger's *The Greenback Era* (1964), which carries the politico-economic history of American finance up to the resumption of specie payments in 1879. Professor Unger in this thoroughly researched and outstanding work has objected to what he calls my "economic determinism," which he regards as even more complete than that of Beard. He has argued that "In the great postwar debate over the currency, ideas and values were often as important as acquisi-

---

[3] Irwin Unger, "Business Men and Specie Resumption," *Political Science Quarterly,* LXXIV (March, 1959); Stanley Coben, "Northern Business and Radical Reconstruction: A Reexamination," *Mississippi Valley Historical Review,* XLVI (June, 1959).

tiveness and 'interest' came to include men united by more than economic ambitions." While admitting the importance and even fascination of ideas and ethics, I would argue that Professor Unger has shown few if any cases where these have diverged from actual economic interest. But in the main, in this and in other cases where Professor Unger and I have disagreed, the arguments boil down to fairly pretty quibbles. The important thing is that both he and I reject the simple dualism of the Beard-Beale interpretation and try to deal with reality in its sometimes awful complexity.

If the material interests of capitalists and other groups were so divergent and conflicting, it becomes obviously impossible to see economic forces as constituting a decisive factor in the determination of Reconstruction policy. One of the effects therefore of the work of Coben, Unger, and myself has been to help to restore primacy to the political interpretation of Reconstruction, a primacy that William A. Dunning had asserted some seventy years ago. Four important works emphasizing political analysis have appeared in recent years. Eric L. McKitrick's *Andrew Johnson and Reconstruction* (1960) delves deeply into the political history of the period and also contains a fascinating assessment of psychological factors. Its net effect is a considerable diminution of the stature of Andrew Johnson and an enhancement of the role of the moderate Congressional Republicans. LaWanda and John H. Cox's *Politics, Principle, and Prejudice, 1865–66* (1963) finds the civil rights issue to be the essence of the Reconstruction drama. Far from being portrayed as either fanatics or agents of capitalism, the Radicals are shown to possess a genuine concern with the welfare of the freedmen. Andrew Johnson is shown to have been the aggressor in his battles with Congress and stands convicted of promulgating thoroughly ambiguous and equivocal policies. W. R. Brock in *An American Crisis* (1963) argues that the driving force behind Radicalism was in essence a powerful ideology pressing relentlessly for the realization of its political principles. He finds Andrew Johnson politically inept and incapable of understanding the major currents of Northern public opinion. Both the Cox's and Dr. Brock accept the general argument contained in *Money, Class, and Party*. Dr. Brock's book contains an excellent treatment of economic issues in a chapter titled, " The Forces Behind Reconstruction." Professor David Donald in his closely reasoned *The Politics of Reconstruction, 1863–67* (1965) addresses himself to the question, " What is a Radical?" Utilizing statistical methods, he argues convincingly that the degree of Radicalism manifested by Congressmen was closely related to the degree of security they felt in their home districts. It is significant in demonstrating the shift back to a purely political interpretation of Reconstruction that all of the votes of the Thirty-Ninth Congress analyzed by Professor Donald relate to the reorganization of the South and have no economic connotations.

The earliest revisionist works took issue with the hostile view of Reconstruction in the South held by the Dunning school of historians. Some of the most important revisionist studies of this type, such as Francis B. Simkins and Robert H. Woody's *South Carolina during Reconstruction* and Roger W. Shugg's *Origins of Class Struggle in Louisiana*, date back to the 1930's. Indeed, in this sense DuBois' *Black Reconstruction* (1935) can also be considered a revisionist as well as a Marxist work. Since that time there have appeared a large number of books and articles on rather specialized aspects of Reconstruction in the South which are revisionist in nature. It is not my purpose here to deal with this sizable body of historical literature, but merely to note three recent syntheses that place emphasis upon the constructive and idealistic aspects of the Reconstruction process without overlooking the negative elements.

James G. Randall and David Donald, *The Civil War and Reconstruction* (1961), is a scholarly updating by Professor Donald of the older work by Randall in which the best results of revisionist research are incorporated. It contains a comprehensive critical bibliography of the Civil War and Reconstruction period. John Hope Franklin, *Reconstruction after the Civil War* (1961), is an excellent survey that sheds new and interesting light on the role of the Negro. Kenneth Stampp, *The Era of Reconstruction* (1965), includes much thoughtful comment on the solid achievements of the Southern Reconstruction governments as well as a timely underlining of the importance of the Fourteenth and Fifteenth Amendments. It is Professor Stampp's judgment that ". . . if it was worth four years of civil war to save the Union, it was worth a few years of radical reconstruction to give the American Negro the ultimate promise of equal civil and political rights."

The word " revisionism " used to describe the work on Reconstruction which has appeared in recent years indicates the reactive nature of the movement. We are still far from achieving for our time an interpretation as serviceable for purposes of explanation as the older Dunning-Beard-Beale synthesis. More thorough historical research, a better understanding of other relevant disciplines, and a more sophisticated methodology no doubt are essential in acquiring a better understanding of the past. But they also exact a price in making ever more remote the establishment and acceptance of those grand theses which once endowed the mind of the historian with certainty and security.

Bologna, Italy
February, 1967

CHAPTER I

ORIGIN OF THE GREENBACKS

Of all the financial laws enacted by Congress during the Civil War, the Legal Tender Acts of 1862 and 1863 were the most momentous and the most controversial. Men who occupied the public stage during the years of war and Reconstruction were almost never neutral about the greenbacks. They either saw eye to eye with Henry Adams and Francis A. Walker who regarded the Legal Tender Acts as " an act of national bankruptcy " and a " calamity involving the credit of every man in whose charge the people then placed the common interests," or they agreed with Senator John Sherman who felt that these measures provided means for "utilizing the wealth of the country " and were the only measures " that could have enabled the government to carry on successfully the vast operations of the war." [1] The truth of either of these extreme positions would be difficult to establish. Adams and Walker took their position behind what they no doubt regarded as the impregnable principles of classical political economy. Senator Sherman, the practical politician, took refuge behind the idea that " necessity knows no law." It is not our task here to pass ultimate judgment on the validity of either of these extreme positions but rather to provide the reader with the facts regarding the origin of the greenbacks in order that the monetary struggle of the post-Civil War years may be placed in its proper perspective.

The Legal Tender Acts resulted from the financial exigencies of war. Thus, in one sense at least, the birth of the greenbacks was legitimate, in that most historical examples of paper money legislation can be traced to periods of war and crisis. Witness the *assignats* of the French Revolution and the issues of the Continental Congress. The temptation of magnifying the im-

---

[1] Henry Adams and Francis A. Walker, " The Legal Tender Act," in Henry Adams, *Historical Essays* (New York, 1891), p. 279; John Sherman, *Recollections of Forty Years in the House, Senate and Cabinet*, 2 vols. (Chicago, 1895), I, 280-281. The article by Adams and Walker originally appeared in the *North American Review* for April, 1870.

portance of the greenbacks as a factor in the financing of the war must be resisted. Total net issues of legal tender notes in the years 1861-1865 amounted to $431,500,000. Total indebtedness which may be attributed to the war amounted in 1865 to approximately $2,600,000,000.[2] The greenbacks, therefore, accounted for less than one-sixth of the total cost of the war. The importance of the paper money issues lies more in the effect upon the political and economic state of the nation than as a resource of war finance. In the financing of the war the Legal Tender Acts represented a stage between the fatuous hope that the war would be of short duration requiring no extraordinary financial measures and the subsequent realization that virtually every resource of the nation would have to be tapped in order to achieve eventual victory.

Two days after his inauguration on March 4, 1861 President Lincoln nominated Salmon Portland Chase of Ohio to be Secretary of the Treasury. The nomination was at once unanimously confirmed by the Senate. Political considerations went a long way toward determining this appointment. Chase's long career in politics including two terms as governor of Ohio and a term in the Senate had brought him little experience in the field of finance. His appointment was a part of Lincoln's plan to achieve a broad representation of factions and interests in the new Republican administration.[3]

Chase realized that his lack of experience would be a serious handicap in undertaking the duties of Secretary of the Treasury. It was with considerable difficulty that the President was able to persuade him to accept the position. Having been selected by the Ohio legislature in February for a second term in the United States Senate, Chase wrote Governor Denison on March 6 pointing out that " It would be far more consonant with my wishes to remain at the post to which the people of Ohio, through the General Assembly, saw fit to call me." He was reluctant to accept the call to " another sphere of duty, more

---

[2] Davis Rich Dewey, *Financial History of the United States*, 10th ed. (New York, 1928), Table, p. 308.

[3] Jacob W. Schuckers, *The Life and Public Services of Salmon Portland Chase* (New York, 1874), p. 207; Wesley Clair Mitchell, *A History of the Greenbacks with Special Reference to the Economic Consequence of Their Issue* (Chicago, 1903), pp. 1-2.

laborious, more arduous, and fuller far of perplexing respon-sibilties." He asserted that he would "accept . . . these new duties, greatly distrusting my own abilities, but humbly invoking divine aid and guidance." [4] As Hugh McCulloch wrote many years later, Salmon Chase was not entirely unequipped to handle the heavy responsibilities of the Treasury as he was " clear-headed, self-possessed, self-confident, patriotic, hopeful, bold, and . . . succeeded when trained financiers, who are usually conservative and cautious, would have failed." [5] Though this judgment is not too wide of the mark in its assessment of Chase's more positive personal qualities, it is nonetheless true that the Ohioan's stubborness, vanity, ambition, and almost total lack of knowledge of the broad principles of war finance were destined to lead him into difficulties on more than one occasion.

When Chase entered the Treasury Department the public debt was $74,985,000. About $18,000,000 of this amount had been incurred since the beginning of the secession movement.[6] Although the total debt was not large when set alongside the tremendous resources of the Northern states, the credit of the nation had suffered grievously in the preceding months. After the November elections which had resulted in the Republican victory, Howell Cobb, Secretary of the Treasury in the Buchanan administration, had reported that " capitalists, in the present conditions of the country, seem unwilling to invest in United States stock at par." [7] Cobb's complaint was well founded, but it is understandable that men of financial means were loth to support an administration whose financial minister was a notor-ious Southern sympathizer and who was soon to become Presi-dent of the first Congress of the Confederacy.[8] Cobb had resigned in December and was replaced by Philip F. Thomas of Maryland, another Southern sympathizer, who remained in office for only a month.[9] The next incumbent was General John

---

[4] Schuckers, *Chase*, pp. 207-208.
[5] Hugh McCulloch, *Men and Measures of Half a Century* (New York, 1889), p. 185.
[6] Dewey, *Financial History*, p. 276.
[7] *Report of the Secretary of the Treasury, 1860*, p. 9.
[8] Robert Selph Henry, *The Story of the Confederacy* (New York, 1931), p. 27.
[9] Albert S. Bolles, *The Financial History of the United States from 1789 to 1860* (New York, 1883), p. 602.

A. Dix who administered the nation's finances during the balance of Buchanan's term of office. Confidence in the public credit had fallen so low that when Dix asked for bids on an issue of treasury notes which Congress had authorized at Cobb's behest several weeks earlier, he was able to obtain money only at ruinous rates of interest, the larger part of the $10,000,000 authorized being taken at rates over 10 per cent and some $4,840,000 being sold at a rate of 12 per cent! [10]

Although the financial climate improved considerably when the Lincoln administration took charge of the nation's destiny, Secretary Chase was confronted at the outset of his term of office with many difficult problems. The revenue of the government was falling far behind its necessary expenditures. For many years the government had been largely dependent upon customs duties for its support. Revenue from this source for the months of January, February, and March of 1861 had totalled $9,772,574. When the frankly protectionist Morrill tariff went into effect on April 1, 1861, the revenue began to drop. Customs yielded only $5,515,552 for the months of April, May, and June.[11] Total revenue from ordinary sources during this final quarter of the fiscal year, 1860-61, was only $5,800,000 whereas expenditures were running at the rate of $23,500,000.[12] Thus the Morrill Tariff Act, a keystone of the Republican economic program, only succeeded in embarassing Secretary Chase in his administration of the finances.[13]

Since revenue amounted to less than 25 per cent of necessary expenditures, recourse had to be made to borrowing. Congress was not in session which meant that Chase could not request new authority to issue bonds or treasury notes. The Secretary, consequently, had to make use of such power to borrow money as existed under previous laws. Authority existed to borrow some $31,000,000 under the Acts of June 22, 1860 and February 8, 1861. Additional authority to issue bonds or treasury notes

[10] Rafael A. Bayley, " History of the National Loans of the United States," *International Review*, XII (February, 1882), 175; Bolles, *Financial History from 1789 to 1860*, p. 602.
[11] *Report of the Secretary of the Treasury, 1861*, p. 30.
[12] *Ibid.*, pp. 30-32.
[13] Mitchell, *History of the Greenbacks*, p. 10; Frank W. Taussig, *The Tariff History of the United States*, 5th ed. (New York, 1910), pp. 158-159.

up to $10,000,000 was contained in the opening sections of the Morrill Tariff Act, but the proceeds of this loan could not be applied to the then current fiscal year. Chase availed himself of this authority to issue $14,412,529 in the form of bonds and treasury notes. In this manner the Secretary managed to carry the government through the difficult months which followed the inauguration of Lincoln. More comprehensive financial measures had to be postponed until the meeting of the special session of Congress on July 4.[14]

Secretary Chase outlined his financial proposals in a message received by Congress on July 5.[15] Overly sanguine about the prospects of early victory, Chase felt that $320,000,000 would be required to support the government for the next twelve months. Of this sum he felt that " not less than $80,000,000 should be provided by taxation, and that $240,000,000 should be sought through loans." [16] Of the amount to be provided by taxation the Secretary thought that $57,000,000 could be obtained from customs, another $3,000,000 from sales of public lands, and $20,000,000 from internal duties or a direct tax as Congress should decide.[17] The suggestion was made at the time that a larger proportion of the money required by the government should be raised by taxation in order to place financial operations on a sounder footing. But as James G. Blaine observed, " unwillingness to create friction and opposition doubtless entered into the considerations which determined the recommendations of the secretary." [18] The failure of Secretary Chase to recommend and of Congress to provide for an adequate and comprehensive program of taxation at the outset of the war was a major blunder, a blunder which Chase recognized in 1863 when he pled that no one at the time realized that the war would be of long duration and that it seemed unwise to " increase the burdens of the people at a time when the sudden

[14] Mitchell, *History of the Greenbacks*, pp. 10-15; Dewey, *Financial History*, p. 276; *Report of the Secretary of the Treasury, 1861*, pp. 30, 37.

[15] *Congressional Globe*, 37th Congress, 1st Session, pp. 11, 13.

[16] *Senate Executive Documents*, No. 2, 37th Congress, 1st Session, p. 6.

[17] *Ibid.*, pp. 8-9.

[18] James G. Blaine, *Twenty Years of Congress: From Lincoln to Garfield with a Review of the Events which Led to the Political Revolution of 1860*, 2 vols. (Norwich, Conn., 1884), I, 402.

outbreak of flagitious rebellion had deranged their business, and temporarily diminished their incomes." [19]

Although nothing was done to provide adequate taxation, Congress hastened to grant the Secretary power to borrow money. By the Acts of July 17 and August 5, 1861 he was authorized to issue various types of securities up to $250,000,000. The securities might be in the form of treasury notes or bonds depending on the discretion of Chase. The rate of interest on the bonds which were to mature in twenty years was set at 7 per cent at par. If the Secretary desired to issue 6 per cent bonds to be sold below par, this might be done provided that the eventual rate did not amount to more than 7 per cent. At his discretion Chase might issue various types of treasury notes, including three year notes bearing 7.3 per cent interest, one year notes bearing 3.65 per cent interest, or demand notes bearing no interest but receivable for all public dues. [20] This latter type of note, which could be issued in denominations as low as $5, was really a form of currency. Chase had requested power to issue such notes but realized their danger, pointing out that " the greatest care will . . . be requisite to prevent the degradation of such issues into an irredeemable paper currency, than which no more certainly fatal expedient for impoverishing the masses and discrediting the government of any country can well be devised." [21] Inasmuch as the Secretary was advocating the issue of just such an irredeemable paper currency within six months, the words above are somewhat ironic, but they do indicate the basic hard-money convictions of Chase, convictions which were destined to emerge strongly some years later when as Chief Justice of the United States Supreme Court, he virtually declared the Legal Tender Acts to have been unconstitutional. [22]

---

[19] *Report of the Secretary of the Treasury, 1863*, p. 10.

[20] Senate Document No. 580, 61st Congress, 2nd Session, *Laws of the United States Concerning Money, Banking, and Loans, 1778-1909*, compilers A. T. Huntington and Robert J. Mawhinney (Washington, 1910), pp. 161-165. (This is one of the publications of the National Monetary Commission. It will be cited hereafter as Huntington and Mawhinney, *Laws*.)

[21] *Senate Executive Documents*, No. 2, 37th Congress, 1st Session, p. 14.

[22] *Hepburn v. Griswold*, 8 Wallace 603. This case involved the tender of notes in settlement of a contract entered into before the passage of the first Legal Tender Act. In his opinion Chase was careful to limit the application of

The second phase of Civil War finance involved the government in negotiations with the banks of New York, Boston, and Philadelphia. The banks of these cities were asked to lend their support to the Treasury in placing a loan of $150,000,000 under the terms of the legislation just enacted by Congress. A conference of bankers held in New York, August 10-17, agreed to come to the aid of the government by advancing $50,000,000 in exchange for a like amount of treasury notes bearing 7.3 per cent interest at par. The banks were further given the option of taking a second $50,000,000 on the same terms on October 15, and a third $50,000,000 on December 15.[23] Although the cooperating banks of the three cities had a total capital of only $120,000,000 and coin reserves of only $63,200,000, they undertook to aid the government in the hope that the treasury notes could be quickly sold to the people, thus replenishing the coin which they must advance to the government.[24] In essence, though not in legal form, the banks were acting as underwriters. This relationship was pointed up by the fact that the Treasury undertook to market the 7.30 notes, appointing agents for this purpose in all the major towns and cities of the Northern states. The notes were sold for the account of the cooperating banks, and the proceeds of these sales were handed over to the banks by the government.[25]

In their negotiations with Secretary Chase the associated banks had supposed that their loan to the government would be handled like a loan to any individual or corporation. In other words the banks would credit the United States with a deposit of $50,000,000 against which the Treasury would draw from time to time as the money was needed. They soon learned that

the decision to such contracts. The opinion, however, leaves little doubt but that Chase felt that Congress had exceeded the limits of its constitutional authority in declaring the United States notes to be a legal tender.

[23] Mitchell, *History of the Greenbacks*, p. 23. For accounts of the $150,000,000 loan, see Don C. Barrett, *The Greenbacks and the Resumption of Specie Payments, 1862-1879* (Cambridge, Mass., 1931), pp. 7-10; Horace White, *Money and Banking Illustrated by American History*, 5th ed. (Boston, 1941), pp. 107-109; Albert S. Bolles, *The Financial History of the United States from 1861 to 1885* (New York, 1886), ch. III; Dewey, *Financial History*, pp. 278-281; Schuckers, *Chase*, pp. 225-228.

[24] Mitchell, *History of the Greenbacks*, p. 24; Bolles, *Financial History from 1861 to 1885*, pp. 24-25.

[25] *Ibid.*, p. 32.

Secretary Chase had no intention of proceeding in this manner. In the mind of Chase the chief obstacle was the Independent Treasury Act of August, 1846.[26] Passage of this act had marked the complete triumph of Democratic hard money philosophy and the absolute separation of the Treasury and the banks.[27] It was still the law of the land in 1861, and, under its provisions, the government could pay out and receive only coin, and this coin must be kept in the various sub-treasuries provided for by the law. By the Act of August 5, 1861, the sub-treasury law had been modified to permit " the Secretary of the Treasury to deposit any of the moneys obtained on any of the loans now authorized by law, to the credit of the Treasurer of the United States in such solvent specie-paying banks as he may select." [28] The purpose of this measure, according to Mr. Elbridge G. Spaulding, one of its authors, " was to relax the rigid requirements of the sub-treasury Act in regard to the receipt and disbursement of coin, and instead of paying solely from coin deposits in the treasury, to allow all the money obtained on these loans to be deposited in solvent banks; the United States treasurer to draw his checks directly on such deposit banks in payment of war expenses, which checks would be paid in State bank-notes then redeemable on demand in gold, or in the ordinary course of business." [29]

Despite the testimony of Spaulding that the Act of August, 1861 was designed to permit the Secretary to use the banks as government depositories, Chase did not choose to construe it that way. He insisted that the specie loaned by the banks be paid directly into the sub-treasury.[30] The Secretary did not feel that the Act of August, 1861 had amended the Independent Treasury Act to the extent that it permitted the government to receive bank-notes, and he knew that if he used the banks as depositories, he would have to acquiesce in having them paid out for government obligations.[31] The failure of Secretary Chase

    [26] Huntington and Mawhinney, *Laws*, pp. 136-141.
    [27] David Kinley, *The History, Organization and Influence of the Independent Treasury of the United States* (New York, 1893), pp. 40-42.
    [28] Huntington and Mawhinney, *Laws*, p. 327.
    [29] Quoted in Bolles, *Financial History from 1861 to 1885*, p. 27.
    [30] Barrett, *Greenbacks and Resumption of Specie Payments*, pp. 8-9; Mitchell, *History of the Greenbacks*, pp. 25-26.
    [31] *Ibid.*, p. 26.

to give a broad interpretation to the obvious intent of Congress to modify the spirit of the Independent Treasury Act placed a great burden on the banks. As a contemporary observer, George S. Coe, President of the American Exchange Bank, observed, " To draw from the banks in coin the large sums involved in these loans, and to transfer them to the treasury, thence to be widely scattered over the country at a moment when war had excited fear and distrust, was to be pulling out continually the foundations upon which the whole structure rested." [32] The necessity of making all payments to the government in coin weakened the specie position of the banks and to some extent at least contributed to the suspension of specie payments.[33]

Despite the Secretary's unwillingness to use the banks as government depositories, all went well for a time. The first $50,000,000 loan was paid by the banks to the government at intervals of about six days. The crucial question was whether or not the specie would return to the banks after having been paid out by the government to contractors, soldiers, office-holders, etc.[34] The question as to whether the specie would return to the banks depended not only on the redeposit of the money paid out by the government but also on the success of efforts to market the 7-30 treasury notes. Any lack of confidence in the government which would lead to the hoarding of specie by individuals and a failure to market the treasury notes would almost inevitably lead to an inability on the part of the banks to maintain coin payments.

During the first few weeks when the associated banks were making payments into the sub-treasury, specie reserves declined precipitously, the New York banks alone losing $13,000,000

---

[32] Quoted in Bolles, *Financial History from 1861 to 1885*, p. 27.

[33] Just how much the banks were weakened by the Secretary's obduracy is a matter of some dispute. Mitchell does not feel that the Secretary's refusal to allow the proceeds of the loans to be deposited with the banks was too important inasmuch as they managed to survive the first and second $50,000,000 loans without much difficulty. *History of the Greenbacks*, pp. 41-42. Bolles and Barrett, on the other hand, feel that Chase's rigid adherence to sub-treasury system was a major blunder. See Bolles, *Financial History from 1861 to 1885*, pp. 26-29; Barrett, *Greenbacks and Resumption of Specie Payments*, pp. 50-51. I am inclined to feel that, while the Secretary's policy weakened the banks, it was not a crucial factor leading to the suspension of specie payments.

[34] Mitchell, *History of the Greenbacks*, pp. 24-25.

from August 17 to September 21. In the latter part of September, however, the tide turned, and the banks began to gain more specie than they were paying out. Both parties to the agreement were encouraged. The Treasury had been able to borrow a large sum of money at what was then considered a cheap rate, and the banks had been able to utilize profitably resources which had been idle since the diminution of commercial demand following the outbreak of war.[35] There was but one element of danger in the situation. Sales of treasury notes under the management of the Treasury Department for the account of the banks were moving very slowly.[36]

Improvement in their specie reserves prompted the banks to take a second $50,000,000 of 7-30 notes on October 1, fifteen days earlier than the time originally agreed upon in August. This time, however, the banks decided to dispose of the securities themselves without the aid of the Treasury Department. Payments into the sub-treasury on the second $50,000,000 loan began on October 29 and proceeded smoothly. The decline in reserves was less precipitous than in August and September, and the banks agreed to take a third $50,000,000 on November 16, a month before the date originally decided upon. Instead of 7-30 notes, however, which were proving difficult to market, the associated banks insisted on receiving 6 per cent bonds which, it was felt at the time, could be profitably sold in Europe. These bonds were taken by the banks at a rate equivalent to par for 7 per cent and consequently netted the treasury only $45,795,478.48. The banks continued to make regular payments to the government and their specie reserve condition remained good. On December 7 they were actually stronger than in August when the first loan to the government was made.[37]

The ability of the associated banks to continue to succor the government with loans in coin was pathetically dependent on the state of public confidence. If confidence were lost in the soundness of government finances, specie would be hoarded, government securities would decline in value, and the main-

---

[35] *Ibid.*, pp. 32-33; Fritz Redlich, *The Molding of American Banking: Men and Ideas*, 2 vols. (New York, 1951), II, 92.
[36] Mitchell, *History of the Greenbacks*, p. 34.
[37] *Ibid.*, pp. 33-37.

tenance of coin payments would become impossible. Until December, 1861 the confidence of the financial community in the government had remained intact, but in that fateful month two events undermined it very badly. The first of these was the publication of the annual report of the Secretary of the Treasury on December 10, a report which "showed that the nation was drifting into financial embarrassments for want of a policy." [38]

In his report to Congress Secretary Chase demonstrated the precarious position of the federal finances, but he failed to provide any plan which seemed likely to improve them. In July, Chase had estimated expenditures for the forthcoming fiscal year at $318,519,582. Revenues from customs and sales of public lands were predicted at $60,000,000.[39] The report of December showed that revenues from customs and land sales were falling far behind the Secretary's previous estimates. Chase predicted that they would provide only about $35,000,000 for the fiscal year which was $25,000,000 less than he had estimated in July.[40] Expenditures, on the other hand, were running far ahead of what the Secretary had estimated. Chase could hardly be blamed for this, inasmuch as few statesmen in the North had foreseen during the summer the dimensions which the war would take. As he pointed out, the basis for his estimates was the understanding that about 300,000 soldiers would be needed to crush the rebellion. Since that time, Congress had authorized the enlistment of 550,000 men. To meet the additional requirements of 250,000 more men, Chase estimated that expenditures for the fiscal year ending June 30, 1862 would be $213,904,427 higher than the $318,519,582 which he had predicted in July.[41]

The figures which the Secretary exhibited were sobering enough, but even greater cause for gloom appeared in his complete failure to recommend a comprehensive program of taxation sufficient to put the finances of the government on a sounder basis. Although Chase recommended new taxes which, he felt, would bring government revenue up to $90,000,000, he placed

---

[38] William G. Sumner, *A History of American Currency* (New York, 1876), p. 193.
[39] *Senate Executive Documents*, 37th Congress, 1st Session, No. 2, pp. 5, 8.
[40] *Report of the Secretary of the Treasury, 1861*, p. 11.
[41] *Ibid.*, pp. 11-12.

his greatest reliance on a scheme to reorganize the banking system of the country so as to compel the banks to buy large quantities of government bonds.[42] This scheme eventually evolved into the National Banking System, but it was obvious at the time that such a system could not be devised in time to meet the most pressing needs of the Treasury. Disappointment with the Secretary's report was keen. James G. Blaine attests to the "discouragement in financial circles" which it produced, while John Sherman wrote that in December, 1861, "the financial condition of the government was more alarming than at any other period during the war." [43]

The second event which led to apprehension in financial circles was the *Trent* affair. The removal of the two Confederate commissioners, Mason and Slidell, on November 8, 1861 from the British steamer *Trent* was the immediate cause for rejoicing and congratulation of Captain Wilkes of the American warship *San Jacinto*. When it became known that the British government took a very stern view of the affair and that war was threatened, the mood of rejoicing gave way to an atmosphere of gloom. The action of the British cabinet in demanding an apology and the surrender of the commissioners caused a panic in the stock market. Government securities fell 2-2½ per cent, while sterling exchange rose two points. This was on December 16. Rumors were abroad that the banks of New York were planning a suspension of specie payments. The next day a meeting of the associated banks was held at which a resolution was adopted that there was "no reason, justification, or necessity for a suspension of specie payments." [44]

Nevertheless, the situation was critical. The *Trent* affair had destroyed any possibility that the banks might sell the 6 per cent bonds in England.[45] Loaded down with unmarketable government securities, the banks witnessed in December a flight of their specie reserves. From December 7 through December 28 the New York banks lost $13,000,000.[46] Money paid by the Treasury to government contractors for supplies

[42] *Ibid.*, pp. 17-20.
[43] Blaine, *Twenty Years of Congress*, I, 407; Sherman, *Recollections*, I, 269.
[44] Mitchell, *History of the Greenbacks*, pp. 37-39.
[45] Barrett, *Greenbacks and Resumption of Specie Payments*, pp. 42-43.
[46] Bolles, *Financial History from 1861 to 1885*, pp. 35-36.

ceased to flow back to the vaults of the banks. Meanwhile the banks of Boston and the West began to draw on their balances in New York, a factor which further weakened the banks of the great metropolis.[47] Inasmuch as hoarding had developed, public confidence in the condition of the Treasury had been undermined, and the market value of government securities had fallen, suspension of specie payments was obviously only a matter of time. The move was finally decided upon at a meeting of the representatives of the New York banks held on December 28, 1861. By a vote of 25 of the institutions represented to 15, the resolution to suspend specie payments on Monday, December 30 was carried. The banks of Philadelphia followed suit as did those of Boston. The action of the banks forced the suspension of coin payments by the Treasury, since the supply of specie was cut off.[48]

As carried out by the banks at this time, suspension was a precaution to prevent further depletion of reserves rather than an absolute necessity. James Gallatin, President of the Gallatin National Bank of New York and a leader of the New York banking fraternity, pointed this out at the time when he said: " The government must suspend specie payments, or we must; and it is only a question of a few more days' time as to who suspends first, and who shall hold the specie in our vaults. If we hold it, the people and the government will be alike benefited. If the government takes it, the whole will be expended and hoarded by a few people." [49] In his annual report of 1862, Secretary Chase said that increased military expenditures and " diminished confidence in public securities " had made a suspension of specie payments " inevitable." [50]

Suspension of specie payments affected two types of currency, bank-notes and demand notes issued by the Treasury. The circulation of state bank-notes at the beginning of the year, 1861, was estimated to be $202,000,000. Of this amount about $150,000,000 represented circulation of banks in states loyal to the Union.[51] This bank-note currency was the principal means

[47] Mitchell, *History of the Greenbacks*, p. 39.
[48] *Ibid.*, pp. 40-41; Bolles, *Financial History from 1861 to 1885*, pp. 36-37.
[49] Quoted in *ibid.*, note, p. 35.
[50] *Report of the Secretary of the Treasury, 1862*, p. 7.
[51] *Report of the Secretary of the Treasury, 1861*, p. 17.

of payment at the time specie payments were suspended. Now that the banks of the country had collectively decided not to redeem their notes in coin, a positive impetus had been given to the forces of inflation. Relieved of the responsibility for redemption, the banks could profitably issue additional millions of their notes without the slightest chance of loss to themselves. As has been pointed out by Professor Redlich, the war could not be financed without the creation of additional purchasing power. The question hinged on how this purchasing power was to be created. If it were created by the banks, it would lead to irredeemable bank notes. If it were created by the government, there would be irredeemable government paper. Naturally, the government chose to take to itself the profit which derived from the creation of new purchasing power, and so the answer was inevitably, government paper.[52]

Demand notes had been issued by the Treasury by the authority of the legislation of July 17 and August 5, 1861. Prior to the suspension of specie payments by the government, they had been redeemable on demand at the sub-treasuries in Boston, New York, and Philadelphia.[53] In his annual report for 1861, Chase stated that up until the thirtieth of November he had issued $24,550,325 of these notes.[54] Since they were receivable for public dues and were issued in denominations as low as $5, they were actually a form of currency. The associated banks had strongly objected to their issue, fearing that they were the prelude to large emissions of government paper money, issues which would eventually drive their own bank-notes out of circulation. Many banks also felt that the circulation of these notes weakened their reserve position, inasmuch as they were expected to receive them on deposit and redeem them in coin, if so requested. As a result, some banking houses refused to accept them except on " special deposit," thus refusing to redeem them in coin.[55] This bone of contention between the banks and the Treasury was removed in December, 1861 when the Treasury itself ceased to redeem the notes in coin.

[52] Redlich, *The Molding of American Banking*, II, 95.
[53] Acts of July 17 and August 5, 1861, Huntington and Mawhinney, *Laws*, pp. 161-165.
[54] *Report of the Secretary of the Treasury, 1861*, p. 10.
[55] Mitchell, *History of the Greenbacks*, pp. 26-27.

THE LEGAL TENDER ACTS

In his report to Congress, Secretary Chase had placed considerable emphasis on his scheme to reorganize the banks of the country. In essence the plan was based on the Free Banking Law of New York which had been enacted in 1838. It envisaged a national bank currency issued by banking associations on the security of government bonds. Chase felt that such a system would not only provide the country with a well secured banknote currency, it would also provide the government with a market for its securities.[56]

The portions of the Secretary's report dealing with this proposal were referred to a sub-committee of the Committee of Ways and Means, of which the chairman was Elbridge Gerry Spaulding of Buffalo, New York, a banker by occupation. The full Committee of Ways and Means, of which the imperious Thaddeus Stevens was chairman, had made a division of its labors and responsibilities in the interest of efficiency. Two sub-committees had been formed. One, headed by Justin Morrill of Vermont, concerned itself with matters relating to the tariff and taxation. The other, headed by Spaulding, dealt with questions relating to loans. Stevens constituted a one-man sub-committee and concerned himself mostly with the writing of appropriation bills.[57]

In the interest of expediting matters, Spaulding requested that Chase provide the sub-committee with a draft bill embodying his suggestions for the proposed National Banking System. On learning from Chase that no such bill had been prepared, Spaulding set to work to prepare one modeled on the Free Banking Law of New York.[58] In his own words Spaulding has described how the idea for a legal tender currency took root in his mind. He states that "upon mature reflection" he came to the conclusion that the bank bill "could not be passed and made available quick enough to meet the crisis then pressing upon the Government for money to sustain the Army and Navy." "He therefore drafted a legal tender Treasury note

[56] *Report of the Secretary of the Treasury, 1861*, pp. 17 20.
[57] E. G. Spaulding, *History of the Legal-Tender Paper Money Issued During the Great Rebellion* (Buffalo, 1869), p. 8.
[58] *Ibid.*, p. 12.

section to be added to the bank bill, hoping, at first, that it might be made available by issuing legal tender notes direct from the Treasury, while the bank bill was put in operation throughout the country." [59]

Upon further consideration, Spaulding came to the conclusion that "the bank bill, containing sixty sections could not, with the State banks opposed to it, be passed through both Houses of Congress for several months, and that so long a delay would be fatal to the Union cause." He, therefore, separated the legal tender section from the body of the bank bill and introduced it as an independent bill with the unanimous consent of the House on December 31, 1861. It was ordered to be printed and was referred to the Committee of Ways and Means. [60]

Considerable opposition to the legal tender clause developed within the Committee. Of the nine members of the Committee, eight attended the meetings at which the bill was discussed. Four members favored the bill, and four opposed it. In support of the measure were Spaulding, Samuel Hooper of Boston, Thaddeus Stevens, and Horace Maynard of Tennessee. Opposed to the measure were Justin Morrill of Vermont, author of the Morrill Tariff, Erastus Corning of New York, Valentine Horton of Ohio, and John Stratton of New Jersey. [61] Finding that the Committee was equally divided on the wisdom of the bill and that most of the opposition impinged on the constitutionality of making anything but gold and silver a legal tender in payment of debts, Spaulding requested an opinion on this point from the Attorney General, Edward Bates. Bates declined to give an official opinion, but in a letter to Spaulding, he tended to support the constitutionality of the proposed measure, arguing that "the Constitution contains no direct verbal prohibition, and I think it contains no inferential or argumentative prohi-

---

[59] *Ibid.*, p. 13. Most contemporaries agreed that Spaulding was the originator of the Legal Tender Acts. Senator Sherman wrote: "Undoubtedly, we owe to him [Spaulding] more than to any other individual Member, the important and radical changes made in our currency system by the act reported by him to the House and amended in the Senate." Sherman, *Recollections*, I, 271. James G. Blaine has stated that "Mr. Spaulding is entitled to rank as the author of the measure." Blaine, *Twenty Years of Congress*, I, 411.

[60] Spaulding, *History of the Legal-Tender Paper Money*, pp. 13-14; *Congressional Globe*, 37th Congress, 2nd Session, p. 181.

[61] Spaulding, pp. 16-17; Mitchell, *History of the Greenbacks*, pp. 46-47.

bition that can be fairly drawn from its expressed terms." [62]
Spaulding read this letter to the Committee, and, although most
of the opposition held its ground, Stratton finally consented to
vote for the bill so that it could be reported to the House. [63]

The bill was reported to the House on January 7 and was
referred to the Committee of the Whole on the State of the
Union. [64] It authorized the Secretary of the Treasury to issue
$100,000,000 of Treasury notes not bearing interest. They
could be issued in denominations as low as $5, and were " re-
ceivable for all debts and demands due to the United States, and
for all salaries, dues, debts, and demands owing by the United
States." They were to be fundable at par for 6 per cent bonds
of the United States, and moreover and most important, they
were to be " lawful money, and a legal tender in payment of
all debts, public and private." In addition, the $50,000,000 of
demand notes which had been authorized by the legislation of
the preceding summer were brought within the scope of the
bill and were also pronounced to be legal tender. [65]

News of the introduction of a legal tender bill produced
consternation among the bankers of New York, Boston, and
Philadelphia. A delegation representing the associated banks
of these cities travelled to Washington in order to make their
opposition felt more effectively. They appointed Singleton A.
Mercer of the Farmer's and Mechanic's Bank of Philadelphia
as their chairman and proceded to invite the Finance Committee
of the Senate and the Committee of Ways and Means of the
House to meet with them at the office of the Secretary of the
Treasury on January 11, 1862. [66] James Gallatin, son of Albert
Gallatin and President of the Gallatin Bank of New York,
made the principal speech on behalf of the bankers and against
the proposed bill. Gallatin offered a plan which, he felt, would
obviate the necessity for resorting to fiat money to carry on
the war. The most important of his proposals were: (1) the

[62] Spaulding, pp. 15-16.
[63] *Ibid.*, p. 16.
[64] *Ibid.*, p. 16; *Congressional Globe*, 37th Congress, 2nd Session, p. 218.
[65] Spaulding, pp. 16-17.
[66] *Ibid.*, pp. 18-20; Mitchell, *History of the Greenbacks*, pp. 47-48; Bolles,
Financial History from 1861 to 1885, p. 47; Redlich, *The Molding of American
Banking*, II, 94.

legislating of heavy taxes which would produce $125,000,000 over and above duties on imports; (2) no further issue of demand notes beyond those already authorized; (3) the issue of $100,000,000 of interest-bearing Treasury notes to run for two years and receivable for public dues except customs; (4) suspension of the sub-treasury act so as to allow the banks to become public depositories; (5) the issue of six per cent twenty year bonds to be negotiated by the Secretary of the Treasury, not necessarily at par but at the price they would bring in the market.[67]

Only on the proposition that there should be more adequate taxation was there agreement between the bankers and the representatives of Congress. Since Gallatin's plan did not even mention a National Banking System, it was not acceptable to Chase. Spaulding and Hooper took exception to the proposal to market government bonds below par. The former expressed himself as objecting " to any and every form of ' shinning ' by Government through Wall or State streets to begin with; . . . to the knocking down of Government stocks to seventy-five or sixty cents on the dollar, the inevitable result of throwing a new and large loan on the market, without limitation as to price; . . . ." Spaulding claimed for legal tender notes at least " as much virtue . . . as the notes of banks which have suspended specie payments." [68]

Here, amid all the drama of a face-to-face meeting were presented two starkly contrasting theories of war finance. Although the Legal Tender Acts were destined to be carried through Congress under the banner of " absolute necessity," it can be deduced from Gallatin's proposal and Spaulding's rebuttal that a great deal more was involved. Almost all the older authorities on this subject have castigated Spaulding for

[67] *Report of the Monetary Commission of the Indianapolis Convention of Boards of Trade, Chambers of Commerce, Commercial Clubs, and Other Similar Bodies of the United States* (Chicago, 1898), pp. 406-407; Spaulding, p. 20; Bolles, *Financial History from 1861 to 1885*, p. 48; Mitchell, *History of the Greenbacks*, p. 48.

[68] Spaulding, p. 21. In objecting to the government's " shinning " through Wall Street, Spaulding meant that he opposed any proposition which would allow capitalists to purchase United States bonds at market prices which would undoubtedly go below par.

his refusal to countenance Gallatin's suggestion that government bonds be sold below par. In their somewhat violent essay on the Legal Tender Act, Henry Adams and Francis A. Walker, looking down from the heights of superior knowledge, say of Spaulding: "Like all ignorant men impatient of resistance or restraint, the moment he saw an obstacle he knew but one resource,—an appeal to force." [69] Words such as these indicate that the essay is itself more an appeal to emotion than to logic and reason. Much more convincing are the arguments contained in the scholarly work of Wesley C. Mitchell. He clearly points out all the inconsistencies in the argument of "necessity" and feels that the government could have obtained the necessary money if it had been willing to sell its securities below par.[70] Spaulding's words above indicate that he knew money could be raised, if the government were willing to have its credit buffeted about in the financial centers. The fact of the matter was that Spaulding and a majority of his colleagues in Congress were not willing to subject the credit of the government to such a trial. Whether they were right or wrong is an exceedingly complex question, as the researches of Professor Mitchell have so clearly demonstrated. Although it may be allowed that there was no very good reason why the government should not have negotiated its bonds at prices considerably below par, it may well be asked if this policy in itself would have been sufficient to meet the situation.

To the present writer it seems that the "necessity" of the situation was not in protecting the credit of the government but in supplying a medium of payment, in other words a currency. At the beginning of the year 1862, there were three types of money in use in the northern states. These were gold and silver coin, the notes of state banks, and the demand notes of the Treasury. A supply of gold and silver coin could in no

---

[69] Adams and Walker, "The Legal Tender Act" in *Historical Essays*, p. 289.
[70] Mitchell, *History of the Greenbacks*, pp. 49-50, 73-74, and *passim*. Other writers have supported Mitchell in his denial of "necessity." See Barrett, *Greenbacks and Resumption of Specie Payments*, pp. 56-57; *Report of the Monetary Commission of the Indianapolis Convention*, p. 406; White, *Money and Banking*, p. 111; Ernest Ludlow Bogart, *War Costs and Their Financing: A Study of the Financing of the War and the After-war Problems of Debt and Taxation* (New York, 1921), p. 310.

way be depended on. It has been noted that hoarding had begun even before the suspension of specie payments.[71] After this event, it seems extremely unlikely that gold could have been brought back into general circulation as suspension certainly exacerbated the tendency to hoard specie. To finance the war with a currency consisting of state bank-notes was not only contrary to public policy as enunciated in the Independent Treasury Act of 1846, but it would have been more dubious in concept than the idea of issuing legal tender notes. The banks would no doubt have been happy to issue an almost unlimited supply of notes, but it would seem that such an expedient, involving vast issues by banks, many of which had little or no real capital, would have been at least as dangerous as the issue of legal tender notes and probably more so. It would, moreover, have been a dereliction of duty on the part of the government to have abdicated this vital power over the currency, placing it in the hands of a horde of private institutions whose chief interest was the profits of their stockholders.[72]

Treasury demand notes authorized by the Acts of July 17 and August 5, 1861 constituted the third type of currency in existence after the suspension of specie payments. Further issues of these notes which were not legal tender but which were receivable for public dues were the most plausible alternative to the issue of legal tender notes. During the debate over the legal tender bill, Congressman Clement L. Vallandigham of Ohio offered a bill giving the Secretary of the Treasury power to issue $150,000,000 of such notes as a substitute for the measure championed by Spaulding.[73] A resort to this proposition would have avoided many of the difficulties incidental to the issue of

[71] *Supra*, p. 27.

[72] I agree here with the conclusion of Professor Redlich, to wit: "The city bankers expected first that the war could be financed like the Mexican War which they all remembered; but it was in fact one of the early modern mass wars, which, like all its successors, could be financed only by the creation of purchasing power. When this fact was sensed by the Secretary and Congressional leaders as well as by the bankers, the decisive question became who should create the additional purchasing power, government or bankers. The bankers wanted the latter, Chase and Spaulding the former. The latters' choice, which prevailed, led to irredeemable government paper money; the alternative would have led to irredeemable bank notes." *The Molding of American Banking*, II, 95.

[73] *Congressional Globe*, 37th Congress, 2nd Session, pp. 614-615.

legal tender notes. Since they would not be legal tender, there would be no change in the standard of value with all the unsettling consequences which such a change entailed. Since no one would have to receive them in payment of debt, there would be no charge that the government was encouraging business immorality and breach of contract. Also no one doubted that the government possessed the constitutional power to issue such notes, since they had been issued many times in the past.[74] The chief difficulty with such a proposition was the fact, quite obvious at the time, that banks would be under no obligation to pay out such notes, and, indeed, could not do so if their customers refused to receive them. Senator Sherman summed up the difficulties inherent in the demand note proposition: " If you strike out this tender clause, you do it with the knowledge that these notes will fall dead upon the money market of the world; that they will be refused, as they are now refused by the banks; that they will be a subordinate, disgraced currency, that will not pass from hand to hand; that they will have no legal sanction; that any man . . . may decline to receive them, and thus discredit the obligations of the government." [75] Such considerations were of controlling importance in the eventual adoption of the legal tender clause.

The meeting of the bankers with the representatives of Congress had been fruitless. The latter refused to agree that United States bonds should be sold below par, and did not feel that the other features of the bankers' plan were adequate to the crisis. In Spaulding's words, they " adhered to the legal tender bill, then pending in the House, as being a more available plan, and on a much larger scale." [76] Letters of support from various bankers and business men pointed up the fact that the opinions of the associated bankers voiced in Washington, by no means represented the sentiments of the business community at large.[77]

On January 20, Spaulding, as Chairman of the Sub-Com-

[74] See, for example, the Acts of December 23, 1857 and December 17, 1860. Huntington and Mawhinney, Laws, pp. 151-152, 156-157.

[75] Congressional Globe, 37th Congress, 2nd Session, p. 791.

[76] Spaulding, p. 22.

[77] See letters to Spaulding from Moses H. Grinnell, Lewis F Allen, J. M. Ganson, Thomas Denny & Co., and John E. Williams, reproduced in ibid., pp. 23-26.

mittee on Loans, reported an additional section to the legal
tender bill. This section, which was approved by the full
Committee of Ways and Means, authorized a bond issue of
$500,000,000 at 6 per cent to run for twenty years. The legal
tender notes, authorized by the first section of the bill, were
specifically made fundable into these bonds. After the bill had
been approved by the full Committee, it was submitted to
Secretary Chase who suggested a few technical changes regarding the engraving and signing of the notes as well as a penal
section dealing with counterfeiting. Chase's suggestions were
adopted, and the bill was once again approved by the Committee. Spaulding reported the measure to the House on January 22. It was read twice and made the special order for
January 28.[78]

Spaulding began the debate on the bill with an elaborate
speech. At the very beginning he indicated his reliance on the
idea of "necessity," arguing "The bill before us is a war
measure—a measure of *necessity*, and not of choice, presented
by the Committee of Ways and Means, to meet the most
pressing demands upon the Treasury, to sustain the Army and
Navy until they can make a vigorous advance upon the traitors,
and crush out the rebellion. These are extraordinary times, and
extraordinary measures must be resorted to in order to save
our Government and preserve our nationality." [79]

At a later point in his speech Spaulding made it clear that
the "necessities" of the situation were not quite what the
vigorous language above would lead us to believe. "Congress
may judge of the necessity in the present exigency. It may
decide whether it will authorize the Secretary of the Treasury
to issue demand Treasury notes, and make them legal tender
in payment of debts, or whether it will put its six or seven
per cent bonds on the market, at various rates of discount, and
raise the money at any sacrifice the money-lender may require
to meet the pressing demands upon the Treasury. In one case
the Government will be able to pay its debts at fair rates of
interest; in the other it must go into the streets shinning for
the means, like an individual in failing circumstances, and sure

[78] *Ibid.*, p. 27.
[79] *Congressional Globe*, 37th Congress, 2nd Session, p. 523.

of being used up in the end by the avarice of those who may exact unreasonable terms." [80]

In other words, the resort to legal tender paper was not a question of " necessity " but one of policy. Spaulding plainly preferred a fiat money policy to one which would subject the government to " shinning through Wall Street." He preferred to " assert the power and dignity of the Government " to issue its own notes rather than resort to such a policy.[81]

Foreseeing that the constitutional power of Congress to pass a legal tender bill would be challenged, Spaulding argued that the bill was " a *necessary means* of carrying into execution the power granted in the Constitution ' to raise and *support* armies,' and ' to provide and *maintain* a navy.' " He interpreted the Constitution liberally, asserting that Congress could pass all " necessary and proper " laws to implement its powers. Inasmuch as the Constitution did not prohibit the issue of legal tender notes, the passage of such a bill in order to execute powers granted to Congress was entirely proper.[82]

Debate on the measure was the principal occupation of the House until it was passed on February 6. A number of able speeches were made both for and against the legal tender provision of the bill. Spaulding's constitutional arguments were challenged by the Ohio Democrat, George Hunt Pendleton, who denied there was any " legitimate connection " between issuing legal tender notes and the power to raise and support an army. The Ohioan took issue with Spaulding's liberal interpretation of the Constitution, arguing that the powers of the federal government were specifically defined, and that just because a power was not actually denied the government by the Constitution, there was no reason to assume that such power existed. Drawing upon a wealth of historical precedent, Pendleton showed that the general government in the past had never considered itself to have the power to make anything but gold and silver legal tender in payment of debts. He also dwelt on the melancholy consequences which had

[80] *Ibid.*, p. 526.
[81] *Ibid.*, p. 526.
[82] *Ibid.*, p. 525.

followed the issue of the Continental currency and the *assignats* of revolutionary France.[83]

Pendleton's constitutional objections were seconded by Representative Clement L. Vallandigham of Ohio, the stormy petrel of Democratic politics during the Civil War decade. Vallandigham denied " the right of the Federal Government to provide a paper currency intended primarily to circulate as money." He offered a substitute for Spaulding's bill which would authorize an issue of Treasury notes to the amount of $150,000,000. The significant difference was that these notes were not to be legal tender, and the purpose envisaged was " to provide a new but temporary medium, receivable for the public dues, and sufficient only to meet the increased fiscal action of the Government." There was no intention " to supersede either gold and silver or bank paper in ordinary business and commercial affairs." [84]

The most prominent Republican to speak against the bill in the House was Justin Smith Morrill of Vermont, a man whose distrust of paper money carried over into the post-war years when he became a leading advocate of Secretary McCulloch's policy of currency contraction. Morrill objected to the bill on the grounds of its "utter impolicy." He painted in glowing colors the saturnalia of inflation which, he felt, would result from the issue of legal tender notes.[85] The Vermonter feared that " having tested this facile mode of paying debts, . . . the stern and honest mode of taxation would be repugnant to many constituencies, and that the doors of the temple of paper money would not soon again be closed." [86]

Sensing that a considerable sentiment was developing against the legal tender provision of the bill, Samuel Hooper, a mem-

---

[83] *Ibid.*, pp. 549-551. Pendleton's opposition to the bill is interesting in light of his subsequent career as leading champion of the " Ohio idea " of paying off the principal of the 5-20 bonds in greenbacks. It was, incidentally, the second section of Spaulding's bill authorizing the issue of $500,000,000 in 6 per cent bonds which was the nexus of the great post-war debate between the advocates of sound money and the greenbackers. The debate evolved out of the fact that the bill was silent on the question of how the principal of the bonds was to be paid, in gold or in greenbacks. Dewey, *Financial History*, pp. 344-345.

[84] *Congressional Globe*, 37th Congress, 2nd Session, pp. 614-615.

[85] *Ibid.*, p. 630.

[86] *Ibid.*, p. 631.

ber of Spaulding's sub-committee, took the floor to defend the measure. The Boston merchant took the position that if Treasury notes of one kind or another must be resorted to, everything possible should be done to make the notes as strong as possible. He argued that the legal tender clause was necessary " to render the Government financially more independent," particularly in time of emergency " when those who are openly or secretly disloyal . . . are found everywhere." [87] Hooper also made the very important point that the country was in need of a medium of payment. Gold was " hoarded by a few speculators," and the notes of a heterogeneous multitude of state banks were hopelessly inadequate as a means of exchange and could not be legally accepted by the government. In this situation Hooper felt that " the issue provided for in this bill will be not only useful to the Government as relieving its temporary necessities but will be essential to the people as a means of supplying them with the currency necessary to pay their taxes." [88]

Debate on the measure continued for over a week. A large number of speeches were made both for and against the legal tender clause.[89] Most of the arguments were variations on the themes noted above. Opponents of legal tender dwelt on the immorality of a resort to paper money, on the economic consequences of inflation, on the " lessons of history " which, they were certain, pointed to the danger of such expedients, and on the doubtful constitutionality of making anything but gold and silver a legal tender. Proponents of the bill said that it asserted the power and majesty of the government, that it

[87] *Ibid.*, p. 617.
[88] *Ibid.*, p. 617.
[89] Speeches in favor of the bill were made by John A. Bingham of Ohio, *ibid.*, pp. 636-640; Frederick A. Pike of Maine, *ibid.*, pp. 656-658; John B. Alley of Massachusetts, *ibid.*, pp. 658-661; William Kellogg of Illinois, *ibid.*, pp. 679-681; Thomas M. Edwards of New Hampshire, *ibid.*, pp. 682-684; Harrison G. Blake of Ohio, *ibid.*, pp. 685-686; James M. Campbell of Pennsylvania, *ibid.*, pp. 686-687; Thaddeus Stevens of Pennsylvania, *ibid.*, pp. 687-689; Samuel Shellabarger of Ohio, *ibid.*, p. 690; and John Hickman of Pennsylvania, *ibid.*, pp. 690-691. Speeches in opposition to the measure were made by Roscoe Conkling of New York, *ibid.*, pp. 633-636; William P. Sheffield of Rhode Island, *ibid.*, pp. 640-642; J. W. Crisfield of Maryland, *ibid.*, Appendix, pp. 47-51; Valentine B. Horton of Ohio, *ibid.*, pp. 663-665; Benjamin F. Thomas of Massachusetts, *ibid.*, pp. 681-682; Albert G. Riddle of Ohio, *ibid.*, pp. 684-685; and Owen Lovejoy of Illinois, *ibid.*, p. 691.

would free the Treasury from dependence on bankers, that it would provide the nation with a badly needed currency, and that furthermore passage of the measure was an absolute " necessity."

The plea of " necessity " was undoubtedly the controlling factor in the passage of the bill, even though, as has been noted, this argument tended to make up in forcefulness what it lacked in logic. Even this argument strongly advanced by Stevens, Spaulding, and others would not have sufficed, had it not been backed up by the Secretary of the Treasury.

Secretary Chase came very slowly and reluctantly to the conclusion that passage of the legal tender bill was a " necessity." A hard-money man of Democratic antecedents, he had found himself at a complete loss when specie payments were suspended. He had promoted the meeting between the associated bankers and the representatives of Congress in hope that a workable policy could be agreed upon. When the meeting failed to produce an agreement, he had surrendered the initiative to Elbridge Gerry Spaulding, the only man in high position who was ready with a concrete plan of action.[90] Though he surrendered the initiative to Spaulding, it was difficult for him to support the legal tender bill wholeheartedly. In a letter to Spaulding on January 22, Chase averred that he " regretted exceedingly that it is found necessary to resort to the measure of making fundable notes of the United States a legal tender." [91] In another letter dated January 29, Chase admitted the " necessity " of the legislation inasmuch as it was " at present impossible . . . to procure sufficient coin for disbursements." He nonetheless again pointed out his great aversion to making anything but coin a legal tender in payment of debts." [92]

A few days later Chase became aware that his failure to come out strongly for the legal tender bill had embarrassed Spaulding in the House debate. In a letter dated February 3 the Secretary left no doubt that he was fully convinced as to the " necessity " of this expedient. " It is true," Chase wrote, " that I came

[90] Mitchell, *History of the Greenbacks*, p. 69; Redlich, *The Molding of American Banking*, II, 95.

[91] Chase to Spaulding, January 22, 1862, cited in Spaulding, *History of the Legal-Tender Paper Money*, p. 27.

[92] Chase to Spaulding, January 29, 1862, cited in *ibid.*, pp. 45-46.

with reluctance to the conclusion that the legal tender clause is a necessity, but I came to it decidedly, and I support it earnestly. I do not hesitate when I have made up my mind, however much regret I may feel over the necessity of the conclusion to which I come. . . . *Immediate action is of great importance. The Treasury is nearly empty. I have been obliged to draw for the last installment of the November loan; so soon as it is paid, I fear the banks generally will refuse to receive the United States notes. You will see the necessity of urging the bill through without more delay."* [93]

The Secretary's support of the " necessity " of the legal tender clause contributed greatly to its eventual triumph. John B. Alley, Congressman from Massachusetts, asserted: " Beneficent as this measure is, as one of relief, nothing could induce me to give it sanction but uncontrollable necessity." [94] Thomas M. Edwards of New Hampshire pointed out that he would vote for the bill only because he believed " that the necessities of the Government today demand of this House that it should come to its rescue." [95] Similar statements were made by other members. [96]

After thousands of words of debate, the House finally came to a vote on February 6. First to be disposed of was a substitute bill offered by Valentine Horton on behalf of the dissident members of the Committee of Ways and Means. This substitute was similar to the one offered by Clement Vallandigham which never came to a vote, but differed from it in that it would have authorized the issue of interest-bearing Treasury notes not a legal tender. [97] The substitute was voted down, 95 to 55. [98] After this, the vote on the legal tender bill was anti-climactic.

[93] Chase to Spaulding, February 3, 1862, cited in *ibid.*, pp. 59-60. See also the letter to William Cullen Bryant from Chase dated February 4, 1862 in which the legal tender clause is asserted to be " indispensably necessary," in Robert Bruce Warden, *An Account of the Private Life and Public Services of Salmon Portland Chase* (Cincinnati, 1874), p. 409.

[94] *Congressional Globe*, 37th Congress, 2nd Session, p. 659.

[95] *Ibid.*, p. 684.

[96] For example, the remarks of William Kellogg of Illinois, *ibid.*, p. 679; of Thaddeus Stevens, *ibid.*, p. 689; of John Hickman of Pennsylvania, *ibid.*, p. 690.

[97] *Ibid.*, p. 693.

[98] *Ibid.*, p. 695.

as its success was assured. The measure was approved by a vote of 93 to 59.[99] The cleavage in the Republican party in the House over the bill was the first of many such cleavages on monetary policy which were destined to occur in the years to follow. It is noteworthy that while leaders like Stevens, Hooper, and Spaulding had supported the bill, other leaders such as Morrill and Conkling had strongly opposed it. The vote on the bill brought out no marked party or sectional divisions, although Republicans tended to support it and Democrats to oppose it. The vote on the substitute measure proposed by the minority of the Committee of Ways and Means was an accurate measure of feeling on the legal tender clause. Of the 95 votes cast against the substitute, 84 were recorded by Republicans, 8 by Democrats, and 3 by " old line Whigs." Of the 55 votes recorded in favor of the substitute and therefore against the legal tender provision, 25 were cast by Democrats, 23 by Republicans, and 7 by " old line Whigs." A sectional analysis shows that New England supported the legal tender provision, 16 to 11; the middle states cast 36 votes for the clause and 18 against it; the southern states opposed it by 7 to 10; the middle western states favored it by 27 to 13; and the western states by 9 to 3.[100]

In the Senate the legal tender bill was debated for only two days. The bill was reported out of the Finance Committee with several amendments. The most important of these provided: (1) that the legal tender notes should be receivable for all claims and demands against the United States *except for the interest on government bonds and notes which should be paid in coin*; (2) that the Secretary of the Treasury could dispose of the $500,000,000 of bonds for coin or for legal tender notes *at the market price*; (3) that customs duties and the proceeds of sales of public lands should be set aside to pay the interest on the public debt in coin.[101]

The Chairman of the Senate Finance Committee, William Pitt Fessenden of Maine, made it clear that, although he was reporting the bill out of the Committee with the legal tender clause intact, he was no friend of that expedient. He objected

[99] *Ibid.*, p. 695.
[100] *Ibid.*, p. 695; Mitchell, *History of the Greenbacks*, pp. 75-76.
[101] Spaulding, *History of the Legal-Tender Paper Money*, p. 100. Italics mine.

to it on a number of grounds. In the first place, he felt that the measure " certainly cannot increase confidence in the ability or the integrity of the country." Secondly, it was, in his judgment, " a confession of bankruptcy,"and moreover was in " bad faith " and encouraged " bad morality in public and private." Furthermore, a legal tender currency would necessarily change and derange all values. The result would be " Inflation, subsequent depression, all the evils which follow from an inflated currency." Despite these objections, Fessenden announced that he was open to conviction, if it could be shown to his satisfaction that the legal tender clause was a necessity.[102]

The constitutional issue, which had played a part in the House debate, was also raised in the Senate where Jacob Collamer of Vermont, quoting extensively from the debates in the Constitutional Convention of 1787, attempted to show that the power to make paper money a legal tender was never contemplated by the founding fathers.[103] The most effective rebuttal to the Pendletons and the Collamers who took this high constitutional ground was delivered in the Senate by Charles Sumner of Massachusetts. Sumner admitted that the Constitution contained no words which expressly gave Congress power to make Treasury notes a legal tender, but he pointed out, " there are no words expressly giving to Congress the power to issue Treasury notes." There is no reason to infer, the Massachusetts Senator argued, that the constitutional denial of power to the states to " emit bills of credit " or make anything but gold and silver coin a tender in payment of debts applies to the general government either directly or indirectly. The fact that the states were denied this power shows that the subject was in the minds of the founding fathers, but " If they failed to extend it still further, it is reasonable to conclude that they left the whole subject in all its bearings to the sound discretion of Congress, under the ample powers intrusted to it." [104] Since Congress had issued Treasury notes at many times in the past, there was no reason to assume that it might not go one step further and declare such notes to be legal tender.

[102] *Congressional Globe*, 37th Congress, 2nd Session, pp. 765-767.
[103] *Ibid.*, pp. 767-771.
[104] *Ibid.*, p. 797.

Most of the amendments to the House bill which had been proposed by the Committee on Finance were adopted on February 12.[105] Almost all the debate on the bill centered on the legal tender clause. One of the strongest speeches in favor of legal tender was made by Senator John Sherman of Ohio, who laid great emphasis on the argument which had been advanced by Samuel Hooper in the House, namely, that the country was desperately in need of some form of currency. He admitted the theoretical possibility of selling bonds for what they would bring on the market. But, " Where," he asked, " will the purchaser of your bonds get the gold and silver coin " which would be necessary under the sub-treasury law? " It is now driven out of circulation. There is no such thing as gold and silver coin circulating in the country to any large amount. It is stowed away." Sherman rightly dismissed the proposal that Congress should finance the war by using the paper money of the State banks. He pointed out to the Senators that to do this would be " to install as your national currency, as your standard of values, the inflated currency of all the local banks in the United States; banks over which you have no control, which you cannot regulate or govern in the slightest degree." [106] This argument, as has been indicated above, provided the strongest defense in favor of the " necessity " of the legal tender clause.

On February 13, the crucial vote was taken on the motion of Senator Collamer to strike out the legal tender clause.[107] The motion was lost by a vote of 22 to 17. Of the 17 votes against the legal tender clause, 9 were cast by Republicans, 6 by Democrats, and 2 by " old line Whigs." Of the 22 votes in favor of the clause, 18 were cast by Republicans, 3 by Democrats, and 1 by an " old line Whig." As in the House, the bill was put through largely by the votes of Republicans, but it is significant that here, also, was presaged the split in the Republi-

[105] *Ibid.*, pp. 771-775.

[106] *Ibid.*, p. 790.

[107] In addition to the speeches already quoted, the bill was supported by Senators Howe of Wisconsin, *ibid.*, Appendix, pp. 51-56; Jacob Howard of Michigan, *ibid.*, pp. 796-797; James Doolittle of Wisconsin, *ibid.*, Appendix, pp. 56-58; James McDougall of California, *ibid.*, Appendix, pp. 58-60. The bill was opposed in speeches by Senators Edgar Cowan of Pennsylvania, *ibid.*, pp. 791-793; James Simmons of Rhode Island, *ibid.*, pp. 793-795; and James Bayard of Delaware, *ibid.*, pp. 795-796.

can party over monetary policy which was to become so notice-able a few years later. Although the legal tender provision was supported by important Republicans such as John Sherman of Ohio, Charles Sumner and Henry Wilson of Massachusetts, and Zachariah Chandler of Michigan, it was opposed by other important Republicans such as William P. Fessenden of Maine, Jacob Collamer of Vermont, Solomon Foot of Vermont, and Preston King of New York.

A sectional analysis of the vote shows that New England opposed the legal tender clause, 6 to 5; the middle states opposed it 7 to 2; the middle west supported it 13 to 0; the West opposed it, 2 to 1; and the South opposed it 2 to 1. There might be some temptation to draw some conclusions from this sectional analysis, particularly from the indecisive nature of the vote by the representatives of New England and the middle states as contrasted with the overwhelming support of the legal tender provision by the middle western Senators. Such a temptation must be resisted, however, for the results of the issue of the greenbacks could by no means be predicted accurately in early 1862, and there had been no chance for sectional or class opinion to coalesce on the issue. Indeed, as has been shown, many of the votes in favor of the legal tender provision were cast only because it was regarded as an absolute " necessity." Senator Doolittle of Wisconsin, for example, said that he cast his vote for the measure " with more misgivings as to its effect at home and abroad than of any other measure for which I have given my vote in this body." [108]

After the move to delete the legal tender clause had been defeated, passage of the bill was a foregone conclusion. The final vote was 30 to 7.[109] Many senators who had opposed the legal tender provision supported the measure on the final vote, because they were unwilling to continue their opposition to the point of obstinacy when it became obvious that the bill would pass.[110]

Because of the amendments which had been engrafted upon

---

[108] Information for an analysis of this vote was drawn from *ibid.*, p. 800 and from Blaine, *Twenty Years of Congress*, I, 316-317. For Senator Doolittle's remarks, see *Congressional Globe*, 37th Congress, 2nd Session, Appendix, p. 58.

[109] *Ibid.*, p. 804.

[110] See the remarks of Senators Latham and Anthony, *ibid.*, p. 804.

the original bill by the Senate, the appointment of a joint conference committee became necessary. There was particular opposition in the House to the amendment which required that interest on the public debt be paid in coin.[111] In conference, however, the opinion of the Senators triumphed with the proviso that import duties should be paid in specie in order that a fund might be accumulated out of which coin interest payments might be paid.[112] Both houses agreed to the report of the conference committee on February 24, 1862.[113] The bill received the signature of President Lincoln and became a law on February 25, 1862.[114]

In its final form the first Legal Tender Act authorized the issue of $150,000,000 of United States notes, not bearing interest. The notes were to be issued in denominations of not less than five dollars and were to be " lawful money and a legal tender in payment of all debts public and private." $50,000,000 of the notes were in lieu of the demand notes authorized by the legislation of July 17, 1861, and it was provided that " said demand notes shall be taken up as rapidly as practicable," and the legal tender notes substituted for them. The legal tender notes were made exchangeable for the six per cent 5-20 bonds which were authorized to the extent of $500,000,000 by the second section of the act. These were the significant provisions of an Act which was destined to have profound and far-reaching consequences for the economic and political history of the United States.[115]

[111] Thaddeus Stevens, for example, asserted that the amendment " makes two classes of money—one for the banks and brokers, and another for the people." Ibid., p. 900.

[112] Ibid., p. 938.

[113] Ibid., pp. 929, 939.

[114] Act of February 25, 1862. See Huntington and Mawhinney, Laws, pp. 165-168. For accounts of the debates on the first Legal Tender Act, see Mitchell, History of the Greenbacks, pp. 51-78; Bolles, Financial History from 1861 to 1885, pp. 51-73; Spaulding, History of the Legal-Tender Paper Money, pp. 29-148; Barrett, Greenbacks and Resumption of Specie Payments, pp. 19-24; Report of the Monetary Commission of the Indianapolis Convention, pp. 408-411; Sumner, History of American Currency, pp. 197-198; A. Barton Hepburn, A History of Currency in the United States with a Brief Description of the Currency Systems of All Commercial Nations (New York, 1915), pp. 185-190; Blaine, Twenty Years of Congress, I, 411-426; Sherman, Recollections, I, 271-279.

[115] Act of February 25, 1862, Huntington and Mawhinney, Laws, pp. 165-168.

FURTHER ISSUES OF LEGAL TENDER NOTES

During the debate on the first Legal Tender Act, Justin Morrill had prophesied that, once opened, "the doors of the temple of paper money would not soon again be closed." [116] The Vermonter's prescience was abundantly demonstrated in the year which followed the passage of the Act of February 25, 1862. By early March of 1863, an additional $300,000,000 of United States notes had been authorized.

The reasons which led to the passage of the second and third Legal Tender Acts were similar to those which brought about the enactment of the first such law, namely, insufficiency of revenue from customs duties, internal taxation, and sales of public lands plus an inability on the part of the government to market its securities successfully. Since the printing of greenbacks was the easiest way for the government to obtain money, it came as no surprise when Chase requested that Congress authorize the issue of another $150,000,000 of legal tender notes. This he did in a letter to Thaddeus Stevens on June 7, 1862 in which the Secretary pointed out that sales of 5-20 bonds had lagged badly. [117]

Congress was not disposed to haggle. Once again the argument of necessity was brought to bear. Spaulding declared: "The ground upon which the secretary of the treasury and upon which the Committee of Ways and Means, rest this issue of notes is the necessity of the case." [118] Once again the argument was implicit that it was better to issue paper money than sell bonds far below par. [119] Chase and Congress shared this opinion, the slight sales of 5-20's indicating that the Secretary was unwilling to throw bonds on the market even though by the Act of February 25, 1862 he possessed the power to sell them at their market value.

The second legal tender bill, authorizing the issue of an

[116] *Supra*, p. 38.

[117] *House Miscellaneous Documents*, No. 81, 37th Congress, 2nd Session, pp. 2-3. Portions of this letter were read by Spaulding on the floor of the House. *Congressional Globe*, 37th Congress, 2nd Session, p. 2768.

[118] *Ibid.*, p. 2768.

[119] Spaulding said: "When money can be obtained at par on six per cent bonds, I would prefer to have that done to the issuing a very large amount of legal tender notes." *Ibid.*, p. 2767.

additional $150,000,000 of greenbacks, passed the House on
June 24 by a vote of 76 to 47. On July 2 it was acted upon
favorably by the Senate, the vote being 22 to 13.[120] The bill
received the signature of the President and became a law on
July 11, 1862.[121] An interesting feature of the second Legal
Tender Act was that the Secretary of the Treasury was authorized to issue $35,000,000 of legal tender notes in denominations
less than five dollars. Chase had requested this power because
of the difficulty encountered by the government in obtaining
means of making change in payments to soldiers. The difficulty
had been accentuated by the fact that almost all gold and silver
coin had disappeared from general circulation.[122]

Despite the fact that the failure of the administration and
Congress to adopt an adequate financial program had led
directly to the first and second Legal Tender Acts, the situation
was destined to get worse before it got better. Chase's second
report to Congress in December, 1862 predicted a deficit for
the fiscal year ending June 30, 1863 of $276,912,517. Despite
this prediction the Secretary suggested no new taxation but
proposed to raise the entire amount by loans. Much of the
report was devoted to a renewed advocacy of a national banking
system.[123]

Shortly after this report was issued, the condition of the
Treasury became so bad that Chase could not find means to
pay the soldiers. This naturally alarmed Congress, and on
December 22, the House passed a joint resolution expressing its
opinion " that immediate steps ought to be taken by the Treasury
Department to pay the sums due to the soldiers in our armies,
and the seamen and marines in our Navy, and that to this end
a preference be given to this class of Government creditors
over every other." [124]

The difficulties of the situation resulted in the passage of the
Act of March 3, 1863 which authorized the emission of another
$150,000,000 of United States notes.[125] The Act also authorized

[120] *Ibid.*, pp. 2903, 3079.
[121] Act of July 11, 1862, Huntington and Mawhinney, *Laws*, pp. 638-650.
[122] *Ibid.*, Also *Congressional Globe*, 37th Congress, 2nd Session, p. 2768.
[123] *Report of the Secretary of the Treasury, 1862*, pp. 12-20.
[124] *Congressional Globe*, 37th Congress, 3rd Session, p. 199.
[125] Act of March 3, 1863, Huntington and Mawhinney, *Laws*, pp. 642-645.

the issue of $750,000,000 of various types of securities including Treasury notes to the extent of $400,000,000 which might be made a legal tender. These were the interest-bearing legal tender notes, which, to some extent, circulated as currency.[126]

Opposition to the legal tender principle had practically died out in Congress. In the House the third Legal Tender Act passed from its first to its third reading in one day and was voted upon favorably with a division on January 25.[127] The Senate passed the bill on a vote of 32 to 4 on February 13. It is noteworthy that Senators Collamer, Cowan, and Fessenden, who had strongly opposed the legal tender clause a year before, all voted for the bill.[128] Now that the country was fairly launched on a paper money policy, even the most recalcitrant hard-money Congressmen sensed that there was no turning back. The fight for specie resumption would have to be postponed until the end of the war.

Under the Acts of February 25, 1862, July 11, 1862, and March 3, 1863, issues of $450,000,000 of legal tender notes were authorized. During the years, 1862-1865, a total of $480,500,000 of these notes was printed, but inasmuch as

---

[126] *Ibid.* According to the terms of the Act, interest-bearing legal tender notes might bear interest at not more than 6 per cent and might run for no more than three years. They were legal tender for their face value, excluding interest. In 1863 and 1864, Secretary Chase, using the discretion granted him by the law, issued $166,500,000 of two-year 5 per cent notes, and in 1864 he issued $44,500,000 of one-year 5 per cent notes. These notes were never expected to circulate extensively as currency. It was rather expected that they would be held as investments by banks. This would probably have been the case except for the fact that interest on the notes was paid twice yearly on detachable coupons appended to the notes. Just before the interest was due, the notes would be hoarded by banks and would cease to circulate as currency. Once the interest had been paid, the banks would immediately pay them out, and once again they would contribute to the volume of the circulation. Chase's successor, Fessenden, recognized the undesirable features of these notes, and under the authority of the Acts of March 3, 1863, and June 30, 1864, he funded them into another type of interest-bearing legal tender note, payable *both interest and principal*, at maturity. These notes were generally referred to as the compound-interest legal-tender notes. At the close of the fiscal year, 1864-1865, $193,800,000 of these 6 per cent three year compound-interest notes were outstanding, along with $42,300,000 of the one and two-year notes originally issued by Chase. Most of the compound-interest notes were held by banks for reserve purposes. See Mitchell, *History of the Greenbacks*, pp. 174-177; Table V, p. 179.

[127] *Congressional Globe*, 37th Congress, 3rd Session, pp. 520-522.

[128] *Ibid.*, p. 945.

$49,000,000 were redeemed by the Treasury during the same period, total net issues during the war amounted to $431,500,000.[129]

GREENBACKS, THE PREMIUM ON GOLD, AND THE PRICE LEVEL

The suspension of specie payments in December, 1861 and the subsequent issue of the greenbacks had profound economic consequences which were felt in one way or another by every citizen of the United States. The specific effects of paper money on the particular economic groups with which we are concerned in this study will be considered in later chapters.[130] At this point it will be useful to devote some attention to the causative influence of the legal tender notes on the price of gold and on the general price level.

Suspension of specie payments necessarily implied the rejection of gold as the general standard of value. The place of gold was taken, first, by the bank-notes of the State banks and the demand notes of the government. After the passage of the first Legal Tender Act, greenbacks became the standard of value in which prices were quoted and in which business was transacted. Gold became just another commodity like cotton or iron, and the price of gold was quoted in greenbacks. It was a very important commodity for two reasons. According to the terms of the first Legal Tender Act, all customs duties had to be paid in gold. It was also important to importers who had to pay for foreign goods in gold, since it was the standard of value in most of the world.

As soon as it was known that the banks and the Treasury were determined to suspend specie payments, there developed a premium on gold. The premium was equivalent to a discounting by the public of the government's promise eventually to redeem its paper money in specie. It was entirely natural and could not have been prevented so long as the government and the banks divorced themselves from the gold standard. The average annual price of gold in greenbacks for the years 1860-1865 is indicated in the table below.[131]

---

[129] Dewey, *Financial History*, Table, p. 308.
[130] See Chapters IV, V, and VI, *infra*.
[131] Wesley C. Mitchell, *Gold, Prices, and Wages under the Greenback Standard* (Berkeley, 1908), Table 74, p. 279.

Year	Price of Gold
1860	100
1861	100
1862	113
1863	145
1864	203
1865	157

It will be noted that gold and currency were at par in 1860 and 1861 before the suspension of specie payments. In 1862, the year of the first and second Legal Tender Acts, it required on the average $113 in greenbacks to purchase $100 in gold. The premium rose in 1863 and 1864 until, in the latter year, it required, on the average, $203 to buy what had formerly been $100 in gold. The prices above are averages and do not indicate the extreme variations in the daily quotations of the premium on gold within a given year. These variations between the highest quoted premium and the lowest such quotation were frequently very great. In 1864, for example, the highest quoted price for $100 of gold in greenbacks was $285. The lowest quoted price during the same year was $151. The difference between these two prices is $134.

There were a number of factors which influenced the course of the premium on gold. The supply of gold and of greenbacks is probably the most obvious of these. Naturally the ratio existing between the supply of gold and the quantity of greenbacks in circulation would tend to affect the premium. Exports of gold which reduced the supply would have a tendency to raise the price of the precious metal. Imports of gold would have an opposite effect. Likewise, additional issues of greenbacks such as were made by the second and third Legal Tender Acts would tend to raise the price of gold. Any contraction of the volume of the legal tenders such as was effected in 1865 would tend to lower the premium on gold. An artificial factor which operated on the supply of and demand for gold was speculation. Throughout most of the greenback period, from 1862 to 1879, this element in the situation was prominent in the public mind. Secretary Chase became so infuriated with the speculation which, he believed, tended to raise the price of gold that he recommended in 1864 the passage of a bill which would outlaw dealings in gold futures and forbid the sale of gold in the " Gold Room " in New York.[132] The law which Congress passed at the Secretary's behest was entirely ineffective, and, by abolishing organized dealings in this commodity, only resulted in raising the price of gold even higher.[133] The law was repealed two weeks after it had received the President's signature.[134]

Although the factors described above all contributed to the sporadic rise and fall in the gold premium, they were by no means the most important influences at work. Of far greater importance were the reports from the various fronts where the war was being carried on. It was on the passage of arms that the confidence of the people in their government actually depended. The greenbacks were issued on the credit of the nation, and it was victory or defeat that determined the standing of that credit. Victory invariably produced a fall in the premium which was the same thing as an appreciation in the value of the greenback currency. A defeat caused depreciation of that currency and a rise in the price of gold.[135]

The rise in the price of gold was matched by a rise in the general price level. The best available index in which prices at wholesale, wages, cost of living, and rents are weighed at 20, 35, 35, and 10, respectively, gives the following results for the Civil War years.[136] 1860 is used as the base year.

Year	General Price Index
1860	100
1861	98
1862	111
1863	135
1864	182
1865	179

[132] See the letter of Chase to Horace Greeley in Warden, *Chase*, p. 603.

[133] Act of June 17, 1864, Huntington and Mawhinney, *Laws*, pp. 182-183. *Congressional Globe*, 38th Congress, 1st Session, pp. 1673, 2937. Mitchell, *History of the Greenbacks*, pp. 228-232.

[134] *Ibid.*, p. 232.

[135] *Ibid.*, pp. 212-238. Professor Mitchell shows indisputably that the premium on gold rose and fell as the prospects of Union victory waxed or waned.

[136] This is the index of Carl Snyder which may be found in United States Department of Commerce, Bureau of the Census, *Historical Statistics of the United States, 1789-1945: A Supplement to the Statistical Abstract of the United*

This is a composite index which provides evidence as to the effect of the issue of the greenbacks on the general price level. Of the elements which entered into the computation of the index, prices at wholesale showed the greatest degree of sympathy with the rise and fall in the premium on gold. This is understandable inasmuch as wholesales prices were determined at the great market centers and were directly influenced by the import-export trade (in which the price of gold was an important factor). Wages and rents, influenced greatly by specific local conditions, did not rise so rapidly during the war years, nor did they fall so swiftly at the close of the conflict. The cost of living, as might be expected, neither rose so rapidly as wholesale prices, nor so slowly as wages and rents.[137]

As had been predicted during the debates in Congress over the first Legal Tender Act, inflation was the primary by-product of the resort to paper money. The statistics presented above demonstrate the magnitude of this inflation. Such a derangement of the pre-war relationship between prices, wages, and the cost of living produced inevitable reactions within the various economic groups which were affected most profoundly. In discussing the climate of opinion which prevailed when the Legal Tender Acts were enacted, Wesley Mitchell commented that " If any one possessed . . . ideas of the beneficence of an irredeemable paper currency as afterwards animated members of the Greenback party, he kept them to himself." [138] This comment is entirely justified, for it would be hazardous and futile to attempt to elicit any class or sectional interpretation from the debates and votes on the Legal Tender Acts. In 1862 and 1863 the full effects of the paper money issues could not be ascertained. By the end of the war, however, it had become apparent that different economic groups had been affected in different ways by the inflation resulting from the issues of the greenbacks. Consequently, definite interests impinged on the question whether the notes should be retained or contracted.

States (Washington, D.C., 1949), Series L 1, pp. 231-233. Snyder's original index used 1913 as the base year. For the years, 1860-65, I have converted the original index, using 1860 as the base year.

[137] More specific information concerning prices, wages, and the cost of living will be presented in Chapters IV, V, and VI, infra.

[138] Mitchell, History of the Greenbacks, p. 68.

These interests it will be our task to investigate in the chapters which follow.

The question as to the " necessity " for the legislation which produced the greenbacks will undoubtedly remain one of those unanswerable conundrums which give rise to innumerable pages of speculative history. It seems apparent that the months between February, 1862 and March, 1863 when the three Legal Tender Acts were enacted marked a phase of the financial history of the war which fell between the fumbling, ineffective efforts of the government to raise sufficient funds in 1861 and the third phase which followed the passage of the third Legal Tender Act in which the nation girded itself financially to fight the war through to eventual victory. The fact that the war was brought to a successful conclusion without the necessity for the issue of more legal tender notes was due to two developments, namely, the success of the government in marketing its securities during the latter stages of the war through the energetic activities of Jay Cooke and his associates, and the adoption by the Acts of July 1, 1862 and June 30, 1864 of a Spartan tax policy which increased revenues from internal sources to $109,000,000 in 1863-64 and to $209,000,000 in 1864-65.[189]

It is conceivable that, had an efficacious system for selling bonds been found early in the war, and had a stringent policy of taxation been adopted in 1861, the war might have been financed on a specie basis without the necessity for a resort to paper money. To the present writer, however, this possibility seems highly unlikely. Effective maintenance of the specie standard during the nineteenth century was largely dependent on public confidence in that standard. The events of 1861-62 including the first battle of Bull Run, the *Trent* affair, the failure of the Peninsular Campaign, and the second battle of Bull Run were hardly calculated to sustain public confidence at a high level. It seems likely, when the precarious military

---

[189] *Ibid.*, pp. 119-122; Dewey, *Financial History*, pp. 302-303; Frederic C. Howe, *Taxation and Taxes in the United States under the Internal Revenue System, 1791-1895* (New York, 1896), pp. 56-57. For the theoretical importance of taxation in war finance, see O. M. W. Sprague, " Loans and Taxes in War Finance," in *Readings in Fiscal Policy Selected by a Committee of the American Economic Association*, eds. Arthur Smithies and J. Keith Butters (Homewood, Ill., 1955), pp. 107-121.

situation in the North at that time is considered, that hoarding would have developed no matter what policy might have been adopted with regard to taxation or selling bonds. If specie went out of circulation, some form of paper currency would have had to be provided. Otherwise business could not have been carried on, taxes could not have been paid, and the enormous bond issues could not have been floated. The choice was between irredeemable bank-notes and irredeemable government paper money. The latter choice was, in my opinion, the correct one. Although it is definitely a minority view, it would seem that a very good case can be made for the " necessity " of the greenbacks.[140]

---

[140] Most of the older authorities on the greenbacks deny the " necessity " of their issue. See footnote # 70, *supra*. The only authority known to the present writer who supports the view that they were necessary is Professor Redlich. See footnote # 72, *supra*.

CHAPTER II

HUGH McCULLOCH AND THE POLICY OF CONTRACTION

In June 1864 the long smouldering conflict between President Lincoln and his ambitious Secretary of the Treasury finally reached a climax. The President had patiently endured the political machinations of Salmon P. Chase for many months. He was well aware that Chase was straining every resource at his command including the patronage of the Treasury Department and his connection with Jay Cooke to attain the prize he valued more than anything else in the world—the presidential nomination in 1864. Lincoln had endured the treachery of Chase because he shrewdly divined that the opposition of the Secretary would be less dangerous inside the cabinet than outside of it. Failing to understand Lincoln's real motives, Chase was convinced that Lincoln felt he was indispensable. This conviction was strengthened when the President refused to accept his resignation after the publication in February, 1864 of the famous Pomeroy circular in which Chase's friends had declared that Lincoln could not be re-elected and that the best available alternative was the eminent Secretary of the Treasury. Chase had denied any prior knowledge of the circular, but Lincoln was not deceived. He refused Chase's proffered resignation, because he knew that the time was not ripe for a break.[1]

In the spring of that year Lincoln had been renominated at Baltimore. No longer was it a matter of crucial importance to avoid an open break with Chase and his Radical friends. Consequently, when the Secretary, in a fit of pique over a matter of patronage in New York, decided to submit one of his periodic resignations, Lincoln surprised Chase by accepting it, pointing out that he and his finance minister had " reached

---

[1] Thomas Graham Belden and Marva Robins Belden, *So Fell the Angels* (Boston, 1956), pp. 100-116; *Inside Lincoln's Cabinet: The Civil War Diaries of Salmon P. Chase*, ed. David Donald (New York, 1954), pp. 210-211.

a point of mutual embarrassment . . . which it seems cannot be overcome or longer sustained consistently with the public service." [2]

The new Secretary of the Treasury was William Pitt Fessenden of Maine, the able chairman of the Senate Finance Committee. Fessenden accepted the position much against his better judgment. He was in bad health and knew that the unremitting labor demanded by the Treasury portfolio would do nothing to improve it. Nevertheless, he was persuaded by Lincoln that he must make the sacrifice because the condition of the country and the Treasury demanded it. Fessenden was one of the best informed men in the country on financial questions. His brief administration of the nation's finances was marked by efficiency and sagacity. Notwithstanding his success, Fessenden was not happy in the job. Having been again elected Senator by the Maine legislature in January, 1865, and finding the condition of the Treasury reasonably good, he sent a letter of resignation to the President on February 6, asking to be relieved as soon as possible.[3]

Fessenden's successor at the Treasury was Hugh McCulloch, the Indiana banker who had become the first Comptroller of the Currency in 1863. In that position he had wielded a decisive influence over the formation of the National Banking System, an influence which will be discussed in a later chapter. As president of the large and important State Bank of Indiana, McCulloch had come to Washington in 1862 to oppose the passage of the national bank bill. After the passage of the act, his opinion underwent a change, and he agreed to accept the position which made him the chief administrative officer of the new banking system.[4]

Hugh McCulloch was a New Englander who went west in 1833 to seek his fortune in the State of Indiana. After travelling by horseback over a good portion of that state, he decided to settle in the little town of Fort Wayne, where he began the practice of law. Shortly after this time, he became the manager

[2] Belden and Belden, p. 122; Warden, *Chase*, p. 619.
[3] Francis Fessenden, *Life and Public Services of William Pitt Fessenden*, 2 vols. (Boston, 1907), I, 315-325; Dewey, *Financial History*, pp. 314-316.
[4] McCulloch, *Men and Measures*, pp. 163-165.

of the Fort Wayne branch of the State Bank of Indiana. Abandoning the practice of law altogether, he became a highly successful banker, and, in 1857, was chosen president of the reorganized State Bank. The confidence was not misplaced, for McCulloch showed prudence and ability in this position. After the suspension of specie payments in 1861, McCulloch took steps to put his bank in an extremely strong situation. He advised all the branch managers to buy gold at the small premium which then existed. When gold rose to fantastic heights in the course of the war, the bank realized a handsome profit on its holdings.[5]

The ideas which McCulloch expressed in his speeches and in his reports as Secretary of the Treasury were derived from his observations and experiences in Indiana. The panic of 1837 and the subsequent depression made a profound impression on him, and he remained convinced to the end of his days that Jackson's "war on the bank" was a vital mistake. In his autobiography he makes the following comment: [6]

> The veto of the bank bill by President Jackson was strongly disapproved by many of the wisest men of his party, but he was the idol of the Democratic masses, and resistance to his iron and misdirected will, even by those who claimed to be their leaders, was impotent. The veto was unquestionably the prime cause of the unparalleled financial troubles, the political effect of which was visited upon the unoffending head of his successor, Mr. Van Buren. That the United States Bank, managed, as it was during its entire career, as a strictly business institution, was of immense utility to the country, is apparent to all who have made its history a careful study. It was useful in a very high degree, not only in what it did, but in what it prevented. It furnished a bank-note currency of uniform value and perfect solvency; it fostered well-directed industry; it regulated exchanges; it created a high standard of mercantile and commercial credit. On the other hand, it stood in the way of the creation of State banks, with unreal capital, and held in check the disposition of its customers to engage in speculative enterprise.

McCulloch was an extremely conservative banker, but he was not a bullionist in the sense that he did not feel it wise or necessary to insist on a one-hundred per cent specie backing for bank-notes. As the passage above makes clear, he favored

[5] Ibid., pp. 35, 78-97, 112-122, 129-138.
[6] Ibid., pp. 60-61.

a well-directed central bank similar to the Bank of England which should control the issue of notes and the discount rate for the entire country. In his opinion the National Banking Act had been weakened by the failure to establish such a bank as the center and prime mover of the system.[7]

As Secretary of the Treasury in the crucial years from 1865 to 1869, McCulloch was the central figure in the financial drama of Reconstruction. The sound and the fury of this drama were destined to be expressed most audibly over the issue of what should be done with the greenbacks or legal tenders. Mc-Culloch's pronunciamentos on this issue reflected the processes of a rigid, conservative, and essentially unimaginative mind. Following his own premises, he could see little merit and much positive evil in the greenbacks. They were controlled by none of the rules of experience and legal restrictions by which a well-secured bank-note currency was made to serve the needs of the business community. Their volume was limited solely by political considerations and the availability of the printing press. In addition, McCulloch felt strongly that the original issue of greenbacks in 1862 had been an unconstitutional exercise of power. This was the orthodox, conservative view of the greenbacks which was shared by a majority of McCulloch's banker colleagues. What it failed to consider was the fact that any tampering with the volume of the greenbacks in the fateful years which followed the end of the war was likely to precipitate a depression. The situation called for the delicacy of a scalpel, but McCulloch brought only the bluntness of a meat axe.

The views of the new Secretary were held up to public view for the first time in a speech delivered at Fort Wayne in October, 1865. On that occasion he strongly challenged those who were disposed to dispense with the older standards of value.[8]

I am not one of those who seem disposed to repudiate coin as a measure of value, and to make a secured paper currency the standard. On the contrary, I belong to that class of persons who, regarding an exclusive metallic currency as an impractical thing among an enterprising and commercial people, nevertheless look upon an irredeemable currency as an evil which circumstances may for a time render a necessity,

[7] *Ibid.*, p. 61.
[8] *Ibid.*, p. 201.

but which is never to be sustained as a policy. By common consent of the nations, gold and silver are the only true measure of value. They are the necessary regulators of trade. I have myself no more doubt that these metals were prepared by the Almightly for this very purpose, than I have that iron and coal were prepared for the purposes for which they are being used. I favor a well-secured convertible paper currency—no other can to any extent be a proper substitute for coin.

This passage illustrates some interesting facets of McCulloch's economic outlook. He along with the majority of his contemporaries who could claim to be well informed on economic matters accepted the idea that the Almighty had ordained the use of gold and silver as money. To such people, the study of economics itself was an attempt to ascertain the will of God. In such vein is much of the economic writing of the time, including the tracts of John Stuart Mill, Amasa Walker, and Herbert Spencer. Is it any wonder that in speaking or writing of the opinions of those who advocated policies of cheap money, whether greenbacks or free silver, the phrase " financial heresy " was frequently used? The moral indignation which such opinions usually elicited leads us to believe that the word " heresy " was used in a proper sense—that orthodox economics rested firmly upon a religious base.

The twin pillars upon which classical, orthodox economics rested were the gold standard and free trade. Both were valid because both expressed the will of God. " Free Trade—The International Common Law of the Almighty " was the proud motto of *The League* which was the organ of the Free Trade League of which William Cullen Bryant was president.[9] As we go further in our study of the monetary history of the post-Civil War years, it will become apparent that those who believed in the holy ordination of the gold standard almost invariably tended toward free trade opinions whereas those who strongly cherished paper money proclivities were usually lined up on the side of high protection to American industry. In this connection it is significant to note that Hugh McCulloch was at heart a free trader as were most conservative bankers of the period. To the end he hoped he would live to see the day when the United States would " remove all restrictions upon international trade." [10]

[9] *The League*, I (April, 1867), 1.   [10] McCulloch, p. 296.

McCulloch's convictions on financial policy were embodied in his first report which was issued in December, 1865. In this report the Secretary made it quite clear that he regarded the legal tender question as the paramount financial issue facing the country. He challenged the power of Congress to make anything except gold and silver a measure of value in time of peace asserting " The present legal-tender acts were war measures, and while the repeal of those provisions which made the United States notes lawful money is not now recommended, the Secretary is of the opinion that they ought not to remain in force one day longer than shall be necessary to enable the people to prepare for a return to the constitutional currency." [11]

The Secretary attempted to counter the arguments of those who maintained that the legal tenders constituted a loan without interest of perfect safety and uniformity. He could not deny that they were a loan without interest, but he strongly questioned their adaptability to the needs of commence. To McCulloch the paper circulation of the country should be flexible, " increasing and decreasing according to the requirements of legitimate business." The greenback currency on the other hand was likely to be " governed by the necessities of the treasury or the interests of parties rather than the demands of commerce and trade." Such currency would also be " greatly in the way of public economy, and would give to the party in possession of the government a power which it might be under strong temptations to use for other purposes than the public good—keeping the question of the currency constantly before the people as a political question, than which few things would be more injurious to business." [12]

As a banker McCulloch naturally favored the national bank-note currency which he regarded as being " secured beyond any reasonable contingency." [13] This was a natural prejudice on his part, though it was not altogether reasonable. The national bank-note currency could not actually respond to the needs of business through expansion and contraction of issue because the total amount was limited by statute to $300,000,000, and

---

[11] *Report of the Secretary of the Treasury, 1865*, p. 4.
[12] *Ibid.*, p. 4.
[13] *Ibid.*, p. 4.

the notes were secured by government bonds, the amount of which available to banks for this purpose was likely to decrease as the national debt was paid. Another important point was the fact that the national currency was by statute *redeemable* only in greenbacks. Under such conditions, it is difficult to see how the national bank-notes could be regarded as a superior form of currency.[14]

Realizing perhaps that his economic arguments were not entirely convincing, McCulloch based his chief objection to the legal tenders on constitutional grounds.[15]

But the great and insuperable objection, as already stated, to the direct issue of notes by the government, as a policy, is the fact, that the government of the United States is one of limited and defined powers, and that the authority to issue notes as money is neither expressly given to Congress by the Constitution, nor fairly to be inferred, except as a measure of necessity in a great national exigency. No consideration of a mere pecuniary character should induce an exercise by Congress of powers not clearly contemplated by the instrument upon which our political fabric was established.

In pointing out what he regarded as the differences between real and apparent prosperity, McCulloch cried out against the trend of the times, asserting that "There are no indications of real and permanent prosperity in our large importations of foreign fabrics; in the heavy operations at our commercial marts; in the splendid fortunes reported to be made by skillful manipulations at the gold room or the stock board; no evidences of increasing wealth in the facts that railroads and steamboats are crowded with passengers, and hotels with guests; that cities are full to overflowing, and rent and the prices of the necessaries of life, as well as luxuries, are daily advancing." To the Secretary these things only proved "that a foreign debt is being created, that the number of non-producers is increasing, and that productive industry is being diminished."[16]

[14] For a discussion of the National Banking Acts and the operation of the National Banking System, see Chapter VI.
[15] *Report of the Secretary of the Treasury, 1865*, pp. 4-5.
[16] *Ibid.*, p. 9. McCulloch's view was somewhat jaundiced and not in accord with the facts. Mr. Warren M. Persons' index of physical production of manufacturing for the years 1865-1870 shows that the manufacturing product rose in each of these years except 1868. The year 1866 was marked by a rise of 34% over the preceding year. *Historical Statistics of the United States*, Series J 13-14, p. 179.

McCulloch's cathartic remedy for returning the nation's economy to a condition of health was enforced contraction of the currency. He recommended that the compound-interest notes be divested of the legal tender quality from the date of their maturity and also that he be authorized at his discretion " to sell bonds of the United States, bearing interest at a rate not exceeding six per cent, . . . for the purpose of retiring not only compound interest notes but the United States Notes." [17]

It will be recalled that the compound-interest legal tender notes had been authorized by the third Legal Tender Act of March 3, 1863 and by the Act of June 30, 1864. Large amounts of these notes had been issued by Secretaries Chase and Fessenden. It was estimated that some $205,000,000 of these notes were outstanding on October 31, 1865. Although a large part of the compound-interest notes were held by banks for use as reserves, they were nonetheless a considerable factor in the inflationary spiral. [18]

To the argument that contraction of the currency might precipitate a business crisis by lowering prices, the Secretary had a ready though not entirely convincing answer. " To this it may be replied, that prices of articles of indispensable necessity are already so high as to be severely oppressive to consumers, especially to persons of fixed and moderate incomes and to the poorer classes. Not only do the interests, but the absolute necessities of the masses, require that the prices of articles needed for their use should decline." [19]

In his report McCulloch estimated that the resumption of specie payments would require the withdrawal of one hundred million or at most two hundred million dollars of the United States notes. This amount, added to the interest-bearing legal tenders which the Secretary wanted to divest of their monetary quality, would mean a reduction of between three hundred and four hundred millions of dollars in the amount of the country's currency. On October 31, 1865 the commerce of the country was being carried on with a little more than nine hundred

---

[17] *Report of the Secretary of the Treasury, 1865,* p. 14.
[18] See Chapter I, *supra,* note #126; Dewey, *Financial History,* pp. 313-314; A. Barton Hepburn, *History of Coinage and Currency in the United States and the Perennial Contest for Sound Money* (New York, 1903), p. 206.
[19] *Report of the Secretary of the Treasury, 1865,* pp. 11-12.

million dollars of legal currency, so that, if other monetary categories received no increase, McCulloch's desire to lower the national price level necessarily involved contracting the currency by at least a third.[20] Despite the violent nature of this economic operation, McCulloch was confident that it would not "injuriously affect real prosperity."[21]

In his first annual message to Congress on the state of the Union, President Johnson supported the opinions of his cabinet minister, declaring "It is our first duty to prepare in earnest for our recovery from the ever increasing evils of an irredeemable currency without a sudden revulsion, and yet without untimely procrastination. . . . The gradual reduction of the currency is the only measure that can save the business of the country from disastrous calamities, and this can be almost imperceptibly accomplished by gradually funding the national circulation in securities that may be made redeemable at the pleasure of the Government."[22]

The depth and sincerity of these sentiments may well be doubted. As will be noted later, Johnson's last message to Congress contained advice of a radically different nature. In the early part of his administration, however, he left financial policy to McCulloch and refrained from interfering.[23]

The Secretary's report was well received by the financial press. The *Commercial and Financial Chronicle* of New York commented: "In this matter of contracting the currency the policy of the government, as expressed by the President, the Secretary of the Treasury, and the Comptroller of the Currency, is approved by the press and by the people, and it will no doubt receive the sanction of Congress."[24] The *Bankers' Magazine* echoed the same sentiments.[25]

The views of the Secretary commend themselves to the earnest con-

---

[20] Other monetary categories did not remain the same, however, and the contraction of the greenbacks and the compound-interest notes was largely offset by the increase in the amount of national bank-notes and the issue of certificates which took the place of the compound-interest notes. See Chapter III, *infra.*

[21] *Report of the Secretary of the Treasury, 1865,* pp. 6, 14.

[22] *A Compilation of the Messages and Papers of the Presidents, 1789-1908,* ed. James D. Richardson (Washington, 1909), VI, 365.

[23] Dewey, *Financial History,* p. 333.

[24] *Commercial and Financial Chronicle,* I (December 9, 1865), 738.

[25] *Bankers' Magazine,* XV (Old Series) (January, 1866), 522.

sideration and the approval of the country. To secure that contraction of the currency which is essential to the great commercial and financial interests of the country, without producing distress to business circles, we conceive that ample time must be given to produce the desired reform. Whether that period be three, or four, or five years, it should be gradual. In view of the condition of the currency at this time, it is to be hoped that Congress will prohibit the issue of any further Treasury or United States notes; and that those now out shall be funded by a gradual process.

In writing to a friend McCulloch expressed pleasure that his report had been "well received and very cordially endorsed by conservative men, as well as by the Press, all over the country." [26] In truth, however, the report was received by the general public with the apathy which Treasury reports usually engender. It was not until the real and imagined effects of the Secretary's policy became uncomfortably evident some months later that the public began to take notice of what was happening in the financial world. There were, however, a few straws in the wind. The *Iron Age*, organ of the high protectionist manufacturers, had commented equivocally two months before McCulloch made his report that "All prudent men and patriotic citizens will rejoice when, naturally and healthfully, the national currency is restored to the same value as gold; but we must remind our readers, that such a change, if introduced at this moment, would prostrate a vast number of manufacturers." [27] When this prophecy was subsequently borne out concurrently with McCulloch's attempts to contract the greenbacks, the *Iron Age* turned to denouncing the Secretary with considerable virulence.

Several correspondents of Senator John Sherman doubted the wisdom of the Secretary's recommendations. One wrote from Philadelphia, "Can you determine the point at which a healthy currency ends and an inflated one begins? Can you determine the standard price for a Bushel of Wheat? Before you can fix a standard, how can you talk of inflation?—of which McCulloch's report is so full. Lincoln said December 1861— ' Labor is the superior of Capital and deserves much the higher

---

[26] McCulloch to John Forbes, December 16, 1865, McCulloch Papers, Library of Congress.

[27] *Iron Age*, October 5, 1865.

consideration ' which is entirely ignored in Treas. Report. His whole aim appears to be to reduce the industry of the country at the feet of Banking Capital." [28] Isaac Welsh of Belmont County, Ohio asserted: " We need not be told that an irredeemable currency is an evil, but there are greater evils than even that. We have the former upon us, let us try and avoid the latter if we can. It is *not* low prices that we need just now, especially low prices forced upon the country as the result of an unnecessary financial crisis." [29] For the moment these dissonant voices were drowned out in the general chorus of approval for McCulloch's desire for a rapid return to the specie standard. They were, however, harbingers of an uncertain future.

On December 18, 1865, John B. Alley, member of Congress from Lynn, Massachusetts, introduced the following resolution in the House of Representatives: " *Resolved* That this House cordially concurs in the views of the Secretary of the Treasury in relation to the necessity of a contraction of the currency with a view to as early a resumption of specie payments as the business interests of the country will permit; and we hereby pledge cooperative action to this end as speedily as practicable." [30]

The resolution was adopted without debate by a vote of 144 to 6 with 32 not voting. The *Commercial and Financial Chronicle* hailed this decisive result as a ". . . pledge that our redundant currency is not only to receive no further increase, but will be steadily contracted from this time forward, until its normal volume is reached and specie payments are resumed." [31]

For the next two months Congress was occupied with questions of political reconstruction. Finally on February 21, 1866, Representative Justin Smith Morrill of Vermont reported out of the Ways and Means Committee of the House a bill which was frankly designed to give Secretary McCulloch the power he desired to contract the currency. Morrill pointed out that

---

[28] W. S. Waldie to Sherman, December 7, 1865, Sherman Papers, Library of Congress.

[29] Isaac Welch to Sherman, December 19, 1865, *ibid.*

[30] *Congressional Globe*, 39th Congress, 1st Session, p. 75. William H. Barnes, *History of the Thirty-Ninth Congress of the United States* (New York, 1868), p. 577.

[31] *Commercial and Financial Chronicle*, I (December 23, 1865), 801.

the bill was actually "but a patch on an old garment" since the Secretary possessed ample power to fund interest-bearing obligations under the Act of March 3, 1865. The present bill was primarily designed to extend that power so as to include the non-interest-bearing portions of the public debt, i. e., the legal tenders.[32] The bill of the Ways and Means Committee provided that the Act of March 3, 1865 should be "extended and construed to authorize the Secretary of the Treasury, at his discretion, to receive any Treasury notes or other obligations, issued under any act of Congress, whether bearing interest or not, in exchange for any description of bonds authorized by the act to which this is an amendment." The bill authorized McCulloch to dispose of the bonds abroad as well as in the United States at such rates as he might think advisable. The power to be given the Secretary was specifically limited to funding. No increase of the public debt was authorized.[33]

In a sense the bill was designed to put the stamp of legality and Congressional approval on a policy which had been put into effect by McCulloch shortly after he entered upon his duties as Secretary of the Treasury. Since July 1, 1865, he had actually contracted the volume of the greenbacks and fractional currency by about $25,000,000.[34] Morrill wanted to give this policy Congressional sanction, and he also desired to give the Secretary sufficient latitude to allow him to retire the greenbacks at the times and in the amounts that McCulloch thought best. The bill contained almost everything that the Secretary wanted with the single exception that it failed to divest the compound-interest notes of their legal tender quality upon maturity. This was not a serious omission, since ample power existed to fund these notes into bonds. Throughout the controversy over contraction Justin Morrill firmly agreed with McCulloch as to the necessity for contraction, and he was supported on the Ways and Means Committee by other strong men of like faith such as James A. Garfield of Ohio, John Wentworth of Illinois, and Roscoe Conkling of New York.

[32] *Congressional Globe*, 39th Congress, 1st Session, p. 971.
[33] *Ibid.*, p. 971.
[34] This has been deduced by comparing relevant figures on the amount of legal tenders and fractional currency in the Secretary's *Reports* for 1865 and 1866. See also Blaine, *Twenty Years of Congress*, II, 320.

In supporting the measure, Morrill left no doubt of his confidence in McCulloch.[35]

Now we have a Secretary—Mr. McCulloch—summoned to his post at a time when its responsibilities presented no paradise to political ambition, whose financial conduct, thus far, has won golden opinions at home and abroad, and whose annual report has been approved not only by a vote in itself unexampled, but a vote of unexampled unanimity, all but six on the part of this House. . . .

The simple question is, will you perpetuate this war-made expansion of the currency and all its illimitable brood of evils, or will you authorize a financier, who shows himself competent for the task, to retire the excess as fast as sound economy will permit? There is no danger that this can or will be done too rapidly. . . .

Those who fear rash attempts at an early resumption of specie payments should be quieted; it is simply impossible to take at once any very long strides in that direction. This is a process only to be sucessfully accomplished by gradual and persistent effort. Haste would mar and retard it. . . .

Morrill advocated funding all of the short-term interest-bearing securities before beginning on the United States notes, but the bill contained no such provision. At the close of his speech, Morrill was interrogated closely by Thaddeus Stevens, the leader of the Radicals in the House and one of the most powerful and consistent advocates of the greenback currency. Stevens took the line that the proposed measure delegated too much power to the Secretary over the financial condition of the country. He also opposed the provision for disposing of bonds in foreign countries.[36]

Congressman Samuel Hooper of Massachusetts who had been one of the chief architects of the first Legal Tender Act in 1862 had definite reservations about the necessity for contraction, although he was very much interested in funding the interest-bearing portion of the debt at a lower rate of interest.[37] Hooper argued that though the necessity for raising vast sums

[35] *Congressional Globe*, 39th Congress, 1st Session, p. 971.

[36] *Ibid.*, p. 973.

[37] *Ibid.*, p. 975. McCulloch feared the opposition of Hooper to the bill. He wrote his Boston friend, John Forbes, February 23, 1866, that "While he [Hooper] favors in general terms contraction, I am apprehensive that his pecuniary interests just now are regarded by him as being opposed to it." McCulloch papers.

of money to carry on a war was no longer present, it would be wise to be cautious in tampering with the volume of money in circulation inasmuch as this question involved " the value of property, . . . affecting the interest of everyone in the community." He asserted that his main objection to contracting the greenbacks besides the expense that would be incurred by converting this currency into interest-bearing bonds was his belief that a " larger amount of money than formerly is now required for the business of the country " and his fear that " some other paper money, not so good, may be allowed to take their place, by which the country would be further than ever from a currency convertible into coin." [38]

William D. Kelley, sometimes known as " Pig Iron " Kelley because of his fanatical devotion to the interests of that industry, was like Thaddeus Stevens, a Radical and a member of the Pennsylvania school of high protection. Like Stevens he took a jaundiced view of the proposed bill and warned: " Let a contraction begin and depositors check heavily upon their balances and it will affect every bank, and the next act of the Secretary of the Treasury will be to notify the banks that, owing to a depreciation in the market value of Government securities, they must increase their deposits to secure the redemption of their notes. I warn gentlemen to withhold from any man the power, at this time, when we are just coming out of such a war, to contract our currency or even to threaten its contraction." [39]

Further consideration of the Loan Bill was postponed until March 15 due to pressing political issues. When debate recommenced, it soon became evident that the money question split the Radical Republican majority right down the middle and that it would not be easy to find a common ground on which action could be taken. Congressman Calvin T. Hulburd of New York pointed out that the substantial sum of $1,109,980,788 in 7-30 notes, compound-interest notes, and other short term obligations which would mature within two years constituted in itself a tremendous funding problem. Why, he asked, should there be a need to worry about the non-interest-bearing legal tenders? " With such heavy interest-bearing liabilities con-

---

[38] *Congressional Globe*, 39th Congress, 1st Session, p. 976.
[39] *Ibid.*, p. 977.

stantly and rapidly maturing, why should the power be asked to call in and pay or fund the non-interest bearing notes? A species of currency everywhere popular and satisfactory surely might be left out until the interest bearing unfunded liabilities of Government have been retired or provided for. Or is the retirement of some $1,200,000,000 of such expected to be of so easy accomplishment that more absorbent power and capacity should be asked?"[40]

"Long John" Wentworth of Chicago strongly favored the bill because of his confidence in McCulloch. "The Secretary of the Treasury has proven himself a cautious man. He would not be precipitate if he could, and he could not if he would. It is because I have this confidence in him that I favor this bill. For the same reason that Congress gave full powers to General Grant when he went out to raise our flag in the rebel States, I am for giving Secretary McCulloch full powers when he goes out to raise our credit."[41]

Taking a cue from Wentworth who had suggested that all members should vote the will of their constituencies on the bill, Congressman Frederick Pike, a representative from one of the rural districts of Maine, asserted that he would oppose the Loan Bill. He doubted that the people of Wentworth's Chicago district wanted to exchange the greenbacks for more bank-notes. "There is not a man in this country, in the Chicago district or in mine, or in any other, that prefers the bank-note to the 'greenback.' All of them, 'without regard to race or color,' are content with the money to which they have become accustomed and which costs the Government nothing but the expense of making."[42]

Hiram Price of Iowa, formerly president of the State Bank of that state, also opposed the bill since he could see no reason for converting $450,000,000 of non-interest-bearing securities into bonds that would cost the government $27,000,000 in interest annually.[43] Coming from a banker, this opinion is of

[40] *Ibid.*, p. 1427.
[41] *Ibid.*, p. 1434.
[42] *Ibid.*, p. 1452.
[43] *Ibid.*, p. 1457. For a brief sketch of Hiram Price, see Redlich, *The Molding of American Banking*, II, 31.

particular interest and is evidence of the divergence of views which frequently existed between bankers of the East and those of the West on the question of currency contraction. A large majority of eastern bankers strongly supported McCulloch's policies, whereas the banking fraternity of the West was far from unanimous in admitting the necessity for his stringent medicine.[44]

Another Iowan, William B. Allison, whose name was later to loom large in the monetary debates of the Senate, supported the measure. He pointed out the fact that the Secretary actually possessed the power to retire the legal tenders by first converting them into 7-30 notes and thence into bonds. The only new powers included in the bill were first that the Secretary could sell bonds on his own initiative instead of waiting to exchange them and secondly that he could sell them, if necessary, below par.[45]

George S. Boutwell of Massachusetts, a leading Radical and later Secretary of the Treasury under Grant, was no great admirer of McCulloch.[46] Boutwell believed that the Treasury should confine itself to efforts to fund the interest-bearing obligations at a lower rate of interest. He pointed out that the addition of four million Negroes to the trading classes of the country meant that a greater volume of currency would be needed. He saw no necessity for contracting the amount of United States notes.[47]

The venerable Stevens threw his powerful influence against the bill. In language which clearly demonstrated his concern with the problem of the manufacturer, he asserted: " I know that two cotton factories that had commenced and were nearly under roof when this bill was introduced, have been suspended, and will be entirely abandoned never to be resumed, if this bill granting this mighty power should become a law. And I venture to say that there is scarcely any branch of business in the country whether in cities or in rural districts, that will not

[44] This divergence of opinion is further dealt with in Chapter VI.

[45] *Congressional Globe*, 39th Congress, 1st Session, pp. 1457-1458.

[46] George S. Boutwell, *Reminiscences of Sixty Years in Public Affairs*, 2 vols. (New York, 1902), II, 125-127.

[47] *Congressional Globe*, 39th Congress, 1st Session, p. 1459.

be immediately so cramped as to reduce all the industrial enterprises of the country and all the great interests of the nation in the revenue-paying department." [48]

Morrill brought the proposed bill to a vote on March 16. The debate had made it clear that there was a strong current of opposition to giving the Secretary unlimited power over the currency. It was not surprising, therefore, that the measure was defeated, though by a narrow margin—nays 70, yeas 65, not voting 49.[49] The vote cannot be taken as a true indication of opinion on the question of currency contraction since several members voted against the bill because of the provision that bonds might be sold in foreign countries. Others wanted to limit the extent of contraction in some definite way. James A. Garfield of Ohio, who was certainly no friend of fiat money, voted against the bill, but only as he explained " for the purpose of moving a re-consideration." [50]

On March 19 Garfield's motion to reconsider was in order.[51] Meanwhile Samuel Hooper had introduced a measure to permit the Secretary to issue bonds for the purpose of funding all short-term obligations of the government but withholding the power to contract the non-interest-bearing legal tenders. " Pig Iron " Kelley introduced a bill which would direct the Secretary to redeem the short-term interest-bearing obligations in greenbacks. This was a move toward inflation, and, if adopted, would have brought the non-interest-bearing currency of the country to well over $900,000,000.[52]

The debate waxed hot over Garfield's motion to reconsider the original bill and the desire of Stevens and Conkling that the bill be recommitted. Boutwell again pronounced himself strongly against contraction asserting that the manufacturing interests of Massachusetts could not stand it. After several hours of debate, Conkling persuaded the House to recommit the bill.[53]

On March 23 Chairman Morrill reported back the revised version of a majority of the Ways and Means Committee. The fear which had been expressed during the debate that too much

[48] *Ibid.*, p. 1459.
[49] *Ibid.*, p. 1468.
[50] *Ibid.*, p. 1468.
[51] *Ibid.*, p. 1496.
[52] *Ibid.*, pp. 1494-1495.
[53] *Ibid.*, pp. 1498-1502.

power was being placed in the hands of McCulloch had apparently received serious consideration from the Committee, for Morrill now reported an amendment to the original bill which provided " that of United States notes not more than $10,000,000 may be retired and canceled within six months from the passage of this act and thereafter not more than $4,000,000 in any one month." [54]

Morrill had the clerk read a letter addressed to him by Secretary McCulloch in which the Secretary argued strongly against tying the hands of the government by inserting in the bill a proviso that bonds could not be sold at less than par. McCulloch argued that such a provision would result in a conspiracy on the part of enemies of the Treasury Department. The Secretary also urged the retention of the provision calling for contraction of the United States notes, asserting it to be " of vast importance to the business of the country." [55]

A brief debate followed in which John Wentworth, James Garfield, Justin Morrill, and John Alley, author of the December resolution, argued in favor of the amended bill and " Pig Iron " Kelley, Samuel Hooper, and Thaddeus Stevens fought against it. The high protectionists Stevens and Kelley were joined in this effort by their colleague, John A. Griswold, the Troy, New York ironmaster.[56] Griswold maintained that in his mind the currency question was not so urgent as the tariff issue. Imports were flooding the country, and little was being done to protect American industry. The New York Congressman made it clear that he felt there were issues of greater moment than the condition of the currency. In this vein he declared: " Of course there is no difference of opinion on one point: every man believes it is our duty, as rapidly as possible, to get back to specie payment. But there are worse things than the mere

[54] *Ibid.*, p. 1609.

[55] *Ibid.*, pp. 1608-1609. McCulloch was making every effort to influence the House in favor of contraction. In a letter to his Boston friend, John Forbes, dated February 23, 1866, the Secretary expressed doubt that much could be done to influence Samuel Hooper, but he added that he would be glad to have Forbes write to Elliott and Ames of the Massachusetts delegation, asserting that " If we can get through the House, I do not anticipate any serious trouble in the Senate." McCulloch Papers.

[56] *Congressional Globe*, 39th Congress, 1st Session, pp. 1609-1614. Barnes, *History of the Thirty-Ninth Congress*, p. 593.

deferring of the resumption of specie payment. I am in favor of its resumption, of course, as every man is or should be, but in arriving at that point I am opposed to any policy which shall crush out and destroy the material and industrial interests of this country. I would clothe no man, not even the present incumbent of the Treasury Department, with that power." [57]

Despite these arguments, the amendments limiting the Treasury's power of contraction together with McCulloch's letter were sufficiently compelling to bring about the passage of the bill. The final vote was yeas 83, nays 53, not voting 47.[58] The table on page 75 presents a sectional and political breakdown of the House vote on this important measure.[59]

The party and sectional characteristics of this vote are enlightening. One fact which emerges with clarity is the importance of the votes of the Democratic Congressmen in producing the substantial majority in favor of contraction. Of the 28 Democrats in the House, all but one voted in favor of gradual curtailment of the volume of the greenback currency. The hard-money sentiments of the Democratic party which had been voiced by leaders such as Pendleton and Vallandigham during the debate over the First Legal Tender Bill proved once again to be the dominant factor in determining that party's vote on the issue of contraction. It will be noted that, without the votes of the Democrats, the Republican majority in favor of contraction would have been very slight indeed, 56 members of that party having been recorded in favor of the measure and 52 opposed to it.

A sectional analysis of the vote shows that the states of the eastern seaboard supported contraction by a vote of 47 to 19, while the votes of the Middle West, and Far West, and the western border states were almost equally divided, 36 votes being cast in favor of the bill and 35 against it. From this evidence Howard K. Beale has concluded in his influential study of the early Reconstruction period that " The East favored

[57] *Congressional Globe*, 39th Congress, 1st Session, p. 1612.
[58] *Ibid.*, p. 1614.
[59] This table was compiled with the aid of the *Congressional Globe*, 39th Congress, 1st Session, p. 1614, and the information concerning party affiliations contained in Blaine, *Twenty Years of Congress*, II, 118-121.

Vote on the Loan Bill, House of Representatives, March 23, 1866

	For Contraction		Against Contraction	
	Rep.	Dem.	Rep.	Dem.
New England States				
Massachusetts	6	0	1	0
Maine	4	0	1	0
Vermont	2	0	0	0
New Hampshire	2	0	0	0
Connecticut	1	0	0	0
Rhode Island	0	0	1	0
Totals	15	0	3	0
Middle Atlantic States				
New York	10	6	4	1
Pennsylvania	6	6	8	0
New Jersey	0	2	0	0
Maryland	0	1	3	0
Delaware	0	1	0	0
Totals	16	16	15	1
Middle Western States				
Ohio	3	2	11	0
Illinois	7	3	4	0
Indiana	3	1	3	0
Minnesota	2	0	0	0
Wisconsin	1	1	1	0
Michigan	1	0	4	0
Iowa	1	0	4	0
Totals	18	7	27	0
Border States				
Kentucky	1	3	1	0
Missouri	3	1	4	0
West Virginia	1	0	1	0
Totals	5	4	6	0
Far Western States				
California	2	0	1	0
Grand Totals	56	27	52	1

contraction; the West was divided, or opposed to it." [60] In a general sense this is undoubtedly true, but because one of the basic tenets of the present study is that the fight over specie resumption was fought out on intra-sectional as well as sectional lines, a second look at the eastern vote on contraction will be instructive. It is clear that the heavy eastern majority in favor of calling in the greenback currency was a product of two striking facts, an overwhelming Republican majority of 25 to 7 in favor of the bill in New England and New York, and the votes of 16 Democrats in the Middle Atlantic states. It is interesting to note that the Republican delegation from Pennsylvania actually opposed contraction by a vote of 8 to 6, and that the 3 Republican members from Maryland all voted against the bill.

The hard-money proclivities of the Democratic party, dating from the Jacksonian period, are sufficient to explain the almost unanimous vote of House Democrats in favor of contraction. But how explain the fact that while the Republicans of New York and New England were voting 25 to 7 in favor of the bill, their colleagues from Pennsylvania and Maryland voted 11 to 6 against it? Analyses of voting statistics will by no means always provide accurate barometers of public opinion nor of the economic facts of life, but in attempting to account for this cleavage among eastern Republicans, it is perhaps significant to bring out some important facts which will be dealt with more fully in later chapters. As the economist and publicist Henry C. Carey later pointed out, inflation was a real problem only in New York and New England.[61] This situation was partially attributable to the higher development of banking and credit facilities in these states which made it possible for one dollar to do the work of several in less developed regions, but even more important was the almost incredible mal-distribution of the national bank currency authorized by the National Banking Act of 1864. Of the $293,000,000 of this currency which had been issued from 1863 through 1866, $170,000,000 had been allotted to New York and New England.[62] This im-

---

[60] Howard K. Beale, *The Critical Year: A Study of Andrew Johnson and Reconstruction* (New York, 1930), p. 242.

[61] The ideas of Henry C. Carey are discussed in Chapter IV.

[62] These figures appear in the report of the Comptroller of the Currency

balance of the national bank currency is one of the keys to understanding the cleavage among eastern Republicans on the issue of contraction.

Another interesting facet of the debate and vote in the House was the fact that the bill was opposed by the leaders of the ultra high protectionist faction, men such as Thaddeus Stevens, " Pig Iron " Kelley, and John A. Griswold. While these men paid lip service to the goal of specie resumption, it was obvious that they regarded efforts at its early attainment as unwise if they tended to react adversely upon the industrial interests of the country. The opposition of the high protectionists to contraction of the currency will emerge as extremely significant at a later stage of this study, when evidence will be presented to show that, because of the complex effects of changes in the premium on gold, contraction of the currency was diametrically opposed to the interests of those who advocated a high tariff policy.[63]

The vote thus brought to light a clear split in the ranks of the Radical Republicans. Voting for the measure were such leaders as James G. Blaine, Roscoe Conkling, James A. Garfield, Justin Morrill, Elihu B. Washburne, and John Wentworth.[64] Voting against the bill were leaders just as strong such as John A. Bingham, George Julian, William D. Kelley, Thaddeus Stevens, Rutherford B. Hayes, John A. Griswold, and James F. Wilson. The non-voters included such names as George Boutwell and Henry Raymond. This split in the ranks of the Radical Republicans on the issue of monetary policy is of crucial importance to this study. Its overall significance as regards the currently accepted interpretation of the history of Reconstruction will be developed in the concluding chapter to this work. At this juncture it is important to note that contrac-

contained in the Report of the Secretary of the Treasury, 1866. Mal-distribution of the national bank currency and its effects will be discussed at length in Chapter VI.

[63] This evidence is presented in Chapter IV.

[64] James A. Garfield had been profoundly influenced by orthodox laissez faire economics and was regarded by the protectionists as little better than a free trader. See Theodore Clarke Smith, The Life and Letters of James Abram Garfield, 2 vols. (New Haven, 1925), I, 402, 454-455. Even Morrill, author of the tariff act of 1861, was at heart only a moderate protectionist. See William Belmont Parker, The Life and Public Services of Justin Smith Morrill (Boston, 1924), p. 254.

tion was opposed in 1866 by a number of Republicans who may be classified as the most ultra of the Radicals and also the most extreme of the high protectionists.

After the Loan Bill had successfully run the gauntlet of the House, passage by the Senate was almost a foregone conclusion. On April 9, 1866, Fessenden, who had resumed his old place as Chairman of the Senate Finance Committee, brought the bill to the floor of the upper house. After a careful consideration by the committee, it had been decided to report the bill as passed by the House without amendment.[65]

Senator John Sherman, a member of the Finance Committee, opposed the measure in an elaborate speech. He believed that the bill gave too much power to the Secretary of the Treasury and maintained that it actually was not needed at all, since the Secretary already had power under previous legislation to fund all of the debt which was pressing at that time. All of these minor objections, however, were secondary to Sherman's real fear—namely, that McCulloch was determined to contract the currency. The Senator pretended to see a conspiracy in the fact that the Secretary had been keeping large balances in the Treasury vaults, asserting that there was no legitimate reason why this money should be kept out of the currency stream.[66] As a representative of the western state of Ohio, Sherman reflected the views of most of his constituents when he said: " With this power, [to contract the currency], the will or whim of the Secretary of the Treasury might destroy all the men of the country who are compelled to go into debt to carry on their business. A sudden contraction or a sudden expansion might build up or tear down fortunes. I think every citizen of the United States has the right to know how much currency, which is the blood of the whole system, shall be in existence for the time being. There should be some limit over this power. . . ." [67]

---

[65] *Congressional Globe*, 39th Congress, 1st Session, p. 1845.

[66] *Ibid.*, pp. 1845-1846.

[67] *Ibid.*, p. 1846. Sherman and McCulloch disagreed basically as to the proper policy to be pursued. In his memoirs Sherman explained their differences. " He was in favor of a rapid contraction of the currency by funding it into interest-bearing bonds. I was in favor of maintaining in circulation the then existing volume of currency as an aid to the funding of all forms of interest-bearing securities into bonds redeemable within a brief period at the pleasure of the

The redoubtable William Pitt Fessenden came to the aid of McCulloch in no uncertain terms.[68]

Now, sir, it is to be supposed that the Secretary of the Treasury is a tolerably honest man, and it is to be supposed that he is a tolerably sensible man. My own opinion is that he is a very honest man and a very sensible man, and understands what he is about. What would be accomplished by overthrowing the business of the country and destroying it, if such would be the effect? In the first place by destroying business he would cut off all the resources of internal revenue, because people cannot afford to do business that breaks them up. In the next place he takes out of the hands of the taxpayers a currency by which alone they are able to meet the obligations upon them to pay taxes. And thus, in order to carry out the favorite idea, according to the Senator, he may, and if the argument means anything he probably will, forget all that, and do precisely the thing which it is not intended he should do, and which it is against the interest of the country, and his own interests as manager of the Treasury, to do.

The Radical Senator Zachariah Chandler of Michigan agreed with Sherman that the bill put too much power in the hands of the Secretary. He asserted: "Certainly, if I were Secretary of the Treasury, I should not be willing to accept the powers contained in this bill. You absolutely authorize him to do what he pleases with the $2,700,000,000, of the public debt." [69]

As the debate went on, Senators Morgan of New York, Cowan of Pennsylvania, and Guthrie of Kentucky spoke in favor of the bill, and Senator Howe of Wisconsin opposed it. When the vote was finally taken, the measure passed by a vote of 32 to 7. The seven votes against the bill were all cast by Republican western Senators. They were Senators Sherman and Wade of Ohio, Chandler and Howard of Michigan, Howe of Wisconsin, and Ramsey and Norton of Minnesota. All the Democrats who voted were recorded in favor of the bill. These included Buckalew of Pennsylvania, Riddle of Delaware, Johnson of Maryland, Davis and Guthrie of Kentucky, McDougall

United States, and bearing as low a rate of interest as possible. Both of us were in favor of specie payments, he by contraction and I by the gradual advancement of the credit and value of our currency to the specie standard. With him specie payments was the primary object, with me it was a secondary object, to follow the advancing credit of the government." Sherman, *Recollections*, I, 376.

[68] *Congressional Globe, 39th Congress*, 1st Session, p. 1848.
[69] *Ibid.*, p. 1848.

of California, and Nesmith of Oregon. The eastern seaboard supported the measure by a vote of 16 to 0; the Middle West, the Far West, and the western border states favored it 16 to 7.[70] The bill was signed by President Johnson on April 12, 1866. The plenary power to contract the greenback currency which McCulloch had requested had been limited by the amendment of the original bill by the House, and the law as passed provided that not more than $10,000,000 of legal tenders could be cancelled within six months of the passage of the act and not more than $4,000,000 in any month thereafter.[71] In this form the Loan Bill fell short of McCulloch's expectations. In his autobiography he commented: " This was not what I wanted, for I knew there would be months in which much more than four millions could be withdrawn without affecting the market; and other months when the withdrawal of a much smaller amount would cause considerable stringency. What I did want was authority to retire the legal-tender notes as rapidly as it could be done, without affecting injuriously industry and trade." [72]

Passage of this measure marked the close of the first round of the great post-Civil War money battle which was to rage until the end of the century. McCulloch had won a limited victory in his fight for an early return to specie payments, but no one realized better than he that an ill wind was blowing. In February he had written to his friend Forbes: " Just now things have a bad look. The quarrel between the President and some of the Radical Members of Congress is an exceedingly unfortunate one. . . . Nothing can be gained and great interests may be put in peril by a serious breach between the President and Congress." [73] With remarkable prescience McCulloch could see that his policies would not fare well in the midst of a duel to the death between Congress and President Johnson, but he did not foresee that the policy of contraction would be equally tried by the vicissitudes of economic depression.

---

[70] *Ibid.*, p. 1854; Blaine, *Twenty Years of Congress*, II, 118.
[71] Huntington and Mawhinney, *Laws*, pp. 648-649.
[72] McCulloch, *Men and Measures*, p. 211.
[73] McCulloch to John Forbes, February 23, 1866, McCulloch Papers.

CHAPTER III

THE POLITICS OF MONEY

Contractionists and anti-contractionists in the post-Civil War years devoted most of their argumentative energies to the greenback issue. As is the case with most controversies which take on a political hue, little effort was made by either side to understand the money problem in all its complexity. By concentrating solely on the importance of the United States notes, the parties to the controversy failed to recognize that contraction of these notes, could not possibly account for all the results usually attributed to this policy. The following table which shows the changes in all the major categories of currency between October 31, 1865 and July 1, 1868 makes this point clear.[1]

	October 31, 1865	July 1, 1868	Net Change
Greenbacks	$428,160,569	$356,141,723	— $ 72,018,846
Fractional currency	26,057,469	32,626,951	+ 6,569,482
National bank-notes	185,000,000	299,806,565 *	+ 114,806,565
Compound-interest notes	173,012,140	28,161,810	— 144,850,330
Three per cent certificates		50,000,000	+ 50,000,000
NET CHANGE IN THE TOTAL VOLUME OF THE CURRENCY			— $ 45,493,129

* This volume of national bank-notes was reached on September 30, 1868.

These figures are significant in that they demonstrate conclusively that the contraction of the greenbacks was by no means the only important change in the total volume of the currency. Actually, the funding of the compound-interest legal tenders was at least equally important; for, although these did not achieve a high velocity of circulation because of their interest-bearing quality, they were nonetheless a significant item since they were especially favored by banks for use as reserves.[2] In

[1] Figures for this table are drawn from the *Reports of the Secretary of the Treasury* for the years 1865 and 1868.
[2] Dewey, *Financial History*, p. 344.

order to counteract the deflationary effect of funding the compound-interest notes, Congress authorized on March 2, 1867 the issue of $50,000,000 in three per cent certificates which could be held by banks for use as reserves.[3] A significant factor in offsetting the contraction of the greenbacks and the funding of the compound-interest notes was the increase in the volume of national bank-notes which almost reached the $300,000,000 statutory limit by September 30, 1868. Since the net reduction in all the varieties of the currency listed above was only $45,493,129 between October 31, 1865 before the policy of contraction has been approved by Congress and July 1, 1868 after it had been abandoned, it might well be asked what all the commotion was about. Actually, the contraction of the greenbacks was more the occasion for the controversy than the cause of it. The real cause was economic depression.

The best available data on business cycles in the United States shows that the wartime boom reached a peak in the month of Lee's surrender, April, 1865. After that time the trend of business activity was downward, and a trough was reached in December, 1867. It is apparent, therefore, that business conditions were deteriorating during almost the entire period when McCulloch was pursuing a policy of currency contraction. Things picked up after December, 1867, and business improved steadily until June, 1869, when another peak was reached.[4] Since McCulloch's policy, which was obnoxious to a great many people, was carried out in the teeth of an economic gale, it is easy to understand why he was subjected to so much opprobrium and ridicule.

It is impossible to determine just what influence the contraction of the greenbacks had on the economic situation from 1866 through 1868. It seems likely that a recession or an economic adjustment at a lower level was inevitable once the stimulus of war production was removed. At the same time the advocacy of an outright policy of deflation by the Secretary of the Treasury was not without its effect. The word advocacy should

---

[3] Bolles, *Financial History from 1861 to 1885*, p. 278.

[4] *Historical Statistics of the United States*, Appendix 1, Table 1, p. 320. This table was taken from Arthur F. Burns and Wesley C. Mitchell, *Measuring Business Cycles* (New York, 1946).

be emphasized, for it seems certain that McCulloch's advocacy of contraction was far more important than any measures taken by him to bring it about. As chief financial officer of the government, the Secretary, through his official reports, his speeches, and statements to newspaper reporters, was able to influence the climate of business activity. The prophecies of doom which issued from the Treasury Department during McCulloch's tenure of office undoubtedly contributed to the depression of 1866-1868. As one financial journal commented in 1866, " A greater power, a more absolute control, over the growth, the enterprise and the activity of a free people was never enjoyed by any executive than is now vested in the Treasury." [5]

Athough the general trend of business activity was downward after April, 1865, the policy of contraction which became law in April, 1866 was destined to enjoy a brief respite from controversy. In May of that year, however, occurred the great Overend-Gurney panic in Lombard Street which sent the Bank of England discount rate to a remarkable ten per cent where it remained for over three months.[6] Within two weeks of the panic over $20,000,000 in gold had been sent from the United States to England and more was to follow.[7] The natural result of this outflow was a rise in the premium on gold. On April 28 gold had been reported at 127. Overends failed on May 10. By May 26 gold was up to 141. Speculation, following its usual course in the wake of a cataclysm, carried the price to a phenomenal 167 in June.[8] It is likely that the premium on gold would have fallen suddenly after reaching this point had not the Austro-Prussian war intervened. Once again large shipments of gold were made to Europe, and the premium was not destined to fall below 140 until November.[9]

Because all prices tended to react sympathetically with

[5] *Commercial and Financial Chronicle*, II (March 31, 1866), 385.
[6] Albert Edgar Feavearyear, *The Pound Sterling: A History of English Money* (Oxford, 1931), pp. 278-281.
[7] *Commercial and Financial Chronicle*, II (May 26, 1866), 642.
[8] *Ibid.*, II (April 28, 1866), 524; II (May 26, 1866), 651; II (June 23, 1866), 779.
[9] *Commercial and Financial Chronicle*, III (July 7, 1066); 3-4; III (November 24, 1866), 651.

changes in the price of gold, the rise of the gold premium in the spring and summer of 1866 due to the shipments of the precious metal to Europe tended to offset and even more than offset any tendencies toward lower prices which might have resulted from the contraction of the currency. The financial press noted the fact that the upward course of gold was improving the condition of business and that it had especially stimulated the export of domestic commodities. The stock and bond markets were firm, and the money market was easy until well into the autumn.[10]

During the latter part of October the confidence which had prevailed for several months in business circles began to be displaced by a feeling of uneasiness. Speculation in stocks, bonds, and commodities had been rampant, and prices had been forced to a level which could not be sustained by legitimate demand. It was reported that "The speculative movement in stocks, during the month, [October] has exceeded in volume anything in the history of Wall Street." [11] At the same time legitimate trade was depressed, manufacturers were shutting down plants, and jobbers were having trouble disposing of goods at prevailing prices.[12] According to a leading mercantile journal, "The obvious explanation of these symptoms is that the high prices of goods are at last compelling a sharp curtailment of consumption." [13] It was apparent that a break in the price level was imminent.

Prices were destined to come down but not without an economic jolt which found its victims in Wall Street and in other financial centers throughout the country. Into the speculative mania there was injected around the middle of November the persistent demand of the West and South for currency to move the crops. In a matter of two weeks call money was up from 4 to 7 per cent. Gold, stocks, and bonds went tumbling down. In less than two months the reserves of the New York City banks were reduced from $92,000,000 to $66,000,000.[14] At

---

[10] *Ibid.*, II (June 2, 1866), 683-684, 688; II (June 9, 1866), 719.

[11] *Ibid.*, III (November 3, 1866), 550.

[12] *Ibid.*, III (October 27, 1866), 527; III (November 3, 1866), 559.

[13] *Hunt's Merchants Magazine*, LV (November, 1866), 396.

[14] *Commercial and Financial Chronicle*, III (October 27, 1866), 523; III (November 10, 1866), 587-588; III (November 24, 1866), 643-644, 650-651.

this point prices began to lose their stickiness. The *Commercial and Financial Chronicle* commented: " It appears to be very generally understood among both manufacturers and merchants, as well as by the consuming public, that we have now passed the climax of high prices, and that henceforth there must be a persistent fall in the value of all products. This idea, of course, produces special caution in the matter of credits and has a depressing effect upon every branch of business; but its tendency is nevertheless to avert any serious convulsions in the markets from a sudden and extreme fall in values." [15]

The decline in the price level continued throughout the year 1867. By way of summarizing this decline, *Hunt's Merchants Magazine* published a list of commodities and their comparative prices on January 1 of each of the years from 1861 to 1868. It was found that the enumerated commodities had declined an average of about ten per cent during the year 1867. The price decline had not affected all commodities equally. Many agricultural products had not declined at all, and some had even increased in price. Among the listed commodities those which had fallen most in price were cotton and iron which declined in value 50 and 28 per cent respectively. Although very few manufactured products were listed, the journal felt that " Were it possible to give comparative prices of manufactures, . . . it would be found that in that department of industry prices have generally declined more than on the products here instanced." [16]

The nature of the commodities which fell most precipitously in price at this time provides an interesting key to the early history of the greenback movement in the United States. Since the tradition of agricultural greenbackism has become almost an *idée fixe* in American historiography, it might be well wondered why so little evidence for its existence can be found

[15] *Ibid.*, III (December 1, 1866), 677.
[16] *Hunt's Merchants Magazine*, LVIII (January, 1868), 60-63. On the discrepancy between the prices of manufactures and agricultural products, this journal commented: " This inequality between the manufacturing and the agricultural interests is one of the derangements bequeathed us by the war, but the losses in the one branch and the handsome profits in the other may be relied upon to effect a more even distribution of labor and capital between the two departments when the values of the two classes of products will be equalized." *Ibid.*, 63.

in the years immediately following the Civil War. The simple and obvious reason is that the prices of agricultural products remained high in this period due to crop shortages in Europe and poor growing seasons in the United States. The greatest declines, as has been noted above, were in the prices of manufactured goods. It seems quite probable that the decline of 28 per cent in the price of iron during 1867 was directly related to the demand of the Pennsylvania ironmasters for higher tariffs and for more greenbacks. The same logic applies to the condition of most manufacturers. An interesting exception, however, would be the New England textile manufacturers who obviously benefitted by the tremendous fall in price of their chief raw material, cotton.

In the public mind the fall in prices and the decline in economic activity were naturally related to McCulloch's policy of contraction. The effect on the public was well summed up by James G. Blaine. " It was easy to see, therefore, that as each month the degree of contraction was made public, the people more and more attributed their financial troubles to its operation. Perhaps, in large degree, this was the result of imagination, and of that common desire in human nature to ascribe one's faults and misfortunes to some superior power. The effect nevertheless was serious and lasting. In the end, outside of banking and financial centres, there was a strong and persistent demand for the repeal of the Contraction Act." [17]

This demand for repeal found expression in Congress early in 1867. On February 4, Josiah B. Grinnell of Iowa introduced a resolution in the House " That the public interest demands that there shall not, during the current year, be a reduction in the amount of the outstanding United States notes commonly called greenbacks." The resolution, which was adopted, called upon the Ways and Means Committee " to report such bill as may be necessary to effect this object." [18]

In accordance with this resolution, Samuel Hooper, on behalf of the Ways and Means Committee, reported out a bill on February 20. In this bill the repeal of contraction had been inextricably linked together with a proposal looking toward

[17] Blaine, *Twenty Years of Congress*, II, 328.
[18] *Congressional Globe*, 39th Congress, 2nd Session, p. 992.

the redemption of the compound-interest notes. As a result the simple question of whether McCulloch's power to contract the greenbacks should be terminated was sidetracked. Debate centered on the problem of how the compound-interest notes should be redeemed, and on this issue a clear-cut line was drawn between expansionists and contractionists. The bill as reported provided that the maturing compound-interest notes should be received on deposit by the Secretary of the Treasury in exchange for certificates bearing 3.65 per cent in interest. Since it was realized that a considerable portion of the compound-interest notes were held by national banks as a part of their reserves, the bill provided that the certificates could also be counted as reserves.[19]

Debate was joined on the issue of whether this expedient should be used or whether the compound-interest notes should simply be redeemed by an issue of greenbacks.[20] This inflationary proposal was backed by Thaddeus Stevens and a fellow Pennsylvanian, Samuel J. Randall, leading Democrat and a convinced opponent of the national banks. Randall saw little reason for providing these banks with a gratuitous opportunity to earn interest upon their reserves. In introducing an amendment very similar to the one already introduced by Stevens authorizing the Secretary of the Treasury to issue up to $100,-000,000 of greenbacks to redeem the interest-bearing legal tenders, Randall pointed out that he would be willing to leave the contraction law just as it stood. "In reference to the contraction or anti-contraction question, it is my opinion this issue of $100,000,000 of legal tenders in place of the present reserves will not produce inflation in the monetary markets of the country. If my proposition be adopted, I think the Senate and House will agree to leave the law as it is for retiring $4,000,000 per month." [21] Although the bill passed the House in the form desired by Stevens and Randall, it did not enjoy a happy fate in the Senate.[22] When the bill was considered by the upper house on February 27, it was attacked by John Sherman. It will be recalled that, although Sherman consistently opposed McCulloch's contraction policy, he was also opposed

[19] *Ibid.*, p. 1417.   [21] *Ibid.*, p. 1420.
[20] *Ibid.*, p. 1419.   [22] *Ibid.*, p. 1426.

to expansion. His position was essentially that the country should be allowed to grow up to the existing volume of the currency. In opposing the bill Sherman stated that " No proposition could be made that would so seriously impair the public credit, that would so seriously derange the value of property, that would strike so much at all the business interests of the people of the United States, as this proposition to increase the legal tenders." [23] The Ohio Senator also opposed the House bill on the ground that the original loan act of 1864 under which the compound-interest notes were issued specifically stated that the amount of legal tenders outstanding should never be greater than $400,000,000.[24]

Impressed with the weight of Sherman's arguments, the Senate rejected the bill which had been passed by the House and substituted another measure which closely resembled Hooper's original House bill. This measure authorized the Secretary of the Treasury to redeem the compounders by issuing up to $100,000,000 in temporary loan certificates bearing interest at a rate of not more than 3 per cent. It was also provided that the national banks could use these certificates as part of their reserves.[25] The Senate version of the bill eventually prevailed and became law on March 2, 1867.[26] The only modification was that the amount of temporary certificates which could be issued was reduced to $50,000,000.[27] Of itself, this piece of financial legislation was of only minor importance, but the debate on this measure in the House and the passage of the Stevens-Randall bill indicated that the contractionist majority of March, 1866 in the lower house had been completely overturned.

Had Hugh McCulloch been of a mind to court popularity in the years 1865 through 1869, he could hardly have chosen a less auspicious position than that of Secretary of the Treasury. In a letter to President Johnson McCulloch asserted in the fall of 1868 that " the palm of being the ' best abused ' man in

[23] *Ibid.*, p. 1870.
[24] *Ibid.*, p. 1870.
[25] *Ibid.*, p. 1869.
[26] *Ibid.*, pp. 1737, 1958.
[27] *Ibid.*, p. 1958.

the country " must be yielded to him.[28] On one occasion Johnson confided to Gideon Welles that there had been more complaints against McCulloch and the Treasury than against all other officials.[29] Congressman Robert Schenck of Ohio accused McCulloch of harboring " a brood of rascals " in the Treasury Department.[30] A popular newspaper accused the Secretary of using his " vast power " to enrich monopolists and " send the laborer's children hungry to bed." [31] One correspondent of Thaddeus Stevens referred to McCulloch as " that Ass of the Treasury Department." [32] It is understandable that McCulloch confessed to Gideon Welles that he was " discouraged " and wrote to Jay Cooke that he considered himself " a dunce for retaining a position in which there is so much of labor and anxiety and so little reward." [33]

McCulloch's difficulties were both political and economic and together constituted an almost overwhelming burden. Abuse centered on his policy of currency contraction, but this was by no means the only financial policy pursued by him which came under attack. It was unfortunate for McCulloch that almost any fiscal action taken by him was bound to have its effect on the money market. The problem of gold sales is a good case in point.

Under the existing tariff laws all customs duties were paid in gold. After it entered the Treasury, the gold was set aside to pay the interest on the bonded indebtedness. The problem was that in the years immediately following the Civil War, more gold was accumulating in the Treasury than was needed for this purpose. Of necessity, McCulloch had to sell gold. The trouble was that gold sales brought about a decline in the gold premium, a fact which was highly disconcerting to ex-

---

[28] Quoted in Herbert S. Schell, " Hugh McCulloch and the Treasury Department, 1865-1869," *Mississippi Valley Historical Review*, XVII (1931), 413.

[29] *Diary of Gideon Welles*, ed. Edgar T. Welles, 3 vols. (Boston, 1911), III, 403-404.

[30] *Congressional Globe*, 40th Congress, 1st Session, p. 723.

[31] Quoted in the *Commercial and Financial Chronicle*, III (November 3, 1866), 547.

[32] D. W. Patterson to Stevens, December 10, 1866, Stevens Papers, Library of Congress.

[33] Welles, *Diary*, III, 16-17; Ellis Paxson Oberholtzer, *Jay Cooke, Financier of the Civil War*, 2 vols. (Philadelphia, 1907), II, 26-27.

porters, merchants, gold gamblers, and stock speculators who were frequently gambling on the maintenance of a high premium. The sales were handled by the Assistant Treasurer in New York, H. H. Van Dyck. Instead of selling the gold publicly to the highest bidder, Van Dyck, with McCulloch's consent, employed a broker to go into the " Gold Room " and sell secretly with the avowed object of keeping the premium at about 130.[34] Although this object seemed reasonable, if not laudable, to Van Dyck and McCulloch, it was detestable to those who were speculating for a rise in gold. Even the conservative *Commercial and Financial Chronicle* deplored the unsettling influence of these secret sales.[35] Feeling that there must be some collusion somewhere, the House of Representatives on May 28, 1866 adopted a resolution directing the Secretary " to inform the House what amount of gold belonging to the United States has been sold by or under his authority since the 1st instant, and at what rates; also, the names of the agent or agents through whom such sales were affected, and what rate of commission has been authorized by the Department for selling the same." [36] McCulloch replied to the resolution by letter on June 4. He appended a lengthy statement by Van Dyck as to just how the sales had been made.[37] The House was not satisfied, however, for on January 21, 1867 it passed a bill prohibiting secret sales of gold, and providing that in the future gold sales should be public and should be advertised in advance in the newspapers of New York and Washington.[38] Although the bill expired quietly in the Senate which was always more considerate of McCulloch's sensibilities, the House was not appeased and continued to be extremely critical of the Secretary's gold sales.[39]

McCulloch was also severely criticised from time to time for hoarding greenbacks in the vaults of the Treasury. During

[34] Letter from Van Dyck to McCulloch reproduced in the *Bankers' Magazine*, XXI (July, 1866), 33-35.

[35] IV (February 16, 1867), 198-199.

[36] *Congressional Globe*, 39th Congress, 1st Session, p. 2857.

[37] Van Dyck to McCulloch, *op. cit.*, pp. 35-39.

[38] *Congressional Globe*, 39th Congress, 2nd Session, pp. 617-618.

[39] *Ibid.*, p. 853. See for example the resolution of General John A. Logan of Illinois, offered on March 18, 1868. *Ibid.*, 40th Congress, 2nd Session, p. 1972.

the debate over the Loan Bill which authorized contraction in the spring of 1866, John Sherman had expressed fear that McCulloch would use this obvious device to bring about contraction. It seemed apparent to the Ohio Senator that the volume of legal tender notes in circulation could be substantially reduced if the Treasury adopted the policy of maintaining a large currency balance.[40] It is doubtful that McCulloch ever consciously adopted this policy, but in the normal course of operations, the Treasury at times did accumulate rather large sums of greenbacks. As this tended to decrease the ratio between gold and legal tenders and contributed to a lowering of the premium on gold, the " locking up of greenbacks " as it was called, was criticised in the financial press. Such criticism was strong in the fall of 1867 when the Secretary was accused of hoarding millions of greenbacks just when the fall movement of currency to the West had set in.[41]

Closely connected with criticism of this sort was dissatisfaction with the way that McCulloch actually carried out contraction. The *Commercial and Financial Chronicle* which strongly subscribed to the principle of contraction did not feel that the Secretary always carried out the operation skillfully. Early in 1867 the *Chronicle* pointed out that the stock market panic which had occurred in January was very likely to be blamed on the contraction which McCulloch had carried out during a period of monetary stringency. The paper believed, and justifiably so, that contraction could only be practiced successfully when the money market was easy and there was no exceptional demand for currency.[42]

McCulloch was by no means insensible to the psychological effects of diminishing the supply of currency, though perhaps he learned his lesson too late. An anecdote from his autobiography illustrates how he once made use of his insight to the country's advantage. During his tenure the Secretary was kept abreast of the condition of the New York money market through daily correspondence with the Assistant Treasurer in that city,

---

[40] Sherman, *Recollections*, II, 381.

[41] *Commercial and Financial Chronicle*, V (October 5, 1867), 413. Similar criticism was made of McCulloch in June after he had taken in $40,000,000 of greenbacks in exchange for 5-20 bonds. *Ibid.*, IV (June 8, 1867), 709-710.

[42] *Ibid.*, IV (February 9, 1867), 165-166.

Mr. Van Dyck. One day he received a letter from that officer informing him that money was becoming tight and that he feared a panic would ensue if the monthly report, which was to be published the next day, showed the usual reduction in the volume of United States notes. As McCulloch explains: [43]

We were just then in the midst of the work of funding the seven-and-three-tenths notes, which would be seriously interrupted by a Wall Street panic; so I sent for the Treasurer, General Spinner, and showed to him the letter and telegram. " Have you," I asked, " the $4,000,000 of United States notes which were to be retired and cancelled this month?" "I have," he replied. "Has the account with the United States notes been credited with the amount?" "It has not!" "Keep them," I said, "in the treasury, with the other currency on hand, so that the report will not show any reduction for the month." This was done, and when the regular monthly report, which was published the next day, showed no reduction in the volume of these notes, although the four millions were in the treasury vaults, Wall Street was relieved, and all indications of a stringent money market disappeared.

As the year 1867 progressed, it became increasingly apparent that the tide of events was setting strongly against the policy of currency contraction. Economic depression had become prevalent, and much of the blame for the distress was placed at the door of the Secretary. A leading Radical Republican organ of the West commented caustically: " It would appear as if Secretary McCulloch was fully determined to paralyze the industrial interests of the country, particularly, those of the West. . . . To all classes this is a very important question; for if this policy of contraction is pursued, it cannot fail to interfere very materially with business prospects for the next year. Of course, it is useless now to attempt to estimate the damage which has already been done to the material interests of the country; but we must look to the future. This work of burning ' greenbacks ' must be stopped." [44] A month later the same journal angrily referred to McCulloch's " insane contraction policy" pointing out that he was nothing but a " tool of Wall Street brokers and capitalists." [45]

The correspondence of Ohio Congressmen reveals the political

[43] McCulloch, *Men and Measures*, p. 212.
[44] The Chicago *Republican*, September 7, 1867.
[45] *Ibid.*, October 24, 1867.

importance of financial issues in that pivotal state in the year 1867. State elections were to be held in the fall, and the Democratic Party, discredited by its opposition to the war, concentrated its fire on the financial legislation of the Republicans. Four main issues were involved. These were McCulloch's contraction policy, the question of whether the 5-20 bonds should be paid in gold or greenbacks, the issue as whether the federal government should tax the income on government bonds, and the question as to whether the National Banking System should be retained. As the campaign waxed hot in the summer of 1867, it became more and more apparent that the Democrats were striking some telling blows at the Republican positions.

A correspondent of Senator Sherman from Eaton, Ohio sent an editorial from a county newspaper which advocated that Congress ". . . restore our circulation at once, by issuing, if necessary, $500,000,000 in greenbacks per annum, and instead of buying up 7.30's with gold interest bonds, let us not only pay off these notes, but also gradually, and as rapidly as we please, pay off the gold bonds also." If it should be objected that this policy would bring about inflation, this paper had a ready-made answer: " When have we been more prosperous as a people, than during the inflation of the war? " The Senator's constituent endorsed these views, pointing out that it represented the views of a majority of Republicans in his county. " This has been brot [sic] about by McCullough [sic] idea of Specie resumption, and if continued, Repudiation . . . will have to be adopted. To hold the People with us, their burthens must be lessened. . . . We can't afford as a party to become the advocates and supporters of a policy that enriches the few at the Expense of the many. With Negro voting and the Bond holders on our backs we are going to have a hard time to get home this fall in Ohio with a decent majority." The writer pointed out that the Cincinnati *Gazette* was waging a relentless campaign against him and advised the Senator to ". . . checkmate this stuff, either in a letter to some of your friends out of the State, or in a well timed speech at home to your friends." [46] Sherman apparently took this advice, although his speech at

[46] A. Denny to Sherman, July 27, 1867, Sherman Papers. The enclosed clipping was probably from the Eaton, Ohio *Register*.

Canton, Ohio on August 20 was not what his correspondent had in mind, for the Senator strongly defended the record of the Republican Party on finance and made a powerful plea for the National Banking System, asserting that ". . . I never was much of a bank man, but while such agencies are demanded, as they are in all new countries when capital is scarce, I believe the present system is far better than we have ever had, and far better than for the United States Government to assume directly the banking operations of the people." [47] It is interesting to note that Sherman received a warm letter of congratulations on this speech from Henry D. Cooke of the banking house of Jay Cooke and Company.[48]

Another worried Republican wrote the Senator late in September: " We are having a *close* canvass in Knox this fall. Great effort will be required to get out our Vote. The *currency* question is now attracting more attention than the Amendment of the Constitution. *Thurman & Pendleton* had a *fair* meeting here Thursday. Their *scheme* of paying Bondholders with ' Greenbacks ' looks plausible to the masses. It must be fully explained & exploded." [49]

When the smoke of battle had cleared and all the votes had been counted, it was found that the Republicans had suffered considerable reverses. The Republican candidate for governor, Rutherford B. Hayes, had been elected over the Democrat, Allen G. Thurman, by the narrow margin of 2,983 votes in a total of 484,603, but the Legislature, on which a successor to Senator Wade would depend, was Democratic. This power was asserted by the Democrats a few months later when they elected Thurman United States Senator from Ohio.[50] These results were considered so ominous to the continued success of the Republican Party that Gideon Welles confided to his diary that they were " hardly credible " and indicated " the overthrow of the Radicals and the downfall of that party." [51]

That the Republicans agreed with these portents of doom is indicated in the correspondence of James A. Garfield and Burke

[47] Cincinnati *Daily Gazette*, August 21, 1867. Clipping in the Sherman Papers.
[48] Henry D. Cooke to Sherman, September 9, 1867, Sherman Papers.
[49] J. C. Devin to Sherman, September 30, 1867, *ibid*.
[50] Charles Richard Williams, *The Life of Rutherford Birchard Hayes*, 2 vols. (Boston, 1914), I, 328.   [51] Welles, *Diary*, III, 232.

A. Hinsdale. Hinsdale wrote on October 22 that ". . . the Fall elections as a whole have settled two things: 1. The negro will be less prominent for some time to come; 2. financial questions will be more prominent. I cannot [know] how prominent these questions have been in the late canvass. Our party must do something to satisfy the people on these questions or the power departs from us. We must have a financial creed if possible. The men who rise to the demands of the time on the money matters will be the men who will make a name for the future." [52]

There was a tendency to scan the horizon in order to determine the direction of the political storm. Schuyler Colfax, Speaker of the House of Representatives, wrote to Sherman: "What is your solution of the causes of the Ohio reverses? You were all over the state and must have some theory. Were we not weakened by Finance almost as much as Suffrage? The Dem. speeches seemed to avoid the issue of Reconstruction in their speeches which I read & preferred Greenbacks. We must profit by these popular indications before '68. I do not mean to yield to them but to study them, influence them & counteract them by pointing out a better way." [53] Senator Wade agreed that the Republicans had been weakened by their financial policies and attributed the Ohio reverses to the " repudiating doctrines preached by our adversaries." [54]

Henry Cooke's letter to Sherman on the subject of the Ohio election reflected the opinion of a conservative banker. He felt that the Republican Party should be more of one mind on financial questions. He asserted that " Such men as Butler and Stevens must be put down—or driven to associate with the Vallandighams and Pendletons of the . . . Democracy and the Republican party must take high ground in regard to the national finances." [55]

---

[52] *Garfield-Hinsdale Letters: Correspondence between James Abram Garfield and Burke Aaron Hinsdale*, ed. Mary L. Hinsdale (Ann Arbor, 1949), p. 112.

[53] Schuyler Colfax to Sherman, October 12, 1867. Sherman Papers. The reference to the " Suffrage " question concerns the amendment to the Ohio Constitution, rejected by the voters, which would have extended the ballot to the Negro. Edward McPherson, *A Handbook of Politics for 1868* (Washington, 1868), pp. 257-258; 353-354.

[54] Benjamin F. Wade to Zachariah Chandler, October 10, 1867. Chandler Papers, Library of Congress.

[55] Henry D. Cooke to Sherman, October 12, 1867. Sherman Papers.

While receiving such high minded conservative advice from the Cookes, Sherman was made aware of other opinions at the grass roots level. A. Denny wrote from Eaton, Ohio that " A few more turns of McCullough's [sic] contraction screw will give us a monetary panic that will eclipse 1840. An issue of fifty millions of Legal Tenders would balance up our financial books and stop the continued cry of a stringent money market by all our business men. Will Congress do it?" [56] A correspondent from Barnesville, Ohio pointed out that " Whether right or wrong the ball set in motion by the Democrats on the Greenback issue will run its course and unless Congress should make some change, the next election will sweep our party out of existence." [57] A constituent from Portsmouth, Ohio wrote: " McCulloch's course will ruin & swamp any man or any party implicated with it. Stop as soon as possible this reduction in the currency, let not a day pass after the assembling of Congress before you take steps to initiate a change." [58]

Some of the strongest advice Sherman received came from Joseph Medill, proprietor of the strongly Republican Chicago *Tribune*. This editor asserted: " The people are exceedingly restive under the present financial system. I think this general discontent had more to do with causing the alarming reaction in politics this fall than all other causes put together." His solution was simple and straightforward. " If the Republican members would come boldly up to the mark and institute greenbacks for bank-notes and tax the bonds, and then cut down taxation to the lowest safe limit and economize appropriations as closely as possible, we shall retain poitical power, otherwise not. This is my candid conviction. The very fact that the reconstruction question is drawing rapidly to a conclusion will hasten the disintegration of our party, unless our leaders reflect public sentiment on financial questions as accurately as they have heretofore done on questions of freedom and personal rights." In regard to McCulloch's contraction policy, Medill added that ". . . the four million a month burning up of greenbacks is

[56] A. Denny to Sherman, October 14, 1867, *ibid*.
[57] C. Davenport to Sherman, October 15, 1867, *ibid*.
[58] R. J. to Sherman, November 11, 1867, *ibid*.

severely condemned by all men of both parties in the West. That policy finds no supporters in any party." [59]

The almost unanimous opinion among Republicans that the Ohio debacle of 1867 had been brought to pass because of the Party's financial legislation was not without its effect on the outcome of the contraction controversy. Of particular importance was the fact that two Ohioans had risen to eminence in the financial committees of Congress—John Sherman, who had opposed contraction in 1866, became in the Fortieth Congress, Chairman of the Senate Finance Committee succeeding the contractionist William Pitt Fessenden. In the House the chairmanship of the powerful Ways and Means Committee, left vacant by the promotion of the contractionist Justin Morrill to the Senate, was assumed by Congressman Robert Schenck of Dayton, Ohio, a man who was described by Garfield as an "inflationist" and an opponent of the National Banking System.[60]

Before turning to the arena of national politics in Washington where the next act in the drama of financial reconstruction was to be played out, it is necessary that some attention be devoted to an aspect of the Ohio election of 1867 which influenced the doctrine of the Democratic Party for years to come, namely, the emergence of that collection of financial ideas which has been variously called the "Ohio rag-baby," the "Ohio idea," and the "Pendleton Plan." No attempt will be made here to describe in detail the development of the Pendleton Plan with all its refinements and shadings. This task has already been brilliantly performed by Professor Destler.[61] It is sufficient to say that the basic idea that the war debt, which had been contracted in depreciated currency, should be paid in the same currency was advocated as early as 1865 by a Radical organ, the Cincinnati *Gazette*.[62] Similar demands were made by Henry Clay Dean, an ultra "peace" Democrat from Iowa who denounced the national banks, the bondholders, and New

---

[59] Joseph Medill to Sherman, November 22, 1867, *ibid.*

[60] Sherman, *Recollections*, I, 433-434; Smith, *Garfield*, I, 415-416.

[61] Chester McArthur Destler, *American Radicalism, 1865-1901: Essays and Documents* (New London, Conn., 1945), chs. II-III

[62] *Ibid.*, p. 34.

England, and called for an immediate issue of greenbacks
large enough to pay the war debt at once.[63]

These ideas were dormant for some time, but early in 1867
they were taken up by the Cincinnati *Enquirer*, an influential
Democratic journal controlled by Washington McLean, party
boss in Hamilton County. The publishers of this paper realized
that their " peace-at-any-price " sentiments had considerably
reduced their influence, even within the Democratic Party.
The idea of paying off the war debt in greenbacks was tailor-
made to their purposes of regaining this influence and providing the Democrats with a winning election issue. At first
McLean attempted to sell the idea to the party leaders at the
Ohio State Democratic Convention, but was unsuccessful. Un-
dismayed he championed the inflationary proposal in the
columns of the *Enquirer*, and the response was gratifying.
Sentiment rapidly began to grow in the Middle West in favor
of paying the war debt in greenbacks.[64]

When the leaders of the party in Ohio began to feel the
popularity of McLean's program, they began to hedge, searching
for a substitute designed to capitalize on the popular feeling on
this issue and yet one which would not leave them open to a
charge of extreme radicalism. The *Enquirer's* program was not
only too radical, but adoption of it would entail surrender of
leadership in the Democratic party to Washington McLean.[65]

The conservative substitute was presented by H. J. Jewett, a
former Democratic candidate for governor, at Zanesville on
July 5, 1867. Jewett criticized the high interest and tax exemption features of the debt, but did not propose repudiation. His
position was very similar to that of Senator John Sherman. He
proposed that bondholders be given two choices, the choice
of accepting taxable, lower interest bonds in place of their
present holdings, or of being paid off in the very greenback
currency with which the bonds had been bought during the war.
Once refunded, the device of a sinking fund could be utilized
to pay off the debt. This sinking fund could be financed partially through the money saved by funding the debt at a lower

[63] *Ibid.*, p. 34.
[64] *Ibid.*, pp. 34-37.
[65] *Ibid.*, p. 37.

rate of interest and by not funding the floating debt (i. e. the greenbacks). Jewett's most radical proposal was the abolition of the National Banking System and the substitution of green-backs for national bank-notes. In this way the interest paid to bankers on the bonds which secured the bank-notes could be saved and could be annually diverted to the sinking fund. In this manner Jewett felt that the entire national debt could be extinguished in eighteen years without increasing taxation.[66]

Skillfully and cautiously the *Enquirer* clique played its devi-ous game. The next important step was to enlist the support of George H. Pendleton whom his adversary Rutherford B. Hayes described as the ". . . most distinguished and perhaps the most influential Democrat now actively engaged in politics in Ohio." [67] As a Congressman in 1862 Pendleton had bitterly denounced the first Legal Tender Act, and his monetary opinions prior to 1867 had always bourne the hard-money stamp of the old Jacksonian.[68] It was only with the realization that this popular financial issue offered the only hope of the Democrats that Pendleton gave himself over to the *Enquirer*'s game. It was, however, Jewett's conservative substitute that he adopted rather than the program of wholesale inflation advocated by Washington McLean.[69]

Pendleton developed his position in a series of speeches in the summer and fall of 1867. In Cleveland on September 18, he described his plan in these words.[70]

The non-interest paying debt, consisting of greenbacks and unliqui-dated debt, amounts to about eight hundred millions of dollars. I do not vouch for the exact accuracy of these figures. They are not far wrong. They serve perfectly well for illustration. The proposition of the Republicans is to convert this debt into bonds which pay interest in gold. The interest on these bonds will be forty-eight millions in gold annually. The result will be to increase by that amount the expenses, to convert active capital into inactive capital, and thus to increase the

---

[66] *Ibid.*, p. 37; Sherman, *Recollections*, I, 376.

[67] Williams, *op. cit.*, I, 296.

[68] Destler, p. 38. Pendleton's opposition to the first Legal Tender Act was described *supra*, pp. 37-38. He had been the vice-presidential nominee of the Democrats in 1864.

[69] Destler, p. 38.

[70] *Payment of the Public Debt in Legal Tender Notes!! Speech of Hon. George H. Pendleton* (Milwaukee, 1867), pp. 15-16.

number of those who do not pay taxes, and to increase the burdens of those who do pay taxes. I maintain that this debt ought not to be so converted—that these forty-eight millions in gold should be saved. There are three hundred millions of these bonds in the Treasury as security for the National bank currency. They are represented by a nearly equal amount of bank notes. They call for eighteen millions of dollars in gold annually as interest.

Now, I maintain that these bonds should be redeemed in greenbacks. The result would be that the greenbacks would take the place of the bank notes, which would be called in, and that eighteen million dollars of interest would be saved. If that eighteen million were added to the forty-eight millions of which I have spoken, you have sixty-six millions in gold annually; and this properly compounded would pay the whole debt, principal and interest in fifteen years. *And now observe that thus far I have not proposed to add one dollar to your taxes, or one dollar to the currency.*

As Pendleton developed his plan, it became clear that it was only the 5-20 bonds which he proposed to redeem in greenbacks. Since the original loan acts under which these bonds were issued were silent as to the medium of payment, this was a defensible position and one which was shared by such influential Republicans as Senators Sherman and Morton.[71] Naturally this plan would have involved a certain amount of currency inflation, but Pendleton was convinced, with good reason, that the business interests of the country could well bear a moderate expansion of the currency.[72] The Ohioan had harsh words for McCulloch's policy of contraction. " To expand the currency when the people are incurring a debt, and to contract the currency when they come to pay it, is public robbery, whether such be the motive or not." [73]

When it had finally jelled, the " Pendleton Plan " was a skillful blend of financial proposals designed to take full advantage of the popular outcry against Republican fiscal policy as enunciated by Hugh McCulloch. By offering to pay the 5-20 bonds in greenbacks, it catered to the popular slogan of " the same currency for the ploughholder and the bondholder." The payment of these bonds in greenbacks would also overturn the hated policy of currency contraction and assure an adequate

[71] Dewey, *Financial History*, pp. 344-348.
[72] Pendleton, p. 16.
[73] Pendleton, p. 16.

supply of money. By the same token, substitution of greenbacks for bank-notes would assure the overthrow of that citadel of special privilege, the National Banking System. No plan could have been better designed to take advantage of the resentment particularly in the West, of all aspects of McCulloch's program. Its strength was sufficient to bring the Democrats a high degree of success in the Ohio election of 1867, while it also succeeded in precipitating alarm in the ranks of Republican politicians.

Why then did the " Pendleton Plan " fail to attain its objective of providing the Democrats with an issue on which they could achieve a return to political power? This is a complex question which calls for more than a superficial answer. In the first place it should be pointed out that the " Pendleton Plan," while popular in the West, was never accepted by the eastern Democracy. It was strongly opposed by eastern leaders such as Horatio Seymour, Samuel J. Tilden, and August Belmont. The latter's Wall Street connections made his stand inevitable, while Seymour and Tilden both possessed impeccable hard-money convictions.[74] One of the few monied men high in the councils of the Democratic Party who favored inflation as a campaign issue was Cyrus McCormick, who was, incidentally, a manufacturer.[75] This split in the party on financial issues made it impossible for Democrats to proclaim unity in a crucial sphere. The ultimate absurdity was presented in 1868 when the gold Democrat, Horatio Seymour, ran for president on a Pendletonite platform which advocated payment of the 5-20's in greenbacks.[76]

The split in the Democratic Party provides us with part of the answer as to why the " Pendleton Plan " failed, but some aspects of the question are still unanswered. Why, it might be asked, did the Democrats, with a Pendletonite plank in their platform, fail so miserably in the Middle West in 1868? Even Seymour during the campaign indicated that he was in sympathy with many of the western grievances against Republican financial policy. In a speech at Chicago, he denounced the

---

[74] Robert Stewart Mitchell, *Horatio Seymour of New York* (Cambridge, Mass., 1938), pp. 387-388; 396.

[75] *Ibid.*, p. 396.

[76] Charles H. Coleman, *The Election of 1868: The Democratic Effort to Regain Control* (New York, 1933), pp. 200-205; 236-245.

concentration of national bank currency in the East, pointing out that Massachusetts had nearly six times the amount of bank currency as did Illinois, but that Illinois had twice the population of Masachusetts. He also played a popular tune when he denounced the contraction of the currency.[77] Why then did the Democrats fail to carry a single middle western state?

It might be answered that no Democratic candidate stood much of a chance against Grant, the great national hero. To this might be replied a financial program posited on genuine economic grievances might well have been expected to win out even against General Grant. Now arises the crucial question. How much genuine economic discontent was there in the years immediately following the Civil War?

That there was genuine economic discontent in these years is hardly to be doubted, but the downturn in the business cycle hit some groups much harder than others. Discontent was rife among manufacturers, a condition which will be discussed in a later chapter.[78] Labor was also restive, although the position of the laboring man in a period of deflation was somewhat better than it had been during the war.[79] Bankers on the whole were prosperous.[80] The key to the political question posited above is the position of the farmer, for if he were genuinely discontented with his economic lot, the Democrats might well have hoped to regain political power in 1868. Even though they had grievances, the manufacturers might be expected to stand with the party of high protection. A majority of bankers had a vested interest in the Republican Party through the National Banking System, and the vote of organized labor was not yet an important factor in the political equation. The farm vote, however, was of decisive importance.

There is evidence to indicate that the relative economic position of the farmer was excellent in the years immediately following the Civil War. One important reason for this was the fact that poor crops in Europe insured a large demand for American breadstuffs.[81] It was complained that the continued

[77] Mitchell, *Seymour,* pp. 472-473.
[78] See Chapter IV.
[79] See Chapter V.
[80] See Chapter VI.
[81] *Commercial and Financial Chronicle,* V (August 10, 1867), 166-167; V (October 12, 1867), 454-455.

maintenance of high prices for agricultural products was
hurting manufacturers in that the average consumer had little
money left for manufactured items after he had purchased the
necessities.[82] Statistical evidence corroborates this view that the
farmer was prosperous, particularly the middle western farmer.
The most important farm products of the Middle West were
corn and wheat.[83] The following table indicates the average
seasonal prices for corn and wheat in the years, 1866-1875.[84]

	Corn for all purposes Price per bushel	All wheat for grain Price per bushel
1866	$0.657	$2.062
1867	0.781	2.012
1868	0.617	1.459
1869	0.725	0.923
1870	0.521	1.042
1871	0.464	1.247
1872	0.383	1.239
1873	0.483	1.168
1874	0.641	0.948
1875	0.419	1.010

High market prices for these two staple crops are the key to
the failure of the "Pendleton Plan." It is evident that the
average seasonal price per bushel for corn and wheat was
considerably greater on the average for the years, 1866-1869
than for the succeeding six years. In the important election
year of 1868, the average seasonal price for wheat was $1.46
per bushel. The same trend is evident when we consider price
statistics on oats, barley, hay, and potatoes.[85] Although it is
evident from the table that the prices for these staples, particularly wheat, were declining from the very high points reached
in 1867, it must be remembered that the prices of the manufactured goods bought by farmers were also declining. The
average seasonal price of $1.46 per bushel for wheat in the

[82] *Ibid.*, V (October 26, 1867), 519.
[83] Solon Justus Buck, *The Granger Movement: A Study of Agricultural
Organization and Its Political, Economic and Social Manifestations, 1870-1880*
(Cambridge, Mass., 1913), p. 7.
[84] This table is derived from *Historical Statistics of the United States*, Series
E 181-195, p. 106.
[85] *Ibid.*, Series E 196-210; E 211-224; E. 225-230; pp. 107-109.

important election year of 1868 represented a considerable decline from the preceding year's average, but it was still a very high price. It was not destined to be that high again until 1916.[86] In general, it can be safely asserted that the farmer had no period of prosperity to compare with 1866-1869 until the First World War. This is corroborated by a leading historian of agriculture who refers to the "years of prosperity immediately following the war."[87] The prosperity of the farmer was one of the decisive reasons why the Republicans managed to retain political power in 1868.

Some writers have emphasized the discontent of the farmers in these years.[88] Though practically no real evidence exists for any acute agrarian discontent prior to 1869, it should not be assumed that the farmer was entirely complacent, for this would not be accurate. The essential point is that the discontent of the farmer was not founded on the real pinch of hard times. Many farmers keenly felt the injustice of paying the 5-20 bonds in gold. They also resented the monopolization of the national bank currency by New England and New York. Few had any use for McCulloch's contraction policy, and most had grievances against the railroads. On the other hand, agrarian revolt does not come to a head in a time of high commodity prices. It was only after the panic of 1873 when the grievances above were combined with actual economic hardship that farmers attempted large-scale organization to achieve their economic and political objectives.[89]

An interesting problem in the history of the Reconstruction period is posed if we seek to understand the reasons why the leaders of the old hard-money Jacksonian Democracy, men such as George Pendleton, William Allen, and Francis Preston Blair, Jr., embraced the soft-money philosophy of the post-Civil

[86] *Ibid.*, Series E 181-195, p. 106. The prices quoted in the table above are currency prices. This is entirely logical since greenback currency provided the standard of value in the United States until the resumption of specie payments in 1879.

[87] Buck, *The Granger Movement*, p. 20.

[88] For example, Beale, *The Critical Year*, pp. 230-231; Destler, *American Radicalism*, pp. 32-33.

[89] Buck, *The Granger Movement*, pp. 34-36, ch. III; Harold Underwood Faulkner, *American Economic History*, 7th ed. (New York, 1954), pp. 366-369. For a fuller discussion of the farmer's negative role in the currency controversy in the period from 1865 to 1870, see the appendix which follows this chapter.

War period. One student of banking has referred to this problem as " one of the most amazing enigmas of American financial history," finding it inconceivable that a man such as William Allen, who had been an intimate friend of Andrew Jackson, could possibly embrace greenbackism.[90] Part of the reason for this complete change of ground was sheer expediency as was indicated above in treating Pendleton's conversion to the *Enquirer's* program. Leading Democrats felt they had found a popular issue, and they did not intend to let it go for the sake of ideological consistency. Pendleton resented the charge of inconsistency, however, and defended himself in his Milwaukee speech of November 2, 1867.[91]

Do not misunderstand me here. I did not vote for that legal tender act. I was in Congress at the time. I opposed it. I voted against it. I believed the policy was bad. We had coin currency, and I believed we should maintain it. I thought the war might have been carried on, as the wars of Napoleon against the world were carried on for years, upon a coin basis and without inflation, and without the issue of notes. I endeavored to the utmost of my feeble ability to enforce that policy upon Congress. I was overruled and a contrary policy was adopted. It became incorporated into the business of the country, and I am now in favor, in good faith, of carrying it out to the end, until every advantage shall be realized, and until we can with safety and ease reverse this policy, as I believe we ought, and return to specie payments in the country.

In other words Pendleton disavowed any connection with the original Legal Tender Act, pointing out that he had opposed it. Once the ball of inflation had been set in motion, however, Pendleton believed that it should be allowed to follow its natural course. To contract the currency before the war debt had been paid was rank injustice. His old hard-money scruples are maintained, for he looks forward to a return to specie payments. The biographer of William Allen seeks to explain the change in the monetary ideas of that old Jacksonian who was elected Governor of Ohio in 1874 on a greenback platform. " True he had been a hard-money man in the thirties; now he was a soft-money advocate. What if he had said that

---

[90] Leonard Helderman, *National and State Banks, A Study of their Origins* (Boston, 1931), p. 159 n.
[91] Pendleton, *Payment of the Public Debt in Legal Tender Notes!!*, p. 9.

metallic money was the only standard of value? Times had changed since then and circumstances molded politics. . . . How could one call the greenbacks irredeemable currency when it paid all debts, public and private, and was legal tender for everything one had to buy? The Democrats in the thirties had opposed the ' wild cat ' state and the local bank issues, which had nothing behind them but a promise to pay their note in specie. They could not oppose the issue of greenbacks by the government of the United States for the same reason, for all real purposes the greenbacks were just as much money as coin and just as good as the precious metals themselves. Allen as a good Democrat of the seventies must be for the greenback! " [92]

An important thread of continuity which linked the pre-war, hard-money Democrats of the age of Jackson and those Democrats, particularly western Democrats of the sixties and seventies whose proclivities were toward soft-money, was a dislike and distrust of banks, bankers, and particularly bank-notes. Since the supply of specie in the country was inadequate to sustain a return to coin payments without drastic deflation, it was only natural that western Democrats should prefer greenbacks, the money of the people, to national bank-notes which was the money of the bankers. This logic is explicit in a letter written by General Francis Preston Blair, Jr. to John Maguire, a labor leader, in 1869. General Blair, who was the Democratic vice-presidential candidate in 1868 and whose very name conjures up the departed glory of the age of Jackson, had this to say about the financial problems of the time: [93]

This golden age [the Jacksonian period when there was no national debt and no United States bank] can never return while a stupendous national debt weighs on the labor of the country, preying on it hourly in the shape of taxation, and converting all the machinery of the Treasury into a paper mint, to create issues for the so-called national banks based by holders of the national debt on the Government credit and deposits, to lay a new and still greater taxation on the people in the shape of loans.

Why may not the Government bank on its own credit, its deposits,

---

[92] Reginald Charles McGrane, *William Allen: A Study in Western Democracy* (Columbus, Ohio, 1925), p. 219.

[93] This letter was printed in the Chicago *Workingman's Advocate*, September 11, 1869.

and its issue of currency, now given to the banks, convert the gains into the means of paying the national debt, instead of surrendering all to stockholders.

In essence, Blair proposed the abolition of the National Banking System and the substitution of greenbacks for national bank-notes. If necessary, the government itself could provide banking services for the people. In the light of such evidence, the attitudes of post-war Democrats toward monetary questions are not completely enigmatic. Founded on expediency these attitudes were still bound up with a strong thread of continuity with the past.

THE END OF CONTRACTION

The temper of the Fortieth Congress, which was elected in 1866 and met on March 4, 1867, was, if anything more radical than that of the preceding Congress. The defeat of President Johnson in the congressional elections of 1866 portended the doom of his southern policy. In the words of James Ford Rhodes, " By an overwhelming vote the people of the North sustained Congress and . . . gave the Republicans enough Senators and representatives to carry out a policy of reconstruction despite any opposition on the part of the President." [94] Just as the tremendous congressional majority of the Radicals augured ill for the program of moderate Reconstruction, so also did it foretell the overthrow of the fiscal policy of Hugh McCulloch.

It has already been noted that in the Fortieth Congress two opponents of McCulloch's policies, Senator John Sherman and Congressman Robert Schenck, had succeeded to the chairmanships of the two most important committees which dealt with financial legislation. If these appointments boded ill for the Secretary, the appearance of certain new Congressmen in Washington was nearly as bad. From Illinois came General John A. Logan, a forceful man and an ardent Radical who quickly rose to a position of prominence in the House.[95] The former commander of the Tenth Corps was no friend to McCulloch, and

---

[94] James Ford Rhodes, *History of the United States from the Compromise of 1850*, 8 vols. (New York, 1899-1919), V, 625-626.
[95] Logan later became one of the seven House managers of impeachment against President Johnson. *Ibid.*, VI, 115.

one of his first acts in the Fortieth Congress was the submission of a resolution inquiring into the Secretary's methods of disposing of 10-40 bonds.[96] What Logan was driving at became clear when he offered another resolution on March 18, 1868. This resolution inquired into " the amount of commmissions paid for the sale or disposal of United States bonds or securities, since the second day of March, A. D. 1861." [97] It was directed against McCulloch's relations with Jay Cooke & Company which was generally thought to have made a great deal of money through its position as agent for the sale of government bonds. Jay Cooke strongly resented the implication that he had profited unduly through this connection. In a letter to his brother Henry, Jay Cooke asserted: " I consider Logan's remarks as a direct insult which ought to be met at once. . . . The question of employing another person to act for the Treasury Department is another matter and if Congress wishes the Secretary to abandon the policy which has prevailed since the commencement of the war we have no complaint to make. We can get along without them if they can get along without us, but I am determined that these attacks upon our honor and our integrity shall be met at once, and indignantly. . . . It is hard that a gallant soldier like General Logan should lend himself to injure the very parties who stood by him and his fellow soldiers, and raised the means for their payment when these very men who are now hounding him on to attack our character and reputation stood by, and speculated in gold, and did all they could do negatively to break up the Union." [98]

Another enemy of McCulloch's financial policy who quickly rose to prominence in the Fortieth Congress was Benjamin F. Butler, ex-Jacksonian Democrat, political general, and now an ultra-Radical Republican. Like many of his Radical colleagues such as Thaddeus Steven and " Pig Iron " Kelley, Butler was a greenbacker. His position was somewhat different from the Radicals of Pennsylvania and the West who had very good economic reasons for their beliefs. Butler was a New Englander, and greenbackers were not too common in that section of the

---

[96] *Congressional Globe*, 40th Congress, 2nd Session, p. 664.
[97] *Ibid.*, p. 1972.
[98] Quoted in Oberholtzer, *Jay Cooke*, II, 32.

country.[99] Gideon Welles maintained that no one but a "knave or a fool" would take Butler's position on paper money, and he knew that Butler was no fool.[100] A careful reading of Butler's pronouncements on this issue, however, leads to the conviction that he was entirely sincere in his belief that the 5-20 bonds should be paid off in greenbacks. In his autobiography Butler has described his position on this question during the campaign of 1866.[101]

I urged that the greenbacks were constitutional currency of the United States, and therefore legal and lawful money of the United States. Upon this question controversy arose, and it was discussed in Congress and the newspapers in the bitterest manner. The legal tender notes were called "rag-baby currency"; it was said that no honest man could stand by it as money; that they were forced loans, broken promises to pay; and that banknotes should be substituted for them, in other words, that the promise of a national bank to pay a given sum was better than the promise of the United States, when all that made a national banknote worth a dollar was, that it was endorsed by the United States to be redeemed in legal tender notes. . . .

Immediately there came a division in my congressional district upon these questions. I proclaimed myself there and everywhere a greenbacker, and that term was applied to me everywhere as the last term of ignominy. The banking interests organized a split in the Republican party. The Democrats had quite a following there, and it was thought better to have a Democrat elected by withdrawing the Republican votes from myself than to have so pestilent a greenbacker represent that solid old Republican district in Congress.

The position of the ultra-Radical Butler on financial issues is thus seen to have been almost identical with that of Democrat George H. Pendleton. Indeed Congressman James G. Blaine of Maine made this point in a debate in the House on November 26, 1867. Butler met the allegation head on. "He [Blaine] has sought to prejudice the argument at this point by coupling the views expressed by me with those expressed by the gentleman from Ohio. Now, why should he do that if he has a good case? My argument, sir, will be neither better nor worse, my views are neither more nor less correct, because they

[99] Wendell Phillips was another notable exception.
[100] Welles, *Diary*, III, 506.
[101] Benjamin F. Butler, *Autobiography and Personal Reminiscences of Major General Benjamin F. Butler; Butler's Book* (Boston, 1892), pp. 920-921.

are agreed to by a gentleman from the West with whom on
other questions I disagree." [102] The case of Benjamin F.
Butler provides another excellent illustration of the fact that there
was no unity of opinion on financial questions among the
Radical Republicans, that, on the contrary, some of the most
ultra-Radical of the species were the loudest advocates of paper
money.

With men like Butler and Logan, Schenck, Stevens, and
Sherman firmly in the saddle, it was clear that the policy of
currency contraction was in for some tough sledding. On
December 7, 1867 Chairman Schenck of the Committee of
Ways and Means reported back to the House floor the following bill with a recommendation that it pass: " That from
and after the passage of this act the authority of the Secretary
of the Treasury to make any reduction of the currency by
retiring or canceling United States notes shall be, and is hereby,
suspended." [103]

Schenck was determined to push the bill through without
debate, and he immediately called the previous question on the
passage of the measure. James A. Garfield, who had studied
the Manchester school of political economy to such effect that
his views no longer reflected those of his Ohio constituents, was
a decided opponent of the bill.[104] Unable to debate under the
rules, he expressed his sentiments very cleverly in the form of
a question to Schenck. " I wish to know if I am to understand
from what the gentleman says that they propose to settle by a
definite law this great question of financial policy, under the
operation of the previous question, without debate, and then
allow members to debate it at their leisure in the Committee
of the Whole after the bill has been passed. I ask him if it is
proposed to revoke and overturn the declared financial policy
of Congress, which has been followed during the last three
years, without debate? " [105]

Mr. Garfield's little scheme for rousing the House to defeat
the motion for the previous question failed, and Schenck was

[102] *Ibid.*, p. 932. *Congressional Globe*, 40th Congress, 1st Session, Appendix,
p. 29.
[103] *Ibid.*, 40th Congress, 2nd Session, p. 69.
[104] Smith, *Garfield*, I, 368-389; 430.
[105] *Ibid.*, p. 429. *Congressional Globe*, 40th Congress, 2nd Session, p. 70.

able to bring the bill to a vote within a few minutes. It passed the lower chamber by a vote of 127 to 32 with 28 not voting. The table on the following page reveals the sectional and political aspects of this vote.[106]

The split in the Democratic Party on monetary policy, a cleavage between eastern and western adherents of that party, which was destined to emerge with greater clarity in later years, can be dated from this vote on the bill to end contraction. It will be recalled that in 1866 every Democrat in the House except one voted for contraction. Since that time the " Pendleton Plan " had swept through the West and become the official doctrine of the Democratic Party in that region. Two years before House Democrats of the middle western and border states had voted 11 to 0 in favor of contraction. Now the votes of these states were recorded 15 to 1 against a continuation of McCulloch's policy. This was certainly a remarkable change of front which marked the demise of traditional hard-money Democratic sentiment in the West. Eastern Democrats, on balance, continued to favor contraction, voting 12 to 8 in favor of that policy.

Republican members of the House opposed further contraction by the decisive margin of 103 to 18. Sentiment against McCulloch's policy was so overwhelming that it engulfed virtually every prominent Radical in the House. Voting for the bill were Ashley, Bingham, Boutwell, Butler, Covode, Julian, Kelley, Logan, Schenck, and Stevens. Among the few contractionist Radicals who upheld McCulloch at this point were Blaine, Garfield, and Elihu B. Washburne.[107]

A sectional analysis of the House vote shows that the middle western and border states suported the bill to suspend contraction by the overwhelming margin of 76 to 5. New England approved the bill by a vote of 14 to 10. The middle Atlantic states supported the measure 35 to 15, while the votes of the far western states were split 2 to 2.[108] The vote demonstrated that the policy of contraction had practically no friends in the

[106] Information used in the construction of this table was derived from *ibid.*, p. 70 and from Blaine, *Twenty Years of Congress*, II, 285-286.

[107] *Congressional Globe*, 40th Congress, 2nd Session, p. 70.

[108] It is significant that 11 of the 15 votes against the bill in the middle Atlantic states were cast by Democrats.

VOTE ON THE ANTI-CONTRACTION BILL, HOUSE OF REPRESENTATIVES,
DECEMBER 7, 1867

	Against Further Contraction		For Continued Contraction	
	Rep.	Dem.	Rep.	Dem.
New England States				
Massachusetts	3		5	
Maine	2		3	
New Hampshire	3			
Vermont	2		1	
Connecticut	1	2		1
Rhode Island	1			
TOTALS	12	2	9	1
Middle Atlantic States				
New York	14	3	1	3
Pennsylvania	12	1	2	5
Maryland	1	2	1	1
Delaware				
New Jersey	2			2
TOTALS	29	6	4	11
Middle Western States				
Ohio	12	4	2	
Illinois	9	2	1	
Indiana	7	3		
Wisconsin	5	1		
Minnesota	1			
Michigan	5			
Iowa	5		1	
Kansas	1			
TOTALS	45	10	4	
Border States				
Kentucky		5		1
Missouri	8			
West Virginia	1			
Tennessee	7			
TOTALS	16	5		1
Far Western States				
California	1	1		1
Nevada			1	
TOTALS	1	1	1	1
GRAND TOTALS	103	24	18	14

West, that it was opposed by better than a two-to-one ratio in the middle Atlantic states, and that McCulloch derived his only important support at this juncture from New England, which nevertheless, on balance, opposed further contraction.

The bill was referred to the Senate Finance Committee on December 9.[109] Eight days later Sherman reported it out of committee with an amendment.[110] The amendment struck out all of the House bill after the enacting clause and substituted the following: " That so much of the act approved April 12, 1866 entitled "An act to amend an act entitled 'An act to provide ways and means to support the Government,' approved March 3, 1865," as provides that the Secretary of the Treasury may retire and cancel United States notes to the extent of $4,000,000 per month be, and the same is hereby, suspended until Congress shall otherwise provide." [111]

As Sherman explained, the purpose of the Finance Committee in changing the phrasing of the House bill was simply to assure the Secretary that he would still possess the power to cancel mutilated or defaced notes and issue others in their stead. Sherman believed this power would be left intact if the contractive provisions of the legislation of April, 1866 were merely suspended.[112]

In the debate which followed Senator Sherman explained the reasons why a majority of the Finance Committee desired that the measure pass.[113]

First. It will satisfy the public mind that no further contraction will be made when industry is in a measure paralyzed. We hear the complaint from all parts of the country, from all branches of industry, from every State in the Union that industry for some reason is paralyzed and that trade and enterprise are not so well rewarded as they were. . . .

Second. This bill will restore to the Legislature their power over the currency, a power too important to be delegated to any single officer of the Government.

---

[109] *Congressional Globe*, 40th Congress, 2nd Session, p. 79.
[110] *Ibid.*, p. 219.
[111] *Ibid.*, p. 407.
[112] *Ibid.*, p. 407.
[113] *Ibid.*, pp. 407-408. It is interesting to note that Sherman speaks only of depression in industry and does not mention agriculture. This tends to support the thesis presented above (pp. 102-104) and in the appendix following this chapter that there was no depression in agriculture.

Third. This will strongly impress upon Congress the imperative duty of acting wisely upon financial measures, for the responsibility will then rest entirely upon Congress and will not be shared with them by the Secretary of the Treasury.

Fourth. It will encourage business men to continue old and embark in new enterprises, when they are assured that no change will be made in the measure of value without the open and deliberate consent of their representatives.

Senator Fessenden, no longer in the driver's seat with regard to financial matters, nevertheless lent his powerful and persuasive voice in support of McCulloch's policy. " Well, sir, I fear the effect of it. I fear that the country can place but one construction on it, and that is that the idea of returning to specie payments is to be abandoned for an indefinite period, and that our policy, instead of being that of returning to what I think the great majority of wise and thinking men suppose to be the true one, that our currency should be founded upon a specie basis and should be in fact specie, is to be anything but that." [114]

The debate began on January 9 and continued through the 15th. Every variety of financial opinion was aired. It was obvious from the first that the Senate amendment was going to pass overwhelmingly, but several of the eastern Senators put up a stubborn fight against it. The opposition came from its natural sources—from Morrill and Edmunds of Vermont, Conkling and Morgan of New York, from Patterson of New Hampshire, Ferry of Connecticut, and Fessenden of Maine. Almost all of the western senators supported the measure strongly. When the vote was finally taken on January 15, the amendment passed by a vote of 33 to 4 with 16 absent or paired. Senate Republicans favored the measure 30 to 4 while the small Democratic contingent in the upper chamber opposed further contraction 3 to 0. The four die-hard contractionist Republicans who opposed the bill were all from New England and New York.[115]

On January 17, Schenck reported the Senate amendment in the House and recommended that it not be accepted. His reasoning, being somewhat involved, was that by previous bills enacted during the war, the Secretary had the power to contract

[114] *Ibid.*, p. 409.   [115] *Ibid.*, p. 537.

the currency any amount at his own discretion. Schenck argued that the Loan Bill of April, 1866 merely limited that power. If then the Senate amendment which suspended the contractive clause of the Loan Bill were concurred in, McCulloch would still possess the power to contract through the previous war measures.[116]

A committee of conference was appointed to iron out the differences. This included Cattell, Morton, and Trumbull of the Senate and Schenck, Hooper, and Niblack of the House.[117]

Senator Cattell reported the compromise of the conference committee on January 22, 1868.[118] The report, which was concurred in by both houses, agreed that the House version should be used but with an amendment, so that the final bill took the following form: [119]

> Be it enacted by the Senate and House of Representatives of the United States of America in Congress Assembled, That from and after the passage of this act, the authority of the Secretary of the Treasury to make any reduction of the currency, by retiring or cancelling United States notes shall be, and is hereby, suspended; but nothing herein contained shall prevent the cancellation and destruction of mutilated United States notes, and the replacing of the same with notes of the same character and amount.

President Johnson did not sign the bill but neither did he veto it, so that it became a law on February 4, 1868 without his signature.[120] The President's failure to sustain McCulloch with a veto indicated a considerable change of mind since 1865 when he had accepted the views of his finance minister without question.[121]

In general the press approved the action of Congress in removing the power of the Secretary of the Treasury to contract the currency, though enthusiasm for the measure varied with the economic predilections of the organs involved. The ultra-Radical Chicago *Republican* asserted that " Had not the Secretary's power of contraction and embarrassment been wisely abated by Congress, the present year would have witnessed the whole Northwest prostrate at the feet of New England, and

---

[116] *Ibid.*, p. 593.
[117] *Ibid.*, p. 675.
[118] *Ibid.*, pp. 674-675.
[119] Huntington and Mawhinney, *Laws*, p. 651.
[120] Blaine, *Twenty Years of Congress*, II, 331.
[121] *Supra*, p. 64.

our growing section an humble suppliant for loans at high
rates of interest, at the counters of her National banks." [122]
James Gordon Bennett's New York *Herald*, which usually took
the anti-Radical side on Reconstruction issues, favored the bill,
pointing out that " Congress did well in stopping any further
contraction of the currency. That simply leaves us where we
are, prevents commercial and financial disturbance, and the
derangement of existing values and contracts, and gives the
country an opportunity to grow gradually and healthfully with
the present currency up to a fixed and sound condition." [123]
The New York *Times* approved the measure declaring that
" the strong argument against a continuance of the discretionary
power which Mr. McCulloch has exercised has been its tendency
to unsettle values and to embarrass all forms of business." This
conservative paper which usually reflected the sentiments of the
mercantile and banking community of New York hoped, however, that the stoppage of contraction was not the prelude to
further expansion, insisting that " Having gained this point of
fixedness by arresting contraction, it would be madness to revive
uncertainty by again resorting to expansion." [124] The attitude
of the *Commercial and Financial Chronicle* of New York,
which accurately set forth the attitudes of the conservative
business men and bankers of that great emporium, was equivocal, to say the least. " We are apparently entering now upon
an epoch of expansion and speculative excitement. Had Mr.
McCulloch been content last Autumn to suspend contraction
as he had done without necessity during the previous Summer,
he would probably have been still in possession of the power
of drawing in and cancelling greenbacks now that contraction
might safely be ventured upon, and would be a healthful relief
of the existing plethora. But for the present the people have
become disgusted with contraction, because it has been so done
as to produce suffering. We shall be surprised, however, if
the evils arising from inflated prices and from the exaggerated
expenses of living do not in a short time call forth a general
demand for renewed contraction." [125]

[122] January 24, 1868.
[123] January 30, 1868.
[124] January 28, 1868.
[125] *Commercial and Financial Chronicle*, IV (February 15, 1868), 198.

Repeal of contraction was a stinging rebuke to McCulloch, but it by no means changed that worthy gentleman's mind on the issues involved. In his *Report* for the year 1868 he insisted that " The United States notes, although declared by law to be lawful money, are, nevertheless, a dishonored and disreputable currency. The fact that they are a legal tender, possessing such attributes of money as the statute can give them, adds nothing to their real value, but makes them all the more dishonorable to the government and subversive of good morals. The people are compelled to take as money what is not money; and becoming demoralized by its constantly changing value, they are in danger of losing that sense of honor in their dealings with the government and with each other which is necessary for the well-being of society."[126] It is interesting that here as in most of McCulloch's writings the moral issue continually takes precedence over the economic. To McCulloch as to most believers in hard-money and free trade, there was something absolutely immoral about using any measure of value other than gold. In reading passages like that above, we can almost visualize generations of McCulloch's New England Calvinist forebears sternly enjoining work and thrift as necessary to salvation. The Secretary's *Reports* make interesting footnotes on the Protestant ethic.[127]

Though touted by some as a victory for inflation, the anti-contraction bill of 1868 was actually a compromise and a triumph of the *status quo*. It satisfied neither expansionists nor contractionists, but the volume of $356,000,000 in green-backs which were outstanding when the bill was passed repre-sented that point, common enough in politics, where people and politicians are content to cease their agitation for a time and turn to other issues. Passage of the bill marked the high point of inflationary sentiment prior to the panic of 1873. For the next few years those who believed in sound money and the sanctity of the public debt would be in the ascendant. The reasons for this are interesting and instructive.

Economic factors are important in explaining the gradual decrease in inflationary sentiment after the passage of the anti-

---

[126] *Report of the Secretary of the Treasury, 1868*, pp. 3-4.
[127] McCulloch's autobiography contains interesting material on his Calvinist upbringing. See *Men and Measures*, ch. II.

contraction bill. It has been noted above that a trough in business activity was reached around December, 1867. After this
time business conditions improved steadily until a peak in
economic activity was reached in the summer of 1869.[128] Since
inflationary agitation was largely a reaction to depressed business
conditions, it might logically be expected to diminish as the
economic climate improved. The course of business activity
goes a long way toward explaining the erosion of inflationary
opinion, but improvement in business was by no means the
only important factor. Political factors were of equal if not
greater importance.

In his first annual message to Congress President Johnson
had strongly supported the policies of his finance minister,
affirming that " It is our first duty to prepare in earnest for our
recovery from the ever increasing evils of an irredeemable
currency. . . ." [129] It is doubtful that this represented Johnson's
real view of the currency issue. Certainly his final message to
Congress in 1868 indicated a definite leaning toward the views
of the inflationists.[130] The important fact is that until the final
months of his administration, the President acquiesced in
McCulloch's policies and pronouncements, and to Congress and
the country at large, McCulloch's policy was Johnson's policy.[131]
A delightfully ironic situation developed in which a majority
of the Radicals vigorously opposed Johnson's financial policies
as enunciated by McCulloch when the actual truth was that
Johnson's convictions on the economic issues of the day were
much closer to those of the extreme Radicals than they were to
those of his Secretary of the Treasury. James G. Blaine felt
that there were two main reasons why McCulloch " failed to
secure cordial support from Congress." The first was his
" official and personal connection with the President." The
second was " his obvious sympathy with the free-traders, who
were already beginning to assault the protective tariff which
the necessities of war had led the country to adopt." [132]

[128] *Supra*, p. 82.
[129] Richardson, *Messages and Papers*, VI, 365.
[130] *Infra*, pp. 122-123.
[131] John Sherman wrote that " President Johnson relied entirely upon Mc-
Culloch, and had no opinions upon financial topics." Sherman, *Recollections*,
I, 384.
[132] Blaine, *Twenty Years of Congress*, II, 332.

McCulloch's connection with Andrew Johnson posed an insoluble dilemma for many conservative businessmen of the eastern seaboard who approved his policies. This dilemma is clearly illustrated in a letter to McCulloch written by Edward Atkinson, the Boston industrialist and free trade propagandist. It is considered so important an indication of the cleavages which existed within the Republican Party that it is reproduced with only minor omissions.[133]

Boston
August 7, 1867

Hon. Hugh McCulloch
Dear Sir:

I am endeavoring in connection with some others who are known as extreme radicals to give such direction to the reorganization of the south as shall prevent the creation of an exclusive black men's party and also to kill the scheme of confiscation. I also hope we may be able to secure the election of a southern delegation who shall not be under Thad Stevens lead on tariff and currency questions, but of this I am not hopeful. The new men from the south will be likely to be the very men who will follow Stevens even to prohibition of imports; they will be misled by the desire to establish manufactures and to diversify employment.

At the risk of being officious and impertinent again, I am led to make certain suggestion to you by the rumors of a diversity of opinion between you and the President. You must now feel assured that the President's policy is dead; even any merit which his views may have had will not be recognized, " he is a dead cock in the pit."

Your fame and reputation will rest on your successful administration of the Treasury. A large section of the Republicans desire to see financial and all revenue questions separated from party issues. If you have real reason to do so, and can separate yourself from A. J. and let it be known that while you do not fully approve the action of Congress, you submit to its decisions and desire to work in harmony, you will be able to secure such support for your plans for administering the Treasury as will insure success. . . .

Only give the Republicans who hold sound views on financial questions a chance to support you as the Secy. of the United States Treasury and not as a member of the present cabinet and you can almost dictate the future policy.

I don't expect an answer to this.

Yours very sincerely,
E. A.
[Edward Atkinson]

---

[133] McCulloch Papers.

Atkinson and men of his persuasion found it very difficult to support McCulloch because of his connection with Johnson. If they could possibly separate him from the President in the same way that Secretary of War Stanton became separated from him, McCulloch's policies would be strongly supported by those Republicans with free trade, sound money views. It will be noted that Atkinson refers to himself as an " extreme radical." This is undoubtedly a reference to his early abolitionist background, certainly not to his economic *Weltanschauung* which bore not the slightest resemblance to the ideas on tariff and currency questions held by leading Radicals such as Stevens, Kelley, Butler, and Logan.[134] On balance, as has been shown above, Radicalism can be identified with a belief in high protection and soft-money, an ideology entirely distasteful to free trade, specie resumptionists such as Atkinson.

The opposition of the New England industrialist to the formation of an "exclusive black men's party" and also the " scheme of confiscation " again demonstrates how far his ideas deviated from those of the true Radicals. While his fear of Negro suffrage was probably not so strong as that of McCulloch who opposed it altogether, it is obvious that Atkinson's ideas on Reconstruction were much closer to those of the Johnsonites than to those of the Radicals.[135] For the purposes of historical analysis Atkinson's brand of conservative Republicanism must be carefully separated from the mainstream of Radical philosophy.

Caught on the horns of a cruel dilemma, conservatives found it very difficult to get their financial ideas accepted in the councils of the Republican Party. In the summer and fall of the year 1868, however, there transpired a series of events which was destined to lay low the scheme of paying the 5-20 bonds in greenbacks and start the country on the road to specie resumption.

The biographer of James A. Garfield has remarked that the election of 1868 " cleared the air marvelously " on financial

---

[134] Atkinson's abolitionist leanings are described in Harold Francis Williamson, *Edward Atkinson: The Biography of an American Liberal, 1827-1905* (Boston, 1934), pp. 3-4.

[135] For McCulloch's opposition to Negro suffrage, see Welles, *Diary*, III, 4.

issues.[136] The principal reason for this clarification was the incorporation of the " Ohio Idea " into the Democratic platform.[137] From that day in 1862 when the Legal Tender Act had been passed over strong Democratic opposition, the greenbacks had been associated with the Republican Party. John Sherman had merely echoed the sentiments of his Radical colleagues when he wrote that they had been " indispensable " to the prosecution of the war.[138] It was consequently with some evidence of confusion that the Republicans awoke to the realization in 1867 and 1868 that the greenback philosophy had been swallowed hook, line, and sinker by the western branch of the Democratic Party and that, indeed, greenbackism was now coupled with a proposition to pay off the 5-20 bonds in paper money. A Benjamin F. Butler could shrug off the charge that his ideas were almost identical to those of George H. Pendleton, but the allegation stuck, nonetheless. Being tarred with a Democratic brush was too much for most Republican politicians, men like Schenck and Sherman whose financial convictions were not rooted in any school of political economy but rather in the quicksand of political expediency.[139] The principled greenbackers, however, stuck to their guns, men like Thad Stevens, Ben Butler, " Pig Iron " Kelley, Benjamin F. Wade, and a new recruit of the soft-money cause, Senator William Sprague of Rhode Island.[140] Thad Stevens was reported to have said that he would vote " for the other side, Frank Blair and all " rather than accept the proposition that the 5-20 bonds should be paid in gold. He would vote for " no such swindle upon the taxpayers." [141]

[136] Smith, *Garfield*, I, 438.

[137] Coleman, *Election of 1868*, p. 201.

[138] Sherman, *Recollections*, I, 378.

[139] Sherman's tendency to act on expediency rather than principle is described in Oberholtzer, *Jay Cooke*, II, 39-43.

[140] Senator Sprague was a rich textile manufacturer from Rhode Island. His radical political views went hand in hand with his belief in high protection and soft-money. He expounded these views in a very interesting speech on the Senate floor, March 15, 1869 during the debate over the Public Credit Act. *Congressional Globe*, 41st Congress, 1st Session, pp. 64-66. For enlightening material on Sprague's motives for making this and other similar speeches, see Belden and Belden, *So Fell the Angels*, pp. 222-240.

[141] Quoted in Coleman, *Election of 1868*, p. 37.

The Republican platform in 1868 took high ground with regard to the sanctity of the public debt, declaring " We denounce all forms of Repudiation as a national crime; and the national honor requires the payment of the public indebtedness in the uttermost good faith to all creditors at home and abroad, not only according to the letter but the spirit of the laws under which it was contracted." [142] This contrasted with the Democratic platform which asserted that the bonds " where the obligations of the government do not expressly state upon their face, or the law under which they were issued does not provide, that they shall be paid in coin, they ought, in right and in justice, to be paid in the lawful money of the United States. . . ." This coupled with an arraignment of the Radical party " for its disregard of right, and the unparalleled oppression and tyranny which have marked its career." [143]

That seasoned politician, James G. Blaine, remarked that " The Democratic party thus determined through its platform and partially through its candidates, to fight its battle on the two issues of paying the debt in depreciated paper currency and overthrowing Reconstruction." [144] The overwhelming victory of General Grant was naturally understood by the Republicans as a public mandate in favor of their Reconstruction policy and for the sanctity of the debt. If the Republicans lacked the impetus and unity required to sanctify the debt by legislative process, President Johnson soon obliged by supplying the necessary motive force. In his last annual message to Congress dated December 9, 1868, the President finally indicated the true tenor of his convictions on financial issues. " It may be assumed," wrote Johnson, " that the holders of our securities have already received upon their bonds a larger amount than their original investment, measured by a gold standard. Upon this statement of facts it would seem but just and equitable that the 6 per cent interest now paid by the Government should be applied to the reduction of the principal in semi-annual installments which in sixteen years and eight months would liquidate the entire

[142] Republican National Committee, *1868 Text Book for the Republican Campaign* (New York, 1868), p. 22.
[143] Henry Steele Commager, ed., *Documents of American History*, 4th ed., 2 vols. in 1 (New York, 1948), II, 54.
[144] Blaine, *Twenty Years of Congress*, II, 404.

national debt. . . ." By proposing to confiscate the interest on
the bonded indebtedness to pay off the bonds, Johnson took a
position on this issue far more extreme than that of the Democratic party in its 1868 platform. But there was more than a
little truth in the President's assertion that his plan " would
afford to the public creditors a fair and liberal compensation
for the use of their capital. . . ." He warned that " The lessons
of the past admonish the lender that it is not well to be over-
anxious in exacting from the borrower rigid compliance with
the letter of the bond." [145]

Thus did Andrew Johnson desert the financial counsels of
his Secretary of the Treasury. In his autobiography McCulloch
sadly noted that the President had " wandered . . . from right
thought " in expressing this opinion " that the holders of the
United States bonds ought not to receive in payment thereof
any more than the Government received for them in real
money." [146] Now that the heretical financial doctrines of
Andrew Johnson had been finally revealed, Congress moved
swiftly to his censure.

On December 14, 1868 the House of Representatives adopted
the following resolution: " *Resoved*, That all forms and degrees
of repudiation of national indebtedness are odious to the American people. And that under no circumstances will their
Representatives consent to offer the public creditor, as full
compensation, a less amount of money than that which the
Government contracted to pay him." No division was taken on
the final vote on the crucial second sentence of the resolution,
but a previous division on a motion to lay the preamble on
the table revealed the partisan nature of the proceedings. The
preamble was simply a recitation of the portion of Johnson's
message quoted above advocating that the interest on the debt
he used to liquidate the principal. Voting to lay the preamble
on the table and thus to vindicate the President were 36 Democrats and one lone Republican from Kansas. All 133 of the
votes against laying the preamble on the table were cast by
Republicans except three, those being the votes of eastern
Democrats, two from New York and one from Connecticut.

[145] Richardson, *Messages and Papers*, VI, 678.
[146] McCulloch, *Men and Measures*, pp. 220-221.

Thus did the airing of the true financial opinions of Andrew Johnson work to bring about a remarkable degree of party unity, both Republican and Democratic, on the question of the sanctity of the public debt. It should be noted, however, that although every western Democrat in the House but one was recorded as voting to uphold the President, six eastern Democrats were recorded as not voting, evidencing perhaps an inclination on their part to avoid a decision when confronted with the question of whether to uphold the President at the expense of seeming to approve his radical financial notions.[147]

In a similar resolution on December 17, the Senate, by a vote of 43 to 6 did " utterly disapprove of and condemn " the proposition of the President. All 43 votes in favor of the resolution were cast by Republicans, whereas the six dissenters were all Democrats.[148] The *Commercial and Financial Chronicle* hailed the action of Congress asserting, " If, therefore, the nation has been humbled by the repudiatory utterances of its chief magistrate, its honor has been promptly retrieved by an unequivocal declaration of the Legislature in favor of the maintenance of the strictest good faith." [149]

So it came to pass in both houses of Congress that the pronouncements of Andrew Johnson managed to effect a more or less strict party division on a financial question, a rare occurrence in post-Civil War politics. Fortified with the gratuitous but heaven-sent opposition of the President to the sanctity of the public debt, conservative Republicans moved to give legal form to their profoundest economic convictions.

On January 20, 1869, Chairman Schenck of the Ways and Means Committee, reacting quickly to the trend of the times, introduced in the House a bill " to strengthen the public credit." [150] As it finally became law some two months later, this measure provided that " the faith of the United States is solemnly pledged to the payment in coin or its equivalent of all the obligations of the United States not bearing interest,

---

[147] For the debate and vote on the resolution see *Congressional Globe*, 40th Congress, 3rd Session, pp. 71-73. Party affiliations for the 40th Congress can be found in Blaine, *Twenty Years of Congress*, II, 284-286.
[148] *Congressional Globe*, 40th Congress, 3rd Session, pp. 123-128.
[149] VII (December 19, 1868), 782.
[150] *Congressional Globe*, 40th Congress, 3rd Session, p. 476.

known as United States notes, and of all the interest-bearing obligations of the United States, except in cases where the law authorizing the issue of any such obligation has expressly provided that the same may be paid in lawful money or other currency than gold and silver. . . . And the United States also solemnly pledges its faith to make provision at the earliest practicable period for the redemption of the United States notes in coin." [151]

The purpose of this bill was to put the Congress squarely on record in favor of the sanctity of the public debt and the resumption of specie payments. The tremendous effect of the election of 1868 on the minds of congressmen was obvious in the debate over the bill. That consistent contractionist and hard-money man, James A. Garfield, emphasized the decisive nature of the public mandate on financial matters. " After the fullest debate ever had on any great question of national politics, in a contest in which the two parties squarely and fairly joined issue on this very point, it was solemnly decided by the great majority which elected General Grant that repudiators should be repudiated and that the faith of the nation should be preserved inviolate." [152] John A. Logan, one of McCulloch's most violent critics in the days gone by, clearly pointed out how the election had changed his mind on financial issues. Confessing that his mind had once tended toward a policy of paying the 5-20 bonds in greenbacks, the General asserted that his constituents had " decided that the bonds of the Government are payable in money—not in paper currency, not in greenbacks, not in bank notes, but in that which is considered money by all civilized nations. The decision of the people of my State on this question was given in such a manner as should satisfy their representatives that the decision must be sustained." [153] In the Senate John Sherman, erstwhile friend of the greenback, now declared: " The gold in the shield of Achilles, the shekels that bought the field of Machpelah, the pieces of silver the price of the blood of our Saviour, will be current coin when the completed history of nations now rising into greatness will be folded away among the records of time." [154] In such manner

[151] Ibid., p. 1830.
[152] Ibid., p. 1880.
[153] Ibid., p. 1536.
[154] Ibid., p. 626.

did the politicians of the Republican Party put themselves on record in favor of financial orthodoxy.

Not all Republicans surrendered to the trend of the times. The consistency of Radical economic philosophy was too strong for some of the principled greenbackers. In the Senate the Public Credit bill was opposed by Wade of Ohio and Sprague of Rhode Island. In a vigorous speech the latter declared: " You have contracted your currency nearly four hundred million dollars in three years for the purpose of enhancing its value. What has been the result of it? Have you enhanced the value of the nation's credit? Not one cent. You have prostrated every interest and every industry in consequence of that most suicidal and most damnable policy. I protest, therefore, in the name of the industries of this country and in their behalf, representing them as I do, and as I know they at present exist, against the additional load that will be put on them by this most unholy and inconsiderate legislation." [155]

Although the leader of the greenback forces in the House, Thaddeus Stevens, was now dead and buried, a number of the old Radicals put up a strong fight against the bill. Among those who voted against the measure were the arch-Radicals Benjamin F. Butler, John Covode, William D. " Pig Iron " Kelley, and Ignatius Donnelly.[156] Speaking of the bill, Butler asserted: " The whole of this thing is simply a stock-jobbing, bill broking, banking, gold speculative concern, and banks have made ten and fifteen millions out of this discussion and the pendency of this bill." [157] Ignatius Donnelly felt that the bill was " altogether in the interest of the creditor class. Their wealth, intelligence, and position will always insure that they will be protected in the work of legislation." [158]

On the crucial votes the Public Credit bill was approved by the Senate, 30 to 16, and by the House, 120 to 60.[159] The table on the following pages presents the sectional and political

[155] *Ibid.*, p. 1831.
[156] *Ibid.*, pp. 1538-1539.
[157] *Ibid.*, p. 1881.
[158] *Ibid.*, p. 1881. Donnelly cannot at this time be considered a greenbacker though he subsequently became such. See John D. Hicks, " The Political Career of Ignatius Donnelly," *Mississippi Valley Historical Review*, VIII (1921).
[159] *Congressional Globe*, 40th Congress, 3rd Session, pp. 1678; 1538-1539.

configuration of the House vote.[160] The results show that the
heavy majority of the previous year in favor of suspending
contraction was now completely reversed and both houses of
Congress were put on record in favor of the sanctity of the
public debt and the resumption of specie payments. Republicans who had opposed the policy of contraction 103 to 18 a
year earlier supported the Public Credit bill 108 to 36. Only
in the Middle West where 20 votes were cast against the bill
was there any substantial Republican opposition, and even in
that section the party vote was 29 to 20 in favor of the measure.

VOTE ON THE PUBLIC CREDIT ACT, HOUSE OF REPRESENTATIVES,
FEBRUARY 24, 1869

	Ayes		Nays	
	Rep.	Dem.	Rep.	Dem.
New England States				
Massachusetts	8		1	
Maine	4		1	
New Hampshire	1		2	
Vermont	2			
Connecticut	1	3		
Rhode Island	2			
TOTALS	18	3	4	
Middle Atlantic States				
New York	15	5		3
Pennsylvania	13	3	3	
Maryland	1		1	2
Delaware				
New Jersey	3			1
TOTALS	32	8	4	6
Mid Western States				
Ohio	9		4	2
Illinois	4		5	3
Indiana	1		6	3
Wisconsin	3		2	1
Minnesota	1		1	
Michigan	6			
Iowa	4		1	
Kansas	1			
Nebraska			1	
TOTALS	29		20	9

[160] Party and state affiliations for this table were derived from Blaine, *Twenty
Years of Congress*, II, 284-286.

| | Ayes | | Nays | |
	Rep.	Dem.	Rep.	Dem.
Border States				
Kentucky	1			5
Missouri	5			1
West Virginia	2			
TOTALS	8			6
Southern States				
North Carolina	4		2	
South Carolina	2		2	
Georgia	2			2
Alabama	4			
Florida				
Louisiana	2			
Arkansas	2			
Tennessee	3		4	
TOTALS	19		8	2
Far Western States				
California	1	1		1
Nevada	1			
Oregon				
TOTALS	2	1		1
GRAND TOTALS	108	12	36	24

The Democratic vote was marked by the same cleavage between East and West which had been so evident in the vote on the anti-contraction bill a year earlier. Every western Democrat except one lone representative from California voted against the Public Credit bill whereas their colleagues from the East supported the measure by a margin of 11 to 6. The two Democratic representatives from the South who had managed to gain admission to the House joined eight Republicans from that section in opposing the bill, but the majority, demonstrating their subservience to whatever Republican dogma might be fashionable at the time, voted in favor of the measure.

In the Senate the same pattern emerged. All 30 votes in favor of the Public Credit bill were cast by Republicans, 14 of the votes coming from the Middle Atlantic States and New England, 12 from the Middle West, the Border States, and the Far West, and 4 from the South. Twelve Republican Senators opposed the bill. Of these, 7 were from middle western, far western, or border states and 5 were from the South. No

Senator from the East voted against the bill.[161] Unlike their colleagues in the House, Democratic Senators from the East took no stand on the bill. All five of them were recorded as absent. The remaining Democratic Senators, Davis and McCreery of Kentucky, Patterson of Tennessee, and Hendricks of Indiana all voted against the Public Credit bill.[162]

President Johnson did not sign the Public Credit bill, thereby applying a pocket-veto to the measure.[163] This action, or lack of action rather, was of little effect. The Public Credit bill was re-introduced and triumphantly passed by both houses of Congress in the first session of the 41st Congress and was the first legislative enactment to receive the signature of President Grant.[164] The Public Credit Act thus became a law on March 18, 1869.[165] A leading journal of commerce hailed the passage of the bill, asserting " The honesty of the policy endorsed by such large majorities in Congress, has had a very direct influence in strengthening the value of every form of Government obligation, and naturally encourages confidence in the purpose of Congress to provide for the earliest practical resumption of payment of its notes, and to oppose the wild schemes for further inflation which have heretofore found advocates." [166]

In his inaugural address General Grant made it clear that he had cast his lot with the adherents of financial orthodoxy, asserting, " A great debt has been contracted in securing to us and our posterity the Union. The payment of this, principal and interest, as well as the return to a specie basis as soon as it can be accomplished without material detriment to the debtor class or to the country at large, must be provided for. To protect the national honor, every dollar of Government indebtedness should be paid in gold, unless otherwise expressly stipulated in the contract." [167]

[161] Sprague of Rhode Island, who had opposed the bill in debate, was recorded as absent.

[162] *Congressional Globe*, 40th Congress, 3rd Session, p. 1678.

[163] *Commercial and Financial Chronicle*, VIII (March 6, 1869), 285.

[164] *Congressional Globe*, 41st Congress, 1st Session, pp. 61; 70. Blaine, *Twenty Years of Congress*, II, 556.

[165] Huntington and Mawhinney, *Laws*, pp. 201-202.

[166] *Hunt's Merchants' Magazine*, LX (April, 1869), 242.

[167] Richardson, *Messages and Papers*, VII, 7.

The Public Credit Act was declaratory in nature and, of itself, did not affect the redemption of a single bond or greenback. It did, however, pledge Congress, or at least the Republican majority in Congress, to a course of action leading to specie resumption, and it did drive the final nail in the coffin of the " Pendleton Plan." Passage of the act marked a recession of inflationary sentiment from the high point which it had reached early in 1868. It is noteworthy, however, that the Public Credit Act made no provision for renewed contraction as a method of achieving specie payments. As John Sherman pointed out in dealing with this period, " The drift of opinion was in favor of resumption without contraction, and funding at low rates of interest on a coin basis." [168] In harmony with this opinion was the new Secretary of the Treasury, George S. Boutwell of Massachusetts, who devoted little time or effort to the currency question, and concentrated primarily on refunding the public debt at a lower rate of interest. Congress agreed with the new Secretary in shifting the focus of financial endeavor to the public debt, and their joint efforts culminated in the passage of the Acts of July 14, 1870 and January 20, 1871. This legislation authorized the issue of $500,000,000 of bonds at 5 per cent, redeemable after ten years, $300,000,000 at 4½ per cent, redeemable after fifteen years, and $1,000,000,000 at 4 per cent, redeemable after thirty years. These bonds were specifically made payable both principal and interest in coin and were exempted from national as well as local taxation.[169]

The struggle over the currency issue from 1865 to 1869 was essentially a battle between different groups within the dominant Republican Party. The importance of the votes of Democratic members of the House and Senate should not be minimized, but they assume significance in these years only because of the wide variance of opinion within the ranks of the Republicans. For example, the original contraction bill could never have been carried in the House except for the almost solid Democratic support which McCulloch was able to enlist. This support was crucial because of the deep split in the ranks of

---

[168] Sherman, *Recollections*, I, 440.
[169] Huntington and Mawhinney, *Laws*, pp. 203-206; Dewey, *Financial History*, pp. 352-354.

the Republicans, only a bare majority of the dominant party voting in favor of contraction. The importance of the Democratic vote, however, tended to be vitiated after 1866 by a developing cleavage on financial policy between the eastern and western wings of that party, a cleavage which was to loom large on the political horizon for years to come. The importance of Democratic opinion was also diminished by the failure of that party to achieve success in the elections of 1866, a failure which assured the Republicans of absolute control over the 40th Congress.

The essence of the fight over specie resumption, therefore, lies in the internecine struggle within the ranks of the majority party. Among the Republicans it is possible to distinguish three different groups, representing three different attitudes toward the financial issues of Reconstruction. One group, represented in Congress by such men as Justin Morrill, James A. Garfield, Roscoe Conkling, and William P. Fessenden, stood for " sound finance " as it was understood in the nineteenth century. This group supported contraction, because it seemed the shortest road to specie resumption. Attainment of this objective was of great importance in maintaining the financial integrity of the nation and in providing business with a stable measure of value not subject to the extreme fluctuations of paper money. Members of this group tended either toward free trade as in the case of James A. Garfield or a moderate form of protectionism as in the case of Justin Morrill. This group tended to adopt most of the maxims of the Manchester school of political economy and felt that opposition to this point of view only tended to reveal abysmal ignorance of the inexorable laws of economic science.

Diametrically opposed to the " sound finance " group was another Republican faction whose leader was Thaddeus Stevens and included such men as William D. Kelley, Benjamin F. Butler, John A. Griswold, Benjamin F. Wade, and William Sprague. This group fought against contraction and supported a soft-money policy. Although paying lip service to the goal of specie resumption, it was obviously little interested in any steps toward this objective which would reduce the currency supply of the country. Men of this persuasion were very sensitive to the opinions of business men, particularly manufacturers, and felt that contraction of the currency was largely responsible for the economic difficulties experienced in 1867. This group possessed a definite economic philosophy colored with extreme nationalism and resting on the twin pillars of paper money and high protection. For purposes of political analysis it is significant that this group enlisted a number of the most extreme Radicals in the Republican Party.

Maneuvering between these two groups and acutely aware of the changing currents of public opinion was another group whose outlook of financial questions was not determined by any theories of political economy but rather by the realities of the political situation. Representative of this group were such men as John Sherman, Robert Schenck, John A. Logan, and George Boutwell. This group held the balance of power between the contractionists and those who advocated a soft-money policy. Reacting to public opinion in 1867 and 1868, these men were sharply critical of McCulloch and voted to strip from him the power to reduce the volume of the greenback currency. Sensing another drift in public sentiment in the latter part of 1868 and in 1869 pointed up by the return of prosperity, the reaction to the financial recommendations of Andrew Johnson, and the election of Grant on a " sound money " platform, this group abandoned any radical financial notions previously held and came out strongly in favor of the sanctity of the public debt and the resumption of specie payments. This group did not advocate a return to contraction, however, because it was understood that public opinion would not approve any further reduction of the greenback currency. Representing the compromise point between contractionists and inflationists, this group demanded that the existing volume of greenbacks be maintained and that resumption be attained without any diminution of the volume of the currency. This was the philosophy which prevailed, and it is noteworthy that it was on these terms that resumption was achieved by the leading member of this group, John Sherman, Secretary of the Treasury, in 1879.[170]

[170] Ibid., pp. 374-378. It would be difficult to place Senator Charles Sumner of Massachusetts in a single one of these three groups. In basic conviction there can be little doubt but that he was a hard-money man. So far as recorded

The divergence of opinion on financial policy which was so
apparent in Congress during this period reflected the conflicting
interests of different economic groups in such questions as the

votes and public posture are concerned, however, he must be numbered with
the fence sitters. A careful analysis of all Sumner's public utterances on the
subject of finance during the years of war and Reconstruction leads this writer
to the conclusion that the basically conservative and orthodox financial opinions
of the Massachusetts Senator were outweighed in his mind by the economic and
political necessities of these turbulent years. In 1862 Sumner supported the first
Legal Tender Act when it was before the Senate on grounds of necessity,
asserting: " If I vote for this proposition it will be only because I am unwilling
to refuse to the Government, especially charged with this responsibility, that
confidence which is hardly less important to the public interests than the money
itself. . . . A remedy which at another moment you would reject is now proposed. Whatever may be the national resources, they are not now within reach,
except by summary process. Reluctantly, painfully, I consent that the process
should ensue." *Congressional Globe*, 37th Congress, 2nd Session, pp. 799-800.
Sumner's votes on the three measures considered in Chapters II and III reflect
the shadow of political expediency. He voted for contraction in 1866, was
recorded as absent on the vote on the bill to suspend contraction in 1868, and
voted for the Public Credit Act in 1869. From the winter of 1865 through the
spring of 1868 Sumner took no part in debate over financial matters on the
Senate floor even though these matters enlisted the attention of the best talent
in both houses. Considering his strong basic convictions on financial questions,
this is remarkable. To the present writer there is only one probable explanation
for this anomaly. Sumner was unwilling to disturb the harmony which existed
among the ultra-Radicals on issues of political Reconstruction by assuming a
firm hard-money position on financial issues. To have done so would have
placed him in opposition to such fellow ultras as Butler, Wade, and Stevens
and in agreement with Andrew Johnson's Secretary of the Treasury. To Sumner
political Reconstruction was all important, so he temporarily swallowed his basic
convictions. By the summer of 1868, however, conditions had changed. The
" Ohio idea " had been seized upon by the western branch of the Democratic
party as a plausible issue. Now Sumner could join with the majority of his
Republican colleagues in castigating the " dishonesty " of the Democrats. Even
then, however, he carefully linked the greenbacks with the war declaring that
" Every greenback is red with the blood of fellow citizens." Furthermore, he
asserted, speaking to his fellow senators on July 11, 1868, improvement in the
nation's finances would not be easy as " there can be small chance for any
success in this direction until after political reconstruction." To Sumner all
blame should be laid upon the opponents of Radical policies, for he declared:
" Andrew Johnson has postponed specie payments, and his supporters of all
degrees must share the responsibility." He added: " You who have at heart
the national credit, on which so much depends, must never fail to cherish the
national freedmen, treating their enemies as if they were your enemies. Every
blow at them will rebound upon yourselves." In thus illogically linking financial
policy with the problems of political Reconstruction, Sumner was probably
justifying in his own mind his previous failure to stand up and be counted
with the Garfields, the Morrills, and the Fessendens. At this point, however, he
left no doubt of his real convictions. He came out four-square against taxation

volume of the currency, the level of the tariff, and the redemption of the public debt. It will be our purpose in the following chapters to analyze these interests and to determine their economic bases.

of the bonds, against redeeming the bonds in greenbacks, and in favor of contraction. In regard to the " Ohio idea " he asserted that those who advocated the plan were " hardly less malignant than war itself," for they would " despoil the Nation of its good name and take from it all the might of honesty." In another attempt to place the blame for financial troubles on another doorstep, he averred: " So long as a great party, called Democratic, better now called Rebel, wars on that political reconstruction, which Congress has organized, there can be no specie payments. So long as any President, or any political party, denies the Equal Rights of the freedman, it is vain to expect specie payments. Who so would have equity must do equity; and now, if you would have specie payments, you must do this great equity." *Congressional Globe*, 40th Congress, 2nd Session, pp. 3961-3965. In a speech delivered in Cambridge, Massachusetts, on October 29, 1868, Sumner left little doubt of his essential convictions on the subject of paper money. The pedantic senator looked far afield for an analogy but his erudition was equal to the task. " Looking into the travels of Marco Polo in the thirteenth century," he declared, " you will find that he encountered in China, paper money on a large scale, being an inconvertible currency standing on the promise of the Grand Khan, not unlike our greenbacks. Describing the celestial city of Kinsai, the famous traveler says: ' The inhabitants are idolators, and they use paper money; ' and then describing another celestial city, Tai-ponzu, he says, ' the inhabitants worship idols and use paper money.' I know not if Marco Polo intended by this association to suggest any dependence of paper money upon the worship of idols. It is enough that he puts them together. To my mind, they are equally forbidden by the Ten Commandments. If one commandment enjoins upon us not to worship any graven image, does not another say expressly, ' Thou shalt not steal? ' " Reported in the *Bankers' Magazine*, XXIII (Old Series) (December, 1868), 465. Although Sumner was, no doubt, essentially a hard-money man, he does not, in the opinion of this writer, deserve any particular credit for standing up for the cause of specie resumption in the summer of 1868. See Moorfield Storey, *Charles Sumner* (Boston, 1900), pp. 356-357; George H. Haynes, *Charles Sumner* (Philadelphia, 1909), pp. 326-327.

APPENDIX I

FARMERS AND THE GREENBACKS, 1865-70

When the original plan for this study was projected, there was included a chapter on the relationship of the farmers to the currency controversy of the early Reconstruction period. Imbued with a conviction derived from readings in American history that farmers are usually debtors and *ipso facto* inflationists, I confidently expected to uncover a wealth of information confirming the preconceived notion that the farmer would be naturally violently opposed to McCulloch's policy of currency contraction. The prospect seemed something less than fascinating.

After a goodly amount of research had been done, it came as a surprise that virtually no evidence had been uncovered to indicate the existence of a group attitude on the part of farmers toward the currency issue in the years 1865-1870. Manuscript collections which yielded considerable evidence of the attitudes of other economic groups were virtually barren of anything that could be labelled farm opinion. The Sherman Papers, for example, which proved a goldmine of information concerning the attitudes of manfacturers and bankers, contained three letters which could conceivably be considered farm opinion on the issue of contraction.[1] Other collections were equally unsatisfactory on this point.

Turning to the early history of the Patrons of Husbandry, there was hope that evidence of economic motivation would emerge as a controlling factor in the founding of that most influential order. Here again confident expectations were shattered. A study of Oliver H. Kelley's account of the founding of the Grange and its early development in the late sixties disclosed no evidence that economic discontent was a moving force in the organizational work of Kelley and his colleagues.[2]

---

[1] Two of these letters opposed contraction (Isaac Welsh to Sherman, December 19, 1865; C. Davenport to Sherman, February 9, 1867) and one favored it (Addison Kelley to Sherman, December 20, 1867).

[2] Oliver H. Kelley, *Origin and Progress of the Order of Patrons of Husbandry in the United States; a History from 1866 to 1873* (Philadelphia, 1875).

There was absolutely no evidence in Kelley's account which would show that the founders of the Grange had the slightest interest in the currency issue. Rather were their motives fraternal and ameliorative. Professor Buck has noted that the original object of the order was " to advance agriculture and bind the farmers together." [3] Kelley's driving motives seem to have been to remove the sense of isolation under which the farmers labored, to give them the sense of belonging to a larger group, to raise the dignity of farming as a vocation, and to improve the techniques of agriculture.[4] It was not until 1869, when the prices of basic agricultural commodities began to slip, that evidence begins to emerge of an increasing concern with broader economic objectives.

A sampling of the agricultural publications which circulated in this period tended in a negative way to confirm a growing suspicion on the part of the author that farmers did not consider themselves vitally interested in the post-war currency debate. A perusal of such farm periodicals of the period as the *Maryland Farmer, Colman's Rural World* of St. Louis, the *American Agriculturist* of New York, the *Minnesota Monthly*, the *Kansas Farmer*, and the *Prairie Farmer* of Chicago uncovered only one article dealing with the money problem.[5] Indeed, if the agricultural press of the period can be said to have mirrored any kind of attitude on the part of the farm group, it definitely reflected a feeling of complacency and prosperity at least until 1869. In October, 1867, for example, the *American Agriculturist* propounded the rhetorical question, " Does farming pay? " The answer was quite definite: " If we could calculate on getting present prices, there can be no doubt that it would pay well." [6] At this time wheat was bringing at the market from $2.00 to $2.71 per bushel depending on the variety.[7]

The high level of commodity prices was well understood to

---

[3] Buck, *The Granger Movement*, p. 41.
[4] Kelley, pp. 17-20.
[5] *Maryland Farmer*, III-VI (1866-69); *Colman's Rural World and Valley Farmer*, XXI-XXII (1868-69); *American Agriculturist*, XXIV-XXIX (1865-70); *Minnesota Monthly*, I-II (1869-70); *Kansas Farmer*, III-VI (1866-69); *Prairie Farmer*, XV-XXIV (New Series) (1865-1869).
[6] *American Agriculturist*, XXVI (October, 1867), 357.
[7] *Ibid.*, p. 348.

be an important economic phenomenon of the period. One astute observer has closely linked high prices with the tremendous increase in production, pointing out that "In 1867, the price of wheat, even on the Chicago market, reached the remarkable level of $2.85 per bushel," and that even this price was not "very greatly above the annual maximum of the period." [8] Writing toward the close of the century, Thorstein Veblen, a close observer of agricultural trends, noted: "The average [price] for wheat, corn, oats, beef, pork, laid, butter, in the New York market was higher for the two years 1867 and 1868 than it has been since that time." By way of illustrating the general condition of farming in these years Veblen pointed out that ". . . the temporary movement of general prices . . . at this precise point (1867-68), was not in the same direction as that of staple farm products. General prices were declining. 1867-8 was a period of depression in business generally. . . . In short, the forces which controlled the situation for American farming were not the same that went to make the general industrial situation. It mattered little whether general business was brisk or dull so long as the seasons favored American crops and prices. And, determined by the character of the seasons, the tone of American farming was . . . buoyant, and distinctly active in 1867-8, when times generally were dull." [9] The prosperity of farmers in these years was thus compounded not only of high prices for staple commodities but also of declining prices for the manufactured goods purchased by the agricultural population.

In his recent study of the movement for railroad regulation in New York State, Mr. Lee Benson has observed that "A span of time several years before and after 1865 constituted the real golden age of New York agriculture—in money terms. . . ." Inasmuch as agitation for lower freight rates and demands for increases in the circulating medium constituted the two chief ways in which farmers expressed their grievances in the post-Civil War period, it is significant that Mr. Benson has noted the debilitating effect of farm prosperity on the movement for

[8] Alexander Dana Noyes, *Forty Years of American Finance* (New York, 1909), p. 3.

[9] Thorstein Veblen, "The Price of Wheat Since 1867," *Journal of Political Economy*, I (December, 1892), 68-70.

cheaper transportation, pointing out that the " antimonopoly revolt " of 1865-66, directed against the railroads, collapsed with the return of prosperity early in 1866. He goes on to add that " Hostility to the railroads in various sections of the West during the nineteenth century, particularly agrarian hostility, was keyed to business cycle fluctuations and was acutely responsive to lowered or raised freight charges relative to commodity prices." [10] The essential idea has been stated by a student of organization among American farmers: " When prices have reasonably compensated the farmers for their labor, they have been satisfied and have allowed their organizations to hibernate. But during each period of low prices the farmers have come forward with a statement of their dissatisfaction and a remedy." [11]

Since agrarian agitation is so closely related to the price levels of basic farm commodities, it is not surprising that the fall in the price of wheat in 1869 brought forth wails of dissatisfaction.[12] One farm journal complained: ". . . times *are* hard. Wheat brings a low price—a price far below the actual cost of production. . . . We have got accustomed to $2@$3.00 a bushel for wheat, and $1.00@$1.50 does not suit us at all." [13] A Kansas organ lamented that agriculture received little consideration in the halls of Congress. The answer was organization. " When every school district has its Farmers' Club; every township and county, its Agricultural Society, and the machinery of organization gathers up the voice of the people, and *whispers* it into the ears of Representatives in *tones of thunder*, then, not till then, will Agriculture command the position it deserves and receive its share of government aid." [14] It is noteworthy that at this time Kelley's efforts to organize the Grange began to show their first tangible and permanent results.[15]

In the *Minnesota Monthly* for December, 1869, there occurs a rare piece of evidence indicating interest in the money problem.

[10] Lee Benson, *Merchants, Farmers, and Railroads: Railroad Regulation and New York Politics, 1850-1887* (Cambridge, Mass., 1955), pp. 17, 81.

[11] John Lee Coulter, " Organization Among the Farmers of the United States," *Yale Review*, XVIII (November, 1909), 293.

[12] See the statistics on the price of wheat quoted in Chapter III.

[13] *American Agriculturist*, XXVIII (December, 1869), 448

[14] *Kansas Farmer*, VI (April 15, 1869), 68.

[15] Buck, pp. 46-47.

The article was probably written by Colonel D. A. Robertson of St. Paul, proprietor of this journal and one of the most active advocates of the Patrons of Husbandry in Minnesota.[16] The article points to a scarcity of credit as one of the factors producing distress among farmers. Inability of wheat growers to borrow money except at exorbitant rates of interest is cited as the reason why farmers cannot hold their crops for higher prices.[17] Minnesota farmers are weak in the market place because they are " too poor in money-capital." " Their want of capital contrains them to mortgage their crops before they are raised, and at rates of interest which their earnings over actual expenses, will rarely pay." [18] The answer to these difficulties would be the creation of a People's National Bank, a government institution which would " receive and pay out the deposits of the United States, and of States, corporations, and individuals, that may so desire. . . ." The main function of the proposed bank would be to " loan its bills of credit, or bank notes to individuals on pledges of improved real estate, at say one-third of its assessed registered cash value, and at a rate of interest not exceeding three per cent per annum." [19] In this manner farmers would be assured an adequate source of credit and would be released from dependence on commercial bankers. The author of the article conceded that these ideas were not original but were contained in the influential work, *Labor and Other Capital* by Edward Kellogg.[20]

There is no evidence that this article reflected any substantial body of farm opinion, and, as the author states, it was merely " submitted to the criticism and consideration of the people." [21] It is significant that the convention of farmers which met in Bloomington, Illinois in April, 1870 concerned itself entirely with agitation for lower freight rates and ventilated no other grievances at all.[22] Grievances against the railroads also monopolized the attention of delegates to the conventions of Illinois

[16] *Ibid.*, p. 46.
[17] *Minnesota Monthly*, I (December, 1869), 409-410.
[18] *Ibid.*, p. 411.
[19] *Ibid.*, p. 411.
[20] *Ibid.*, p. 413. The ideas of Edward Kellogg are discussed in Chapter V.
[21] *Ibid.*, p. 413.
[22] John R. Commons *et al., A Documentary History of American Industrial Society*, 10 vols. (Cleveland, 1911), X, 42-46.

140

140   MONEY, CLASS, AND PARTY

farmers held at Kewanee in October, 1872, Bloomington in January, 1873, and Springfield in April, 1873. At none of these conventions was any resolution passed which even remotely touched on the condition of the currency or on the National Banking System.[23] It therefore seem evident that the grivances which began to be felt by western farmers around 1869 were directed almost completely against the railroads and definitely involved no identifiable group opinion on the money situation. With these facts in mind it seems safe to say that in the years from 1865 to 1870, which is the period of this study, farmers were the least concerned of all economic groups in the general question as to whether the volume of currency should be expanded or contracted.[24]

[23] *Ibid.*, pp. 46-59.

[24] In her study of Minnesota wheat farming, Henrietta M. Larson generally supports this conclusion. With regard to the post-Civil War period, she writes: " The fact that very little was said about currency is significant. In 1869 there was some suggestion of increasing greenbacks as a means of raising prices. But until 1875 the preponderating influence was with the hard money element, which saw inflated currency as an evil at a time when wheat was sold on a non-inflated world market while the price of what farmers bought was affected by a high tariff and inflated currency." Henrietta M. Larson, *The Wheat Market and the Farmer in Minnesota, 1858-1900* (New York, 1926), p. 103 n. I agree with Miss Larson's conclusion that little was said about the currency question, but I tend to feel that the principal reason for this was that farmers were generally prosperous. I doubt that many farmers had a clear understanding of the mechanics of international finance, and, as will be pointed out in chapter IV, the interaction between the gold premium, greenbacks, and the general price level was far more complex than Miss Larson's statement would tend to indicate.

CHAPTER IV

THE MONETARY RATIONALE OF HIGH PROTECTIONISM

For the American manufacturer the years 1861-1865 had been years of unprecedented prosperity. In order to meet the needs of a nation at war, a huge increase in productive capacity had been necessary. Large government orders combined with a rising level of prices had virtually guaranteed large profits. It was reported by Dun's Mercantile Agency in 1864 that "The average profits on trade range from 12 to 15 per cent." [1] Even in the cotton textile industry which was supposedly suffering from a cotton famine, profits for the mills which were able to continue operations were sometimes phenomenal. During the four years 1863-1866 the stockholders of the Pepperell Manufacturing Company of Biddeford, Maine received dividends on shares of $500 par value averaging $256.25 per year. [2] Of the woolen manufacture inordinately stimulated by the scarcity of cotton, an economic historian has this to say: "The progress of the woolen factories, most of them located in New York and New England, was enormous; every mill was worked to its fullest capacity, many working night and day, Sunday included. In all 2000 sets of new cards were erected, representing many new mills. As the report of the New York Chamber of Commerce said, the progress seemed scarcely credible. Profits were enormous, thanks to the high prices of government contracts and to the scarcity of cotton." [3]

In the newly important oil-producing industry conditions were much the same. "Stimulated by enlargement of the market, the advance in the value of gold, and a temporary slackening of output, the price of oil at the wells rose from $3 or $4

---

[1] *Hunt's Merchants' Magazine*, LII (February, 1865), 147.

[2] Evelyn H. Knowlton, *Pepperell's Progress: History of a Cotton Textile Company, 1844-1945* (Cambridge, Mass., 1948), pp. 115-116.

[3] Emerson David Fite, *Social and Industrial Conditions in the North During the Civil War* (New York, 1910), p. 84.

in the first weeks of 1864 to $13.75 in midsummer. It continued high. Well owners could pay all expenses and make profits of $3 to $7 a barrel. Many of them rolled in wealth. Men were feverishly boring fresh wells in old areas, and prospecting and 'wildcatting' new fields. Investors who heard that the Columbia Oil Company had paid dividends of $26 a share in the latter half of 1863 rushed to pour more money into speculative enterprises." [4]

The historian of Reed & Barton, silversmiths of Taunton, Massachusetts, has recorded the substantial prosperity which that old firm enjoyed during the war. Sales rose from $148,000 in 1862 to $256,472 in 1863, and in 1864 to $341,456. Merchants and jobbers would visit Taunton begging for goods of any description. There was little or no necessity for maintaining a sales organization of any kind, and many manufacturers in the electro-plating industry abandoned their retail contacts altogether and depended entirely on jobbers. [5]

Iron and steel manufacturing presented a similar picture. In one year six extensive iron mills were erected in Pittsburgh, while in the last year of the conflict $26,000,000 of iron and steel were manufactured. [6] Other manufacturing interests such as glass, leather, agricultural implements, meat packing, and machine tools also benefited enormously from the combination of high prices, high protection, and large scale government buying. [7] The leading authority on manufacturing in the United States has cited opinion that the year 1865 was "the most profitable year known in the history of the New England states." [8]

The unsettlement of the standard of value which followed the issue of the greenbacks in 1862 presented difficulties to which some manufacturers found it difficult to adjust. These difficulties were compounded in the case of producers who

[4] Allan Nevins, *Study in Power: John D. Rockefeller, Industrialist and Philanthropist*, 2 vols. (New York, 1953), I, 42.

[5] George Sweet Gibb, *The Whitesmiths of Taunton: A History of Reed & Barton 1824-1943* (Cambridge, Mass., 1943), pp. 181-182.

[6] Fite, *Social and Industrial Conditions*, p. 92.

[7] *Ibid.*, ch. IV.

[8] Victor S. Clark, *History of Manufactures in the United States*, 1929 ed., 3 vols. (New York, 1929), II, 37.

contracted in advance to deliver goods at a specified price. The chronicler of the Whitin Machine Works of Whitinsville, Massachusetts has given us an account of some of the difficulties encountered by John C. Whitin, a pioneer in the manufacture of textile machinery. " At first Whitin sought to maintain his machinery prices at prewar levels in terms of gold; he asked only that his customers pay the greenback equivalent. Since gold fluctuations were erratic, he seems to have attempted standard gradients at which his prices automatically changed. Even this expedient did not prove to be feasible, however. The inflationary spiral was rising so steeply that up-to-date prices became hopelessly obsolete before machinery could be delivered. Soaring costs quickly wiped out profit margins. Finally during the hectic summer of 1864, Whitin abandoned all effort at price quotations, requiring instead that his customers pay the price dictated by the level of gold at the date of delivery." [9]

Most entrepreneurs seem to have been nimble and shrewd enough to avoid the losses which might be entailed by committing themselves to deliveries at certain prices in advance, and, as Mitchell has observed, such evidence as we possess indicates that profits were " uncommonly large." [10] It is extremely significant that business failures which numbered 5,935 in 1861 declined to 495 in 1863, 510 in 1864, and 500 in 1865.[11] Undoubtedly a good deal of this prosperity was fictitious, and the enormous profits of many manufacturers would not have seemed so impressive had they been calculated on a gold rather than a paper money basis, but as Mitchell has pointed out the climate of opinion regarding business conditions is rarely influenced by the real value of the monetary unit in which profits are calculated. Entrepreneurs find it difficult to resist a feeling of prosperity when their money incomes are rising even though sober second thought may convince them that much of their good fortune is ephemeral.[12] It is also true that, while a good slice of the wartime profit pie represented paper gains, a healthy portion was made up of real gains obtained by entrepreneurs

[9] Thomas R. Navin, *The Whitin Machine Works Since 1831: A Textile Machinery Company in an Industrial Village* (Cambridge, Mass., 1950), p. 78.
[10] Mitchell, *History of the Greenbacks*, p. 389.
[11] *Ibid.*, table LXIII, p. 389.
[12] *Ibid.*, pp. 394-395.

at the expense of other economic groups. Laborers, capitalists, and landlords in the Civil War years all made their contributions to the profits of the entrepreneuring group whose most important component was the manufacturers. The failure of wages and rents to keep pace with the general rise in prices redounded to the benefit of the manufacturers, who, as residual claimants, were able to pocket what laborers and landlords had lost. Similar gains were made by manufacturing entrepreneurs at the expense of capitalists whose loans were repaid in a constantly depreciating currency.[13]

When the war ended, the logic of this situation was completely reversed for there began a strong downward movement in prices which was not to be significantly arrested for thirty years.[14] After producing at peak capacity for several years, the nation's manufacturers were confronted with a tremendous falling off in government purchasing which had guaranteed their prosperity even against inefficiency and waste. The prevailing business attitude was summed up by a writer in *Harper's Magazine.* " When the war ended we all knew we should have a panic. Some of us . . . expected that greenbacks and volunteers would be disbanded together. Others expected gold to fall to 101 or 102 in a few days. Others foresaw a collapse of manufacturing industry, owing to the cessation of government purchases. But we all knew a " crisis " was coming and, having set our house in order accordingly the ' crisis ' of course never came." [15]

The mood was one of pessimism. Trade assumed a feverish unsettled aspect. It was reported that there were " so many contending influences upon the markets, that there is no regularity to the course of prices, and no steadiness in demand." [16] Early in 1866 it was lamented that the fall in gold had " totally defeated the anticipations of those who looked for activity and buoyancy with the commencement of the new year." [17] At first the business community seemed to mirror the near complete

[13] *Ibid.*, p. 382.
[14] N. S. B. Gras and Henrietta M. Larson, *Casebook in American Business History* (New York, 1939), pp. 706-707.
[15] " The Great Gold Conspiracy," *Harper's Magazine*, XL (April, 1870), 747.
[16] *Commercial and Financial Chronicle*, I (December 16, 1865), 784.
[17] *Ibid.*, II (January 13, 1866), 47.

unanimity with which the House of Representatives had resolved in favor of a contraction of the currency in order to return to specie payments.[18] After all the gold standard was right and honest. Had not the Secretary of the Treasury said that paper money was "undermining the morals of the people"?[19] Did not the integrity of business demand a return to gold, the only natural determinant of value? These sentiments were native to conservative men of business and continued to be held by those whose interest would be served by contraction of the currency. Within a few months, however, the real and imagined effects of contraction which was authorized by the Loan Bill of April 12, 1866 raised up a host of businessmen and manufacturers who violently opposed such a policy.

There has been a tendency on the part of historians to assume that manufacturers generally favored deflation and a rapid return to specie payments in the years following the Civil War.[20] Because this assumption lies at the core of that interpretation of Reconstruction which identifies the interests of the Radicals in Congress with "big business" generally and sees the latter as the principal force advocating both high tariff rates and a return to the gold standard, it is of great importance that we actually examine the opinions of manufacturers on the financial questions of the Reconstruction period.[21] In this examination and analysis we shall be chiefly concerned with manufacturing opinion of the high protectionist variety, and an attempt will be made to describe a system of thinking on financial matters which, for want of a better name, we shall call the monetary rationale of high protectionism.

In order to make clearer the position of the manufacturing interest in the years 1860-1870, it is convenient at this point to reproduce a portion of a table from Wesley Mitchell's work on the economic data of the greenback period. This table indicates the "average annual price of gold, the average of quarterly medians of relative prices at wholesale, medians of relative

[18] *Congressional Globe*, 39th Congress, 1st Session, p. 75.
[19] *Report of the Secretary of the Treasury, 1865*, p. 9.
[20] See, for example, Beale, *The Critical Year*, p. 278.
[21] The ramifications of the prevailing interpretation of the financial aspects of Reconstruction will be discussed in Chapter VII.

prices at retail, medians of cost of living, and average of January and July medians of relative rates of wages. . . ." [22]

An asterisk has been used to indicate the highest point reached by each series. It is seen that some degree of sympathy with the rise in gold is shown in each case. Wholesale prices, determined in the great market centers and directly influenced by the import-export trade (in which the price of gold was an important factor) show the greatest correlation. Retail

Years	Gold	Wholesale Prices	Retail Prices	Cost of Living	Wages
1860	100	100	100	100	100
1861	100	97	104	103	100
1862	113	103	115	112	101
1863	145	133	143	129	112
1864	203*	180	170	156	130
1865	157	185*	176	168	150
1866	141	177	180*	170*	161
1867	138	162	172	168	168
1868	140	158	174	161	169
1869	133	157	164	156	175*
1870	115	139	157	150	175*

prices, influenced by distance from the market centers and local custom, show a lesser degree of sympathy. Cost of living rose more slowly than retail prices probably because of the slow rise in rents.[23] Wages reacted more slowly to the rise in gold than any other price, but it is significant that they continued to rise throughout the period of this study reaching a high point in 1869-70.

The prices which manufacturers could obtain for their products is indicated generally by the trend of wholesale prices. In order to put the position of the manufacturing interest in these years in clearer focus, it will be helpful to reproduce portions of wholesale price indexes relating to five key industries for the years, 1860-1870. These indexes were compiled by George F. Warren and Frank A. Pearson. The base period used is 1910-1914.[24]

[22] Mitchell, *Gold, Prices, and Wages*, Table 74, p. 279.

[23] *Ibid.*, p. 90.

[24] *Historical Statistics of the United States*, Series L 7, L 8, L 9, L 10, L 11, p. 232. These indexes appeared originally in George F. Warren and Frank A. Pearson, *Prices* (New York, 1933), table 3, pp. 25-27.

The highest point reached by each series is marked by an asterisk. Although the course of prices varies somewhat among these product groups, the same general pattern emerges. From 1860 to 1861 prices of these products remained stable, falling slightly in building materials and chemicals, somewhat more precipitously in fuel and lighting products, and rising slightly in textiles and metals. In 1862, the year in which the greenbacks were issued, a general rise in prices is evident in each category. In four of these product groups the rise in prices continues throughout the war years, reaching a peak in 1865 for textiles, fuel, and chemicals, and 1866 for building materials.

Years	Textile Products	Fuel and Lighting	Metals and Metal Products	Building Materials	Chemicals and Drugs
1860	119	98	149	65	175
1861	120	80	152	63	174
1862	147	87	180	69	206
1863	206	125	236	88	234
1864	264	197	354*	114	297
1865	266*	214*	306	118	300*
1866	245	160	278	128*	283
1867	220	144	248	120	229
1868	197	149	225	116	204
1869	194	166	227	110	227
1870	179	134	200	101	199

Metals and metal products reached an earlier peak in 1864. In each category the rise in prices is tremendous compared with 1860, amounting to over one hundred per cent in textiles, fuel, and metals, to very nearly that in building materials, and to seventy-one per cent in the case of chemicals and drugs. Each product group except building materials shows a fall in prices after 1865. In the case of metals and metal products this declination began in 1864; for building materials it is postponed until 1866. The fall in prices continues throughout the period of this study except for the year 1869 in which some temporary improvement is evident in three of the product groups.

The effect of these price fluctuations on the manufacturer is fairly obvious. The war years of high prices and high profits were followed by years of readjustment to a peace economy in which manufacturers saw the prices which they could obtain for their products declining almost constantly. While prices were falling, it is apparent from Mitchell's table above that the most important cost of production, wages, was rising throughout the post-war period. This was putting great pressure on the manufacturers and, in many cases, forcing them to produce at a loss. Not only was the laboring class adamant in refusing to accept a reduction in wages, the wage-earners were actively agitating for greater increases.[25] A financial journal commented pessimistically: "We have then, on the one hand, producers under an imperative pressure to reduce wages, in order to produce goods for prices at which consumers will buy them; and, on the other hand, laborers making a directly opposite demand. This antagonism between employers and operatives is too decided to admit of the hope that it will be adjusted as early as the interest of business requires. For the capitalists to yield is impossible, for in doing so they inevitably incur loss; and while the workmen appear so little to comprehend the situation of affairs, and the laws which control wages, that they are not likely to meet the views of employers until compelled by the fruitless result of strikes.[26]

Depression was the common lot of manufacturers from 1866 through 1868. The historian of Reed & Barton records that "the pinch of hard times" hit the electroplating industry in 1866 revealing an "inherently ugly competitive condition." Sales for this company declined from $475,800 in 1865 to $350,890 in 1867.[27] Professor Nevins has described conditions in these years in an industry which had enjoyed a high degree of wartime prosperity. "The depression swiftly spread to the refining industry. . . . In 1867 and still more in 1868 cobwebs gathered on dozens of refinery doors in Cleveland and Pittsburgh. The price of refined oil had fallen as heavily as that of crude; the average per gallon in New York in 1867-68 was 28 and 29 cents. Small establishments, inefficiently managed, winked out all over the country." [28]

[25] Strikes for higher wages were reported in 1867 among the miners of Luzerne County, Pennsylvania and the iron molders of Pittsburgh. In New England great resistance was met by employers who tried to reduce wages. *Commercial and Financial Chronicle*, IV (April 13, 1867), 455.

[26] *Ibid.*, II (March 31, 1866), 387.

[27] Gibb, *Whitesmiths of Taunton*, pp. 185-187.

[28] Nevins, *Rockefeller*, I, 55.

Caught between the Scylla of declining prices for their products and the Charybdis of increasing labor costs, is it indeed likely that manufacturers would have supported a contraction of the currency which led directly to even lower prices? The nature of the stock and commodity markets was "bearish" in 1866 and 1867. "All are sellers; few care to buy" was the laconic report of a leading financial journal.[29] Purchasing was almost at a standstill; no one wanted to be caught with goods on hand while prices were declining. Is it any wonder that the organ of the iron and steel manufacturers commented that "The expressions about contraction of a portion of the press are very far from the opinions of the business community, and it is widely known here that the most loud-mouthed of these contractionists is a very heavy bear operator in Wall Street, and the outcries of that newspaper are but the echoes of transactions in the Stock Board."[30]

By contributing to the declining premium on gold, contraction had a secondary effect on the import-export trade more or less separable from its more obvious effect on the domestic price level. This effect has been noted by an outstanding economist, but almost nowhere do we find a full appreciation of how the declining gold premium affected the monetary philosophy of high protectionism.[31]

[29] *Commercial and Financial Chronicle*, II (January 20, 1866), 79.

[30] American Iron and Steel Association, *Bulletin*, I (January 16, 1867), 156.

[31] See Frank D. Graham, "International Trade Under Depreciated Paper: The United States, 1862-79," *Quarterly Journal of Economics*, XXXVI (February, 1922), 220-273. The effect has also been noted by Howard K. Beale, "The Tariff and Reconstruction," *American Historical Review*, XXXV (1929-30), 276. Professor Beale presents Graham's findings in regard to the effects of international borrowing on the gold premium, but he does not draw the conclusion which to me is unavoidable; namely, that the declining gold premium was important in causing manufacturers to oppose contraction. Since this chapter was first penned, two articles have appeared in which the importance of the fluctuating premium on gold is pointed out. See Irwin Unger, "Business Men and Specie Resumption," *Political Science Quarterly*, LXXIV (March, 1959), 46-70 and Stanley Coben, "Northeastern Business and Radical Reconstruction: A Re-examination," *Mississippi Valley Historical Review*, XLVI (June, 1959), 67-90. The first article evidences a certain confusion in dealing with the working of the gold premium. At one point (p. 47) Mr. Unger identifies the interests of importers with a rising premium; on another page he notices the attractiveness to American manufacturers of the "tariff effect produced by the gold premium" (p. 57). It could not be had both ways. Actually, as is pointed

To the economic science of the present day, currency depreciation is a well know device for stimulating exports. As one authority has put it, " If the foreign exchange value of the local currency depreciates faster than its domestic purchasing power, exporting will be rendered more profitable." [32] This is precisely what happened during the Civil War. From Mitchell's table above it is evident that the greenbacks depreciated far more in terms of the currency used by most of the rest of the world, namely gold, than it did in terms of domestic purchasing power. Consequently exporters found it very easy to sell to foreigners those surplus products of manufacturers and farmers which were not required for the war effort. The economist David A. Wells noted this phenomenon and rightly attributed it to the effect of the advancing premium on gold.[33] As long as the premium was rising, it contributed to the manufacturers' prosperity in that it made it easier to sell in foreign markets and more difficult for European manufacturers to sell in the American market, since the high gold premium would force them to sell at very high currency prices, if they wanted to show a profit.[34]

out above, the interests of importers were served by a declining not a rising premium on gold. In the second article Mr. Coben deals briefly with the effects of the fluctuating premium (pp. 81-82) and correctly points out that a rising premium served the interests of American manufacturers through the additional protection which it afforded.

[32] Harold L. Reed, *Money Currency and Banking* (New York, 1942), p. 296.

[33] Wells, writing in 1872 said: " Another anomaly of this period was the extraordinary increase in the exportation of many articles of domestic produce, notwithstanding the greatly increased cost of their constituent materials and of labor. Thus, the export value of carriages increased from $472,080 in 1861 to $803,000 in 1864-5, gold valuation; glass and glass-ware, from $277,000 in 1860 to $627,000 in 1864-5; clothing, do., from $402,000 to $756,000; boots and shoes, do., from $782,000 to $1,038,000. . . . The aggregate exports of wheat and wheat-flour from the United States rose to the unprecedented figure of 67,000,000 bushels, or an average of over 33,000,000 bushels per annum. [In 1863-1864] The explanation of this increased movement may be found, first, in the fact that the premium on gold often rose with great rapidity, and for periods was often unquestionably from fifty to seventy per cent in advance of the currency prices of the labor and materials employed in many branches of domestic production, the effect of which was to increase the purchasing power of the foreign consumer dealing only with gold; or, what was the same thing, to decrease the relative cost of such articles of American product as were available for export and sale in a foreign market." David A. Wells, *The Recent Financial, Industrial and Commercial Experiences of the United States: A Curious Chapter in Politico-Economic History* (New York, 1872), p. 25.

[34] The protective influence of the gold premium was understood by manu-

The logic of this situation was completely reversed when the price of gold began to fall. As is evident from Mitchell's table, it fell faster than any other price. This was equivalent to currency appreciation and meant that the importer of foreign manufactures could sell at a much lower price in currency, convert the currency back into gold at a much lower premium, and show a good profit. It also meant that the importer of foreign manufactures could undersell the American manufacturer whose costs were not declining with gold, but were actually increasing due to the rising cost of labor. A contemporary writer for the most important manufacturing journal saw this situation clearly: [35]

An English knife, the price of which in New York, in July, 1864, would have been, say, $1.50 per dozen, in gold, would have cost, in U. S. money, about $3.75 per dozen, and, at the present rate of duty, would have paid about *ninety cents* in currency. Now the same knife will cost about $2.00 per dozen, and the duty will be about *forty eight* cents in currency; the importer being thus enabled to sell his goods at nearly half the price he did then, and being relieved of nearly half the duty he paid then.

At the same time, the home producer experiences no similar reliefs; he pays the same wages as he did then, he pays the same taxes as he did then. The cost of living is the same as it was then; and while the foreign agent can reduce his price according to the decline in gold, without loss, the American manufacturer is compelled, if he would meet this competition, to do it at a loss—a loss that was never contemplated in the framing of the tariff of '64 and which is occasioned by the fact that gold has declined in value, while wages have advanced.

As this article suggests, the declining gold premium nullified much of the wartime tariff legislation. The various tariff acts which followed the enactment of the Morrill tariff law of 1861 had boosted the average duty on commodities (other than those

---

facturers. In a paper read before a meeting of Pittsburgh manufacturers and representatives of the coal interest on April 13, 1865, one James M. Cooper asserted: "It is obvious that with the enormous cost of labor and materials the American manufacturer could not have contended with his English rival but for the incidental *or accidental* rate of premium upon gold and foreign exchange. This unsteady and precarious security is about all the protection the former receives, and as this continues to decline, his ability to maintain the struggle declines with it." James M. Cooper, *The Government the Partner of the Manufacturer* (Pittsburgh, 1865), p. 7.

[35] *Iron Age*, February 7, 1867.

on the free list) to 47% by 1864.[36] The existence of these decidely protective statutes has tended to conceal the fact that after the war they did not keep foreign manufacturers from sending in vast quantities of goods to compete on the domestic market. Professor Graham's figures indicate that merchandise imports exceeded merchandise exports in the years 1865-1869 by $466,799,000.[37] A protective tariff generally induces higher real costs of production. During the war wasteful and extravagant methods had become the rule in many factories. No one had to suffer for it then, because military needs meant high profits for even the marginal producer. But when the war was over and gold began to decline, the tariff did not suffice to keep out a growing flood of imports. Too much has been made of the idea that greedy manufacturers combined to obtain even higher protection in the Reconstruction period.[38] Not enough has been made of the declining premium on gold, the internal revenue taxes, and the high costs of production which went a long way toward nullifying the protection afforded by the tariff laws.

If the equilibrating mechanisms of international trade had been allowed full play during the early Reconstruction period, the great excess of imports would have brought about an outflow of gold which would, in turn, have raised the gold premium and the foreign exchange rates, making it unprofitable to import more goods. That this did not happen is largely due to the fact so well enlarged upon by Professor Graham that the United States floated loans in Europe in the fiscal years, 1865-1869, totalling $424,000,000.[39] In other words the United States paid for its adverse merchandise balance by selling Europe stocks and bonds. This was probably the most important single reason why the exchanges did not turn against us and force a cessation of merchandise imports. In the public mind, however, and in the minds of businessmen and manufacturers, this factor was not generally accorded the attention which it deserved. As the historian of manufacturing in the United States has observed

---

[36] Taussig, *Tariff History*, p. 167.
[37] Derived from the table in Graham, *op. cit.*, p. 231.
[38] See, for example, Herbert Ronald Ferleger, *David A. Wells and the American Revenue System, 1865-1870* (New York, 1942), chs. VI and VII.
[39] Derived from the table in Graham, *op. cit.*, p. 231

of this period, " Among the general domestic conditions having direct bearing upon industrial prosperity at this time, the currency situation probably ranked first." [40] The process of contraction put into effect by Hugh McCulloch was actually directed to the destruction of a large part of the medium of circulation. This contributed directly and obviously both to lowering the prices of manufactured goods and to causing a decline in the gold premium resulting in diminishing protection. Is it true then that manufacturers favored contraction of the currency, or is it more likely that high protection was congenial with a philosophy looking toward expansion of the currency? To answer this question we must consider the contemporary opinions of the high protectionists themselves.

The onslaught against McCulloch's contraction policy was led by the high priest of protection himself, Henry Charles Carey of Philadelphia. Several writers have commented upon the soft-money ideas of Carey. One has pointed out that it was ". . . hopeless to rear any enduring tariff wall upon the shifting sands of an inflated currency . . ." and that " Even Henry C. Carey failed to recognize the menace, and simultaneously advocated high protection and cheap currency; an attempt to reconcile the irreconcilable which led many of his contemporaries . . . into strange realms of economic fallacy." [41] It should be pointed out, however, that although Carey's linkage of the ideas of high protection and soft-money may have been inconsistent before 1862 when the country was on the gold standard, the two ideas became wholly consistent once the currency began to depreciate in terms of gold. Carey and his school hated the gold standard because, to their way of thinking, it left the American manufacturer at the mercy of the importer of foreign and particularly British goods. " Of all the commodities in use by man, there are none that contribute so little to his comfort or convenience as gold and silver. . . . Ten furnaces and rolling-mills, capable of producing in a year three millions of dollars' worth of iron, may close without producing even a passing remark from a newspaper, but no

---

[40] Clark, *History of Manufactures*, II, 139.
[41] Malcolm Rogers Eiselen, *The Rise of Pennsylvania Protectionism* (Philadelphia, 1932), p. 269.

vessel can arrive or depart, with fifty thousand dollars in gold, without the arrival being noticed in half of the papers of the Union." [42] Monetary independence was the goal of Carey and his followers. The effect in the United States of the Overend-Gurney panic in England which caused a large export of gold from the United States in the summer of 1866 struck Carey as most significant. " The crash was terrific, yet it never affected our domestic operations for even a single hour. Our monetary independence had been established. Our machinery of exchange being a non-exportable one, we had no use for gold, and if it were needed abroad, we could say, ' Why let it go! ' Accordingly, $30,000,000 were at once dispatched; the bank was saved [the Bank of England] and injury was thus avoided to an extent that would scarcely be exaggerated were it counted by hundreds of millions ot pounds; and thus did Britain benefit by the fact that the currencies of the two countries were different." [43]

That this view has considerable validity was admitted by the free trade, contractionist *Commercial and Financial Chronicle* of New York which, though maintaining that " A paper currency not redeemable in coin is a curse to any country where it prevails, . . . the curse is not without its blessing. Our paper money is unsettled and unstable in its value; that is its evil; but our paper money system is not liable to derangement from foreign demand for specie; that is its compensating good." [44]

Carey was essentially a domestic free trader. He wanted to erect a wall of protection around the United States so as to make possible the fullest development of human and material resources. To his mind the " British monopolists " would stoop to any trick to prostrate American manufacturers and open the way to a deluge of imports. Carey saw a British agent behind every tree, laboring through such organizations as the Free Trade League to breach the protectionist wall erected with such difficulty during the Civil War. [45] Within his scheme of a har-

[42] Henry C. Carey, *The Harmony of Interests, Agricultural, Manufacturing, and Commercial* (Philadelphia, 1872), p. 190.

[43] Henry C. Carey, *Monetary Independence. Letter of Mr. H. C. Carey to the Hon. Moses W. Field, Chairman of the Committee of Invitations for the Detroit Convention* (Philadelphia, 1875), p. 2.

[44] *Commercial and Financial Chronicle*, II (May 26, 1866), 642.

[45] Carey's attitude toward the British is best summed up by the title of one

mony of interests between manufacturers, laborers, farmers, and capitalists, there was need for a plentiful supply of money to keep interest rates low, and to stimulate production and consumption. With approval, he quoted Hume on money: " In every kingdom into which money begins to flow, in greater abundance than formerly, everything takes on a new face; labor and industry gain life; the merchant becomes more enterprising; the manufacturer more diligent and skillful; the farmer follows his plow with more alacrity and attention." [46]

In 1867 and 1868 Carey made a frontal assault on McCulloch's contraction policy. In a public letter to Senator Henry Wilson of Massachusetts, he warned: " The Fort Wayne decree of Secretary McCulloch, likely to prove of far more enduring importance than the Berlin and Milan decrees of the Emperor Napoleon, is now nearly two years old. As it stands it constitutes the great financial blunder of the age, having already, by the paralysis of which it has been the cause, cost the country more than the whole amount of the national debt. Let its policy be persevered in and it will constitute the greatest in history, for *it will have cost the Union its existence*." [47]

In a pamphlet published in 1868, Carey maintained that there was no inflation except in New York and New England and that this was more the fault of McCulloch himself than anyone else, for it was McCulloch as Comptroller of the Currency who had allotted to New England and New York nearly 60 per cent of the circulation authorized under the National Banking System. With a population of about 7,000,000, New York and New England, the " trading states " as Carey called them, had far more bank currency than the rest of the " producing" states and territories with a population of about 30,000,000.[48] Given the superior credit facilities of banking centers like New York and Boston, it was clear that inflation

of his pamphlets, *Commerce, Christianity, and Civilization Versus British Free Trade. Letters in Reply to the London Times.* (Philadelphia, 1876).

[46] Abraham David Hannath Kaplan, *Henry Charles Carey, A Study in American Economic Thought* (Baltimore, 1931), pp. 59-60.

[47] Henry C. Carey, *Reconstruction: Industrial, Financial, and Political, Letters to the Hon. Henry Wilson, Senator From Massachusetts* (Philadelphia, 1867), no. 12, p. 58.

[48] Henry C. Carey, *The Finance Minister, the Currency, and the Public Debt*, 2nd ed. (Washington, 1866), pp. 6-7.

should be much greater in the "trading states." Because
McCulloch was largely responsible for this money monopoly,
Carey argued: "He, therefore, it is who is to be regarded as
the great 'inflationist'; yet does it please him to style as such
all those who fail to see that the resumption of specie payments
can by any possibility be attained by means of measures tending
to total destruction of the societary circulation." [49]

It was Carey's messianic zeal and powerful pen which rationalized the needs of the mining and manufacturing interests of
Pennsylvania and the western states. In correspondence with
Senators and Congressmen, these manufacturers raised their
voices against the policy of contraction which, they felt, was
paralyzing business. John McManus, an iron manufacturer of
Reading, Pennsylvania, wrote Thaddeus Stevens: "I find in
conversing with my business friends I am not alone of the
opinion that the report of the Secy of the Treas. is suited more
to dazzal [sic] the Benton School than to meet the wants of
the situation . . . I beg your early consideration of the policy
the Secy proposes particularly his recommendations to withdraw
200,000,000 bills from circulation—he will by doing so reduce
the cost of living at the expense of reducing their ability to
consume. . . . It is a fallacy that we have too much money in
circulation; if we had, interest would not be from 7 to 9 per
cent. If not interfered with, all can be employed well and
profitably." [50] N. G. Olds, a spoke and hub manufacturer of
Fort Wayne, Indiana, sent Senator John Sherman several anti-
contractionist clippings from local newspapers, asserting, "We
the people endorse every word contained in the slips herewith
enclosed. We demand that something be done for the improvement of our finances at once. We think it quite as necessary
to look after Hugh McCulloch as His accidency A. J." [51]

In a letter to Congressman James A. Garfield late in 1867,
Burke A. Hinsdale passed on the opinions of two prominent
representatives of the oil refining interest. He wrote: "Business
men are hungry for more money. The Phillips Bros. took
dinner with me yesterday; they join in the common cry—green-

---

[49] *Ibid.*, p. 8.
[50] January 2, 1866, Stevens Papers.
[51] December 11, 1866, Sherman Papers.

backs, greenbacks or the country is ruined! They say you are trying to govern this country according to the precedents of history, and the trouble is there are no precedents for it. I should not wonder if the cries of the people, reinforced by the extreme stringency of the money market, would extort from Congress an inflationary policy." [52]

F. W. Blatchford, a Chicago manufacturer, explained to Lyman Trumbull the effect contraction was having on business in the Middle West.[53]

You can hardly conceive what a feeling of despondency has settled down again upon manufacturers and business men in view of the probable defeat or postponement of the three great financial measures, *Internal Tax, Tariff, & Currency Bills*. For months now everything has been in suspense, and until definite action is taken the same condition must continue. Preparations were made in December for many enterprises involving the activities of our Machine Shops and other manufactories; but the estimates and bids all remain unaccepted because no man knows what Congress will do. . . . It is well known that most manufacturing business proved disastrous last year & that the Income returns of 1866 will afford little revenue but if we are to have a repetition of last year's legislation, still more heavy must be the losses & greater the derangements. Scarcely a business man we have conversed with feels that the Contraction policy should be enforced at present and all are equally firm in the conviction that the Compound Interest Notes should be redeemed in *plain legal tenders*. . . . We write in behalf of a dozen firms who have spoken to us about the matter.

D. W. Patterson wrote Stevens from Lancaster late in 1866: " Now I hope you will not let that Ass of the Treasury Department ruin the country by his speedy contraction or withdrawal of the currency, and the early resumption of specie-payments. He will crush the business of the country if you and Congress do not restrain him." [54] Whitely, Fassler & Kelly of Springfield, Ohio, manufacturers of mowing and reaping machines, viewed McCulloch's course as an " Effort at the utter prostration of all kinds of business of every department." They begged Senator Sherman to " do all that lies in your power . . . not

[52] Mary L. Hinsdale, ed., *Garfield-Hinsdale Letters*, p. 119. The Phillips brothers of New Castle, Pennsylvania, were prominent men in the oil refining industry before its absorption by the Standard Oil Company.

[53] February 25, 1867, Trumbull Papers, Library of Congress.

[54] December 10, 1866, Stevens Papers.

only to avoid the further contraction of our currency but to pass an act whereby the great & increasing demand of the people can be obtained." [55] In a letter to Senator Fessenden an official of the Elmira and Williamsport Railroad Company expressed the opinion that "McCullough [sic] is an arrant humbug—& more than that he is either what most believed him to be—a scoundrel, or he is the *dupe of scoundrels*. He has *ruined* the Spring trade all over the Country—Agricultural, Commercial & Manufacturing & by so doing has cost the country at least two hundred & fifty millions." [56]

John Williams' *Iron Age*, the leading manufacturing journal of the time, asked while the Loan Bill was being discussed: "Why then, contract our circulation, already seen to be so much less than that of our European peers? Is it not rather the course of wisdom to keep it in rapid and profitable motion, stimulating and maintaining a home market, by which it will pass promptly from hand to hand, dispensing comfort and independence through all classes of the community?" As the shades of depression deepened, Williams laid much of the blame for the situation on McCulloch and referred to the contraction policy as "the most vicious that has ever been proposed by any finance minister the world as yet has seen." [57] In October, 1867 the organ of the iron and steel trade complained bitterly, "It ought not to be necessary to the prosperity of an American iron maker, that the national credit should be at a discount, but so the short-sighted policy of the government has made it. If gold is at a premium, then iron can be made to profit, but if it descends much below its present point, then can the British come in at prices that render its production unprofitable." [58]

Two months later the same publication saw little hope for relieving the dullness of trade unless Congress should adopt measures for "securing an increased supply of currency." [59] At the annual meeting of the American Iron and Steel Association

[55] December 24, 1867, Sherman Papers.
[56] T. Kimber, Jr. to Fessenden, March 14, 1866. Fessenden Papers, Library of Congress.
[57] *Iron Age*, March 22, 1866; October 31, November 7, 1867.
[58] American Iron and Steel Association, *Bulletin*, II (October 9, 1867), 36.
[59] *Ibid.*, II (December 11, 1867), 108.

held in Washington in January, 1867, the membership resolved against any attempt at an immediate return to specie payments.[60]

John Williams of the *Iron Age*, Daniel J. Morrell, Congressman and manufacturer from Pennsylvania, John A. Griswold, also a Congressman and manufacturer from Troy, New York, Stephen Colwell, and others of the high protection, soft-money school organized the American Industrial League in May, 1867, to combat the proselytizing activities of William Cullen Bryant's Free Trade League. The grand old man of American industry, Peter Cooper, was elected President.[61] Speaking before this organization in May, 1868, Cooper denounced those " whose pecuniary interests, as importers, agents, and merchants, are directly and deeply identified with those of the manufacturers of Great Britain and Continental Europe . . . ," those who are making " efforts most zealous and persistent . . . to circulate among the masses of our people the unsound and impracticable theories of free trade and an immediate return to specie payment, while we are a debtor nation . . . with a balance of trade against us in gold of $136,000,000 during the year 1867." [62] In an address before the Union League Club in 1867, Cooper had pled for a " national currency, issued solely by the authority and supported in circulation by the taxing power and solvency of our Government." [63] Predicted Cooper, " It will increase indefinitely the country's exporting power. We will then pay our balances with other nations with our surplus products, and have but little occasion for the use of gold and silver to pay balances of trade." [64]

[60] *Iron Age*, January 16, 1867.

[61] *Ibid.*, May 23, 1867. Morrell made a speech in Congress in which he said that the friends of contraction were " all in high places, and . . . enemies of the workingman." He believed that most of McCulloch's followers were " moneyed men, who wish to give their money more power over labor and its products." *Ibid.*, February 6, 1868. Colwell attributed the premium on gold to speculation and not to any distrust of the currency. *Ibid.*, April 12, 1866.

[62] Peter Cooper, *Ideas for a Science of Good Government, in Addresses, Letters and Articles on a Strictly National Currency, Tariff and Civil Service* (New York, 1883), p. 341.

[63] *Ibid.*, p. 10.

[64] *Ibid.*, p. 11. It is interesting that Cooper had been an advocate of the Benton-Jackson doctrine of hard-money and had enlisted with " Old Hickory " in the war on the Second Bank of the United States. The thread of continuity with the past, which has been noted in the cases of other old Jacksonians such

This high protectionist, soft-money ideology had its natural home in Pennsylvania, but it also had great influence in the western states and in New York where manufacturers such as John A. Griswold and Peter Cooper espoused its doctrines. The natural whipping boy of those whose thinking fell into these lines was New England, for this section was regarded as unsound on the tariff in addition to being completely selfish with the currency. In the summer and fall of 1867, Henry C. Carey lashed out at New England in a series of public letters to Senator Henry Wilson of Massachusetts.[85] Dipping into his vast store of miscellaneous erudition, Carey enunciated his thesis that the " Producing" states were being forced into thraldom for the benefit of the " Trading" states of New England and New York. He brought forth quotations from eminent statesmen and businessmen of New England to show that the allegiance of this section to protectionism was only lukewarm—that the real interest of the manufacturers of Massachusetts and Rhode Island lay in buying raw materials cheap and selling finished goods dear.[66] Since two of these raw materials were coal and iron, the backbone of the economy of Pennsylvania, Carey was violently opposed to such a policy. According to the Philadelphian, the elements which entered into the calculations of New England textile manufacturers were completely different from those of the manufacturers of the " Producing" states. Because of the tendency toward monopoly in New England, the overriding consideration had become the suppression of domestic competition.

as F. P. Blair, Jr., George Pendleton, and William Allen, was the same, a hatred of banks, bank-notes, high interest rates, and debt. In his business Cooper had for years refused to have anything to do with banks and to the end of his days held them responsible for the recurring cycles of boom and bust endemic to nineteenth century American economic history. Allen Nevins, *Abram S. Hewitt with Some Account of Peter Cooper* (New York, 1935), pp. 281-282.

[65] Henry C. Carey, *Reconstruction: Industrial, Financial, and Political. Letters to the Hon. Henry Wilson, Senator from Massachusetts.*

[66] *Ibid.*, nos. 13, p .69; 4, p. 21. That this view was common to those of the soft-money, high protection persuasion was indicated by Thaddeus Stevens' denunciation in 1866 of the tariff bill prepared by New Englander David Wells and supported by New Englander Justin Morrill " as a free trade bill from beginning to end" because it reduced duties on coal and scrap iron. Edward Stanwood, *American Tariff Controversies in the Nineteenth Century*, 2 vols. (Boston, 1903), II, 153.

It may be asked, however, if the Boston capitalist engaged in the cotton manufacture does not suffer equally with those elsewhere engaged in other industrial departments? He does not. Having secured an almost entire monopoly, all he desires is that nothing shall be done that will ' stimulate domestic competition '; and to that end, as I understand, New England men have shown themselves inflexibly opposed to the granting of any more protection than that which they themselves required, or little more than that now allowed them. With them capital abounds, interest is low, and machinery exists in great perfection. Just now, they suffer in some small degree; but they find their compensation in the fact that . . . their competitors in the purchase of cotton and sale of cloth, are being ruined beyond redemption. . . . The more frequent the crises, the more dangerous the trade; and the more the free trade cry can be raised, as is now being done throughout New England, the less is the danger of ' domestic competition ' for the purchase of cotton and for the sale of cotton cloth; and therefore is it that Eastern cotton manufacturers have been enabled to build up the immense fortunes that we find recorded. The system here pursued by them closely resembles that of the great British iron-masters, . . . the latter being as much intent upon having a monopoly of the supply of iron to the world as are the capitalists of Boston upon monopolizing that of cottons for the Union.[67]

To Carey and his school the New York-New England monopoly of sixty per cent of the circulation of the National Banking System was an integral part of the plot to impoverish the " Producing " states for the benefit of the " Trading " states. A writer in the *Iron Age* summarized the reasons why the New England states were so anxious to get back to gold: [68]

The New England States, as represented in Congress, are urgent for an early return to specie payments. Why? Because, with little more than a *twelfth* of the population, they have secured to themselves more than a *third* of the great money monopoly that, under the new banking law, has been created! Because, to those States, small as they are, there has been granted an average circulation of no less than seventeen millions! Because, the large amount of capital that has been allowed to be there invested in banking prevents necessity for the overtrading that exists in the less favored States of the centre, the South, and the West! . . . Because being creditor States, they desire that all existing claims shall be paid in gold, the commodity of highest value! Because, being purchasers of wool, cotton, and other raw materials, they desire that the agricultural and mining States may find themselves compelled to accept the lowest prices! For all these reasons the votes of eastern

---

[67] Carey, *Letters to the Hon. Henry Wilson*, no. 5, p. 25.
[68] *Iron Age*, November 14, 1867.

members are almost unanimously favorable to the Treasury policy of contraction.

The evidence partially supports the assertions of the high protectionists that New England manufacturers wanted contraction as opposed to their Pennsylvania and western colleagues. The moving force for a return to specie payments among the New England manufacturers was Edward Atkinson of Boston. It was Atkinson who advised McCulloch to separate himself from Andrew Johnson, so that the Radical high protectionists could not identify McCulloch's contractionist financial policies with Johnson.[69] Atkinson's biographer states that for him the great economic goals of Reconstruction were an approach to free trade and the re-establishment of the specie standard.[70] Atkinson described expansion of the currency in a letter to William B. Allison as " folly, fraud, treachery, dishonor, theft, stupidity and everything else that is weak, miserable and cowardly combined." [71]

Despite his powerful propaganda efforts, it is doubtful that Atkinson represented the views of all New England manufacturers on the question of specie resumption. Evidence on this point is not easy to come by, for on questions of finance New England producers seem to have maintained virtually a conspiracy of silence. At the convention of manufacturers held at Worcester, Massachusetts in January, 1868, it was resolved that the deliberations of the delegates be confined to the specific purpose of securing removal of the internal taxes.[72] No extraneous issues were allowed to reach the floor, possibly because it was realized that on such questions as expansion or contraction of the currency or the tariff, it would be impossible to achieve the unity which was so evident on the internal taxation issue. Certainly, if this were not the case, it might be expected that Edward Atkinson, who was secretary of the Committee on Resolutions, would have attempted to commit the convention to a firm stand in favor of the early resumption of specie

---

[69] *Supra*, Chapter III.

[70] Williamson, *Edward Atkinson*, p. 87.

[71] *Ibid.*, p. 84.

[72] *Proceedings of the New England Manufacturers' Convention Held at Worcester, Mass., January 22, 1868* (Boston, 1868), p. 16.

payments.[73] The same lack of commitment on financial policy appears in the proceedings of the conventions of cotton manufacturers and planters held in New York in 1868 and 1869.[74] At these meetings in which planter interest was purely nominal and New England influence was dominant, discussions were largely confined to problems of production.[75] No mention was made of the currency issue, though there was some consideration of the tariff. Opinions expressed in the convention of 1869 tended toward a position of moderation on the tariff, one delegate declaring " It is not an extreme protective tariff that we want, but something permanent and reliable. . . ." [76] Sentiment in favor of high protective duties was not in evidence.[77]

It is probable that the wealthier and well-established manufacturers of New England supported the policy of contraction and a moderate tariff; for if they were not monopolistic, they controlled enough of the market to fear unbridled domestic competition. As for the newer entrepreneurs who were not so well-established, it is not likely that they looked with favor upon contraction. A writer in the Boston *Post* in the winter of 1869 analyzed the differences between these two groups.[78]

The trouble and the danger are not based on the question of a tariff, but simply on that of cheap money. To go on with their enterprises, our manufacturers must have that. The other corporations find it comparatively easy to go along with their business, on the basis of their large accumulated resources, which have been steadily piling up in their possession from one generation to another; but the large, active, working and progressive element of New England business . . . finds itself manacled by the heavy rates of interest demanded for money, and, after a stout struggle with fate begins . . . to succumb. These young and enterprising establishments, that are so seriously menaced by the present

[73] *Ibid.*, p. 21.

[74] *Proceedings of a Convention Held in the City of New York, Wednesday, April 29, 1868, for the Purpose of Organizing the National Association of Cotton Manufacturers and Planters* (Boston, 1868) ; *Proceedings of the First Annual Meeting of the National Association of Cotton Manufacturers and Planters Held in the City of New York, Wednesday, June 30, 1869* (Boston, 1869).

[75] The president of the Association was Amos A. Lawrence of Massachusetts. The Treasurer and the Secretary were also from New England. *Proceedings of the First Annual Meeting . . .* , pp. 51-52.

[76] *Ibid.*, p. 36.

[77] *Ibid.*, pp. 33-38.

[78] Quoted in *DeBow's Review*, VII (New Series) (December, 1869), 1077-1078.

monetary policy and system of management, are the ones that make and multiply business.

Carey's attack on New England was accompanied by a proposition that all the "Producing" states of the South, the West, and the Center meet in a convention to decide upon measures to circumvent the policies of New England.[79] The organ of the American Free Trade League took note of this proposition and replied in kind. "After setting forth the grounds upon which he bases his opinion that New England is unsound on the tariff question, Mr. Carey brings forward a plan to punish that refractory section of the Union, and to put things to rights again. His scheme is to form an alliance between Pennsylvania and the South, whose ruling idea shall be to pass laws adverse to New England; to establish nonintercourse with her; to construct railroads and canals expressly to carry trade away from her; to build a high fence about her; to impose taxes on her, and to make faces at her." [80] Despite the mutterings of the free traders there were indications that some elements in the South were well disposed to listen to Carey. A writer for the most influential Southern economic journal commented: [81]

There is great danger in hearkening only to those who are in harmony with our previous sentiments, for they confirm error, and strengthen us in conclusions which have been overthrown by arms, and which have been rendered inapplicable by defeat. We must recast our practical philosophy to make it harmonize with altered necessities. We cannot do this by feeding upon the past, and renewing a dissipated dream. We must turn, though with no credulous ear, to those whose whole habit of thought is diverse from our own, but more accordant with the changed systems under which we have to live and work. To no one can we recur with more confidence of receiving valuable and intelligent suggestions than to the distinguished gentleman who has rebuked the selfishness and blind exclusiveness of New England domination in these letters to Senator Wilson, of Massachusetts.

The preachings of the high protectionist school did not fall on wholly unresponsive Southern ears. That earnest propagandist for the Pennsylvania way of life, William D. " Pig

[79] Carey, *Letters to the Hon. Henry Wilson*, no. 13, p. 66.
[80] *The League*, February, 1868.
[81] *DeBow's Review*, V (New Series) (July, 1868), 586.

Iron " Kelley went South in the spring of 1867 and made speeches in Montgomery, New Orleans, and other cities. He extolled the beauty and latent wealth of the section and predicted that thrift, industry, and free labor would be its resurrection.[82] His audiences were sometimes hostile, but he struck popular notes whenever he lashed out at the Northern Democrats, those " false and unprincipled friends of the South," and also when he pled for industrialization and diversification.[83] He advised the citizens of Montgomery to " build furnaces, forges, rolling mills, machine shops, and factories," to " spin and weave your own cotton, and create an Alabama Lowell or Manchester." [84] Kelley's teachings were alien and unfamiliar, but many of the thinking people of the South were profoundly disenchanted with the nature of the region's economy. The needs of war had made them finally cognizant of the crucial importance of industry, and they were willing to turn, as the article above suggests, to " those whose whole habit of thought is diverse from our own " for instruction and guidance.

It has been shown that economic and ideological considerations point toward a close correlation between high protection and soft-money in the years immediately following the Civil War. The effect of a falling price level on manufacturers holding inventories of raw materials is too obvious to need clarification. The effect of a falling gold premium on the volume of imports is more subtle and has been explained at some length. These economic facts of life were the central cause for the onslaught on the free trade-gold standard school of thought by the high protectionists. The latter regarded Henry C. Carey as their intellectual standard bearer, and Carey's doctrines were carried into the political arena by men like " Pig Iron " Kelley, Thaddeus Stevens, John A. Griswold, and Daniel J. Morrell. One has only to read manufacturing journals such as the *Iron Age* or letters from manufacturers to their Congressmen in order to understand the enormous influence Carey had on the thinking of the manufacturing group. The three cardinal principles of the Pennsylvania school were high protection, an

---

[82] William D. Kelley, *Speeches, Addresses and Letters on Industrial and Financial Questions* (Philadelphia, 1872), pp. 146-184.
[83] *Ibid.*, p. 152. [84] *Ibid.*, p. 166.

abundant money supply, and the union of all producing classes. This union of producers was a logical outgrowth of Carey's idea of the harmony of interests.

To Carey there was no essential antagonism between farmers, laborers, and manufacturers. The farmers would benefit from high protection and easy money because such policies would guarantee them the domestic market for their crops as well as low interest rates for money. Such a policy would also ensure the prosperity of manufacturers who would expand their plants, hiring more labor to consume more food grown by American farmers. Laborers, on the other hand, would gain by a policy which excluded the products of the " pauper " labor of Europe. This protection would enable manufacturers to pay higher wages than employers in any other country. Thus the philosophy of high protection and easy money was calculated to draw together all of the producing interests of the country, creating a solid front against deflationary capitalists anxious to increase the value of their money, railroad owners anxious to import cheap rails from England, and all those who had been seduced by the " sophistries " of the British free trade school of political economy.

Carey held that " The tendency of the whole British system of political economy is to the production of discord among men and nations." [85] It is certainly true that the Marxian theory of classes owes a great deal to classical economics which placed great emphasis on the separate nature of land, labor, and capital and their oftimes separate interests. At the hands of Marx, the Ricardian theory of rent evolved into the theory of surplus value, one of the great justifications for class warfare. At the hands of the conservatives in the United States after the Civil War the wages-fund doctrine became a justification for holding down the wages of labor. The following extract from a leading free trade-gold standard publication shows how the doctrine that wages were controlled by the amount of capital was translated into the struggle between capital and labor: " Manufacturers cannot produce at current wages without incurring a serious loss. Operatives say, ' capitalists have made large profits during the war and can well afford to lose now a portion of

---

[85] Henry C. Carey, *The Harmony of Interests*, preface, p. iii.

their late gains.' But can it possibly be to the interest of the operatives that employers should lose any part of their capital? Suppose manufacturers should run into bankruptcy by paying higher wages than they can afford, there is then no capital for giving employment to labor; the operatives are thrown out of work, and employers and employees suffer in a common disaster." [86]

The high protectionists rejected the idea that wages were set either by the fund of capital or by the minimum cost of reproducing human beings. In fact, some of them held very advanced views and advocated profit sharing as a device to check labor unrest. John Williams set forth a plan whereby manufacturers would share profits with their employees after ten per cent interest had been paid on the capital invested in machinery and plant.[87] On every front the efforts of the propagandists of the high protectionist persuasion were directed to show that there was no essential divergence of interests among the producing classes. They would also bring farmers, laborers, and manufacturers into harmony with government by advocating a broad distribution of national securities. The *Iron Age* asserted: " Democratic stumpers are in the habit of telling the ' industrial class ' that they fight the battles and pay the taxes of the Government. Why do they never credit them with buying its bonds in its emergencies? Is it because that would kick the bottom out of the Democratic distinction of classes? " [88]

The high protectionists had no more sympathy with strikes and labor combinations than did the free traders.[89] A strike was a demonstrable negation of the idea of the harmony of interests. Their credo was designed to stimulate laborers and farmers to agitate in favor of a highly protected national economy. It was an attempt to channel labor unrest arising from economic grievances into a broad river of political agitation. The success they achieved will be discussed in the following chapter.

The question now comes to mind to what extent the demand

[86] *Commercial and Financial Chronicle*, II (March 31, 1866), 387.
[87] *Iron Age*, June 13, 1867.
[88] *Ibid.*, March 12, 1068.
[89] For Peter Cooper's unenlightened view of labor agitation, see Edward C. Mack, *Peter Cooper, Citizen of New York* (New York, 1949), pp. 361-362.

for easy money among the high protectionist manufacturing interest tended to create an alliance with those who favored the greenback as a superior form of currency and advocated an increase in the supply of money by simply resorting to the printing press. It must be admitted that the monetary rationale of the high protectionists would have carried them inevitably into the greenback movement of the seventies. As a corroboration of this, it is extremely significant to note that Henry Carey, Horace Greeley, and Peter Cooper all became disciples of the Kellogg currency school which advocated a greenback currency interconvertible with bonds bearing a low rate of interest.[90] In 1876 Peter Cooper was the Presidential candidate of the Greenback party.[91] These men were increasingly concerned with the problems we have outlined here—insufficient currency, rising interest rates, an adverse balance of trade, stagnation and depression.[92]

In general, however, the manufacturers did not rally around the greenback standard. Nor did Carey or Cooper or Greeley until the great depression following the panic of 1873 made it seem the only way out. The reasons are not hard to find. They are bound up with the word " repudiation," a word well calculated to make the manufacturers, a group which had bought the bonds of the United States during the Civil War, think twice about any expansion scheme dependent upon paying off the 5-20 bonds in greenbacks. The spokesmen for the high protectionist school were just as virulent in denouncing the " repudiation " schemes of Pendleton and Vallandigham as any Wall Street banker. The *Iron Age* referred to the " wickedness and folly in the project of Mr. Pendleton " and predicted that the American people would realize that it involved a " hideous scheme not only for the dishonor of the National credit but for the universal ruin of the people and the consequent disruption of the country." It was a scheme designed to

[90] For the views of Carey and Greeley, see Henry C. Carey, *Currency Inflation: How It Has Been Produced, and How It May Profitably Be Reduced. Letters to the Hon. B. H. Bristow, Secretary of the Treasury* (Philadelphia, 1874), pp. 15-20. For Cooper's similar view, see Mack, *op. cit.*, pp. 358-359.

[91] *Ibid.*, pp. 365-369.

[92] Henry C. Carey, *Letters to the Hon. B. H. Bristow*, pp. 4-5; 15-17.

achieve "the objects of certain political demagogues, and accomplish the restoration to power of the Democratic party." [93]

The mean between the extremes of flagrant greenback inflation and "repudiation" on the one hand and McCulloch's contraction and deflation on the other lay in an expansion of the amount of the National Bank currency sufficient to meet the needs of business. The $300,000,000 already authorized was held to be wholly insufficient, especially since, as we have noted, it was largely concentrated in New York and New England. The National Manufacturers' Association, meeting in Cleveland in May, 1868, advocated enlarging the National Bank currency on the basis of new low-interest gold principal bonds which should be used to fund the 5-20's.[94] John Williams and the *Iron Age* swung over to this position early in 1868. In an open letter to General Schenck, Chairman of the House Ways and Means Committee, Williams outlined his solution to the currency problem: "Remove the restriction at present imposed by the law upon the issue of National Bank currency. Let that be allowed to extend to any amount for which the proper security may be deposited, whether that amount be three hundred millions or a thousand millions. If, to meet the prejudice of those who fear an excessive circulation, some restriction should be thought desirable upon the amount of National Bank notes circulated, let the amount be limited to a thousand millions, and all other circulation (except gold or silver) absolutely prohibited." [95]

A week later the same journal asserted that "The present injustice to the West and South is too palpable and gross to be longer borne. . . . Why place any restrictions at all upon the amount of currency issued for which United States bonds have been pledged? Why not let every locality have just as large an amount of National Currency as it feels the need of?" [96] The *Commercial and Financial Chronicle* saw this scheme as just another subterfuge for inflating the currency and hopefully predicted that "The national cry for a sound currency will

[93] *Iron Age*, August 22, 1867.
[94] The New York *Times*, May 29, 1868.
[95] *Iron Age*, January 2, 1868.
[96] *Ibid.*, January 9, 1868.

certainly be heeded . . . by Congress that no further depreciation is to be attempted, nor any new emissions of any sort of paper money, especially of bank notes." [97] The point of view expressed by Williams and the National Manufacturers' Association eventually prevailed, for the Funding Act of July 12, 1870 authorized a $54,000,000 increase in bank-note circulation, and in 1875, the Resumption Act removed all limitations upon the amount of bond-secured currency which could be issued.[98] Ironically, this had no effect on increasing the supply of currency, because the rising premium on government bonds made it unprofitable to invest in them for currency issuing purposes when such currency could be issued to only ninety per cent of their par value.[99]

The foregoing analysis has demonstrated that the rationale of the high protectionist manufacturing interest tended inevitably toward a soft-money philosophy. After all reservations have been made and all deviations noted, the fact remains that in the period covered by this study, businessmen who held either free trade or low tariff views almost invariably lined up behind the gold standard. Conversely, those who favored protection almost to the point of prohibition were generally vacillating or soft in their attitude toward money. The heart of high protectionist-soft-money agitation lay in Pennsylvania. The most important non-agricultural products of the Keystone State were iron and coal. Their primacy was threatened in the domestic market by the pig iron of Scotland and the coal of Nova Scotia. Both are raw materials which enter largely into international trade. The fact that Pennsylvania had more to fear from foreign competition than Massachusetts or Rhode Island goes far toward explaining the economic ideas of Henry Carey and " Pig Iron " Kelley.

Historians who have identified sound money with high protectionism and the Republican Party would do well to reexamine the economic logic of the manufacturers as a producing group, particularly during the period of the greenback standard from 1862 to 1879. These years marked a late stage in the

---

[97] VI (June 6, 1868), 709.
[98] Dewey, *Financial History*, pp. 386-387.
[99] Redlich, *The Molding of American Banking*, II, 120-121; 123.

development of industrial capitalism in the United States and preceded the era of large scale business combination under the hegemony of finance capitalism. The desiderata of most manufacturers in these years were high prices, low interest rates, and a highly protected domestic market. High prices and low interest rates could according to the Careyite philosophy, best be achieved through an adequate and expanding volume of currency and credit. This soft-money position was perfectly consonant with high protectionism so long as paper money represented the standard of value and there was a premium on gold. Henry Carey had a perfect understanding of the linkage of the gold premium with protection to American industry and declared in 1865 that he would be happy to see gold remain at 200 for seven years as the " premium afforded a protection that even false invoices would not enable the foreigner to avoid." [100] The logic of this position eventually carried most of the intellectual apologists for high protection such as Carey, Cooper, and Greeley into a frank espousal of the doctrines of the Kellogg currency school. The more conservative manufacturers pressed the fight for expansion of the currency by agitating for an increase in bank-note circulation. Both factions agreed that the policy of currency contraction was ruining the industry of the country.

[100] Henry C. Carey, *Letters to the Hon. B. H. Bristow*, p. 7.

APPENDIX II

LETTER TO SENATOR JOHN SHERMAN FROM JONATHAN STURGES

One of the crucial factors which tended to bring manufacturers into the soft-money camp was the operation of the falling gold premium after 1865. It had a subtle effect and has largely been ignored or misunderstood by later generations. The following letter addressed to Senator John Sherman by Jonathan Sturges, a New York capitalist, gives a good account of how the falling gold premium adversely affected the American manufacturer.

New York
Dec. 29th, 1866

Hon. John Sherman
My dear Sir,

I regret not seeing you when you were last here. I should have been glad to have had a little talk with you about the Tariff, and the finances of the country, as each will have to be considered as more intimately connected with the other than ever before. What the industry of the country needs, is to be relieved from the shackles which the internal taxes have thrown around it, more than it does *increased protection*. It does not seem wise to me, to reduce the tariff on articles not produced in this country and not used in manufactures, if this necessitates the continuance of taxes on our own industry. There are some elements operating against our manufactures, which are not generally understood, and they will continue to act, so long as *money* is *cheap* in *Europe*, and *Gold* is *dear here*. All articles manufactured in Europe, are purchased upon a *Gold* basis, labor is paid for at Gold rates, so that all these manufactures are laid down here on a Gold basis. They are sold here on a *Currency* basis, which has been forty or fifty per cent above *Gold*. When sold for the account of European manufacturers, remittances are not made while Gold is up, but the money is borrowed in Europe at their *low rates*, until Gold falls here; this gives them a great advantage over our manufacturers, and, I have no doubt, is a serious cause of our present embarrassment. As soon as Gold falls twenty or thirty per cent, the foreign houses rush in and buy for remittances; and this puts gold up and enables them to go through the same operation again.

Our own manufactures are all on a Currency basis, (materials and labor) and are sold for *Currency*. When Gold falls, the manufacturer loses the difference on the stock on hand. Gold has fallen 20 per cent in 60 days. The foreign manufacturer, all things being equal, can sell 20% cheaper than we can goods manufactured before Gold fell. This may be remedied by increasing the duty on foreign manufactures until Gold falls, say for two years, and Foreigners will lose the advantage which they now have, just so soon as Gold is permanently lower. But our manufacturers need to *lessen production*, more than they need further protection. . . .

[The author goes on to advocate the public sales of gold in order to steady the movements of the premium.]

Very truly yours,

Jon. Sturges [1]

---

[1] Sherman Papers. Sturges was a merchant engaged in the importation of tea and coffee, a founder and director of the Bank of Commerce, and a director of several railroads.

CHAPTER V

LABOR IN TRANSITION

It should be confessed at the outset that of the economic groups considered in this study, manufacturers, labor, bankers, and farmers, the attitude of labor is easily the most difficult to understand from the standpoint of continuity. Why was the Locofoco hard-money attitude of workingmen of the pre-Civil War era abandoned in favor of the greenback expansion creed of Reconstruction? What Helderman has referred to as ". . . one of the most amazing enigmas of American financial history"[1] in noting the conversion of such old Jacksonians as George Pendleton and William Allen to the philosophy of paper money, applied with no less force to the labor movement, for labor had stood forth in the thirties and forties for hard-money and against the paper issues of banks both state and national.[2] Such an attitude was entirely consistent with the economic facts of life, for wage-earners were among those who believed themselves " regularly cheated by paper money." Workingmen who received their wages in bank-notes frequently discovered that these notes had depreciated in value, while some unscrupulous employers " even bought up depreciated notes and palmed them off on their workingmen at face value."[3] Is it any wonder that laboring men had come to put their trust only in specie? How then do we explain the about-face of the late sixties when a large majority of the leaders of the labor movement espoused the doctrine of paper money? Is this conversion truly an insoluble enigma or is it possible to discern a thread of consistency connecting pre-war and post-war attitudes? In order to answer such questions, it is necessary to go back to the impact of war on the labor organizations as they existed in 1861.

---

[1] Helderman, *National and State Banks*, p. 159n. *Supra*, p. 105.

[2] Arthur M. Schlesinger, Jr., *The Age of Jackson* (Boston, 1946), chs. 10, 15-16 .

[3] *Ibid.*, p. 120.

THE CIVIL WAR BACKGROUND

The prospect of civil strife in 1861 met with little enthusiasm in the ranks of organized labor. The leaders of the movement, men such as William Sylvis of the iron molders and Jonathan Fincher of the machinists and blacksmiths, were convinced that no real interest of labor could be served through war. After the prostrating panic of 1857 which brought unemployment or starvation wages to thousands of American workingmen, these men had pioneered the formation in 1859 of what were soon to become two of the most important national unions, the National Molders' Union and the International Union of Machinists and Blacksmiths. They were well aware that fratricidal strife would probably bring the destruction of the organizations they had put together with such difficulty.[4]

Important demonstrations of the attitude of workingmen toward the impending conflict took place in Louisville and Philadelphia. In the former city a mass of workers was addressed by the molders Robert Gilchrist and William Llorian. At this meeting it was resolved that the welfare of the workmen depended on the preservation of the Union and that slavery was but an "abstract issue" used to divide the masses.[5] To implement these sentiments a call was issued for a workingmen's convention which should take action to avert war.[6]

In Philadelphia plans were set in motion by William Sylvis and others to hold such a convention. Justifying this step in a letter published in *United Mechanic's Own* on February 12, 1861, Sylvis asserted: "Under the leadership of political demogogues and traitors scattered all over the land, north and south, east and west, the country is going to the devil as fast as it can. And unless the masses rise up in their might and teach

---

[4] John R. Commons *et al.*, *History of Labour in the United States*, 2 vols. (New York, 1918), II, 5-12.

[5] *Ibid.*, p. 10; Jonathan Philip Grossman, *William Sylvis, Pioneer of American Labor: A Study of the Labor Movement During the Era of the Civil War* (New York, 1945), pp. 45-46.

[6] James C. Sylvis, *The Life, Speeches, Labors, and Essays of William H. Sylvis, Late President of the Iron-molders' International Union; and Also of the National Labor Union* (Philadelphia, 1872), pp. 42-46.

their representatives what to do, the good old ship will go to pieces." [7]

A committee of thirty-four Philadelphia workingmen made all the arrangements for the convention. Scheduled to meet on Washington's birthday, it was thought appropriate to stage a parade before the delegates got down to business. Lining up shop by shop and trade by trade, the mechanics of the city marched through the streets bearing banners with such legends as " Concession not secession." [8] After the parade came the speeches. The convention was called to order by Sylvis, and a resolution was made in favor of the Crittenden compromise of " some other full and clear recognition of the equal rights of the South in the Territories by such enactment for constitutional action as will finally remove the question of slavery therein from our National Legislature. . . ." In another statement which well expressed the attitude of labor on the eve of conflict, the convention resolved " That our government never can be sustained by bloodshed, but must live in the affections of the people; we are, therefore, utterly opposed to any measures that will evoke civil war, and the workingmen of Philadelphia will by the use of all constitutional means, and with our moral and political influence, oppose any such extreme policy of fratricidal war thus to be inaugurated." [9]

Fear of competition from Negro labor was one of the most important reasons why many workingmen of the North were hostile to any war which would have as its object the overthrow of slavery. This fear was played upon by Democratic politicians and by newspapers opposed to the policies of the Republican party. On election day, 1860, James Gordon Bennett of the New York *Herald* made a last minute appeal to workingmen on behalf of the Democrats which attempted to capitalize on this fear. " If Lincoln is elected to-day, you will have to compete with the labor of four million emancipated negroes. . . . The North will be flooded with free negroes, and the labor

[7] Quoted in Terrence V. Powderly, *Thirty Years of Labor, 1859-1889* (Columbus, Ohio, 1890), p. 45.
[8] Grossman, *Sylvis*, p. 46; Powderly, *Thirty Years of Labor*, pp. 45-46.
[9] Commons *et al.*, *History of Labour*, II, 11-12.

of the white man will be depreciated and degraded." [10] A student of labor has pointed out that this sort of propaganda made a deep impression on the working people of New York, laying an insidious foundation for the viciously anti-Negro draft riots of 1863 in which many workingmen, chiefly Irish, participated.[11]

Labor opposition was of little effect against the tide of events which was leading inexorably toward conflict. The beginning of hostilities in the spring of 1861 dealt a heavy blow to labor organizations throughout the country. In a patriotic response to the firing on Fort Sumter, thousands of laborers and mechanics volunteered for service in the Army. In Philadelphia where one union enlisted to a man, the following entry was made on the records of the organization: " It having been resolved to enlist with Uncle Sam for the war, this union stands adjourned until either the union is safe or we are whipped." [12] In Illinois one of the first companies raised in St. Clair country consisted of coal miners, organized as the St. Clair County Miners and Sappers.[13] Martin Boyle resigned his post as "lecturer" for the American Miners' Association to form a company of volunteers of which he was elected captain.[14] In the molders' organization ex-president Isaac J. Neall was wounded, re-enlisted, and became a captain. Ex-treasurer Francis Rosche sacrificed his life for his country. Sylvis joined with other Philadelphia molders in forming a company to help repel Lee's invasion of Pennsylvania in 1863.[15] Taken altogether the record of the unions and of the union leadership in 1861 and 1862 is a commendable one. It is true, however, that as the war dragged on, certain new factors appeared which affected the attitude of labor leaders toward a conflict initially regarded as a selfless struggle for the preservation of the union.

[10] Quoted in Albon P. Man, Jr., "Labor Competition and the New York Draft Riots of 1863," *Journal of Negro History*, XXXVI (October, 1951), 379.

[11] *Ibid.*, p. 381. For another discussion of the hostility of Northern workingmen toward the idea of Negro competition, see Williston H. Lofton, "Northern Labor and the Negro During the Civil War," *Journal of Negro History*, XXXIV (July, 1949), 251-273.

[12] Powderly, *Thirty Years of Labor*, p. 57.

[13] Edward A. Wieck, *The American Miners' Association: A Record of the Origin of Coal Miners' Unions in the United States* (New York, 1940), p. 113.

[14] *Ibid.*, p. 113.   [15] Grossman, *Sylvis*, pp. 54, 48-49.

Disillusionment with the conduct of the war, the draft with its obnoxious exemption features, repression of labor organizations by employers and by the government, and the tremendous rise in the cost of living were all factors which caused some labor leaders to take a harder look at the effects of war upon their interests. Apathy and disillusionment with the war, of course, were not confined to the laboring classes in 1863 and 1864. In the latter year defeatism became the official doctrine of the Democratic party, and even stalwart Republicans such as Horace Greeley were infatuated with the idea that the war could be ended through negotiations. Dissatisfaction with the draft was especially prevalent among workingmen, for it was felt that the $300 exemption provision discriminated against the poor. " A poor man's blood for a rich man's money " was a popular slogan of the time.[16] This dissatisfaction culminated in the terrible New York draft riots in the summer of 1863 in which Irish workingmen were conspicuously prominent. Though hatred of the draft was an important factor in these riots, the real root of the trouble was the replacement of striking Irish longshoremen by Negro scabs, an action which contributed to the vicious anti-Negro flavor of these riots.[17]

Repression of labor organizations by employers and by the federal and state governments was fairly general throughout the Civil War. Particularly galling to workingmen were numerous cases of interference by the military. In St. Louis General Rosecrans intervened decisively in a strike of tailors and machinists through his famous General Order No. 65 which ordered among other things that " No association or combination shall be formed or continue, or meeting be held, having for its object to prescribe to the proprietors of any . . . establishment whom they shall employ therein, or how they shall conduct the operations thereof." [18] In this strike the leaders of the workingmen were arrested as a means of " securing the military power of the nation." At Cold Springs, New York a strike at the Parrot Shot and Shell Works was crushed by soldiers. The strike leaders were imprisoned without trial, and

[16] *Ibid.*, pp. 49-50.
[17] Man, *op. cit.*, pp. 375-405.
[18] Grossman, *Sylvis,* pp. 51-52, Appendix III, pp. 128-131.

upon release, made to leave town. General Burbridge in Louisville was another officer who felt it necessary to drive workers
back to their jobs with bayonets.[19]
Employers beset by strikes had recourse to the state legislatures during these years. Strikes in the Illinois coal fields led
to the passage of the notorious " LaSalle Black Laws " in
1863. The Act prohibited any two or more persons from combining " for the purpose of depriving the owner or possessor
of property of its lawful use and management," or preventing
" by threats, suggestions of danger, or other means," any workers from being employed by such employers.[20] The phrase " or
other means," of course, left a wide latitude of discretion. In
Massachusetts and New York anti-strike laws were introduced
in the state legislatures but were defeated largely because of
the efforts of labor.[21]
    In addition to the grievances of labor described above should
be mentioned labor's strenuous opposition to the breakdown
of the apprenticeship system and the related grievance of unrestricted immigration. The molders lost an important strike in
Philadelphia on the former issue, which can be briefly described as an attempt by employers to introduce into the shops
more than the usually prescribed number of apprentices and
thereby throwing journeymen out of work. It also tended to
create a surplus of journeymen upsetting the demand-supply
relationship within a given trade.[22] Unrestricted immigration
was a running sore which irritated labor leaders for years.
Employers in difficulties with intransigent workers found that
one of the most effective ways to deal with labor organizations
was to import thousands of docile foreigners to take the places
of those prone to heed the advice of labor agitators.[23] That this

[19] Ibid., pp. 51-52.
[20] Wieck, The American Miners' Association, pp. 128-131.
[21] Grossman, p. 52.
[22] Fite, Social and Industrial Conditions, pp. 188-189. For a discussion of the
molders' strike and the apprenticeship system in the molders' organization, see
Frank T. Stockton, The International Molders Union of North America (Baltimore, 1921), pp. 102, 170-185. For an interesting contemporary discussion of
the effects of the loose apprenticeship system, see James Dawson Burn, Three
Years Among the Working Classes in the United States During the War (London,
1865), pp. 182-190.
[23] Fite, pp. 190-196.

policy was considered eminently respectable is attested by the fact that the American Emigrant Company chartered under the laws of Connecticut in 1863 had as its sponsor many politicians and businessmen of more than local importance.[24]

These grievances were real and were deeply felt by the majority of American workingmen. They furnish the background from which there can emerge a clearer understanding of the root issue and grievances of the war years, the tremendous rise in the cost of living which followed hard upon the issue of the greenback currency in 1862. One authority on industrial conditions during the Civil War has characterized this as an issue ". . . of far more influence than any other, one in fact that created the atmosphere through which all other possible grievances quickly loomed large." [25] The consequences of the tremendous inflation of the war years would not have been so serious for the working class if wages had kept pace with the rise of prices. This, however, was not the case. Prices outdistanced wages throughout the war years, and it was only at the close of the conflict when prices fell rapidly that labor began to improve its relative position. In order to obtain a clearer picture of the position of workingmen during the Civil War decade, it will be helpful to reproduce once more that portion of Mitchell's table which furnishes indices for the general level of wages and the cost of living. Represented are medians of the cost of living and the average of January and July medians of relative rates of wages for the years 1860-1870.[26]

It is apparent that wages rose much more slowly than the cost of living in the early years of the war, that the discrepancy was greatest in 1864, and that the gap began to be closed in 1865. The natural consequence of the failure of wages to keep pace with rising prices was considerable suffering. Fite has produced illustrations of this suffering considerably more graphic than anything which could be deduced from a series

[24] Commons et al., Documentary History of American Industrial Society, IX, 75.
[25] Fite, p. 183.
[26] Mitchell, Gold, Prices, and Wages, Table 74, p. 279. For another statistical treatment, see Edith Abbott, The Wages of Unskilled Labor in the United States, 1850-1860 (Chicago, 1905), Table X, p. 363.

of index numbers. Most pitiable was the case of the seam-stresses who were employed in the making of clothes for the Army. Through a vicious system of contracting and sub-contracting which the Government did nothing to control, wages fell to incredible levels. For example, in 1864 when prices of the necessities of life were at a very high level, some contractors were paying only eight cents for making a shirt. In this same year a woman in New York using a sewing machine and supplying her own thread and working fourteen hours a day

Year	Cost of Living	Wages
1860	100	100
1861	103	100
1862	112	101
1863	129	112
1864	156	130
1865	168	150
1866	170	161
1867	168	168
1868	161	169
1869	156	175
1870	150	175

was able to make the princely sum of sixteen and three-fourth cents per day. An average week's wage paid by the contractors in 1865 was $1.54.[27] As Fite points out, "Employers were wont to appropriate to themselves all or nearly all of the profits accruing from the higher prices, without being willing to grant to the employees a fair share of these profits through the medium of higher wages."[28]

Although there can be little doubt of the very real suffering of the laboring class during the war, it is possible that Mitchell's statistics make the situation seem a bit worse than it actually was. This is likely, as one writer has observed, because Mitchell did not take into account the economic principle of substitution.[29] By including such items as cotton goods, tea, and coffee

[27] Fite, p. 184.

[28] *Ibid.*, p. 184. The tendency of active men of business to make economic gains at the expense of other social groups has been discussed. *Supra*, pp. 143-144.

[29] Barrett, *Greenbacks and the Resumption of Specie Payments*, p. 125.

in his list of commondities, Mitchell tended to distort the actual picture. Cotton almost disappeared from the economic horizon in the North during the war, and the price of what was available was naturally very high. Tea and coffee, being imported articles subject to taxes and the effects of Southern privateering also became very expensive. Substitution, however, could be employed in each case. Linens and woolens could be used in place of cotton goods and tea and coffee gave way to chicory, sassafras tea, and other cheap beverages.

It is apparent from the table that the relative position of the workingman began to improve in 1865. By 1867 real wages were the same as they had been in 1860. For the next three years the position of the laboring class improved as wages rose and the cost of living fell. This gain in real wages was accomplished despite the fact that thousands of soldiers returned from the battlefields to compete for jobs on the labor market. It has already been noted above that, with the sufferings of the war years a matter of recent experience, labor adamantly refused to accept placidly any attempt on the part of employers to cut wages after the war and frequently resorted to strikes to enforce their demands.[30] Although the relative position of labor improved in the post-war years, it must be remembered that there was considerable unemployment, particularly in the years 1866-1868. It was estimated by one labor leader in 1868 that there were 20,000 unemployed in New York City alone.[31]

During the war years the laboring man had witnessed a deterioration in his own economic position and consequently had considerable reason to feel himself aggrieved. While he suffered the loss of a substantial portion of his real income, other groups benefitted enormously, particularly as Mitchell points out " the active employer, who found that the money wages, interest, and rent he had to pay increased less rapidly than the money prices of his products." [32] Fite says that at the end of the war labor regarded itself as " persecuted, still arrayed against capital, still on the defensive and probably . . . worse off than in 1860. But . . . there had been improvement.

---

[30] *Supra,* p. 148.
[31] Commons *et al., History of Labour,* II, 123.
[32] Mitchell, *History of the Greenbacks,* p. 350.

Industrial wages had advanced from the low figure of 1863, the laborer was more sure of his daily bread from this source and of decent comfort than at the middle period of the war; his ability to lay by a part of the wage for a rainy day was improved, but he was still far from the good times of the previous decade. . . . With paper currency, and rising prices, scarcity of labor, and extreme industrial activity, an unusual set of new conditions arose, to which it behooved labor as well as capital to seek adjustment." [33] Only in the light of the new conditions created by the war can the history of the labor movement during the Reconstruction period be properly understood.

THE NATIONAL LABOR UNION

The years 1865-1870, which form the period of this study, coincide almost exactly with the rise and fall of the National Labor Union, for, although this organization lasted until 1872, its activities after 1870 were of little or no importance.[34] The impulse toward national unity in the labor movement had been strong at the outbreak of the Civil War. In 1860 President Isaac Casson of the machinists' and blacksmiths' union had suggested in his address " the cooperative alliance of all trades, and the erection of Trades' Assemblies to represent them, subordinate to a National Trades' Congress." [35] In 1861 this union resolved at its annual convention that ". . . this National Union appoint a committee . . . to request the appointment of a similar committee from other national or grand bodies to meet them, fully empowered to form a National Trades Assembly, to facilitate the advancement of the interests of labor. . . ." [36] This impulse foundered for the next three years on the shoals of war. It was only in 1864 when laboringmen throughout the country were organizing to fight for higher wages and better working conditions that national solidarity became feasible and desirable. This time the call came from the Trades' Assembly of Louisville. Published in *Fincher's Trades' Review* and signed by Robert

[33] Fite, p. 212.
[34] Commons *et al., History of Labour*, II, 153.
[35] *Ibid.*, p. 33.
[36] Commons *et al., Documentary History*, IX, 117.

Gilchrist, the anti-war labor leader referred to above, the call took cognizance of the fact that employers and capitalists throughout the country were combining to combat the aspirations of labor. "Are we to shrink with fear when we behold this spectacle? We answer, no; but it should stimulate us to powerful exertion; we ought to work with renewed energy and labor zealously to organize the mechanics of every branch, and if necessary, laboring men into protective unions, and draw these unions into international bodies, the same as the molders, machinists and blacksmiths, printers, etc." [37] The call asked that the various Trades' Assemblies send delegates to a convention to be held in Louisville on September 21, 1864. When the convention met, there were twelve delegates from eight city assemblies. Various resolutions were passed, and a constitution was drawn up which promulgated the International Industrial Assembly of North America. Although this organization was national in scope and similar in method and purpose to the National Labor Union, its life was limited to this one meeting. A possible explanation of this was the failure of the Industrial Assembly to enlist the support of the powerful Trades' Assemblies of Philadelphia in which Sylvis and Fincher were dominant figures.[38]

Two rival types of labor organizations pioneered the formation of the National Labor Union. The initial impetus came from the Trades' Assemblies, particularly those of New York and Indiana.[39] The decisive action was taken, however, by the leaders of the national unions. Sometime in February, 1866, Sylvis, president of the powerful Iron Molders' International Union, met in Philadelphia with William Harding of Brooklyn, president of the Coachmakers' International Union.[40] This meeting resulted in a preliminary conference of presidents of the various national labor organizations held in New York on

[37] *Fincher's Trades' Review*, August 13, 1864.
[38] Commons *et al.*, *History of Labour*, II, 33-39; Norman J. Ware, *The Labor Movement in the United States, 1860-1895: A Study in Democracy* (New York, 1929), pp. 2-3; Philip S. Foner, *History of the Labor Movement in the United States from Colonial Times to the Founding of the American Federation of Labor* (New York, 1947), pp. 360-362.
[39] Commons *et al.*, *History of Labour*, II, 95.
[40] Grossman, *Sylvis*, p. 224.

March 26. This conference issued a call for a national convention to be held in Baltimore on August 20, 1866. It was thought particularly desirable that members of labor organizations from the southern states take part ". . . as an evidence of a revival that is to give us new strength and power in the future." [41]

Seventy-seven delegates from thirteen states and the District of Columbia met in Baltimore on the appointed date. Fifty of these represented local trade unions. Seventeen were delegates from Trades' Assemblies, and seven represented eight-hour leagues. Only two of the national unions were represented as such since the leaders of these unions, having been largely responsible for initiating the convention, desired to stay in the background in order not to antagonize the Trades' Assemblies. [42]

From the outset the deliberations of the National Labor Union exhibited a political flavor. Wage conscious unionism was at a discount during the history of this organization. This was brought out in Baltimore in the report of the Committee on Trades' Unions and Strikes of which A. C. Cameron of Illinois, editor of the Chicago *Workingman's Advocate*, was chairman. This report was adopted by the convention and gave it as the " deliberate opinion " of the committee that strikes ". . . have been productive of great injury to the laboring classes; that many have been injudicious and ill-advised, and the result of impulse rather than principle. . . ." The committee advised that strikes be discountenanced ". . . except as a *dernier* resort, and when all means for an amicable and honorable adjustment have been exhausted." [43]

The questions which animated the proceedings of the convention were those of land reform, political action, and the eight-hour movement. The last two were the most important. Although political action was not favored by some of the delegates, particularly those under the influence of Jonathan Fincher, a consistent trade unionist and opponent of political

[41] *Iron Molders' International Journal*, I (April, 1866), 19; Powderly, *Thirty Years of Labor*, p. 63; Grossman, *Sylvis*, p. 224.

[42] Commons *et al., History of Labour*, II, 96-97.

[43] *Iron Molders' International Journal*, I (September, 1866), 180. The proceedings of the 1866 convention will also be found in Commons *et al., Documentary History*, IX, 127-168.

agitation, the majority was in favor of it. A resolution was adopted to the effect that ". . . the history and legislation of the past had demonstrated the fact that no confidence whatever can be placed in the pledges or professions of the representatives of existing political parties so far as the interests of the industrial classes are concerned: . . ." and that "the time had come when the workingmen of the United States should cut themselves aloof from party ties and predilections, and organize themselves into a National Labor Party, ..." [44]

The primary purpose of political action was ". . . to secure the enactment of a law making 'eight hours' a legal day's work by the national Congress and the several states legislatures, and the election of men pledged to sustain and represent the interests of the industrial classes." [45] The eight-hour movement was largely the work of one man, Ira Steward of Massachusetts, a monomaniac who was able to elicit something of a philosophy of life from the central idea of shortening the hours of labor. [46] It need not concern us here except to note that it preceded currency reform as the dominant cause of the National Labor Union. The convention adjourned after electing officers and providing for an organizational structure in which each trade union, workingmen's association and eight-hour league should be entitled to one delegate for the first five hundred members or less, and one delegate for each additional five hundred or fraction thereof. Each national or international union was also allowed one delegate. It was also provided that a convention of the National Labor Union be held each year. [47]

Between the conventions of 1866 and 1867 the doctrine of currency reform captured the labor movement in America. It would be a mistake to regard this doctrine which inspired the leaders of the National Labor Union as simple greenbackism, for this term tends to connote a purely inflationary point of view. [48] Inflation was an incidental and not even a particularly

---

[44] *Iron Molders' International Journal,* I (September, 1866), 181.

[45] *Ibid.,* I (September, 1866), 181.

[46] Ware, *The Labor Movement,* pp. 4-8; Commons *et al., History of Labour,* II, 87-94.

[47] *Iron Molders' International Journal,* I (September, 1866), 180-181.

[48] This is the term used by John B. Andrews in describing Kellogg's doctrine. See Commons *et al., History of Labour,* II, 119-124. As indicated above, the

desirable concomitant of the ideal of currency reform. The key to the doctrine was an exposition of the role of the rate of interest in determining the disposition of labor's product among the various classes of society. It was a typically American approach to the problem of the growing concentration of wealth. Similar problems in Europe had given rise to the scientific socialism of Karl Marx.

The idea which inflamed the leaders of the various labor organizations in 1867 traced its origin to an obscure New York businessman of the pre-Civil War era. His name was Edward Kellogg, and for want of a better name we shall call his philosophy Kelloggism. It was a genuinely American philosophy of action in the economic sphere which was designed to satisfy the aspirations of the petty bourgeoise, of what both William Sylvis and Henry Carey could refer to as " the producing classes " as opposed to bankers, stockjobbers, and usurers.

Edward Kellogg was born in Norwalk, Connecticut in 1790. He was one of many children of a typical Yankee farmer. Helping his father on the farm during his boyhood, he was early noticed for his energy and resourcefulness. When he came of age, he began to buy goods in New York and sell them to country storekeepers in New Jersey, Pennsylvania, Maryland, and Virginia. Around 1820 he set himself up in business in New York City as a wholesale dry goods merchant. Kellogg prospered until the panic of 1837 when he was unable to collect from some of his debtors and was forced to suspend. It was at this time that he began his analysis of the existing monetary system in light of his own experience. A small merchant in trouble, he had found himself unable to obtain bank credit in an emergency except at usurious rates. He devoted long hours of thought to problems of finance and finally arrived at a solution to these problems which he described at length in a work published in New York in 1849 entitled *Labor and Other Capital: The Rights of Each Secured and the Wrongs of Both Eradicated. Or, An Exposition of the Cause Why Few Are Wealthy and Many Poor, and the Delineation of a System,*

present author believes the term " greenbackism " tends to distort the real meaning of Kellogg's program.

*Which, Without Infringing the Rights of Property, Will Give
to Labor Its Just Reward.* Until his death in 1858, Kellogg
strove constantly to gain recognition for his work but was
unsuccessful. It was only after the issue of greenbacks in 1862
that certain reformers could see merit in many of his arguments.[49]

As is the case with many works in political economy whose
essential object is reform, Kellogg's work is part analysis and
part panacea.[50] At the outset he disassociates money from
value.[51] Value accrues only to property, which is the product
of nature or of labor making use of natural resources. Money
is simply a legalized agent to represent property.[52] Since its
usefulness depends upon its legal qualities, there is no reason
why money must be made from gold or silver. " The fact that
it takes many thousand times more labor to mine the gold and
silver and coin them into money, than it does to make the
paper and engrave the bank-notes, makes no difference in the
market value of the money, because the value of the money depends on its immaterial power—that is, upon its legal authority,
and not at all upon its material substance." [53]

Besides being the legal representative of value, money is also
the measure of value. " The government reserves the right to
fix the length of the yard, the weight of the pound, the size
of the bushel, and the value of the dollar, that they may be
fitted for public use. Money is the public measure of value;
and the government is bound to make it just and uniform,
that it may correctly determine the value of all commodities." [54]
How then is this measuring power itself to be determined?

[49] This biographical material is drawn from a sketch by Mary Kellogg Putnam
in Edward Kellogg, *A New Monetary System: The Only Means of Securing the
Respective Rights of Labor and Property, and of Protecting the Public from
Financial Revulsions*, ed. Mary Kellogg Putnam, 6th ed (Philadelphia, 1878).
This book was a revision of Kellogg's earlier work *Labor and Other Capital* and
is the work cited here in discussion. It is interesting to note that the 1878 edition
was published by Henry Carey Baird & Co., publishers of the works of Henry
Carey and William D. " Pig Iron " Kelley. An interesting discussion of Kellogg
and his theories can be found in Destler, *American Radicalism*, Ch. IV.
[50] For example the works of Karl Marx and Henry George.
[51] Kellogg, *A New Monetary System*, p. 44.
[52] *Ibid.*, p. 44.
[53] *Ibid.*, p. 55.
[54] *Ibid.*, p. 59.

" Money," wrote Kellogg, " is valuable *in proportion* to its power to accumulate value by interest. A dollar which can be loaned for twelve per cent interest is worth twice as much as one that can be loaned for but six per cent, just as a railroad stock which will annually bring in twelve per cent, is worth twice as much as one that annually brings in six per cent. . . . Any increase or diminution of the power of money to accumulate by interest, increase or diminishes proportionably its value, and consequently its power over property." [55]

According to Kellogg it is incumbent upon the government to set a rate of interest which will fairly determine the measuring power of money. The next question is what constitutes a fair rate of interest. Kellogg's criterion is the amount of increase in the national wealth which should be properly and fairly distributed to labor. " The money of a nation, instead of being a power by which a few capitalists may monopolize the greater part of the earnings of labor, ought to be a power which *should distribute products to* producers, according to their labor expended in the production." [56] Kellogg believed that high rates of interest were the means by which capitalists appropriated to themselves a lion's share of the national income.[57] The wealth of the country increased by a certain percentage each year, probably about two or three per cent. [The rate is nowhere stated but is implicit.] If capitalists are able to extort rates of ten or twelve per cent for their money, it was obvious to Kellogg that not only would the entire normal annual increase in national wealth accrue to them but inevitably the property of labor as well.[58] Thus would the producing classes become pauperized and the capitalists grow richer and richer. In this manner Kellogg made the rate of interest the key to the financial problem of the country.

After analysis follows the remedy. " The plan requires the General Government to establish an institution, with one or more branches in each State. This institution may appropriately

[55] *Ibid.*, pp. 61-62. Kellogg denies that money has value, but here he says that it is " valuable." What he means is that money has no inherent value but that it can be invested with market value through the action of the state.

[56] *Ibid.*, p. 37.

[57] *Ibid.*, p. 181.

[58] *Ibid.*, p. 237.

be called the NATIONAL SAFETY FUND: first, because the money of this institution will constitute a legal tender of uniform value for the whole people, and will always be safe; second, because the interest being fixed at a just rate it will secure the respective rights of labor and capital; and third, the supply of money being always commensurate with the wants of business, it will effectually protect the nation from financial revulsions." [59] The Safety Fund would lend money on real estate mortgages to half the value of the property mortgaged. These loans of Safety Fund legal tenders would be made at a rate of one and one-tenth per cent which Kellogg adjudged a fair rate to offset the costs of the banking operation. The Fund would also issue notes or bonds bearing interest at one per cent.[60] It would consequently be impossible for the rate of interest to rise much above one and one-tenth per cent, since any property owner could borrow from the fund at that rate. An oversupply of money would also be impossible since, if the commercial rate fell below one per cent, holders of legal tenders could always invest them in the notes or bonds of the Safety Fund.[61]

As was pointed out earlier, this scheme was throughly bourgeois in method and outlook. It was geared to meet the needs of the farmer, the mechanic, and the small businessman. Kellogg emphasized this aspect of his program. "Who are those directly interested in the adoption of the Safety Fund? All agriculturalists, manufacturers, mechanics, planters, in short, all who wish to earn a support by honest industry. Merchants will do a safe business in exchanging products, and their profits will be moderate and sure. Nine-tenths of our whole population will receive the pecuniary benefit which is justly their due, and the remaining one-tenth will be left in undisturbed possession of their present wealth, and like their fellow-citizens, at liberty to increase it by any useful employment." [62] He disavowed any radical notions. "The Safety Fund contemplates no agrarian distribution. It asks for no distribution of lands and property, and for no contributions of money by either the Government or individuals to the support

[59] *Ibid.*, pp. 274-275.
[60] *Ibid.*, p. 276.
[61] *Ibid.*, pp. 284-285.
[62] *Ibid.*, p. 320.

of laborers. Laborers will need no favors. They only require that the Government establish a just standard of value, which will allow them to possess an equitable share of the fruits of their labor." [63]

Kellogg firmly believed that his interconvertible bond-currency scheme would bring about the millenium. Unfortunately he did not live to see the influence of his ideas on the labor movement of the sixties. The issue of the greenbacks in 1862 followed by the passage of the National Banking Acts in 1863 and 1864 allowed critics to compare the two systems of currency. It was in this context that Kellogg's ideas first began to receive notice.

In 1864 there was published in Chicago a pamphlet by Alexander Campbell, an obscure labor and currency reformer, which supplied the necessary link between the ideas of Edward Kellogg and the new financial conditions created by the Civil War.[64] In the first half of his treatise Campbell used all Kellogg's arguments with regard to the nature of value and its distinction from money. He also used similar arguments and examples to show that the rate of interest was too high and that this factor was causing the wealth of the country to be concentrated in fewer and fewer hands.[65] By using some actual and some hypothetical statistics, Campbell computed that the annual rate of increase in the capital of the country from 1790 to 1860 had been four per cent.[66] He pointed out, however, that this rate was above normal and due to exceptional circumstances such as the acquisition of large amounts of new territory. The true rate of capital gain, he felt, was about three per cent.[67] In Campbell's system which he called "The True American System of Finance," this rate would be the rate of interest on government bonds. The system was outlined in the following manner: "The issue of Treasury Notes, without interest, made a legal tender for the payment of all public and

[63] Ibid., p. 320.
[64] A. Campbell, The True American Sysem of Finance; The Rights of Labor and Capital, and the Common Sense Way of Doing Justice to the Soldiers and Their Families. No Banks: Greenbacks the Exclusive Currency (Chicago, 1864).
[65] Ibid., pp. 1-27.
[66] Ibid., pp. 12-13.
[67] Ibid., pp. 12-13.

private debts, in denominations to meet all the wants of business interests, and convertible, at the option of the holder, into Government Stocks bearing three per cent interest per annum, payable annually in lawful money of the United States. These stocks to be made reconvertible into legal tender Treasury Notes, at the option of the holder, at any time after one year from the date of the issue of said stocks." [68]

Writing in 1864, Campbell guessed that the national debt at the end of the war would be around two billion dollars.[69] He proposed that another $600,000,000 of greenbacks be issued and used to retire a like amount of the debt, leaving the debt at $1,400,000,000. The interest on the latter would be set at three per cent.[70] Greenbacks and bonds would be interconvertible. If the commercial rate of interest rose above three per cent, bonds would be converted into legal tenders and the rate would be driven down. If the commercial rate fell below three per cent, greenbacks could be converted into bonds. Unlike Kellogg, however, Campbell did not propose that the government loan money on real estate mortgages.[71] He apparently felt that if the soldiers and suppliers of war materials to the government were given the opportunity to buy government bonds, it would insure a wide enough distribution to guard against a manipulation of the bonds and the currency by capitalists.

There is evidence that Campbell's ideas began to be influential in reform circles as early as the summer of 1866. In June of that year a mass meeting of farmers and laborers was held in Bloomington, Illinois.[72] A Declaration of Principles

---

[68] *Ibid.*, p. 27.

[69] *Ibid.*, p. 29.

[70] *Ibid.*, p. 30.

[71] *Ibid.*, p. 32.

[72] It is interesting that farmers were mentioned as being in attendance at this meeting although it is clear that their influence and interest was slight. Throughout the history of the National Labor Union efforts were made to enlist the support of farmers though with scant success. In the Chicago convention of 1867 Sylvis hotly denied a report in the *Tribune* which pointed out that the farmers of the country were unrepresented. The credentials of the delegates, however, make it clear that no farm organization was represented as such. Commons *et al.*, *Documentary History*, IX, 169-171, 188. It is significant that in dealing with the charges made by the *Tribune* that farmers had no interest in the labor congress, George E. McNeill, a contemporary New England labor leader, admitted

was adopted containing passages which are the same, word for word, as passages in the Declaration of Principles subsequently adopted by the National Labor Union in August, 1867. Among the tasks essayed by the Bloomington meeting was the interpretation of history along radical lines. The Declaration asserted that bankers and capitalists ". . . have dictated every monetary, financial, and revenue measure that has passed Congress excepting alone the issue of treasury notes [the greenbacks]. To this measure and to it alone is the government indebted for its financial success. When this just, reasonable and practicable measure was first presented it met with their [the bankers] opposition. . . . The Secretary of the Treasury (their agent) in his report to Congress, presented some of the advantages that the government would derive from the issue of treasury notes but said he did not recommend the measure, and dwelt at considerable length on the advantages and importance of the so-called National Banking System, for which a bill was immediately introduced into Congress but kept in obeyance [sic] until the fate of the rebellion was clearly decided. . . . They went on demanding increased rates and warring on the credit of the government until the interest on the government securities averages full nine per cent. When it became evident that the rebellion would be overthrown at an early day, they brought forward their bank scheme, and forced it through Congress under the pressure of necessity." [73]

When the convention of the National Labor Union met in Chicago in August, 1867, the committee on political organization was headed by A. C. Cameron, editor of the Chicago *Workingman's Advocate.* It is more than likely that Cameron was responsible for the Declaration of Principles adopted, a fact which would explain its similarity to the Bloomington Declaration with which Cameron was familiar. The Declaration was modelled on the Declaration of Independence and followed the same form in attributing iniquity to capitalists

that this was "measurably true of that day." George E. McNeill, *The Labor Movement: The Problem of Today* (Boston, 1887), p. 136. This substantiates the position taken in Appendix I above that farmers had little interest in monetary reform and other radical schemes.

[73] This meeting and the Declaration of Principles adopted were reported in the Chicago *Workingman's Advocate,* June 30, 1866.

just as Jefferson chronicled the sins of George III. It denounced
the National Banking System as ". . . a delegation by Congress
of the sovereign power to make money and regulate its value
to a class of irresponsible banking associations, thereby giving
to them the power to control the value of all the property in
the nation, and to fix the rewards of labor in every department
of industry, . . ." It asserted that ". . . this money monopoly
is the parent of all monopolies—the very root and essence of
slavery—. . . ." As long as ". . . these unrighteous laws of
distribution remain in force, laborers cannot, by any system of
combination or cooperation, secure their natural rights." [74] But
how was this yoke of servitude to be removed? Here the
Kellogg-Campbell scheme is brought to bear.[75]

We hold that this can be effected by the issue of treasury notes made
a legal tender in the payment of all debts public and private, and convertible at the option of the holder into government bonds, bearing a
just rate of interest, sufficiently below the rate of interest in the
national wealth by natural production, as to make an equitable distribution of the products of labor between non-producing capital and labor,
reserving to Congress the right to alter the same when, in their judgment the public interest would be promoted thereby; giving the government creditor the right to take the lawful money or the interest bearing
bonds at his election, with the privilege to the holder to reconvert the
bonds into money or the money into bonds, at pleasure.

There was some debate upon the adoption of the interconvertible bond-currency scheme. Several of the delegates held
to the old pre-war bias in favor of gold and silver as a measure
of value, but after a speech by Richard Trevellick, representing
the Detroit Trades' Assembly and the ship carpenters' union,
in favor of the Declaration, it was adopted.[76]

There can be little doubt but that most of the important labor
leaders present at the 1867 congress regarded the money question as the supremely important issue of the time. Sylvis,

[74] Commons *et al.*, *Documentary History*, IX, 178-179. The proceedings of
the 1867 congress are also recorded in the Chicago *Workingman's Advocate*,
August 24-31, 1867.

[75] Commons *et al.*, *Documentary History*, IX, 180.

[76] *Ibid.*, IX, 183. Trevellick was certainly the most consistent and long suffering of the advocates of the Kellogg-Campbell scheme. As late as 1893 he was
still propagandizing in its behalf. See Richard F. Trevellick, *Money and Panics*
(Detroit, 1893).

Trevellick, Cameron, J. C. C. Whaley, who was president of the National Labor Union in 1866 and 1867, John Hinchcliffe of the American Miners' Association, John Maguire of the Workingmen's Union of Missouri, Susan B. Anthony, and others were agreed on this point. Jonathan Fincher was the only important leader present who deprecated the prevailing belief in the Kellogg-Campbell financial panacea, and even he admitted that paper money was a necessity.[77] Sylvis was so convinced of the validity of the Kellogg-Campbell analysis that he wrote in 1868 that ". . . when a just monetary system has been established, there will no longer exist a necessity for Trade Unions. . . ."[78]

The thread of consistency which connects the monetary ideas of the pre-Civil War and post-Civil War labor movements is a general hatred and distrust of banks, bankers, and bank-notes. The importance of this thread as a means of understanding the two movements cannot be overemphasized. Experience with the worthless shinplasters issued by the state banks during the Jacksonian period as well as with the political overtones of central banking as practiced by Nicholas Biddle had convinced the leaders of the labor movement that the workingmen could put their confidence only in gold or silver. The Civil War introduced a new set of conditions to which adjustment had to be made. Gold and silver virtually disappeared from circulation after the suspension of specie payments in December, 1861.[79] The only thing laboring men knew of gold during the war years was what they read in the newspapers about the activities of the gold gamblers in New York, activities which had a considerable effect on the price level.

In 1862 came the first issue of paper money. Greenbacks rapidly became the money of account, the money of trade, and the money in which wages were paid. It became the money of the people. In the meantime the National Banking Acts were passed by Congress, and in 1864 national bank currency came into general circulation. It was understood that the issues of these banks were based on government bonds and that many

---

[77] Commons et al., Documentary History, IX, 209.
[78] Quoted from his letter addressed to the "Working People of the United States," Chicago Workingman's Advocate, December 12, 1868.
[79] Barrett, Greenbacks and the Resumption of Specie Payments, p. 55.

of these bonds, bearing six or seven per cent interest *in gold* had been purchased by " patriotic capitalists " at fifty or sixty cents on the gold dollar in 1863 and 1864. Not only did these bankers draw gold interest on the non-taxable bonds they had deposited with the government, but they also got interest on the bank-notes they issued as well.[80] Workingmen felt that the war on greenbacks was only a tactic designed to insure that control of the entire currency supply should fall into the hands of bankers.

Just before the meeting of the labor congress of 1867 the Chicago *Workingman's Advocate* compared the two types of currency and found that " The advantages of greenbacks or treasury notes over every other sort of currency are so obvious, that the popular preference for, and determination to have them, is not at all surprising." [81]

The day has gone by when the people will ever submit to a State Bank currency and the taxations and discounts inseparable from it. The circulating notes of the National Banks have this quality of equal value everywhere in the country, which the people, taught by the losses of half a century, have come to demand as the essential quality of a currency; but this system is not only costly, but in creating special privileges for a special class in the community, is repugnant to the principles of free government and odious to the feelings of the American people. Every man who has a United States bond has just the same right or ought to have, to deposit it at Washington and receive notes for it, all the while drawing interest upon it as well as speculating with the money thus received, as the bankers. So long as any man who holds a bond which is the basis of the issue of the national currency, cannot receive money for his bond as well as interest on it, so long does the law discriminate against him, simply because he is not a banker, and in favor of another because he is a banker. Legislation which thus respects class and persons, must either yield to the democratic principle of our political institutions, or those institutions must conform to the nature of monarchical government.

Over a year later the same paper could find even less virtue in the National Banking System, arguing that since it was ". . . plainly impossible to have gold and silver in quantities sufficient for the commercial needs of the country, the question is whether the government shall furnish the paper issues, which

[80] Dewey, *Financial History*, pp. 326-328.
[81] Chicago *Workingman's Advocate*, August 3, 1867.

shall have all the qualities of money, and which, in fact, shall be made money by the same unquestionable authority which makes gold and silver money or whether the government shall abdicate this power . . . into the hands of a small class of men chartered by act of law to furnish a wildcat currency, to engross and speculate upon the products of labor, to swindle and cheat without restraint. This system of banking the nation is fully acquainted with. It has so wrought its curse upon the industrial classes that they had come to think there was no safety to them except in an exclusive gold and silver currency." [82]

Since gold and silver as money was obviously impractical, the solution was greenbacks infinitely preferable to the bank-notes of the " swindling and cheating " bankers. Considered from this viewpoint it is not difficult to explain the transition of labor leaders from the hard-money attitudes of the age of Jackson to the soft-money radicalism of Reconstruction. Another point which should be borne in mind is that the period from 1860 to 1870 was one of nationalization in many phases of economic life. It was the period of the National Banking System, the national income tax, the draft laws, the high protective tariff, the Homestead Act, the various railroad land grant acts, and the creation of an enormous public debt. The old *laissez faire* attitudes of the forties and fifties had given way to new concepts of government. Various interests came to the fore and demanded special favors. Through the agency of the Legal Tender Acts the government had taken a long step toward nationalizing the medium of circulation. It was only natural that the laboring class should endeavor to make its voice heard in preserving the " money of the people " as opposed to the money of the bankers.

The motives which impelled the leaders of the National Labor Union to embrace the soft-money philosophy are thus seen to have been the same as the motives which drove old Jacksonians such as George Pendleton, Francis Preston Blair, Jr., and William Allen to the same conclusion. In both cases a dislike and distrust of bankers and bank-notes plus a conviction that the sovereign power of providing a monetary medium should not be abdicated to any group of businessmen supplies

[82] *Ibid.*, December 19, 1868.

the thread of consistency which enables us to understand what has been referred to as ". . . one of the most amazing enigmas of American financial history." [83]

Reform of the currency became the *cause celebre* of the National Labor Union in 1867. It maintained its hold on the leaders of the N. L.U. until the practical demise of that organization in 1870.[84] There is evidence that in the years from 1867 to 1870 currency reform was not just the ruling passion of a group of labor leaders but that it penetrated to the level of the rank and file as well. Understanding on the part of workingmen of the economic effects of an insufficient money supply and support for the principle of monetary reform appears in the columns of correspondence of the *Workingman's Advocate*, the leading labor journal of the period and the official organ of the National Labor Union. Correspondents from many sections of the country digressed on the importance of the currency question. A correspondent from Philadelphia wrote that " The want of sufficient money to properly transact the business of the country is making itself more seriously felt in this section than ever before and hundreds are daily being thrown out of employment without having been able during the summer . . . to lay away a dollar." [85] A correspondent from North Carolina opined that if there ". . . is too much money in circulation why is it that none of it finds its way to us? " This writer pointed out that wages at the Highshoals Iron Works in his state were 75 cents per day.[86] A letter from Illinois contained the statement that " The amount of greenbacks should be increased to accommodate the business of the country and made receivable for all dues to the Government and individuals, including duties on imports." [87] From the Mississippi valley came the opinion that " The monetary reform is the fundamental principle. Let that be secured and the whole is easy." [88] Similar conclusions were reached by other correspondents.[89]

[83] *Supra*, pp. 105, 174.
[84] See the debates and resolutions of the conventions of 1868, 1869, and 1870 in Commons *et al., Documentary History*, IX, 206-218, 234-236, 262-266.
[85] Chicago *Workingman's Advocate,* December 19, 1868.
[86] *Ibid.*, January 16, 1869.
[87] *Ibid.*, May 8, 1869.
[88] *Ibid.*, September 18, 1869.
[89] See letters of the correspondent from Philadelphia in *ibid.*, January 16, 1869;

Workingmen's meetings also provide some indication of the influence of the money issue on the rank and file. At such a meeting held in Cincinnati in September, 1867 a resolution was passed ". . . in favor of contracting the National bank currency, and expanding with equal step, the legal tender (greenbacks), until the National banks shall be entirely wound up. . . ." [90] At a rally of workingmen held in Cooper Union in the summer of 1868, an address was made advocating the payment of the national debt in currency.[91] A meeting of Labor Union # 1 of Elkader, Iowa in 1869 adopted a straight National Labor Union program calling for the abolition of the National bank currency and the payment of the 5-20 bonds in greenbacks.[92]

THE SITUATION IN NEW ENGLAND

Just as the New England manufacturers failed to present that solid front in favor of soft-money and high protection which was typical of their colleagues in other sections, so did the labor movement which centered around Boston fail to lend its wholehearted support to the Kellogg-Campbell currency reform program. This is not to say that no support for currency reform existed in New England, for such a statement would not be accurate. A strong movement in favor of the monetary program of the National Labor Union actually developed in 1869 and centered around the New England Labor Reform League, but this support began to gain momentum two years after the basic principles had been enunciated at the labor congress of 1867. In the years 1866 through 1868 when the National Labor Union was most active and most viable, New England labor's interest in the currency issue was virtually non-existent.

New England labor's failure to become enamoured of currency reform in the years when the Kellogg-Campbell philosophy became the official doctrine of the national labor move-

from a writer in New York, April 10, 1869; from a correspondent in Missouri, July 10, 1869.
[90] *Ibid.*, September 21, 1867, in which the Cincinnati *Times* of September 13 is quoted.
[91] *Ibid.*, July 11, 1868.
[92] *Ibid.*, August 7, 1869.

ment was not due to a lack of interest in labor reform generally but rather to commitment to a rival philosophy. This was the eight-hour doctrine, which, in the hands of Ira Steward, certainly attained all the dimensions of a philosophy.[93] To Steward the sole object of labor organizations should be agitation for the eight-hour day. He was impatient with and contemptuous of other objectives. In a letter published in the leading labor newspaper of New England just before the Chicago convention of 1867, Steward deprecated the concern which the previous Baltimore congress had shown for a wide variety of issues. He hoped that the Chicago congress would show more wisdom. " Until we learn, therefore, to narrow down our platform to the real and only issue, we must expect nothing but evasion from the opposition. . . . If . . . the Chicago Convention resolved to present the great Labor Reform movement to the country upon the single issue of *more time for the workers* free from all local, narrow, partisan, and obscure questions, it will find enough to do to make that successful." [94]

Steward's influence was very great in New England, and he did not stand alone in his efforts to keep the labor movement of his section on the straight and narrow course toward the eight-hour goal. He was seconded by his friend and fellow eight-hour enthusiast George E. McNeill who agreed with Steward that the hours of labor was the only issue worthy of strenuous effort.[95] McNeill was active in the publication of the Boston *Daily Evening Voice*, and it was more or less inevitable that the journal should reflect the bias of the eight-hour movement.[96] The *Voice* tended to take a somewhat dim view of the activities of the National Labor Union. Reporting on the deliberations of the Chicago congress it opined: " So far the doings of the Congress have a rather foggy aspect. Little appears to have been maturely considered." [97] When the Chicago congress recommended that workingmen become active politically and run their own candidates for office, the *Voice*

[93] Commons *et al.*, *History of Labour*, II, 87-96.
[94] Boston *Daily Evening Voice*, August 1, 1867.
[95] McNeill, *The Labor Movement*, pp. 124-132; Commons *et al.*, *History of Labour*, II, 92.
[96] *Ibid.*, II, 92n.
[97] Boston *Daily Evening Voice*, August 27, 1867.

was strongly opposed, asserting that there was not enough "coherence" among New England workingmen to sustain a political party.[98]

Although the *Voice* never actively opposed the currency reform doctrine of the National Labor Union, its sympathies did not lie in the direction of soft-money. In an editorial entitled "The Financial Evils We Suffer" published in the fall of 1866, the paper asserted that what was needed was "Resumption of specie payments, so that a dollar will mean a dollar, and we shall know what it is worth in London or Paris. . . ." Another thing needed in the opinion of the *Voice* was a reduction of the tariff.[99] In May of 1867 the thought was expressed that the ". . . paper money system, high tariffs, exemption of government bonds from taxation, etc. . . ." was "imposing upon the laboring classes the exclusive burden of paying off the public debt. . . ."[100] Such an attitude precluded sympathy for the paper money crusade of the National Labor Union.

The New England labor movement was unique in this period in that it was profoundly influenced by the thought and activities of a group of reform conscious intellectuals including Ezra A. Heywood, Amasa Walker, Wendell Phillips, Josiah Warren, William B. Greene and others. After the war these intellectuals, who were mostly men of superior education and good social position, attained commanding positions in various labor organizations, frequently making speeches and engaging in political activity in behalf of the labor movement. As early as November, 1865, for example, that great American radical, Wendell Phillips, turned from the cause of abolition to the cause of labor. In a speech in Faneuil Hall in which he championed the eight-hour movement, Phillips reflected: "It is twenty-nine years this month since I first stood on the platform of Faneuil Hall to address an audience of the citizens of Boston. I felt then that I was speaking for the cause of the laboring man, and if tonight I should make the last speech of my life, I would

[98] *Ibid.*, September 19, 1867.
[99] *Ibid.*, September 28, 1866.
[100] *Ibid.*, May 24, 1867.

be glad that it should be in the same strain,—for laboring men and their rights." [101]

Until at least 1869 the intellectuals were in fundamental agreement with Ira Steward that the currency reform panacea was a delusion and a snare. According to Steward Phillips advised in 1866: "Don't meddle with ethics, don't discuss debts, keep clear of finance, talk only eight-hours." [102] At this time Amasa Walker, the economist, and Ezra Heywood, the anarchist, agreed that the paper money creed boded no good to the cause of labor. In a speech delivered before a mass meeting of workingmen at Worcester in September, 1867, Walker argued that laboring men are being "robbed by a redundant currency." [103] A week later Walker and Heywood addressed another mass meeting at Worcester. On this occasion Heywood asserted that "Labor reform will stand the test of the hard coin of reality, and welcomes to its service the accurate precision of sound finance. . . . Hard-money, free trade, supremacy of the people to government, these are labor principles." [104] Such admonitions must have had their effect for among the resolutions of the second meeting was one which noted that ". . . an irredeemable paper currency is a most active and prevalent invasion of the common welfare." [105]

After 1867 Heywood and Phillips began to abandon the high ground they had taken on financial issues and emerged eventually on the extreme left of the monetary reform party. In this position they joined the Boston anarchist, former Army officer, philosopher, theologian, and lawyer, William B. Greene, who had been a monetary reformer for some twenty years.[106] Why Heywood should have abandoned his 1867 sentiments on "sound finance" is something of a mystery. The probable explanation is that like William B. Greene he had been influenced by the ideas of the French philosopher, Pierre-Joseph

[101]Wendell Phillips, "The Eight-Hour Movement," *Speeches, Lectures, and Letters,* Second Series (Boston, 1891), p. 139.

[102] Quoted in Commons *et al., History of Labour,* II, 143n.

[103] Boston *Daily Evening Voice,* September 25, 1867.

[104] *Ibid.,* October 2, 1867.

[105] Chicago *Workingman's Advocate,* October 12, 1867.

[106] Joseph Dorfman, *The Economic Mind in American Civilization,* 3 vols. (New York, 1949), III, 36-37.

Proudhon, who advocated the establishment of mutual banking, a scheme which would allow groups of producers to gain credit by issuing non-redeemable notes based on pledges of property.[107] Such a scheme, of course, was totally inconsistent with a hard-money philosophy.

In 1869 Heywood became president of the New England Labor Reform League, an organization which derived support both from the intellectuals and the labor unions. In his opening address to the League in June, 1869 Heywood emphasized the financial question, and a series of resolutions was offered in which it was asserted that " the use of one's credit as of his conscience or his vote, is a natural right, antecedent to, and independent of government," but that the government by " its claim to dictate the nature and amount of money, especially to restrict it to gold and silver, naturally scarce, and easily hoarded enables the privileged few in control to make interest and prices high, wages low, and failures frequent, to suit their speculative purposes." [108] The specific remedy which the League prescribed for these evils was enunciated at a meeting held in Boston in October. The organization demanded " the immediate withdrawal of the exclusive national bank-notes to be replaced with treasury certificates of service receivable for taxes and bearing no interest and the provision of free banking laws whereby money based on commodities may be furnished anywhere at cost." [109] The League in its program thus coupled a demand for government issues of greenbacks with Proudhon's scheme of mutual banking.

Wendell Phillips' conversion to currency reform postdated that of Heywood by about two years, and the main influence on the great Massachusetts Radical was that of Edward Kellogg rather than Proudhon.[110] In the post-Civil War period Phillips was the most prominent American who advocated the cause of

---

[107] *Ibid.*, III, 37.

[108] *American Workman*, June 5, 1869, quoted in Commons *et al., History of Labour*, II, 138-139.

[109] Chicago *Workingman's Advocate*, October 23, 1869.

[110] Foner, *The Labor Movement*, p. 426. A copy of Kellogg's *Labor and Other Capital* in the possession of the present writer is inscribed " Wendell Phillips Esq. With the respects of Mary E. Kellogg Putnam." Mary Kellogg Putnam was the daughter of Edward Kellogg and was prominent in the labor movement of the sixties.

labor. Nor was his advocacy lukewarm or detached. The same fanaticism which made Phillips' phrase, " One, on God's side, is a majority " more than just a motto but the guiding principle of his life projected the zealous Boston Brahmin into the mainstream of the labor reform movement. In September, 1870 Phillips was the nominee of the Labor Reform Party for the governorship of Massachusetts. In acknowledging the nomination Phillips asserted: " Capital and labor—partners, not enemies—stand face to face, in order to bring about a fair division of the common profits. I am fully convinced, that hitherto legislation has leaned too much—leaned most unfairly —to the side of capital. Hereafter it should be impartial." [111]

A year later Phillips had moved closer to a radical financial position. At the Labor Reform Convention which assembled at Worcester, September 4, 1871, Phillips presided and presented the platform which resolved, " That we declare war with the wages system, which demoralizes alike the hirer and the hired, cheats both, and enslaves the workingman; war with the present system of finance, which robs labor, and gorges capital, makes the rich richer, and the poor poorer, and turns a republic into an aristocracy of capital; war with these lavish grants of the public lands to speculating companies, . . . ; war with the system of enriching capitalists by the creation and increase of public interest-bearing debts." [112] Early in 1872 Phillips moved completely into the Kellogg-Campbell camp. In address before the International Grand Lodge of the Knights of Saint Crispin in April, the great Radical made his position clear.[113] " I say, let the debts of the country be paid, abolish

[111] Wendell Phillips to Charles Cowley, Esq., September 12, 1870. Reproduced in George Lowell Austin, The Life and Times of Wendell Phillips (Boston, 1901), p. 259.

[112] Wendell Phillips, " The Foundation of the Labor Movement," in Speeches, Lectures, and Letters, Second Series, pp. 152-153.

[113] From the point of view presented in this study Wendell Phillips is almost the " ideal type " of Radical Republican. His Radicalism on the Negro question is of course well known, but more significant from our point of view is his economic Weltanschauung. In this connection it is fascinating to note that Phillips coupled his soft-money views with a belief in protection. One of his biographers has found this fact " paradoxical," but, of course, from the viewpoint of this study, it is completely consistent. See Ralph Korngold, Two Friends of Man, The Story of William Lloyd Garrison and Wendell Phillips and Their Relationship with Abraham Lincoln (Boston, 1950), pp. 378-388. It is also

the banks, and let the government lend every Illinois farmer
(if he wants it), who is now borrowing money at ten per cent,
money on the half-value of his land at three per cent. The same
policy that gave a million acres to the Pacific Railroad, because
it was a great national effort, will allow of our lending Chicago
twenty millions of money, at three per cent, to rebuild it." [114]

Phillips would thus rescind the note issuing privileges of the
national banks, replace the national bank-notes by greenbacks
issued by the government, and require the government to make
loans to producers at low rates of interest. In putting the government in the banking business and permitting loans on real
estate security, Phillips was closer to the original program of
Edward Kellogg than to the Campbell modification of the
National Labor Union, but the general objective is the same,
namely the overthrow of the "money monopoly" by guaran-
teeing credit to producers at low rates of interest. [115]

The currency reform issue was not simply the hobby horse of
the intellectuals in the New England labor movement. It was
considered the paramount question of the day by such union
leaders as Samuel P. Cummings and President William J.
McLaughlin of the Knights of Saint Crispin, the shoemakers'
organization which in the late sixties and early seventies was
one of the strongest labor organizations in America. [116] The
importance of the currency issue to the political labor movement
in New England is attested by the election of William B.
Greene, the long-time money reformer, as president of the
Massachusetts Labor Union. [117]

interesting to note that in 1871 Phillips ardently supported his fellow Radical
and money reformer, Benjamin F. Butler, in his bid to secure the Republican
party's nomination for Governor of Massachusetts. Phillips liked Butler because
of his fight against the "money power" and his natural inclination toward the
cause of the common man. *Ibid.*, pp. 370-372.

[114] Wendell Phillips, "The Labor Question," in *Speeches, Lectures, and Letters*,
Second Series, p. 176.

[115] At a speech before the financial department of the American Social Science
Association in 1875, Phillips added a further refinement to the Kellogg scheme,
suggesting that bondholders be allowed to deposit their bonds with the government, borrow full value on them at three or four per cent, and continue to
receive the interest on the bonds. Phillips thought that individuals should be
able to have the same privileges as national banks. Austin, *Wendell Phillips*,
pp. 308-309.

[116] Commons *et al.*, *History of Labour*, II, 76-79, 140.

[117] *Ibid.*, II, 142.

Though the currency reform issue had attained hegemony over the minds of a number of the leaders of the labor movement in New England, it was a divisive rather than a unifying force. Ira Steward and George McNeill were incensed that the financial issue had become so prominent to the neglect of the eight-hour movement. Failing in their attempt to dominate the New England Labor Reform League in the interest of the eight-hour reform, they established in 1869 the Boston Eight-Hour League as a rival organization. At one of its conventions it was " Resolved, That the Boston Eight-Hour League records its most emphatic protest against the discussion or the consideration of financial theories, in the name of Labor Reform." The resolution went on to declare that such questions as taxation, currency, interest, protection and free trade, railroad and banking management, and civil service were " economical humbugs, the settlement of which the best way, still leaves the laborer a laborer, and the captalist a capitalist, between whom there is an irrepressible conflict which must continue until all are laborers and all are capitailsts." [118]

The gulf between the eight-hour advocates and the currency reformers was unbridged, despite occasional attempts at cooperation such as occurred in 1870 when both groups joined in an unsuccessful campaign to elect Wendell Phillips Governor of Massachusetts. By 1872 the political labor movement in Massachusetts was of little consequence and consisted of two small and hostile groups, one led by Steward and McNeill which continued its fanatical advocacy of eight-hours, and the other led by Phillips which accorded the currency issue first place among desired reforms.[119]

THE ESSENTIAL CONGRUITY OF SOFT-MONEY PHILOSOPHIES

It is significant at this point to consider the similarities which existed between the theories of the high protectionists and the ideas which dominated the leaders of the American labor movement in the sixties. No evidence has been found that Henry Carey or his disciples were ever regarded as spokesmen for the

[118] The resolutions are reproduced in McNeill, The Labor Movement, pp. 140-141.
[119] Commons et al., History of Labour, II, 142-143.

laboring class. On the contrary, John Williams, editor of the *Iron Age* and one of the chief expositors of Carey, was strongly denounced for his sponsorship of the American Emigrant Company whose object was to stimulate emigration from Europe in order to break the back of labor organizations in the United States.[120] It is likely that Carey and his followers were far more profoundly impressed by the theories of Edward Kellogg than the labor movement was ever influenced by the ideas of Henry Carey.[121] On the other hand there is a tremendous similarity in phraseology and ideas between the Careyites and the leaders of the National Labor Union. This can only be explained if we understand that there was a fundamental congruity between the soft-money philosophies, a congruity which led both the Careyites and the followers of Kellogg and Campbell to the same conclusions.

Carey's theory of the union of the producing classes could almost have been lifted intact from the pages of the *Workingman's Advocate*. Beneath the title in every issue was carried the legend, " Dedicated to the Interests of the Producing Classes of the Northwest." Both the Careyites and the Kelloggites were convinced that the cause of industrial distress lay in the high rates of interest. Both were convinced that the " producing classes " were paying tribute to bankers and usurers. Both felt that New England and New York, where banking capital was largely concentrated, were exacting tribute from the rest of the country. The following paragraph written by William Sylvis a few months prior to his death in 1869 could well have come from the pen of the high priest of Pennsylvania protectionism, so similar in tone are the sentiments expressed.

" The manufacturer, the farmer, the business man of any kind needing money, must pay from 10 to 30 per cent for the use of it. In many cases the profits of his business are less than the rate of interest demanded. To borrow would be ruinous, therefore, his business must languish, or what is very frequently the case, a reduction of wages is made. This reduction does not always, as is supposed, go into the pocket of the employer,

---

[120] Chicago *Workingman's Advocate*, February 13, 1869. For evidence of Williams' part in this project, see Commons *et al.*, *Documentary History*, IX, 75.
[121] *Supra*, p. 168.

but into that of the money-lender. Thus do employer and
employee suffer from this system of legal robbery, called interest
on money." [122] And again from an editorial dealing with the
regional aspects of the problem. " By gold paying laws, including the payment for public lands as well as impost duties,
. . . gold was largely circulated at New York City, and by the
humbug, or rather the robbery of the gold basis system, she
was able to make the whole country pay her the tribute demanded." [123]

Compare Carey's well known views on English classical political economy with those of Sylvis. " The whole system of
political economy, from beginning to end, is an apology for
tyranny, and the whole tribe of political economists are humbugs;
they are such because they have humbugged the people, and
at their head stands the prince of humbugs, John Stuart Mill." [124]

Striking similarities are evident between the two schools of
thought in the foregoing instances. It is, however, the issue of
protection versus free trade which provides us with the key
to ascertaining the fundamental congruity of the two points of
view. The attitude of the leaders of the labor movement on this
issue is particularly interesting because, unlike manufacturers,
the workingmen had no real and tangible interest in the question. Probably as much can be said to support the view that
labor is better off under conditions of free trade as can be said
for the other side of the coin. The point is that men like
Cameron, Sylvis, and Trevellick were led to a moderate support
of protectionism by the inherent logic of the soft-money
philosophy. The journal of Sylvis' own union presented the
case for protection late in 1866. Noting that there had been
a substantial balance of imports over exports in recent years,
workingmen were asked ". . . to look well into these facts, and
ask themselves what the result of such a condition of things
must be. The simples question is this:—is it better for the
workingmen of America that we pay $100,000,000 in gold for
goods made in foreign countries, and by labor at one-third the

[122] Chicago *Workingman's Advocate*, March 20, 1869. This is from a series of
articles entitled " What is Money? " which also appears in James C. Sylvis, *Life
of William H. Sylvis.*
[123] Chicago *Workingman's Advocate*, August 10, 1867.
[124] *Ibid.*, May 1, 1869.

price paid here, and the same goods to be sold at a less price than the same articles can be made for here, or to make these goods themselves?" The article went on to point out that " It is a well known fact to every intelligent man, that there exists among us a ' ring ' or combination, composed almost exclusively of foreign importers, and the agents of foreign manufacturers, who have millions of dollars to spend to defeat any effort made by Congress for the protection of our industry." The author of this article (who may well have been Sylvis himself inasmuch as he was editor of the journal) felt that the best interests of the workingmen would be served by " a well-regulated protective system, and a fair home competition." [125] The case for protection could hardly have been better stated by Henry Carey himself.

It is not implied here that labor was united in favor of a protective tariff. The *Workingman's Advocate* pointed out that ". . . there is no political question upon which there is a greater diversity of opinion than the mythical question of ' Free Trade,' . . . there are thousands of mechanics who have given this subject careful consideration . . . who are honestly convinced that the present protective tariff means protection only to monopoly, protection to the manufacturer and capitalist." But the article continued ". . . a large number of our mechanics entertain the very opposite opinion, and believe that protection to American industry is a panacea for the wrongs of the workingman. . . ." [126] The position of William Sylvis and Andrew Cameron, co-editors of the *Workingman's Advocate*, on this issue was presented in an editorial entitled " Protection or Free Trade " which appeared in the summer of 1869.[127]

We have purposely omitted any reference to the " all engrossing question of ' Free Trade,' " because we have been opposed to the intro-duction of any issue not germane to the principles of the National Labor Union. But as we have no wish to dodge the matter we reply, " We are in favor of a *protective tariff* for the benefit of the American mechanic, and opposed to a New England prohibitory tariff for the enrichment of the American capitalist." As a great diversity of opinion exists, however, among our readers on this much vexed question, we have

---

[125] *Iron Molders' International Journal*, I (December, 1866), 276.
[126] Chicago *Workingman's Advocate*, August 4, 1866.
[127] *Ibid.*, July 24, 1869.

deemed discretion the better part of valor, and preferred to confine our efforts to the attainment of a system by which both Free Trade and Protection will become obsolete issues.

This last reference, of course, is to the Kellogg-Campbell interconvertible bond-currency panacea.

Diversity of opinion on the question of free trade versus protection is borne out by the debates and resolutions on the subject at the annual congresses of the National Labor Union. At the 1867 convention, two motions, one in favor of protection, the other in favor of free trade, were tabled, indicating that there was little desire to go into the subject. There was little discussion of the issue at the congresses of 1868 and 1869, but in 1870 a mildly protective tariff was favored in a resolution which was adopted calling on Congress to lay duties ". . . upon such articles of manufacture, as, we having the raw material in abundance, will develop the resources of the country; increase the number of factories, give employment to more laborers, maintain good compensation, cause the immigration of skilled labor, the lessening of prices to consumers, the creating of a permanent home market for agricultural products, destroy the necessity for the odious and expensive system of internal taxation, and will soon enable us to successfully compete with the manufacturers of Europe in the markets of the world." [128]

The attitude of labor leaders on the tariff issue is, of course, an interesting phenomenon in itself. What makes it doubly interesting is the fact that the strongest advocacy of the protective principle in the labor movement of the sixties came from the very elements who were staunchest in their support of the currency expansion platform of the National Labor Union. The essential congruity of the philosophy of high protectionism with that of the leaders of the National Labor Union is apparent. In fact, in all that is fundamental, in the emphasis on low interest rates, an adequate supply of currency, distrust of the "money monopoly," the union of the producing classes, and the principle of the protected home market—the outlook of the high protectionists and the Kelloggite leaders is virtually identical.

[128] Commons et al., Documentary History, IX, 266.

LABOR AND POLITICS

It remains to consider how labor viewed those political issues of the day which related to the financial portions of the platform of the National Labor Union. The picture which emerges shows quite clearly that financial policy was the key issue which determined labor's attitude toward political parties and politicians. Actually, the N. L. U. had little regard for either of the two great parties. In the Baltimore convention of 1866, a resolution was offered and adopted to the effect that ". . . the history and legislation of the past has demonstrated the fact that no confidence whatever can be placed in the pledges or professions of the representatives of existing political parties so far as the interests of the industrial classes are concerned." The remedy was for laborers to ". . . organize themselves into a National Labor Party. . . ." [129] Similar resolutions were offered in succeeding congresses, though it was not until 1870, when the N. L. U. had virtually disintegrated, that a procedure was devised for creating such a party.[130] The most effective demonstration during this period that workers could with proper organization send their own representatives to Congress took place in Cincinnati where labor managed to elect Samuel F. Cary as Representative from the second district.[131] Some transitory success was also achieved in Massachusetts in 1869 when the Labor-Reform Party elected one of its candidates to the state senate and twenty-two to the lower house of the state legislature.[132]

Although the National Labor Union did not support either of the two major parties, there were individuals within both parties who were supported by the labor press. Praise was meted out to those politicians, Republican and Democratic, whose financial views either conformed or were similar to those contained in labor's platform. Among Republicans Thaddeus Stevens and Benjamin F. Butler were singled out for special consideration. " Butler and Stevens, and many others, are nobly striving to induce the payment of the federal bonds in accord-

[129] Commons et al., Documentary History, IX, 135.
[130] Ibid., IX, 175, 204, 232.
[131] Commons et al., History of Labour, II, 130.
[132] Foner, The Labor Movement, p. 425.

ance with the plan proposed by the Labor Congress; and the
votes which have been already given indicate that the infamous
scheme of Blaine, Morrill, and others, who propose to increase
forty per cent the public debt, the burden of which now op-
presses every productive industry, and paralyzes every effort of
honest labor, will be defeated." [133] Even in this period of his
chameleon-like career when Butler was regarded as one of the
most ultra of the Radical Republicans, he was elevated to the
pantheon of labor heroes. The Philadelphia correspondent of
the *Workingman's Advocate* wrote: " The supporters of the
National Labor Union owe General Butler a debt of gratitude for
his assumption of their cause and for the able manner in which
he has forced its consideration upon the country." [134] Butler's
speech of January 12, 1869 delivered in Congress in favor of
a national paper currency was adjudged " an intellectual treat "
which all workingmen should read.[135] Butler avowed in an
interview that ". . . the National Labor Union platform will
find in him an unwavering and unflinching advocate." [136] The
particular scheme advocated by the General (and it must be
confessed that devising new currency systems was one of the
favorite hobbies of the post-Civil War generation) differed
somewhat from the Kellogg-Campbell program. Butler proposed that the national banks be abolished, but that every man
be afforded the privilege once accorded the bankers, namely,
that citizens be allowed to deposit their bonds with the government and receive 90 cents in greenbacks for every $1.00 in
bonds so deposited. Since the amount of bonds outstanding
was something over two billion dollars, a generous supply of
currency would be assured.[137]

Other Republicans who were regarded as having views very
sympathetic to labor were Senators Sprague of Rhode Island
and Wade of Ohio. In March of 1869, Sprague introduced a
bill in Congress which would have required all government
deposits to be withdrawn from the national banks and re-

---

[133] Chicago *Workingman's Advocate,* December 7, 1867.
[134] *Ibid.,* January 30, 1869.
[135] *Ibid.,* January 30, 1869.
[136] *Ibid.,* December 26, 1868.
[137] *Congressional Globe,* 40th Congress, 3rd Session, 303-310. This was
similar to the plan proposed by Wendell Phillips in 1875. See *Supra,* p. 205 n.

deposited in the sub-treasury in New York. These government funds would then be used to create poor men's banks which would make loans at a low rate of interest. Sprague, himself a prominent textile manufacturer, was convinced that American business was suffering from foreign competition because of high rates of interest.[138] Although his scheme differed from that of the National Labor Union, its emphasis on the nefarious influence of high interest rates was in the right spirit and Sprague gained labor support. After the bill was introduced, Washington workingmen serenaded the Senator and congratulated him on his bill.[139]

Senator Ben Wade was regarded as a man sympathetic to labor. Jay Cooke, a banker with banker's prejudices, accused Wade of being a " reckless demagogue " who tried to " array labor against capital." [140] In 1867 the leading New England labor journal referred to Wade as a " true man and a patriot " and asserted that " if the workingmen make a nomination for the presidency, this man of all others should be their choice." [141] Invited to lecture before the Workingmen's Institute of Boston, Wade found himself unable to accept, but in a letter to George McNeill he averred that now that the question of slavery had been settled, there was nothing to " prevent the laborer's attaining that dignity and consequence in the community to which he is entitled." The Senator " rejoiced to see the almost universal awakening of the laboring classes." [142] A few months before the *Voice* reprinted a report of an interview with Wade in which the Ohioan had said: " That system of labor which degrades the poor man and elevates the rich, which makes the rich richer and the poor poorer, which drags the very soul out of the poor man for a pitiful existence is wrong. We must

---

[138] *Ibid.*, 41st Congress, 1st Session, pp. 64-66. See also Belden and Belden, *So Fell the Angels*, p. 223.

[139] Chicago *Workingman's Advocate*, May 1, 1869.

[140] Oberholtzer, *Jay Cooke*, II, 28.

[141] Boston *Daily Evening Voice*, September 16, 1867. Alexander Campbell, the currency reformer of the N. L. U., took occasion to write to Wade in the summer of 1867 because the Senator's speeches " clearly indicate that you believe labor has rights—as well as money, or non-producing capital which our law-makers are bound to recognize and respect." Alexander Campbell to Wade, June 29, 1867. Wade Papers, Library of Congress.

[142] *Ibid.*, September 16, 1867. Chicago *Workingman's Advocate*, September 21, 1867.

elevate the laborer, and give him a share in the proceeds of his labor." [143] Such sentiments led labor leaders to feel that in Ben Wade the workingman had found a sincere champion. With regard to the Johnson administration the perceptions of labor journalists were quite acute. The impeachment proceedings were regarded as a " fizzle to amuse the public " while the plans were made by politicians under the influence of bankers and capitalists to push through bills providing for the gold payment of the 5-20 bonds. [144] Johnson himself was treated rather sympathetically, especially after he received a delegation from the National Labor Union after the Baltimore convention of 1866. [145] On the other hand, the Secretary of the Treasury, Hugh McCulloch, was thought to be an agent of the bankers and was consequently subjected to considerable abuse. The following bit of sarcasm from the pages of the *Workingman's Advocate* is a good case in point. " ' The legal tenders are a contrivance for cheating the laboring classes,' says the Secretary of the Treasury, his tender heart gushing over with sympathy for the welfare of these classes. From his vantage ground he has witnessed with painful emotions the losses which farmer and mechanic have endured from the legal tenders, and he sighs for a return to the system of wild catting pursued so profitably by a few gentlemen in Indiana and where his first laurels as a financier were won." [146] Opposition to McCulloch's contraction of the currency was strenuous and sustained. When the Chicago *Tribune* made a reference to the Secretary's policy, the *Advocate* exclaimed, " It is unfortunate for the *Tribune* to refer to Secretary McCulloch's policy; it should be frank and say the ' bankers' and usurers' policy,' for the Secretary is but their agent; and that paper knows their policy will be the one that will lay the heaviest burdens on the tax payers for the benefit of the ' Christian bankers and usurers! ' " [147]

Among Republicans heaviest fire was leveled at the gold redemptionists. Chief devils were Justin Morrill and James G.

[143] Boston *Daily Evening Voice,* June 29, 1867. The interview was originally printed in the Cincinnati *Commercial.*
[144] Chicago *Workingman's Advocate,* June 6, 1868.
[145] Commons *et al., History of Labour,* II, 103.
[146] Chicago *Workingman's Advocate,* December 19, 1868.
[147] *Ibid.,* August 3, 1867.

Blaine referred to above as well as Senator Morton of Indiana.[148] Opinion on the powerful Senator from Ohio, John Sherman, who was Chairman of the Senate Finance Committee, varied with the opinions of the Senator which, to say the least, were extremely vacillating. In 1868, Sherman found favor with labor after he had introduced a bill providing that 10-40 bonds be made convertible into greenbacks at the discretion of the holder.[149] Later on, however, Sherman was associated with the passage of the Public Credit Act of 1869 which in unequivocal language pledged the faith of the United States to pay the 5-20 bonds in gold.[150] The Ohio Senator was bitterly attacked for his part in this legislation.[151]

The attitude of labor toward the presidential campaign of 1868 was mixed and skeptical. Evidence emerges of a predisposition in favor of the Republican party. In reporting a convention of workingmen held in Ottawa, Illinois in the fall of 1867, it was asserted: " Three-fourths of the convention were Republicans, men who have done much for the success of that party, but when that party turns a deaf ear to all petitions for relief against lavish expenditure, excessive rates of interest, curtailment of the currency, and kindred measures which oppress the industry of the nation, these men are forced to abandon their party predilections and form another whose object shall be the good of the country." [152] Another editorial condemned the attitude which seemed to prevail among the Republican leadership that payment of the 5-20's in greenbacks was wrong just because it was supported by Democrats. " If Democracy presents arguments correct in themselves, but which they are sure opponents will not accept, in them they have the most effective engine for the destruction of the Republican party. But if the latter would at once accept whatever is just and right as readily for toiling whites as for Southern slaves, Democracy would be thoroughly disarmed of its sharpest and most potent weapons, and the party of political progress would quietly march in the road of uninterrupted success." [153]

[148] *Ibid.*, October 5, 1867.
[149] *Ibid.*, April 11, 1868.
[150] *Supra*, pp. 125-126.
[151] Chicago *Workingman's Advocate*, April 24, 1869.
[152] *Ibid.*, September 7, 1867.
[153] *Ibid.*, October 5, 1867.

There was a definite disinclination to trust the Democrats on financial questions. The reason for this was the complete realization by labor leaders that the Democratic party was strongly influenced at the top echelons by a group of hard-money New York bankers and capitalists. The fact that August Belmont, American agent of the Rothschilds, was Chairman of the Democratic National Committee was sufficient evidence on this point.[154] Disillusion with parties and with politics in general was summed up in an editorial published in the *Advocate* early in 1868.[155]

. . . If it should appear how much stock Congressmen own or have owned in the various railways which have been built by grants of public lands, one reason would be manifest for the lavishness of those grants. If it should appear how much bank stock Congressmen own, one reason would appear why the National Bank System should be considered the best in the world. If the precise relations between Wall Street and the Secretary of the Treasury were known, the public would have the key to his contraction policy, and similar relations would explain why the Senate Finance Committee think the Federal bonds, payable by law in greenbacks, should be paid in gold.

By February, 1868, it had become apparent that General Grant was an odds-on favorite to receive the Republican nomination. This prospect was viewed with little enthusiasm. General Grant was asserted to be a " toady of the monied aristocracy " and labor would support " the devil on a People's platform in preference to Gen. Grant or Gabriel on a platform framed by the bondholders." [156] Later on it was stated that the General ". . . has studied the signs of the times to little purpose, if he imagines for a moment that his name, great as it is, can bolster up a rotten cause, or wheedle the people into a support of our present financial system." [157]

As the campaign gathered momentum, there was a definite swing toward the Democratic party. The reasons are not hard to find. In April the Illinois State Democratic Convention passed resolutions in favor of paying the 5-20 bonds in greenbacks, against the National Banking System, and in favor of

---

[154] Coleman, *Election of 1868*, p. 39.
[155] Chicago *Workingman's Advocate*, January 18, 1868.
[156] *Ibid.*, February 1, 1868.
[157] *Ibid.*, February 22, 1868.

taxation of income from government bonds. The Republican State Convention came out in favor of paying the 5-20's in gold. The *Workingman's Advocate* lauded the action of the Democrats while deploring that of the Republicans.[158] In May the Republican National Convention meeting in Chicago adopted a platform which denounced repudiation in all its forms, though it failed to point out in which repudiation consisted.[159] The chief organ of labor reform denounced the Republican platform as having been written in the interest of the bondholders.[160] The secret of "their enigmatical platform" was said to be a desire to introduce the "consol system" of bonds running "forty or fifty years, bearing some five or six per cent interest, and interest and principal payable in gold." [161] On the other hand, the Democratic National Convention which met in July adopted a platform containing "out-and-out greenback planks." [162] Rapid payment of the federal debt was endorsed, and where they "do not expressly state upon their face, or the law under which they were issued does not provide, that they shall be paid in coin . . . ," the bonds "ought in right and justice to be paid in the lawful money of the United States." [163] The Democratic platform also called for taxation of government bonds and demanded one currency for the government and all the people, including the laborer and the bondholder.

Given the two platforms, it was only natural that labor support tended to swing toward the Democrats, although there was considerable dissatisfaction with Horatio Seymour, the Democratic standard bearer, who was known to possess strong hard-money-anti-repudiation sentiments. In September, the *Advocate* came very close to saying that labor should endorse the Democratic ticket at the forthcoming New York convention of the National Labor Union.[164] It became known in August

[158] *Ibid.*, April 18, May 9, 1868.
[159] Coleman, *Election of 1868*, p. 39.
[160] Chicago *Workingman's Advocate*, May 23, 1868.
[161] *Ibid.*, June 6, 1868.
[162] Coleman, p. 39.
[163] *Ibid.*, p. 39.
[164] The N. L. U., however, did not endorse either party. Commons *et al.*, *Documentary History*, IX, 195-227. Chicago *Workingman's Advocate*, September 19, 1868.

that labor's congressional champion, Samuel F. Cary, was supporting the Democrats.[165] Despite this trend, labor had few illusions about the real nature of the Democratic party. The *Advocate* quoted approvingly the analysis of the New York *Democrat* that George H. Pendleton had not been asked to speak in New York City because ". . . Mr. Pendleton's paper money ideas were antagonistic to the interests of the Rothschilds and their agents here. . . ."[166] This was a direct reference to August Belmont.

When the results of the election became known, labor once more retreated into its "plague on both your houses" attitude. A long impassioned editorial pointed out that Seymour would have won the election had he come out strongly against paying the 5-20's in gold and in favor of greenbacks as against the national bank-notes.[167] A Pennsylvania correspondent ruefully acknowledged that many workers had voted Republican because they regarded the Democrats as the party of "Southern supremacy."[168]

Passage of the Public Credit Act in 1869 was the occasion for an indignant outburst. "The keynote of the present administration is the legalization of gold contracts, or virtually legislating out of the people one hundred dollars, with six per cent gold interest for every forty dollars furnished by the capitalists. This kind of legislation has a gold basis and a specie-returning in it with a vengeance and is only equalled in enormity by furnishing to capitalists the cash means to build the Pacific Railway at enormous profits, in the shape of depreciated gold bearing and gold principal paying bonds, charged over to the people, and re-duplicated by enormous donations of public lands."[169]

The influence of labor in the campaign of 1868 was not strongly exerted in favor of either the Republicans or the Democrats. Within each party there were men whose financial views were similar to those expressed in the platform of the National Labor Union. In the Republican party these views were held by a group of arch-Radicals including Thaddeus

[165] *Ibid.*, August 1, 1868.
[166] *Ibid.*, September 6, 1868.
[167] *Ibid.*, December 19, 1868.
[168] *Ibid.*, October 31, 1868.
[169] *Ibid.*, August 21, 1869.

Stevens, Benjamin Butler, William Sprague, and Ben Wade. The same views were represented in the Democratic party by George H. Pendleton and Francis P. Blair, Jr. In neither party, however, could the advocates of paper money gain control. The election of Grant had been interpreted as a mandate for "sound finance," and the gold payment-specie resumptionists were firmly in the saddle.

The primary purpose of this chapter has been to ascertain the views of the leaders of the labor movement toward the financial issues which vexed the nation in the years 1865-1870. The grievances of the war years are seen as the background which conditioned the attitudes of workingmen during Reconstruction. Repression of strikes and labor organizations, the breakdown of an apprenticeship system, unrestricted immigration, the failure of wages to keep pace with the rise in the cost of living, and a general feeling among laboringmen that they had not received a fair share of wartime prosperity—all these grievances spurred the movement for national organization at the close of the war. The result of this movement was the National Labor Union, labor's answer to the dominant trend of nationalization in almost every phase of American life.

In 1867 the interconvertible bond-currency scheme emerges as the paramount labor reform issue. Despite some opposition, particularly from New England in the early years, this issue continues to dominate the deliberations of the National Labor Union until its final dissolution. The explanation of why the currency question should obtain such prominence is seen to be complex. The ideas of Edward Kellogg as interpreted and modified by Alexander Campbell are seen to provide the ideological basis for labor's platform. The experience of the war years had provided the context in which Kellogg's ideas could become meaningful, for in comparing greenbacks, the people's money, with national bank-notes, the bankers' money, the workingman had come to prefer the former. It is from this standpoint that the great transition between pre-war hard-money Locofocoism and the post-war advocacy of paper money can best be considered. The central thread of consistency connecting the pre-war and post-war attitudes is shown to be a continuing distrust and hatred of bankers and bank-notes. This, combined with the practical unavailability of sufficient gold and silver to meet the currency needs of the nation, led to a firm advocacy of a national greenback currency issued directly by the government with no intermediaries and made convertible into bonds bearing a low rate of interest.

Control of the rate of interest rather than inflation is seen to be the desideratum of the program of the National Labor Union. By making credit easily available to all, class distinctions would be eradicated. Through cooperative effort under a reformed currency system, laborers could become capitalists, and the power of the money monopoly would be broken. Such a program was thoroughly bourgeois in outlook and totally lacking in class consciousness. Indeed, the ideas which motivated the leaders of the National Labor Union are seen to be remarkably similar to the ideas of the high protectionist school of Henry Carey. Both philosophies emerged during a period of industrial capitalism when the independent entrepreneur was still a force to be reckoned with. Both are philosophies of independent enterprise in which low interest rates are seen as a key tool with which to combat the growing influence of the finance capitalists centered in New York. The most impressive similarity is the fact that the inherent logic of the nationalist soft-money position brought leaders like Sylvis, Cameron, and Trevellick into the protectionist fold. Though anomalous perhaps from the Marxian point of view, the idea of the " union of the producing classes " was more than just an idle slogan but provided a basis upon which both laborers and employers could join to do battle with the common enemy, the " money monopolists " of Wall Street.

In the realm of politics it is seen that financial policy rather than such questions as Negro suffrage and Southern Reconstruction was the paramount issue which most concerned the leaders of the labor movement. Although both major parties were controlled at the top by specie resumptionists, labor could find in both parties men whom it could support. It is interesting in the light of the theory of the " Second American Revolution " that the pantheon of labor heroes included those arch-Radicals, Thaddeus Stevens, Benjamin F. Butler, and Ben Wade.

CHAPTER VI

BANKERS AND THE CURRENCY

Since money is always the lifeblood of banking, the monetary opinions of the American banking fraternity in this period were naturally better informed and more refined than, say, those of the leaders of the labor movement. This is certainly true of the leaders of the profession. Men such as James Gallatin and George S. Coe based their opinions on great knowledge and vast experience in the sphere of finance. At the same time it must be admitted that the opinions of bankers on monetary matters were not particularly enlightened. On the whole the bankers failed to understand the reasons for the demand for more currency in the back country and also overlooked the tremendous development of credit instruments in the large cities which reduced the need for currency. Professor Redlich has pointed out that bankers in the years following the Civil War did not respond creatively to the difficulties with which they were faced and that Henry Carey understood the real situation much better than his contemporary critics.[1] It is also ironic that this " informed opinion " was infinitely more diverse than the opinions of labor leaders. Whereas labor seemed to agree pretty well on one panacea (the Kellogg-Campbell interconvertible bond-currency scheme), the bankers had almost as many panaceas as there were bankers. Despite this confusion it is refreshing to discover that opinions and panaceas rarely strayed from the immediate vicinity of group interest.

THE NATIONAL BANKING SYSTEM

The climate of banking in the period of this study was determined to a large extent by the institutional arrangement known as the National Banking System. Like the greenbacks, the protective tariff, and internal taxation, the National Banking System was a product of the war. Though in theory the

[1] Redlich, *The Molding of American Banking*, II, 120, 124.

System owed much to such pre-war experiments as the Suffolk Banking System in New England and particularly to the Free Bank System of New York, only the exigencies of war could provide a sufficiently compelling reason for Congress to act to rationalize the completely unrational condition of state banking as it existed in 1861.[2]

A lengthy description of the various systems of state banking which preceded the National Banking System would be beyond the scope of this study, but since the defects of state banking provided the great arguments in favor of the Acts of 1863 and 1864, it may be helpful to survey the scene briefly. In the first place it should be noted that state banking as it was carried on prior to the Civil War can by no means be condemned outright and in all its forms. Some of the state banking systems were eminently respectable and tended to foster sound banking practices. This was particularly true of the systems which prevailed in New York and several of the New England states. The model for many of the state banking systems was the New York Free Bank System which was established in 1838. The keystone of this system was the principle of bond secured note issues. By law the bank-notes of New York banks had to be secured by the deposit of approved securities with the Comptroller of the Currency at Albany. The notes themselves were issued to the banks by the Comptroller and were stamped " secured by the pledge of public stock." The list of approved securities included bonds of the United States, New York, or other states approved by the Comptroller, as well as real estate mortgages on unincumbered land in New York worth twice the amount of the mortgage. Failure on the part of a bank to redeem its notes in specie left it liable to payment to the note-holder of a fourteen per cent annual interest charge on the amount of the bill. Continuing failure to redeem resulted in an auction of the bank's deposited securities, the proceeds of which were applied to the redemption of the notes. Another important feature of the Free Bank System of New York was the requirement of a specie reserve against note issues. Although the

<hr/>

[2] For accounts of the Suffolk system, see Helderman, *National and State Banks,* pp. 29-34 and N. S. B. Gras, *The Massachusetts First National Bank of Boston, 1784-1934* (Cambridge, Massachusetts, 1937).

original provision in the law of 1838 calling for a twelve and one-half per cent specie reserve against outstanding circulation was repealed in 1840, the principle of maintaining an adequate reserve was gradually being accepted by conservative men as a necessary ingredient of sound banking.[3]

The integrity of the Free Bank System depended to a very large degree upon the soundness of the securities pledged against the note issues of the banks. In New York the security requirements were rather stringent, but such was not the case in several of the western states. In Illinois, Indiana, Wisconsin, and Missouri the laws were seemingly designed expressly for the proliferation of banks of issue. Almost any type of bonds could be pledged as security including the highly questionable securities of many southern states. Such security was doubtful even in good times, and any crisis was likely to involve ruin to note-holders.[4] Hugh McCulloch, for many years a banker in Indiana, has given us a graphic illustration of the way free banking worked in that state.[5]

An enterprising gentleman, whose cash capital did not exceed ten thousand dollars, in connection with two others who were utterly impecunious, bought, mostly on credit, fifty thousand dollars of the bonds of one of the Southern states. These bonds he deposited with the treasurer, and as soon as they could be engraved he received an equal amount of notes, with which he paid for the bonds. This transaction having been completed, more bonds were bought and paid for in the same manner; and the operation was continued until the financial crisis of 1857 occurred; at which time this bank, which had been started with a capital of ten thousand dollars, had a circulation of six hundred thousand dollars, secured by State bonds, on which the bank had for two or three years been receiving the interest.

McCulloch goes on to describe how these notes " died without a struggle " when they were presented for redemption after the panic of 1857, for there was no reserve whatever behind them, and the so-called " bank " was an issuer of notes pure and simple.[6]

The faults and excesses of the western systems made it neces-

[3] Helderman, pp. 19-24.
[4] Fite, *Social and Industrial Conditions in the North*, pp. 110-111.
[5] McCulloch, *Men and Measures*, p. 125.
[6] *Ibid.*, p. 126.

sary that something should be done to provide the nation and the people with a sounder circulation. Although over $200,-000,000 of state bank currency was in circulation in 1861, none of this could legally be accepted in payments to the government.[7] The issue of the greenbacks in 1862 provided a badly needed national currency, but Chase's well known dislike for this expedient led him to seek other alternatives. His plan as outlined in December of 1861 called for the adoption of the free bank principle on a national scale. In his Report Chase defined the principal features of the system as ". . . a circulation of notes bearing a common impression and authenticated by a common authority; . . . the redemption of these notes by the associations and institutions to which they may be delivered for issue; and . . . the security of that redemption by the pledge of United States stocks, and an adequate provision of specie."[8]

Chase felt that in this plan the people would find " the advantages of uniformity in currency; of uniformity in security; of effectual safeguard, if effectual safeguard is possible, against depreciation; and of protection from losses in discounts and exchanges; while in the operations of the government the people would find the further advantage of a large demand for government securities, of increased facilities for obtaining the loans required by the war, and of some alleviation of the burdens on industry through a diminution in the rate of interest, or a participation in the profit of circulation, without risking the perils of a great money monopoly."[9]

By proposing that bank circulation be secured by deposits of the United States bonds and by arguing for a specie reserve requirement, Chase met the two main objections to free banking as it had been practiced in the West. The Secretary continued to press the plan, and in December, 1862 President Lincoln gave it his blessing in his second annual message in which he said that he knew of no other proposal " which promises so certain results and is at the same time so unobjectionable as

---

[7] Charles A. Conant, *A History of Modern Banks of Issue, With an Account of the Economic Crises of the Nineteenth Century and the Crisis of 1907*, 4th ed. (New York, 1909), p. 397.

[8] *Report of the Secretary of the Treasury, 1861*, p. 19.

[9] *Ibid.*, p. 19.

the organization of banking associations, under a general act of Congress, well guarded in its provisions." [10]

A bill to implement this plan was introduced into the Senate by John Sherman on January 26, 1863, and it was reported out from the Finance Committee a week later.[11] It was largely through the efforts of the Ohio Senator that the bill eventually became a law, for the forces against the idea of a National Banking System were many and powerful, and it required all of Sherman's logic and eloquence to whip his Republican colleagues into line. In his speech of February 10, 1863, Sherman advocated the bill on a number of grounds, pointing out that banks formed under its provisions would furnish a market for United States bonds, that it would provide a uniform currency which would be difficult to counterfeit, that the newly formed banks would provide public depositories, and that their notes could be received by the government for public dues without loss. In addition Sherman saw the Bank Bill as a contribution toward a growing American nationalism.[12] He later expanded upon this idea in his memoirs, declaring that the lack of a national currency had contributed to the growth of the states' rights dogma which contained the seeds of civil conflict.[13]

The Bank Bill passed the Senate by a narrow margin, the vote being 23 to 21.[14] True to their anti-bank proclivities, the Democrats were largely opposed to the bill, only two of their number being recorded in the affirmative. Nine Republicans were also opposed, and according to Sherman, it was only the last minute conversion of Senator Anthony of Rhode Island which assured passage of the measure.[15] The bill was sponsored in the House by Samuel Hooper and Elbridge G. Spaulding.

[10] Richardson, *Messages and Papers*, VI, 130.

[11] *Congressional Globe*, 37th Congress, 3rd Session, pp. 505, 666.

[12] *Ibid.*, pp. 840-846. " That Mr. Sherman's speech was powerful and effective is undoubtedly true, and to him more perhaps than to any other person Mr. Chase owed the successful passage of the bill at this time." Andrew McFarland Davis, *The Origin of the National Banking System* (Washington, 1910), p. 79.

[13] Sherman, *Recollections*, I, 298.

[14] *Congressional Globe*, 37th Congress, 3rd Session, pp. 896-897.

[15] Sherman, *Recollections*, I, 299.

It was passed on February 20, 1863 by the close vote of 78 to 64 and was signed by the President on February 25.[16] There had never been any great enthusiasm for the bill, but Chase had demanded it as an instrument of war policy and hinted that he would resign if the scheme did not receive Congressional approval.[17] As in the case of the Legal Tender Acts, the needs of a nation at war were, of course, preeminent in the minds of Congressmen. As one writer has pointed out, "It seems exceedingly doubtful if the act could have passed Congress without the war emergency to serve as an excuse, for that body was neither anxious to legislate on banking nor conscious of the full significance of their action when they did legislate." [18]

Opposition to the bill came from varied and antithetical sources. Thaddeus Stevens was the most powerful enemy of the bill and was able to block its progress in the House for months.[19] An ardent friend of the greenback, Stevens saw the national currency proposal as just another scheme of the money monopolists. The banks were by no means in favor of the bill. State bankers saw that the system would raise serious obstacles to their profitable privilege of issuing notes without restraint. Hugh McCulloch, later closely associated with the system, went to Washington in 1862 to fight the bill on behalf of the State Bank of Indiana.[20] One authority states: "The opposition of the state banks had been continuous from the outset." [21]

The forces against the new system were especially strong in the City of New York. When Secretary Chase went to New York in 1861 to attend a meeting of the Associated Banks, he was strongly advised by James Gallatin, leader of the banking fraternity of that city, not to come out in favor of a national banking system based on the Free Bank System of New York.[22]

[16] *Congressional Globe*, 37th Congress, 3rd Session, p. 1148; Blaine, *Twenty Years of Congress*, I, 478.

[17] Davis, *Origin of the National Banking System*, p. 88.

[18] Margaret G. Myers, *The New York Money Market: Origins and Development* (New York, 1931), p. 218.

[19] Davis, *Origin of the National Banking System*, pp. 56, 61, 87.

[20] McCulloch, *Men and Measures*, p. 163.

[21] Davis, p. 87.

[22] Redlich, *The Molding of American Banking*, II, 103.

Late in 1863 Gallatin urged that National bank-notes be treated as " uncurrent money " by the New York Clearing House and not to be accepted at par. This sentiment was echoed by John Earl Williams, president of the Metropolitan Bank, who argued that greenbacks would be preferable to national bank-notes.[23] The outcome of it all was that the New York Clearing House resolved that " all National Bank currency be treated as uncurrent money unless the bank [in question] redeem at par through a member of this Association." [24] Not all bankers acted like the leaders of the New York Clearing House, but it can be said with a fair degree of certainty that only in some states of the West, where the excesses of wildcatting were best remembered, was there any real enthusiasm for the new system in banking circles.[25] The factor of great importance in passing the National Bank Act of 1863 was not the wisdom of rationalizing an illogical and heterogeneous lot of state banking systems, but the critical nature of the military situation which led Senators and Representatives to support a measure which many of them basically opposed, because it had been advocated as a necessity by the Secretary of the Treasury.

Organization of national banks under the new law went forward slowly. The next session of Congress gave its attention to several amendments which helped facilitate the conversion of state banks into members of the national system.[26] This legislation of June 3, 1864 put the finishing touches on the system which survived until the inauguration of the Federal Reserve in 1913. It will be helpful at this point to consider briefly the most important provisions of the law as it emerged from Congress in 1864.

The execution of the Act was placed in the hands of an officer to be known as the Comptroller of the Currency appointed by the President for a term of five years.[27] This officer was responsible for supervising the initial organization of national banking associations and also for making certain that the associations held to the letter of the law after they were

[23] *Ibid.*, II, 107.
[24] Quoted in *ibid.*, II, 107.
[25] *Ibid.*, II, 109.
[26] Bolles, *Financial History from 1861 to 1885*, pp. 224-223.
[27] Huntington and Mawhinney, *Laws*, p. 330 (Act of June 3, 1864, Sec. 1).

organized. These associations were designated corporate bodies and could be formed by no less than five persons with a minimum capital of $50,000.[28] They were granted the right to carry on the business of banking " by discounting and negotiating promissory notes, drafts, bills of exchange, and other evidences of debt; by receiving deposits; by buying and selling exchange, coin and bullion; by loaning money on personal security; by obtaining, issuing and circulating notes. . . ."[29]

When the organizational features of the law had been complied with, the association was required to deposit with the treasurer of the United States registered government bonds " to an amount not less than thirty thousand dollars nor less than one-third of the capital stock paid in. . . ."[30] In exchange for these bonds the association received " circulating notes of different denominations, . . . equal in amount to ninety per centum of the current market value of the United States bonds so transferred and delivered, but not exceeding ninety per centum of the amount of said bonds at the par value thereof. . . ."[31] The registered bonds were held by the treasurer as security for the circulating notes of the bank in the fashion described above for the Free Bank System of New York. The amount of notes which could be issued under the law was limited to $300,000,000.[32]

It is obvious that great attention was paid by the law to the security of notes issued by the national banks. This was only natural since most of the banking troubles of the past had been associated with unsound or fraudulent note issues. It was, however, symtomatic of the growing importance of demand deposits that the requirements dealing with reserves included deposits as well as notes in computing those liabilities of national banks against which reserves must be held.

Three different categories of banks were recognized in the sections of the law which dealt with reserve requirements. The first category embraced the so-called " country banks " usually located in towns of small population. These banks were re-

[28] *Ibid.*, p. 333 (Sec. 7).
[29] *Ibid.*, pp. 333-334 (Sec. 8).
[30] *Ibid.*, pp. 337 (Sec. 16).
[31] *Ibid.*, p. 340 (Sec. 21).
[32] *Ibid.*, p. 340 (Sec. 22).

quired to "have on hand, in lawful money of the United States, an amount equal to at least fifteen per centum of the aggregate amount of its notes in circulation, and of its deposits."[33] This did not mean, however, that the country bank had to keep this amount in its till, for it was also provided that three-fifths of the fifteen per cent could consist of balances due from a national bank in one of the seventeen designated reserve cities. In the amended Act of June 3, 1864, these cities were St. Louis, Louisville, Chicago, Detroit, Milwaukee, New Orleans, Cincinnati, Cleveland, Pittsburgh, Baltimore, Philadelphia, Boston, New York, Albany, Leavenworth, San Francisco and Washington. Charleston and Richmond could be added at the discretion of the Comptroller.[34] National banks in these cities were required to maintain a reserve of twenty-five per cent against note issues and deposits. But here again it was provided that one-half of this amount could consist of balances deposited with a correspondent bank in the central reserve city of New York.[35]

Organization of national banks under the new system continued to be slow until the passage of the Act of March 3, 1865 which laid a punitive tax of ten per cent on the note issues of the state banks.[36] After this enactment, most of the state banks saw the handwriting on the wall and made plans to convert to the national system. The power to tax was obviously to be used as the power to destroy, for no state bank could profitably issue notes and pay a ten per cent tax for the privilege of doing so. The conflict between state banking and national banking was thus brought to an end, and the new system had clearly gained the field. Progress was greatest during 1865 when 1,014 new national banks were organized, bringing the total number to 1,601.[37]

In many ways the National Banking System was a great improvement over the old heterogeneous state banking systems. Certainly this was true in regard to the national bank-notes

[33] *Ibid.*, p. 345 (Sec. 31).
[34] *Ibid.*, pp. 345-346 (Sec. 31).
[35] *Ibid.*, p. 346 (Sec. 32).
[36] *Ibid.*, pp. 362-363 (Act of March 3, 1865).
[37] This information is contained in Comptroller of the Currency Freeman Clarke's annual report in the *Report of the Secretary of the Treasury, 1865*, p. 62.

which, backed by bond security and reserve requirements, were vastly superior to the old note issues of the state banks. On the other hand the system contained grave faults which became apparent in the first years of its operation. The central weakness of the system was inherent in the structure created by the laws of 1863 and 1864. By legalizing the practice of redepositing reserves, a practice which had been common in the pre-war years, Congress had created a pyramidal reserve structure in which the strength of the base represented by the country banks was, to a large extent, dependent on the shifting fortunes of the apex, represented by the banks of the financial center of New York. There is no disposition here to go into an involved discussion of this grave weakness in the National Banking System. It is sufficient to say that the desire of the outland banks to earn interest on their reserves combined with the intimate relationship which existed between the central reserve banks of New York and the call money market produced a situation in which the withdrawal of reserves by country banks at harvest time, when the demand for money in the interior was great, was likely to bring about a curtailment of loans to brokers and consequent panic in the stock market. Despite the fact that almost all competent observers recognized the weakness inherent in a system which concentrated a large part of the nation's banking reserve in New York for use on the call loan market, legislation to remedy the defects was not forthcoming. The pyramiding of reserves continued to be a contributing factor to periodic panics and crises in the money market until the passage of the Federal Reserve Act brought a measure of elasticity to the banking system.[38]

[38] A leading financial journal commented in 1867: "The needless intricacy of this system [of national banking] is almost wholly due to one prolific cause—namely, the anxiety of the banks to earn interest on reserves. We have often expressed disapproval of this weak feature of the national system, and are not without hope of seeing it gradually disappear, to be replaced by the simple provision that the reserve of no bank shall consist of anything but cash actually in hand, or cash in the hands of its redeeming bank. And by cash we mean lawful money ready to be paid out at any moment if called for." *Commercial and Financial Chronicle*, V (November 16, 1867), 615. For a discussion of the problem of concentrating reserves in New York, see Myers, *The New York Money Market*, pp. 240-250; Bolles, *Financial History from 1861 to 1865*, pp. 349-351; *Report of the Monetary Commission of the Indianapolis Convention*,

In addition to this crucial defect in the reserve structure of the National Banking System, there were other faults more germane to the subject of this study. These relate to the arbitrary limit placed on the amount of the national bank-note circulation, the irredeemability of that circulation and its mal-distribution. The first of these is important because an increase in the amount of national currency provided a rallying point for those who were opposed to deflation and currency contraction but nevertheless fought against further emissions of greenbacks.[39] The issue of central redemption is significant because it mirrors the same differences between big city bankers and their country colleagues which also appear in the debates among bankers on the greenback issue. The mal-distribution defect is important because it was on this issue that the Careyites levelled their most damning accusations against New York, New England, and the National Banking System in general.[40]

As the price for his support of the original banking law of 1863, John Sherman insisted on the provision that the bank-note circulation be limited to $300,000,000. The Ohio Senator pointed out that a good part of the wartime inflation could be attributed to the expansion of the note issues of the state banks, and he had no desire to unleash more inflation through the agency of the new national banks.[41] Sherman's logic was probably sound in 1863, but it could certainly be argued that there was no essential reason why the national circulation should be limited arbitrarily to $300,000,000 for years to come. A common meeting ground for bankers all over the country (except for some eastern metropolitan bankers) who were almost unanimous in their opposition to any further emissions of greenbacks was the proposal that the $300,000,000 limit be abandoned in favor of free banking, that is, that bank-notes

pp. 213-218; Reed, *Money, Currency and Banking*, pp. 237-239; Esther Rogoff Taus, *Central Banking Functions of the United States Treasury, 1789-1941* (New York, 1943), p. 112; Oliver Mitchell Wentworth Sprague, *History of Crises Under the National Banking System* (Washington, 1910), pp. 15-24.

[39] The National Manufacturers' Association and the *Iron Age* had taken this position in 1868. *Supra*, pp. 169-170.

[40] *Supra*, pp. 155-156.

[41] Sherman, *Recollections*, I, 296-297; Davis, *Origin of the National Banking System*, pp. 75-76.

be issued to any amount provided that they were backed by the usual bond security.[42] This point was finally gained by the legislation of 1875, but by that time the high prices of government bonds had led to a decline in the profit on note circulation.[43] Banks found it more profitable to sell their bond security at a good profit and retire their note issues rather than issue more currency. Newly organized banks or older banks which by law may have been entitled to additional circulation found the note issuing privilege unprofitable when they were required to pay a sizeable premium on government bonds in order to issue currency up to ninety per cent of their par value.[44] The free banking legislation of 1875, consequently, did not have the desired effect, and the national currency outstanding even decreased by about $50,000,000 between 1874 and 1877.[45]

The central redemption issue was a bone of contention between bankers of New York and those of the interior. The former desired that all national banks be required to redeem their currency in lawful money (greenbacks) at the counters of correspondent banks in New York. In this manner the banks of the metropolis would be relieved of the plethora of national bank-notes which tended to accumulate there. If the banks of the interior were required to maintain reserves in New York for the purpose of redeeming their notes, there would be obviously less incentive for issuing an excess of bank-notes.[46] The same forces which supported contraction of the greenback currency tended to support the idea of central redemption. This is entirely logical inasmuch as both concepts were deflationary in application. Central redemption was supported in the years 1865 through 1870 by Secretary McCulloch, the two Comptrollers of the Currency, and the majority of the bankers of New York City.[47] Among the latter group the idea was

---

[42] See the speech of Elbridge G. Spaulding and the remarks of Theodore M. Pomeroy in the *Proceedings of the National Bank Convention Held in New York City, Wednesday, June 23, 1869* (Syracuse, 1869).

[43] Huntington and Mawhinney, *Laws*, pp. 422-423 (Act of January 14, 1875); John Jay Knox, *A History of Banking in the United States*, Rev. ed. (New York, 1903), pp. 116-117.

[44] *Ibid.*, pp. 116-117; Redlich, *The Molding of American Banking*, II, 120.

[45] Knox, *History of Banking*, p. 117.

[46] Redlich, *The Molding of American Banking*, II, 114.

[47] See the letters of Hugh McCulloch and Freeman Clarke, Comptroller of

championed by James Gallatin, President of the National Bank and long-time foe of the National Banking System. As Professor Redlich has written, it was the " deflationary aspect of the scheme which . . . must have appealed to the big city bankers." [48] Advocacy of the idea was also part of a continuing hostility to the National Banking System on the part of the New York bankers, a hostility which dated back to the unfriendly reception of the new system by the New York Clearing House in 1863.[49]

The constitution of a proposed National Bank Note Redemption Association was published in November, 1865. The purpose of the Association as explained in the constitution (drawn up by a committee of which James Gallatin was chairman) was to gather up and send home for redemption the notes of all banks which did not redeem in New York.[50] Although this Association never became operative, the idea stirred up opposition in many quarters. Roswell S. Burrows, president of a small national bank in Albion, New York, doubted the motives of the big city bankers. " I do not believe that our city bankers are so disinterested as some may be led to suppose from their efforts to establish and maintain an Assorting House Association, ostensibly for the purpose of improving our currency. They very well know, if the interior banks shall be compelled to redeem their notes in the cities at par, that they must keep their funds at the place or places of redemption, and that therefore the redeeming banks and their associates will hold, measure, control, and use nearly all the available funds of the country." [51]

Western bankers were decidedly opposed to legislation which

the Currency, to the Committee of the New York Clearing House, printed in the *Bankers' Magazine*, XX (Old Series) (November, 1865), 402-404. Comptroller H. R. Hulburd's similar opinion appears in the *Report of the Secretary of the Treasury, 1866*, pp. 68-72.

[48] Redlich, II, 114.

[49] *Supra*, pp. 226-227.

[50] This constitution appears in the *Bankers' Magazine*, XX (Old Series) (November, 1865), 415-417.

[51] " The Redemption of National Bank Currency. Letter from Roswell S. Burrows, Esq., President of the National Bank of Albion, N. Y., in Opposition to the Assorting-House Association," *Bankers' Magazine*, XX (Old Series) (December, 1865), 461-464.

would require them to redeem their notes in greenbacks on the eastern seaboard. They considered that attempts to force such measures through Congress in the name of sound currency were merely maneuvers in a campaign to render the banks of the interior subservient to those of New York, Boston, and Philadelphia. Bankers who were opposed to central redemption retained several lawyers connected with the Merchants' Union Law Company of New York to argue their case before Congress and the people. Petitions were circulated which asked that legislators " refrain from the enactment of any law, compelling all National Banks, wherever located to redeem their notes in New York. . . ." [52] Concern over this issue was evident at the convention of western bankers held in Chicago in September, 1866. A resolution was adopted which expressed " decided disapprobation " of the proposed amendment to the banking law which would require national banks to redeem their notes in New York, Boston, or Philadelphia. The resolution held that " the effect of such amendment, if substituted for the provision of the law as it now exists concerning redemption, will be to seriously embarrass and impede the commercial and financial interests of the entire West and Southwest, by the forced concentration in the eastern cities of a very large portion of the means of the banks which the commercial necessities especially of the West, require to be used at home." [53]

The central redemption issue illustrates the same cleavages between bankers of the East and bankers of the West, between small town bankers and big city bankers which were also reflected on the greenback issue. It continued to be a point of dispute until 1874 when Congress resolved the issue by providing that bank-notes should be redeemed in lawful money by the United States treasurer at Washington. The banks were required to deposit five per cent of their circulation in lawful money which could be counted as part of their reserve. Although Washington was not the most desirable redemption

[52] C. L. Boalt sent one of these petitions to John Sherman on January 4, 1867. Sherman Papers.

[53] The proceedings of this convention appeared in the Bankers' Magazine, XXI (Old Series) (November, 1866), 321-333. The resolution in question is found on p. 326.

city since it was not a financial center, the new law did serve
to silence the proponents of central redemption.[54]

The most serious criticism which could be levelled at the
national bank currency was its brazen mal-distribution. It was
this feature more than any other which made the system a force
for sectional discord. There is sometimes a tendency to speak
and write of the demand for more currency in the less com-
mercially favored sections of the country during the sixties,
seventies, and eighties as though it were a pure and simple
demand for currency inflation by the debtor classes. What is
not so readily apparent is the fact that Henry Carey was right
when he pointed out that real inflation existed only in New
York and New England.[55] This was largely due to two causes.
One of these was the fact that the transfer of demand deposits
by check had advanced to a high degree of perfection in these
states, and particularly in New York City.[56] Since such transfers
tended to diminish and economize the use of currency, they
constituted an inflationary force. The second cause of inflation
in these states was the apportionment of the national currency,
which, as carried through by Hugh McCulloch as Comptroller
of the Currency from 1863-1865, allocated some $170,000,000
out of a total of $293,000,000 to New England and New
York.[57] In 1866, when almost all of the authorized $300,000,000
had been apportioned, the *per capita* circulation in Rhode Island
was $77.16 whereas that of Arkansas was fourteen cents. The
per capita circulation of ten southern states averaged $1.70
against a *per capita* average of $33.30 for New England and
New York. A low *per capita* circulation might be expected in
the South since the Civil War was raging while much of the
currency was being allotted, but that reason will not explain
the discrepancy which existed between the Middle West and
the more favored states of the East. The *per capita* circulation
of seven middle western states averaged $6.36, about one fifth
of that of New England and New York.[58]

[54] Huntington and Mawhinney, *Laws*, p. 418 (Act of June 30, 1874).
[55] *Supra*, pp. 155-156.
[56] Redlich, *The Molding of American Banking*, II, 118-119.
[57] These figures are derived from a table in the annual report of the Comptroller of the Currency which appears in the *Report of the Secretary of the
Treasury, 1866*, p. 65.
[58] These figures have been derived from a table giving *per capita* circulation

This misapportionment of the currency in the formative years of the National Banking System was not part of a plot by Hugh McCulloch to secure the advantages of the national currency to the northeastern states. It arose simply from a combination of circumstances and poor judgment. In his report for 1866 Comptroller H. R. Hulburd attempted an explanation for the obvious injustices which had arisen.[59]

The original act of March 25, 1863, provided for an apportionment of the national currency to the several States and Territories as follows: one hundred and fifty millions according to representative population, and one hundred and fifty millions according to banking capital, resources, and business.

This requirement was repealed by the act of June 3, 1864, which left the distribution to the discretion of the Comptroller of the Currency. By the amendment of March 3, 1865, the clause requiring an apportionment to be made was reenacted, but at the same date an amendment to section 7 of the internal revenue act provided that all existing State Banks should have the right to become national banks, and should have the preference over new organizations up to the 1st day of July, 1865.

These two amendments were not in harmony; for, if the apportionment was made as required by the amendment to section 21, the State banks then in existence could not have been converted without exceeding in many instances the amount of circulation apportioned to the different States. But, as it seemed to be the intention and policy of the act to absorb all existing banking institutions rather than to create new banking interests in addition thereto, the Comptroller of the Currency so construed the amendments as to permit the conversion of State banks without limitation. The effect of this action was to make a very unequal distribution of the currency, some of the States receiving more than they were entitled to by the apportionment, and leaving but a very limited amount to be awarded to the southern and some of the western states.

Hugh McCulloch was a stubborn man. His intransigence was demonstrated not only in his persistent advocacy of the unpopular policy of contraction, but in his refusal to admit that grave injustices had been done in the apportionment of the bank currency. McCulloch defended his actions in a letter to W. P. Fessenden, Chairman of the Senate Finance Committee, asserting, " One hundred and seventy-five thousand of the rural

by states of the national currency in the *Bankers' Magazine*, XX (Old Series) (June, 1866), 953.

[59] Hulburd's explanation appears in the Comptroller's annual report in the *Report of the Secretary of the Treasury, 1866*, p. 72.

population of Ohio or Illinois do not need a tenth part of the circulation required by the manufacturing and commercial community of Rhode Island. A well-to-do farmer may not receive for his products more than $5,000 in the whole year, and a community of farmers require but little in the way of banking facilities; but skilled labor, capital, and machinery combined produce millions. The value of manufactures produced annually in Massachusetts exceeds by more than one hundred and forty per cent the combined manufactures of Illinois and Ohio, while the combined population of those States exceeds that of Massachusetts by more than two hundred and twenty-five per cent. Hence any fixed ratio betwen circulation and population is an arbitrary ratio, and impracticable." [60] This position was untenable. As Professor Redlich has observed, "The maldistribution of note issues . . . was doubly unjust because the back country needed more currency than the advanced regions where checks and credit instruments could be used instead. Because of the survival of traditional business methods in the back country this unfortunate maldistribution alone was bound to impede in the less advanced sections the establishment of banking, because banking there was still identical with note issue as it once had been throughout the land." [61]

The Act of July 12, 1870 made an attempt to remedy the obvious injustice of the original apportionment. An increase of $54,000,000 in the national currency was authorized, this amount being reserved exclusively for those states which had not received their proper share.[62] The difficulty was that interest rates were so high in the West and South that there was little incentive to form national banking associations when the profit which could be made on circulation was estimated at only 2.65 per cent in 1878.[63] There was some improvement by 1874,

[60] This letter was published in the *Bankers' Magazine*, XX (Old Series) (June, 1866), 945-946.

[61] Redlich, *The Molding of American Banking*, II, 118. The whole subject of the misapportionment of the currency receives comprehensive treatment in George Laverne Anderson, The National Banking System, 1865-75: A Sectional Institution. This is an unpublished manuscript in the library of the University of Illinois.

[62] Huntington and Mawhinney, *Laws*, p. 369; Knox, *History of Banking*, p. 109.

[63] Redlich, *The Molding of American Banking*, II, 119; Knox, *History of Banking*, p. 110.

but at that time New England and the Middle States still accounted for about two-thirds of the bank-notes outstanding.[64]

BANKERS AND INFLATION

We turn now from an institutional description of the National Banking System to consider the question of how the banking interest fared during the violent price fluctuations of the Civil War years. Superficially at least it would seem that bankers were prosperous. In the financial center of New York deposits of the banks associated in the New York Clearing House increased from $79,988,633 on June 30, 1860 to $218,535,824 on December 30, 1865. Total liabilities in the same period increased from $193,897,638 to $413,978,500. The annual exchanges at the Clearing House rose from $7,231,143,056 to $26,032,384,341. At the same time it is interesting to note that during the period of frenetic inflation the capital of the Associated Banks actually diminished in amount, it being $69,758,777 on June 30, 1860 and $69,204,350 on December 30, 1864. The fact that new capital was obviously not going into banking during these years leads us to question this apparent prosperity. It is true that the capital of these banks increased to $80,770,200 by December 30, 1865, but 1865 was a year of deflation and falling prices and presented an entirely different face to the banking interest.[65] The table below gives the average dividends paid by the New York banks in the years 1860-1865.[66]

1860	7.80%	(53 banks reported)
1861	7.63%	(52 banks reported)
1862	7.51%	(50 banks reported)
1863	8.47%	(53 banks reported)
1864	10.74%	(60 banks reported)
1865	11.88%	(66 banks reported)

Here again it would appear superficially that the banks prospered. Particularly significant are the average dividends for 1863 and 1864 for these were the years of greatest inflation.

---

[64] *Ibid.*, p. 118.

[65] These banking statistics are found in the *Eighth Annual Report of the Chamber of Commerce of the State of New York for the Year 1865-'66* (New York, 1866), Part II, pp. 135-138.

[66] Average dividends of the New York banks were derived from a table which appears in *Hunt's Merchants' Magazine*, LIV (January, 1866), 87.

On first glance an average earning rate of 8.4% in 1863 and
10.7% in 1864 would seem more than adequate compared with
the rate which had prevailed before the war. Such figures,
however, are quite deceiving, for the rapid decline in the purchasing power of money in 1863 and 1864 meant that bank
stockholders were actually receiving far less in terms of real
income than they received in 1860 and 1861. The banker
dealing in money was in exactly the reverse position of the
entrepreneur dealing with goods. Whereas goods were rapidly
appreciating in terms of money, money was just as rapidly
depreciating in value in terms of goods.

Although it might logically be expected that bankers would
possess a more sophisticated outlook on the mechanics of
inflation than any other economic group, it becomes obvious,
as Professor Mitchell has pointed out, that persons who derived
their income from capital lent at interest were hurt by the
inflation even more than wage-earners.[67] This phenomenon
is borne out in the rates of interest charged on call loans and
short-term commercial loans, types of business in which the
banks were traditionally interested. On call loans the rate in
1863 and 1864 varied between 5 and 7 per cent, never rising
above the latter figure. On sixty day loans the highest rate
quoted through 1864 was 9.3 per cent.[68] Such rates could
hardly begin to compensate the banks for the tremendous loss
in the purchasing power of money. Professor Mitchell has
estimated that for a lender to have shown a gain of 6 per
cent in terms of real purchasing power on a loan made in
April, 1862 for one year, the rate of interest should have been
50.5 per cent. This would have compensated for the 30 per
cent decline in the purchasing power of money which occurred
in that period. Similarly a lender making a one-year loan in
April, 1863 should have charged 30.9 per cent, a rate which
would have compensated for a drop of 19 per cent in the
purchasing power of money during this period and allowed
the lender to show a six per cent real gain.[69] Since such rates

---

[67] Mitchell, *History of the Greenbacks*, p. 368.

[68] *Ibid.*, Table LVIII, p. 367. For corroborating evidence on short term rates,
see *Bankers' Magazine*, XVIII (Old Series) (July, 1863), 86; *ibid.*, (May,
1864), 925; *ibid.*, (June, 1864), 1005.

[69] Mitchell, *History of the Greenbacks*, p. 372.

were never charged by bankers in these years, it is not difficult to see how bankers and bank stockholders were badly hurt by the wartime inflation. The relatively high dividends paid by the New York banks in 1863 and 1864 pale into insignificance if the loss in real purchasing power is taken into consideration.

1865 was a profitable year for the banks of New York. The large average dividends of 11.88% which were reported represented a considerable gain over 1863 and 1864. In addition the purchasing power of money was increasing. This change of fortune in the banking business can best be illustrated in conjunction with index numbers which show the great price fluctuations of the period. Carl Snyder's index converted to a base in which 1860 equals 100 gives these results for the Civil War decade.[70]

Year	General Price Index
1860	100
1861	98
1862	111
1863	135
1864	182
1865	179
1866	173
1867	165
1868	161
1869	156
1870	144

It is apparent that the inflation reached its peak in 1864, and that thereafter the course of prices was downward. The decline in the price level meant an appreciation in the value of money. Such a situation obviously worked to the advantage of the banking interest. Loans made after 1864 would necessarily be repaid in dollars worth more than they had been when the loan was contracted.

After the bonanza year of 1865, bank dividends slipped back to a more reasonable level. In 1866 forty New York banks

[70] Carl Snyder's general price index was referred to *supra*, pp. 52-53. It appears in *Historical Statistics of the United States*, Series L 1, pp. 231-233.

reported dividends which averaged 5.56 per cent.[71] In 1868 the share earnings of fixty-three such banks averaged 5.26 per cent.[72] Although such earnings may not seem impressive compared with the 10.74 per cent figure of 1864, they were actually far more impressive to bank stockholders, for, they represented money which was increasing rather than decreasing in value. Five or six per cent in the post-war years meant a very substantial gain whereas eight or ten per cent in 1863 and 1864 meant a very definite loss.

It thus appears that in the years following the Civil War, the banking interest generally had a vested interest in deflation. A predisposition in favor of Hugh McCulloch's policy of contraction would be a logical consequence of this interest. There are, however, other factors to be considered. The mal-distribution of the national currency and the general dearth of money of any kind in many areas of the West are particularly important in understanding the varying attitudes toward contraction which appeared among bankers. The nature of these attitudes it will now be our task to consider.

BANKERS AND GREENBACKS

In a sense it is perhaps ironic that the great proprietors of inflation, the bankers of New York and New England, were by and large the loudest advocates of contraction. Though the inflation which prevailed in those states was to some extent of their own making, the banking interest had not reaped the tremendous benefits which had accrued to the manufacturers. It is therefore not surprising that many eastern bankers should support the deflationary policy of the Secretary of the Treasury, a policy which was largely in their own economic interest. Those financial journals which mirrored the opinions of the New York banking community were steadfast in their support of the policy of contraction. While these journals advocated that contraction of the greenbacks be carried out cautiously and with due regard to the business interests involved, there

[71] This average is derived from a list of reported dividends in the *Bankers' Magazine*, XXI (Old Series) (August, 1866), 153.

[72] This average is derived from a table of reported dividends in the *Bankers' Magazine*, XXIII (Old Series) (June,1869), 995.

was no hedging on the fundamental issue. Early in 1866 the *Bankers' Magazine* heartily endorsed McCulloch's *Report*, asserting, "The views of the Secretary commend themselves to the earnest consideration and the approval of the country. To secure that contraction of the currency which is essential to the great commercial and financial interests of the country, without producing distress to business circles, we conceive that ample time must be given to produce the desired reform. Whether that period be three, or five years, it should be gradual. In view of the condition of the currency at this time, it is to be hoped that Congress will prohibit the issue of any further Treasury or United States notes; and that those now out shall be funded by a gradual process." [73]

McCulloch's firm advocacy of the policy of contraction was followed by the overwhelming adoption on December 18, 1865 of a resolution in favor of this policy.[74] The *Commercial and Financial Chronicle* noted this action with approval: "The decisive vote of 144 to 6 by which this conservative and sound policy was adopted naturally seals the fate of the mischievous schemes of further inflation which of late have been urgently pressed forward in certain quarters; and gives a pledge that our redundant currency is not only to receive no further increase, but will be steadily contracted from this time forward, until its normal volume is reached and specie payments are resumed. . . ." [75] After the Act of February 4, 1868 which suspended McCulloch's power to contract the currency, the same journal asserted irritably, "No mistake can be more gross, and no confusion of thought more deplorable than to suppose that because contraction of the currency has been thus converted into a gambling operation by recklessness and knavery, therefore contraction of the currency in the hands of honesty and statesmanship must be intolerable." [76] The *Bankers' Magazine* was even more convinced of the rectitude of contraction, arguing early in 1869 that "through contraction, and through this alone, can we escape-the terrible evils which await us under

[73] *Ibid.*, XX (Old Series) (January, 1866), 522.
[74] *Supra*, p. 66.
[75] *Commercial and Financial Chronicle*, I (December 23, 1865), 801.
[76] *Ibid.*, VII (November 21, 1868), 645-646.

the present system; that such contraction will *never* be voluntary, but must be enforced; that any distress and disaster which it may cause is equally inevitable under the present method of *laissez aller*, without the accompanying advantages; . . . ." [77]

Letters written to Hugh McCulloch during his tenure as Secretary of the Treasury indicate that many New York and New England bankers were behind his policy of contraction of the legal tenders. E. G. Binkam of the City Bank of New York wrote the Secretary on October 10, 1867 expressing concern that McCulloch was in danger of being removed. " I am convinced that there is a combination composed of stock speculators, Gold Gamblers, with others who are determined to have you removed before Congress convenes. No man in this nation is so much in the way of the combination as yourself. Millions of dollars, I believe, can be raised to have you removed. Your contraction policy is death to those who now hold large amounts at high prices, and the most unscrupulous and infamous means will be resorted to. . . . I am confident that a majority of the substantial and conservative business men of this city—of the whole country—of both political parties, are, in the main, with you on the question of finance." Binkam asked McCulloch to write him immediately " if, in your opinion, the President needs any advice upon the subject of your removal, . . . for I am confident that such men as Moses Taylor [President of the large and important City Bank] and others of substance, who really wish the best man in the place, and who, though disinclined to appear prominent in matters of this kind, yet, for the sake of the country, would join in, and say to the President what they believe to be right." [78]

George Walker, a former bank commissioner of Massachusetts and President of the Third National Bank of Springfield, expressed agreement with the policy of contraction and expressed the hope that no more bank currency would be issued until the greenbacks were on a firmer basis.[79] In an article in the *Bankers' Magazine* this same gentleman asserted: " To get back to specie payments is the first object; and I know no other

---

[77] " The Currency of the United States," *Bankers' Magazine*, XXIII (Old Series) (March, 1869), 698.

[78] McCulloch Papers.

[79] *Ibid.*, December 4, 1866.

way of doing it than by the way once attempted and afterwards suspended, namely by the painful process of contraction." [80]

Commenting on McCulloch's *Report* for the year 1867, W. H. Y. Hackett, President of the First National Bank of Portsmouth, New Hampshire, wrote that it had "the genuine ring of an old Spanish milled Dollar." [81] David Snow, President of the Boston National Bank of the Republic, endorsed the *Report* and pointed out that his banker friends wanted contraction not expansion of the currency. "There are no sympathies in New England with inflation and nothing could operate more disastrously on the industry of the country." [82] Letters from other eastern bankers echoed the same sentiments. [83]

That McCulloch's general economic outlook was shared by the great majority of eastern bankers can hardly be doubted. The great desideratum among this group was a return to specie payments, for distrust of paper as a measure of value was almost universal among bankers. It was, therefore, McCulloch's denunciation of the greenbacks, of inflation, and his desire for a return to coin payments which struck sympathetic chords among bankers. Contraction was a means to an end, and not all bankers even in the East agreed with the *Bankers' Magazine* that it was the only means. It should be emphasized that, although bankers generally had a vested interest in deflation and that by and large eastern bankers constituted the greatest single group interest in favor of the policy of contraction, this interest did not extend to a crisis producing type of deflation which would involve them and their customers in general ruin. A majority of bankers in this period would probably have desired a gradual deflation in which the value of money slowly appreciated. Such a situation would be all to the benefit of a creditor group, but any panic involving forced liquidation would most certainly not be to the benefit of the banking interest. There was therefore considerable disagreement among bankers over the policy of contraction.

[80] George Walker, "The Currency Systems of the United States and Europe," *Bankers' Magazine*, XXIII (Old Series) (March, 1869), 738.

[81] December 6, 1867. McCulloch Papers.

[82] *Ibid.*, December 21, 1867.

[83] For example, P. F. Kelly of Philadelphia to McCulloch, August 2, 1867. *Ibid.*

Some believed that it was an absolutely necessary step on the road to specie resumption and that it could be accomplished without seriously disturbing the money market, while others believed that it was a remedy too radical for the times and that the country should be allowed to grow up to the volume of currency outstanding.

To exhibit the flavor of eastern banking opinion in this period, the opinions of several outstanding bankers will be considered. Those whose testimony on the greenback issue is sufficiently explicit to deserve such consideration include Jay Cooke, the great government loan agent of the Civil War; James Gallatin, son of Albert Gallatin and President of the Gallatin National Bank of New York; George S. Coe, President of the American Exchange Bank of the same city; George Opdyke, one-time President of the Fourth National Bank and Vice-President of the New York Chamber of Commerce; Elbridge Gerry Spaulding, Buffalo banker well known as the " father of the greenbacks," and Henry Clews, a private banker of New York.

Jay Cooke was associated with the National Banking System from the very beginning. His wholehearted support of the legislation of 1863 had at times been crucial. After John Sherman's great speech of February 10, 1863 in which he came to the support of the proposed system, Henry D. Cooke wrote to his brother: " It will be a great triumph, Jay, and one to which we have contributed more than any other living men. The bank bill had been repudiated by the House, and was without a sponsor in the Senate, and was thus virtually dead and buried when I induced Sherman to take hold of it, and we went to work with the newspapers." [84] Immediately after the bill had been passed, the House of Cooke threw its energies into the business of organizing national banking associations. By July, 1863 charters had been granted to two banks dominated by the Cooke interests, the First National Bank of Philadelphia and the First National Bank of Washington, D. C.[85] The efforts of Jay Cooke were also directed toward organizing

[84] Quoted in Davis, *Origin of the National Banking System*, p. 78.
[85] Oberholtzer, *Jay Cooke*, I, 340-343; Henrietta M. Larson, *Jay Cooke, Private Banker* (Cambridge, Mass., 1936), pp. 139-140.

national banks in the smaller towns of the West and South. His subsidiary loan agents in these areas followed his instructions in stimulating such development. Although the House of Cooke was not directly interested in these banks, there was considerable incentive for such activity since Cooke, as government loan agent, sold them the 5-20 bonds to secure their circulation.[86] Cooke's activities gave him a much more national and less parochial point of view than the great New York bankers. His great success plus his almost complete monopoly of the placing of the great government loans of the Civil War years led to considerable hostility between the Cooke firm and some of the banking fraternity of that city.

Shortly after the National Banking System had become operative, the need for a large national bank in New York became apparent since many country banks would need a correspondent in that city. Initial efforts to organize such a bank resulted in failure, and Chase and McCulloch turned to Jay Cooke to supply the necessary leadership and driving force.[87] Although three national banks had already been organized in New York, none had the requisite capital and prestige to serve as the capstone of the national system. Cooke went to work with energy and determination and within a matter of days he had raised a capital of five million dollars for the new Fourth National Bank.[88] A large amount of the capital for this venture came from outside New York, and it is evident that the enormous prestige of the Cooke name was the difference between success and failure.[89]

In the post-war years Jay Cooke continued to be a leading exponent of the National Banking System. Unlike the bankers of New York, Cooke had great faith in the national currency. Faith in this type of paper money, however, did not extend to a belief in the greenbacks. In 1863 Cooke had strongly opposed any further issues of legal tenders, and after the war he was " in the foreground in the movement for a speedy return to specie payments." [90] McCulloch leaned heavily on Cooke for

[86] Oberholtzer, I, 353-355; Larson, pp. 142-143.
[87] Redlich, The Molding of American Banking, II, 110-111.
[88] Ibid., II, 111; Oberholtzer, I, 343-349; Larson, pp. 140-141.
[89] Oberholtzer, I, 345-346.
[90] Oberholtzer, II, 4; Larson, p. 135.

advice in 1865, and the Philadelphian counseled a return to the gold standard which he thought could be achieved by 1867.[91] Since McCulloch consulted Cooke before he issued his *Report* of 1865 which recommended contraction and since Cooke strongly supported the Loan Bill of 1866 which gave the Secretary power to call in the greenbacks, it is apparent that Cooke supported contraction at this time as the quickest way to specie resumption.[92] Late in 1867 Cooke denounced the greenbacks in a letter to the press, asserting that he regarded " the issue by the government of legal tender notes, to be used as a circulating medium, as an anomaly in finance. It was purely a war measure, justified because necessary to the life of the nation, and, like other war measures, should end with the return of prosperous peace." It is evident, however, that though Cooke was unrelenting in his opposition to the greenbacks, he had some doubts about the wisdom of any further diminution in the total volume of the currency, for he added: " It is not desirable that the greenbacks be immediately or suddenly withdrawn, but they should be gradually and surely replaced with a currency which is legitimate and permanent." [93]

Cooke believed that as greenbacks were withdrawn, they should be replaced dollar for dollar with national bank currency.[94] He would consequently repeal the legal limit of $300,000,000 in issuing bank-notes. In a pamphlet issued by Jay Cooke in 1865 which was generally thought to contain many of his views, the assertion was made that " That is not a hazardous opinion which declares that in less than twenty years our National Bank-note circulation will be One-Thousand Millions of Dollars." [95] This attitude was in contrast with conservative financial opinion in New York as expressed by the *Commercial and Financial Chronicle* which expressed the hope in 1868 that " no further depreciation is to be attempted, nor any new emissions of any sort of paper money, especially of

[91] Oberholtzer, II, 4.
[92] *Ibid.*, II, 4-8; Larson, p. 204.
[93] Philadelphia *Inquirer*, October 24, 1867, quoted in Oberholtzer, II, 58.
[94] *Ibid.*, II, 193.
[95] Samuel Wilkeson, *How Our National Debt May Be A National Blessing. The Debt Is Public Wealth, Political Union, Protection of Industry, Secure Basis for National Currency* (Philadelphia, 1865), p. 9.

bank notes." [96] It is evident that Cooke's opposition in 1867 to any diminution in the volume of the currency was closely related to his own interest in marketing government bonds. In a letter to his brother Henry, the financier made this clear: " As to getting back to specie payments," he wrote, " the least said about that the better as it is the premium on gold that enables us to sell the 5-20's. If purchasers of 5-20's supposed that we will get back to specie payments within a year or two they would not touch them at present prices." [97]

Jay Cooke continued to oppose any plan of specie resumption involving a curtailment of the circulating medium. His natural predilection toward coin payments, however, was made manifest in 1869. Late in that year he recommended that Congress announce that specie resumption would take place on January 1, 1872. He felt that certain preparatory steps should be taken. Among these would be the flotation by the government of a $100,000,000 gold loan in order to accumulate gold in the Treasury, building up of the specie reserves of the banks by forcing them to conserve the gold interest on their pledged bonds, the withdrawal of $100,000,000 in greenbacks to be replaced by an equal amount of national bank-notes.[98] Cooke's natural bias against the greenbacks was again evident, but also apparent was his desire to achieve resumption without deflation.

Because of its national outlook, the easy money requirements of its bond selling business, and its close connection with many smaller banks in the hinterland, the House of Cooke never shared the prejudices of conservative New York banking. Jay Cooke's dislike of the greenbacks was never in question and his initial support of contraction was simply the conditioned reflex of this attitude, but it is also clear that Cooke was no deflationist and that if the greenbacks were to be contracted, they should be replaced dollar for dollar by national bank-notes.

The hostility of many New York bankers to the National Banking System has been noted. This hostility was both logical and emotional. Emotional antagonism stemmed from the conflict between Secretary Chase and these gentlemen during the

[96] Commercial and Financial Chronicle, VI (June 6, 1868), 709.
[97] Quoted in Larson, p. 204.
[98] Ibid., p. 206.

Civil War when the Treasury and the great New York banks found it impossible to agree on such issues as whether government bonds should be sold at par or at market price and whether the Treasury should demand amounts due it from the banks in gold or whether these balances should be drawn down by check.[99] The New York banking fraternity was also irritated by Chase's directive that all national banks should be known by numerals, forcing banks of considerable prestige such as the Bank of Commerce or the Merchants' Bank to be known as the First or Second National Bank.[100] This issue was eventually resolved by compromise, but at the time it had contributed to bad feeling. Antagonism was also due to the feeling on the part of the New York bankers that the government was attempting to ram the new system down their throats, a system whose features they did not like and in which they saw little profit for themselves.

It is not difficult to understand the reasons for this point of view. The most important advantage of the national system was the currency issuing privilege. In this privilege the New York banks were not particularly interested. One authority has remarked that " If the city banks saw little advantage for themselves in the change from state to national charter, they at least had little to fear from the competition of the new currency. They derived little profit from circulation, and two of the largest banks, the Bank of Commerce and the City Bank, had abandoned the issue of notes altogether because they found the trouble and expense greater than the return." [101] Not only were these banks initially disinterested in the currency issuing privilege, they profoundly distrusted banks which sought such a privilege.[102] After the passage of the legislation of 1863, Augustus Ely Silliman, President of the Merchants' Bank, had commented: " If the theory of the Secretary of the Treasury be

[99] *Supra*, pp. 21-23, 31-33.
[100] Redlich, *The Molding of American Banking*, II, 106.
[101] Myers, *The New York Money Market*, p. 221.
[102] It is significant to note, however, that the banks of New York City later became more interested in this privilege and that by October 1, 1866, fifty-eight national banks in that city had issued $30,427,414 of national currency on the basis of a paid up capital of $75,009,700. *Bankers' Magazine*, XXI (Old Series) (February, 1867), 608-609.

successful, we shall have a thousand banks spread over the whole Continent, initiated and managed, in the majority of cases, by inexperienced men, without saying anything of unprincipled adventurers, who will flood the country with a currency essentially irredeemable. . . ." [103]

An explicit and comprehensive statement of the views held by what Jay Cooke's brother Henry called the " old fogy bank men of New York " is contained in an article written by James Gallatin and published in 1868.[104] An acknowledged spokesman for the New York banking fraternity, Gallatin had since 1862 voiced strong objections to the financial policies of the Republican party.[105] It is significant that Gallatin's article is in the form of a letter addressed to none other than " His Excellency, Andrew Johnson, President of the United States." At a time when tensions between the President and Congress were rapidly becoming acute, leading to the resolution by the House of Representatives of February 24 that Johnson be impeached, it is noteworthy that Gallatin took occasion to congratulate the President on his recent message to Congress which " has made a profound impression upon my mind by the many truths in political economy which it enunciates." [106] The hard-money views of the Tennessee Democrat found a friendly reception in Wall Street.[107]

Gallatin bases his arguments on what he calls " The Truths

[103] Quoted in Redlich, The Molding of American Banking, II, 141-142.

[104] This epithet is contained in a letter from Henry Cooke to John Sherman, September 9, 1867. Sherman Papers.

[105] Supra, pp. 31-33.

[106] James Gallatin, " Letter on the Financial Economy of the United States, With Suggestions for Restoring Specie Payments," Hunt's Merchants' Magazine, LVIII (March, 1868), 188-202. The quotation is from p. 188.

[107] Gallatin is referring to the views expressed in Johnson's third annual message to Congress of December 3, 1867. When this message was written, Johnson's financial views were still those of Hugh McCulloch. At this time the President argued for the " necessity of retiring our paper money, that the return of gold and silver to the avenues of trade may be invited. . . ." Johnson also quoted approvingly the maxim of Daniel Webster: " Of all the contrivances for cheating the laboring classes of mankind, none has been more effectual than that which deludes them with paper money." Richardson, Messages and Papers, VI, 573-574. For further evidence that the mercantile-financial community of New York City was favorably disposed toward both the political and economic policies of the Johnson administration, see Appendix III which follows this chapter.

of Financial Economy." Among the propositions which he held to be indisputable were the "Truths" that "There is no authority in the Constitution for making paper money the national standard or measure of value," and that "the power to make it such standard of value . . . is to be *sought* in the *war power,* outside of any expressed constitutional authority." Gallatin held that "The making of an irredeemable paper money a legal tender, or compulsory payment, is at any time an act of questionable propriety, but it is more than questionable when no provision is made for funding such money in the public securities bearing interest." "Every government," the New Yorker asserted, "has an unquestionable right to use its credit . . . but no civilized government claims the right to take the property of its loyal people without compensation, and hence the custom of enlightened governments, in modern times, of providing for the funding of paper credits, bearing no interest, in the public securities bearing interest." [108]

These propositions based on constitutional interpretation and a statement of the powers of government were followed by arguments based on economic reasoning. In an early statement of what has come to be known as the equation of exchange, Gallatin argued that "Money of any kind, made a legal tender, creates prices in proportion to its amount in use and the activity of its circulation. . . ." [109] The trouble with legal tender paper money was that it could be "created at will, free from the intrinsic value of coined money." As a result, "the fluctuations which it produces in prices are much more rapid than those peculiar to the movements of the latter." "Hence," the banker argued, "the great and violent expansions and contractions of prices prevailing under legal tender paper money that is neither redeemable nor fundable; in such expansions and contractions the capital of people of limited means is swept away, and the whole nation in the aggregate becomes impoverished, to the advantage of the people of other nations having monetary systems based upon intrinsic values. . . ." [110]

[108] Gallatin, p. 189.
[109] *Ibid.,* p. 190. For a discussion of the equation of exchange, see George N. Halm, *Monetary Theory: A Modern Treatment of the Essentials of Money and Banking,* 2nd ed. (Philadelphia, 1946), pp. 77-82.
[110] Gallatin, p. 190.

Gallatin's economic arguments are followed by a denuciation of the greenbacks on moral grounds. He warns that "The passion for gain saps the foundation of public credit in any nation which resorts to the prolonged use of legal tender paper money. . . ." In phrases very much like those used by his fellow banker, Hugh McCulloch, Gallatin asserts: "The demoralization of society progresses steadily under the blighting influence of an irredeemable legal tender paper money. Religion, virtue, and honor decline. Vice becomes fashionable. Gambling prevails in the marts of trade and the financial centres, from the very necessities of the case, because the slow process of honesty, prudence, forethought and plodding industry are impracticable in occupations subject to the licentious reign of such paper money." [111] Such was the New York banker's indictment of the evils brought to pass through the issue of the greenbacks.

After enunciating these "Truths," Gallatin considers some of the other results of Civil War finance. Although he concedes that the National Banking System "has been greatly improved," his dislike of that institution crops out. "Not content with a large volume of government paper money, we made it the basis of another volume of auxiliary money in the form of bank issues. We built paper upon paper. Our paper house topples to its foundation, yet we are advised to build it higher, with more paper. . . ." [112] Gallatin lashes out at the tariff legislation of the war and significantly notes the addiction of

[111] *Ibid.*, p. 191.

[112] *Ibid.*, p. 192. It has been noted above that a hatred of the National Banking System was shared by many New York bankers. In the case of John Earl Williams, President of the large and important Metropolitan National Bank, this dislike of the new system even transcended the normal New York banker's distaste for the greenbacks. In fact, Williams definitely preferred greenbacks to national bank-notes. In a letter to Senator Fessenden, he admitted that " I have shocked some of my banking friends by saying that I was in favor of withdrawing every dollar of National Bk. currency & instituting therefor U. S. Treasury notes." If this could be done, the New Yorker felt " we shall have 5 or 600 banks instead of 1600 and quite enough to do all the banking business of the country. Again, if the U. S. could add 300 millions to its own notes as a substitute for N. Banknotes withdrawn—and then add one hundred million to the specie now in the public treasury, the U. S. could resume specie payments any day it chose to do so, provided, the balance of trade was not in favor of Europe." John Earl Williams to Fessenden, Feb. 6, 1867, Fessenden Papers. It is curious than an important banker should have taken a position so close to that of the Pendletonites and the leaders of the labor movement.

the protectionists to soft-money ideas. " By a false system of taxation upon foreign imports, aiming at the so-called protection of home industry, we unduly stimulated domestic manufactures, and the greediness for gain of those who urged that false system, even at a time when we were struggling for our national existence,—overlooking revenue for protection,—having thus overreached itself, it is painful to read the humble confessions which these people are now making. *It is a remarkable phenomenon in economical science, that the theory in favor of protection to home industry should be found to go hand in hand with the theory in favor of paper money.* These ' twin relics of barbarism ' continue to have their followers among our leading public men, men who are leaders in legislation and literary culture." [113]

After considering all of the evils which beset the country, Gallatin goes on to consider some of the solutions which have been offered. It is not necessary to go into all of these, but it is extremely important to note that he explicitly endorses the policies of both Johnson and Hugh McCulloch including " The restoration of the Southern States to their proper relations to the Federal Government " as well as " The funding or payment of the interest-bearing notes and a continual contraction of the paper currency." [114] The former is important because it indicates the distrust with which a conservative banker like Gallatin viewed the Radical policy of keeping the Southern states in limbo; the latter is significant as it demonstrates the sympathy felt by conservative New York bankers for McCulloch's policy.

Gallatin noted with concern the moves in Congress toward removing from the Treasury Department the power to contract the greenbacks, warning that such action would mean " a practical maintenance of the paper money inflation and the premium on gold at existing amounts." The banker asserted: " No immediate approach to specie payments is possible, if these measures are to prevail. . . . We shall continue to flounder on amid the storms and wrecks of irredeemable paper money." [115]

---

[113] *Ibid.*, p. 193. Italics mine. Perhaps nowhere is there to be found a more explicit statement by a contemporary of the general thesis propounded in Chapter IV.

[114] *Ibid.*, pp. 195-196.

[115] *Ibid.*, p. 197.

The remedy for the monetary malady afflicting the nation was about what could have been expected from an extreme conservative such as Gallatin. " Maintain the highest standard of value possible in the Government paper money by permitting it to be funded. In other words, if the forcible contraction must be repealed, then repeal the law prohibiting the funding of the legal tender paper money; permit the funding of it in the natural way, in some interest-bearing stock." [116] In order to facilitate the funding of the greenbacks and the resumption of specie payments, Gallatin proposed " A Specie Resumption Loan at such rate of interest and such number of years to run as the Secretary could dispose of *for gold*, at not less than par, with the view of drawing out the hoards of gold in the country into the Treasury." Specie payments would be resumed when the amount of gold in the Treasury equalled the amount of greenbacks outstanding. Gallatin did not feel that this hoarding of gold in the Treasury would seriously inconvenience the money market, for he thought the whole process could be accomplished quickly. After specie payments had been declared, " The banks and the people would send to the Treasury and get gold for the legal tenders they might hold, and these latter, as they went into the Treasury, would be destroyed, the banks resuming and the Government having paid for its notes in coin, would therefore cease to interfere with the currency, and be freed from the most dangerous and seductive power and influence of paper money." [117]

Although Gallatin attempted to make his financial pill sweeter by calling this destruction of greenbacks " funding " rather than contraction, it differed in no essential way from the policy of McCulloch. The economic and political *Weltanschauung* of James Gallatin was typical of that of the conservative New York bankers, of what Henry Cooke called the " old fogy bank men of New York." The essential ingredients of Gallatin's outlook consisted of a hatred of the greenbacks, a distrust of the National Banking System, opposition to a high protective tariff, and a desire for a rapid return to specie payments via a contraction of the currency. His political views were very

[116] *Ibid.*, p. 200.
[117] *Ibid.*, p. 201.

similar to those held by Andrew Johnson and Hugh McCulloch, particularly on the subject of Southern Reconstruction.

The monetary opinions of George S. Coe, President of the American Exchange Bank of New York, are of particular interest, because Coe was one of the best informed and most constructive bankers of his time.[118] It is nonetheless true that Coe's monetary ideas are a disappointment. His conception of the nature of currency is extremely limited, and the distinction he draws between money and currency is not valid. He also considered the quantity theory of money as a " mathematical truth " even in its crudest form.[119]

To Coe money was an " unvarying object " with an intrinsic value. The adoption of the precious metals as such was due to " human instinct and necessity tantamount to Divine ordination." Paper instruments were not money, but currency, and a valid currency must partake of certain attributes. " All true currency," he wrote in 1868, " is in the nature of bills of exchange. These are legitimate only when drawn against products of industry, which they represent and convey through the channels of commerce and trade, and of which they are the title deeds. As such, they can never be in excess of the public want, because their amount is the measure of the property of the nation, passing into trade and commerce. The more there is of such currency the greater is the evidence of prosperity. A currency thus truly representative, also expresses the amount which the nation may expend without embarrassment or financial disorder. It is limited to the value of the products of labor, which could be exchanged by barter, without the intervention of any paper currency whatever. The legitimate office of currency is simply to facilitate such exchange and distribution, and the genuineness of all forms of paper promises, used as currency, may be tested by this one standard, *that they repre-*

[118] Students of American banking are particularly indebted to Professor Redlich for his skillful portrait of Coe which appears as an appendix to *The Molding Of American Banking*, II, 424-438. Coe's economic ideas emerge very clearly as does his great role in the development of American banking, particularly his role in the development of the clearing house loan certificates. The reader is referred to this article for a comprehensive treatment of Coe's ideas. We are here concerned narrowly with some of his monetary opinions and particularly his ideas on how to achieve specie resumption.

[119] *Ibid.*, II, 436.

sent and transfer some specific property, resolvable into money in the commerce of the world, and pledged for their redemption." [120]

Given this theory of the nature of currency, it is not difficult to see how Coe found the greenbacks unacceptable. He argued that they differed from a legitimate bank-note in " that having been given for articles consumed in war, it had not, when emitted, the essential attributes of true currency. It represented no equivalent in commerce or trade, nothing passing to secure its redemption. It was simply a debt: the evidence of want, not of wealth; of the absence not of the presence, of redeeming power." Coe held that "Suspension of specie payments was the inevitable consequence of thus injecting into trade an element not the growth of its natural operations. Every dollar issued was a step from specie value. It expressed the absence of any present equivalent for its redemption, and therefore lacked the indispensable commercial property of currency." [121]

Despite his exclusion of the greenbacks from the categories of either money or currency, Coe's proposals for action in returning to specie payments were rather mild. He was in favor of contraction of a very gentle sort, but thought that it should be preceded by his pet panacea, the legalization of gold contracts. Contraction of the greenbacks when it was the only legal instrument of trade would tend to produce commercial confusion. Before embarking on such a course, it would be both desirable and necessary to provide for some means by which gold could come back into use as the money of commerce. This, Coe felt, could be accomplished by legislation enabling buyers and sellers, borrowers and lenders, to contract for payment on an individual basis in gold. [122] By this means gold would once again become familiar as money. Demand for it would cause an influx from abroad as well as dishoarding. He

---

[120] George S. Coe, "The Natural Road to Specie Payments," *Bankers' Magazine*, XXII (Old Series) (March, 1868), 732. Italics are Coe's. Several congratulatory letters on this article from bankers were received by Coe. See Redlich, II, 444. Coe's idea that bank-notes cannot be overissued was similar to the opinions of some members of the Banking School in England, particularly Thomas Tooke. See Feavearyear, *The Pound Sterling*, p. 247.

[121] Coe, p. 733.

[122] *Ibid.*, p. 735.

realized that for a time there would exist two standards of value, but in time the country would, he felt, adjust to gold, and greenbacks would be in demand no longer.[123]

But what eventually should be done with the greenbacks? Coe answered this question more explicitly in another article which appeared late in 1868.[124] He argues once more the case for the legalization of gold contracts and this time couples it with a plea for central redemption of the national currency. This he feels will cause a certain amount of contraction since it will force the banks to hold a great amount of greenbacks in reserve for redemption purposes. After these two steps have been taken, Coe argues that the greenbacks should be funded though not directly. He attempts to make the pill of contraction much sweeter by proposing that the greenbacks be funded first into other legal tenders *bearing interest* and that these in turn be gradually funded into bonds. " It is confidently believed," he wrote, " that . . . the operation of the law giving legal protection to coin contracts, would so increase the metallic currency, and the beneficial result of the redemption system would render the banks so strong and reliable, that the legal tenders could be gradually retired, first by conversion into interest bearing notes, if need be, and these again into gold bearing five per cent bonds; and that the process of financial restoration would be effected with greater facility than now seems possible. At all events the process we suggest is a natural one, and the steps in it those which afford the best protection to all the great interests involved." [125] It might be noted that though this process had much to recommend it as a method of returning to specie payments, it only proposed to make contraction more bearable by making it more " natural." [126] In operation it would have been deflationary, and consequently Coe's proposals would have had the same effect as those of James Gallatin. In thus arguing for a return to specie payments through contraction, Coe like Gallatin was representative of conservative New York banking opinion.

[123] *Ibid.*, pp. 735-736.
[124] G. S. C. (George S. Coe), " The Currency and the Public Debt," *Hunt's Merchants' Magazine*, LIX (December, 1868), 418-420.
[125] *Ibid.*, p. 420.
[126] This plan had been advocated as early as 1865 by the *Commercial and Financial Chronicle*.

Less representative of the right wing of New York banking was George Opdyke whose interests were broader than those of Gallatin or Coe. Before the war Opdyke had been a manufacturer of clothing, a retailer, and a writer on economic subjects. In 1862-1863 he had been mayor of New York. In 1864 he became the first president of the new Fourth National Bank organized by Jay Cooke. After the war he continued to be a director of that bank as well as a Vice-President of the Chamber of Commerce of the State of New York. The variety of his interests as well as his association with the House of Cooke helps explain the fact that Opdyke's opinions on the currency issue were less parochial than those of the arch-conservative New York bankers.[127]

Opdyke's views on monetary questions were presented in a speech delivered before the Richmond meeting of the National Board of Trade in December, 1869. Opdyke's speech followed an argument in favor of contraction presented by Joseph S. Ropes, representing the Boston Board of Trade.[128] Because the New Yorker's opinions were delivered *ex tempore*, they do not possess the degree of cogency and close reasoning which might be desired. At the same time they provide a good statement of a moderate position on the currency issue.

At the outset of his speech Opdyke took a position which would appear to lead inevitably to an argument in favor of contraction, for he made the rather arbitrary statement that no nation could maintain a convertible currency which exceeded ten dollars *per capita*. All his experience had tended to confirm this belief. To prove the proposition it was only necessary to study past events. In 1836 and 1837, when the banking system was much extended, the circulation had reached thirteen dollars and a half *per capita*. "What was the consequence? The most disastrous collapse and failure, not only of the banks, but of the commercial community, and a period of industrial prostration extending to the year 1843, at which time the volume of currency had been again reduced to about seven dollars and a

---

[127] Biographical information on Opdyke is derived from Redlich, *The Molding of American Banking*, II, 152. See also *Bankers' Magazine*, XVIII (Old Series) (April, 1864), 842 and XXIV (Old Series) (April, 1870), 793.

[128] *Proceedings of the Second Annual Meeting of the National Board of Trade Held in Richmond, December, 1869* (Boston, 1870), pp. 150-161.

half *per capita*, the previous expansion thus compelling a succeeding contraction as far below the point of gravitation [i. e. ten dollars *per capita*] as it had at first been carried above." [129] As for the condition of the currency in 1869, it was even worse, for Opdyke found that the volume of money in circulation was equivalent to seventeen and a half dollars *per capita* which he held was " seventy five per cent more currency than it is possible for any commercial country in the world to float and maintain its convertibility." [130]

Despite these facts, Opdyke did not advocate contraction of the circulating medium, at least not in an absolute sense. The growing business of the country would, he felt, gradually accommodate itself to the volume of currency outstanding, and this growth of trade itself would mean relative contraction. Absolute contraction would be a mistake for it would bring about a business crisis.[131]

. . . Five per cent per annum of increase of commerce, with a currency of seven hundred millions to facilitate the operations of that commerce, is equivalent to a contraction of thirty-five millions a year, compounded. Now, the question is whether we shall wait that slow process by letting the growth of our commerce slowly, gradually, but surely, climb up to the volume of our currency, or whether we shall attempt to bring about an equilibrium by a rapid contraction of the currency. The uniform method of the nations, including our own, has been to bring about an equilibrium by contraction. We did it in 1837, in 1857, and in every other banking crisis in the country. Great Britain did it; other commercial nations have done it; and in every case, without a single exception, it has been attended by universal commercial disaster, arresting the progress of industry, arresting, in a word, the entire prosperity of the country which has attempted it. . . . For one, I am fully persuaded that the only path of safety is to maintain with all possible care, the equilibrium of the currency as it exists to-day, neither expanding it nor contracting it, and let the business of the country grow up to it.

Opdyke regretted the fact that the country had departed from the specie measure of value, but pointed out there was little to be gained from bewailing the fact. The question was how

---

[129] *Ibid.*, pp. 166-167. By currency Opdyke means the entire circulating medium including gold coin, bank-notes, and greenbacks but excluding bank reserves.

[130] *Ibid.*, p. 167.   [131] *Ibid.*, pp. 167-168.

to get back to specie payments. In that connection, he averred, " Now, if any gentleman can devise a plan by which we can shrink our currency seventy-five per cent at least, the excess over its natural volume, without producing those disasters to which I have referred, I shall be most happy." [132] For his part he felt that the actions of Congress with regard to the currency since the war were " wise and judicious." " We have already . . . got rid of about three hundred and fifty millions of our circulating money, including the compound interest notes. That is accomplishing a great deal. We have done that without any interruption to the prosperity of the country. It is getting better every year, every month, every day, and the prosperity of the country continues. There is no large profit made now, because there is a virtual contraction going on, and sooner or later, by some means or other, prices have got to come down; they will come down." [133] He concluded: " I hope we can go on and avoid any interruption to our prosperity until we reach the period when the volume of business and of currency will be on the same level, when we can resume specie payments just as naturally as the ripe fruit drops from the tree." [134]

The opinions of James Gallatin, George S. Coe, and George Opdyke represent a fair sampling of the sentiments of the New York City banking fraternity. In the main this sentiment was favorable to McCulloch's policy of contraction. Even Opdyke had supported contraction in 1867 and had argued in favor of a resolution adopted by the Chamber of Commerce of the State of New York in April of that year to the effect that ". . . it is the dictate of public interest and national honor, that the Federal Treasury should cautiously, but steadfastly, adhere to the policy of contraction, in so far as it can be done without adversely affecting the business and industrial interests of the country." [135] A similar resolution in favor of contraction was adopted in January, 1869.[136] Since the Chamber of Commerce

[132] *Ibid.*, p. 168.
[133] *Ibid.*, pp. 170-171.
[134] *Ibid.*, pp. 171-172.
[135] *Ninth Annual Report of the Chamber of Commerce of the State of New York for the Year 1866-'67* (New York, 1867), p. 75.
[136] *Eleventh Annual Report of the Chamber of Commerce of the State of New York for the Year 1868-'69* (New York, 1869), pp. 47-53.

was largely composed of members of the mercantile-financial community of New York City, it is fair to assume that these resolutions expressed the convictions of a large majority of the metropolitan bankers.[137]

The post-war views of " the father of the greenbacks " would be interesting, if only to ascertain how the "father" then regarded his controversial children. Elbridge Gerry Spaulding, however, has greater claims to our consideration than his role in originating and carrying through the Legal Tender Acts. Spaulding was a banker and a banker of more than ordinary importance. Not only was he President of the Farmers and Mechanics' National Bank of Buffalo, New York, but also a writer on financial topics as well as a recognized spokesman for the national banking interest as was evidenced by his election as Chairman of the National Bank Convention in 1869.

Spaulding never disavowed his role in the passage of the Legal Tender Acts. As late as 1870, he defended himself against the vicious attack made upon him by Henry Adams and Francis A. Walker in the *North American Review*, asserting that the first Legal Tender Act " was passed in a great emergency as a ' war measure '. . . ." As such, " it proved a success, and has therefore vindicated itself." At the same time Spaulding made it clear that he had never envisaged the greenbacks as a permanent form of currency, pointing out that the legislation of 1862 and 1863 had been passed during an emergency and " not with a view of having it continued indefinitely as a permanent policy of the Government in time of peace." [138]

The Buffalo banker's attitude toward the policy of contraction was one of acquiescence tinged with mild approval. In an article published in 1866, Spaulding wrote: " The avowed policy of the Government is to retire the legal-tender greenback currency,

[137] There can be little doubt but that the New York Chamber of Commerce fairly represented the banking interest of that city. In the years 1867-1869, the first vice-president of the Chamber was George Opdyke. The secretary was John Austin Stevens, a director and one-time president of the Bank of Commerce, whose capital of $10,000,000 was the largest in the nation. The original resolution of 1869 in favor of contraction was offered by Abiel Abbott Low, formerly President of the Merchants' Bank.

[138] E. G. Spaulding, "War Legal Tender Vindicated," *Bankers' Magazine*, XXIV (Old Series) (June, 1870), 973. For the attack of Adams and Walker upon Spaulding and the Legal Tender Acts, see *supra*, pp. 1, 33.

issued during the war, and bring the business of the country back to a gold standard, and a resumption of specie payments. This policy is avowed by the President in his annual message, and by the Secretary of the Treasury in his Fort Wayne speech, and in his annual report. As the policy will sooner or later be carried out, it is important we should look ahead and be prepared for the change. It will take time to accomplish so great a result, and it must be done with great prudence and discretion, or it will produce a shock to the legitimate business of the country, which will paralyze our business operations and thereby diminish the revenues that will be so much needed to maintain the public credit. Whatever measures will aid in promoting the healthy and legitimate business of the country during the process of contraction will be of essential service both to the Government and the people." [139] It thus appears that Spaulding looked upon contraction without any real enthusiasm but as a bitter but healthful medicine which must be taken. His pet panacea which he urged at this time was that national bank-notes be made a legal tender. By investing the notes with this quality, the Buffalo banker believed that contraction could be carried out and specie payments attained more easily, because if bank-notes were legal tender, there would be less demands on the banks for gold which would thus be economized.[140]

Though Spaulding's role in the issue of the greenbacks was such that he could not sincerely adopt the attitude of a man like James Gallatin in denouncing them, it is apparent that he did not approve their continued use in peacetime at least not in an irredeemable form.[141] That the Buffalo banker approved of McCulloch's policy is made evident by a letter written to the Secretary by Spaulding late in 1867 in which the banker asserted: "You are doing a good service to the country, and I trust that your financial policy will be sustained by Congress." [142] Like most of his fellow bankers in the East, Spaulding

---

[139] E. G. Spaulding, "The National Currency A Legal Tender," *Bankers' Magazine*, XX (Old Series) (April, 1866), 762.

[140] *Ibid.*, pp. 767-768.

[141] It will be recalled that Gallatin and Spaulding had clashed in 1862 over the proper financial policy to be pursued by the government. *Supra*, pp. 31-33.

[142] E. G. Spaulding to McCulloch, December 5, 1867, McCulloch Papers.

approved of contraction providing it could be carried out without a business crisis.

This attitude is apparent in the speech delivered by Spaulding before the National Bank Convention of 1869. On this occasion he averred that the Convention had as its object the formation of a new organization which would aid in perfecting the National Banking System. One of the ways in which the national banks could be improved would be to secure " a prompt redemption of their currency in gold and silver." But the man from Buffalo asserted: " It is very obvious that the country must pass through an important crisis before we reach specie payments, and that there must be mutual aid and co-operation by all parties in accomplishing that result." [143] The national bankers, he declared, approved the financial policy of President Grant as outlined in his inaugural address which included " economy, the payment of the public debt in coin, and as early a return to specie payments as possible without materially affecting the debtor class." [144] He found it cause for congratulations that the Secretary of the Treasury was now in a position to use surplus revenue to make a monthly reduction in the public debt. This, he asserted, was evidence of " the ability of the Government to . . . make adequate preparation for placing all the neglected and misused greenback currency on a par with gold, the redemption of such portion of it as may be necessary for that purpose, the inauguration of regular and certain methods of managing the finances, giving stability to the business of the country, which is so essential to success at this time." [145] It was, however, a fact to be regretted that the Secretary possessed no power to redeem and cancel greenbacks. " We are now in this anomalous condition. While all the funded debt, amounting to over $2,100,000,000, is placed by law upon a gold basis, *so that it will readily pass out of the country for imported goods of little real value to the country*, and an ample fund provided to pay the interest in coin, the Secretary of the Treasury is prohibited from paying the greenback currency at all. It seems almost incredible that the finances should have

[143] *Proceedings of the National Bank Convention Held in New York City, Wednesday, June 23, 1869*, p. 7.
[144] *Ibid.*, p. 8.   [145] *Ibid.*, pp. 8-9.

been so shaped, that ample provision should have been made for paying all the public debt in coin, except that which is now due, and which is greatly depreciated because no provision is made of its payment. It is not at all to be wondered that a debt thus dishonored, should be so depreciated that a dollar in gold will purchase $1.37 in greenbacks. . . ." [146]

Because of the Act of February 4, 1868 which denied to the Secretary of the Treasury the power to contract the currency, Spaulding felt that that officer was " much restricted " in the influence he could wield on the financial situation. Even though the Secretary's power had been curtailed, however, there were certain things he could do to improve the situation. The most significant move he could make in the direction of specie payments would be the building up of a gold reserve in the Treasury against the day when coin payments would be feasible.[147] At the same time the Buffalo banker agreed with George S. Coe that some way must be found to bring gold back into circulation. " Whatever else may be done to improve the finances, it is perfectly plain to every practical business man, that the greenback currency cannot be redeemed in coin until the Government is able to let the coin flow in and *again circulate as money*, the same as it did previous to the war. Coined money must resume its place in the business of the country simultaneously with the withdrawal of the greenbacks, so that there shall be no material contraction, and so that there shall be no material disturbance to legitimate business, when resumption takes place. . . ." [148] Like Coe, Spaulding felt that the reintroduction of gold as a medium of payment would be necessary to counteract the deflationary effects of contraction. Spaulding also agreed with Coe and Gallatin that contraction was a necessary step along the road to specie payments.

The interests of Henry Clews must be sharply distinguished from the interests of the national bankers previously discussed. The distinction arises from the essential difference in the nature of private banking as contrasted with conventional banking under the national system. Whereas the large national bankers

---

[146] *Ibid.*, p. 14. Italics are Spaulding's.
[147] *Ibid.*, pp. 10-11.
[148] *Ibid.*, p. 16. Italics are Spaulding's.

of the East possessed something of a vested interest in deflation, no such consideration applies to the typical metropolitan private banker of the period.

Henry Clews was an Englishman who came to the United States at an early age and received his business training in New York in a firm of woolen importers. He soon became independent and emerged in Wall Street as a private banker and broker, working with various partners under various firm names. As Professor Redlich notes, he was for most of his life " a stock trader and broker and a typical Wall Street banker, financing his clients' trading on margin." [149] Clews solicited the balances of out-of-town banks and paid interest thereon. He acted as a broker in the buying and selling of stocks, bonds, and gold. These interests alone would have given him something more than an academic concern with the course of the stock, bond, and gold markets, and it is significant to note that this interest was intensified by the fact that Clews frequently dealt in gold and securities on his own account.[150] Now it is true that as a speculator Clew's interests would not necessarily be inextricably tied to inflation. It is also true, however, that speculation generally prospers during periods of rising prices and frequently suffers in a reverse situation. As a trader in gold and securities, Clews definitely did not feel that his interests were being served by McCulloch's policy of contraction.

The opinions of Henry Clews on the currency question were brought to public attention in an open letter to the Secretary of the Treasury published in the spring of 1867.[151] Clews minced no words on the subject of McCulloch's financial policy. He averred that business was being " paralyzed and demoralized " by the contraction of the currency, and that " after the heavy losses sustained by the business firms through the entire country, it would require but little further pressure to cause very many of them to become bankrupt." [152]

The New Yorker made a frontal attack on one of McCulloch's

[149] Redlich, *The Molding of American Banking*, II, 361.
[150] *Ibid.*, II, 76-77.
[151] Henry Clews, " The Currency Question. Letter to the Secretary of the Treasury, from a New York Banker," *Bankers' Magazine*, XXI (Old Series) (May, 1867), 822-825.
[152] *Ibid.*, p. 822.

principal positions, namely, that contraction was necessary to bring about a reduction in the high level of prices. Clews pointed out what he regarded as the weaknesses of this point of view: " One of the most important requisites to a decline in prices is the encouragement of production, as the abundance of products is practically synonymous with cheapness. It is, however, the misfortune of the policy of contraction, that it directly tends to discourage production." [153] A public spirited concern with the health of the economy having been demonstrated, Clews was impelled to consider interests of a more personal nature, asserting that " The contraction of about eighteen millions of greenbacks during the last three months of 1866 produced a succession of small panics in the stock market, and caused a general depression of business; not so much from the loss of that amount of circulation, but from the fact that this depletion of the vital current of commerce begat a general alarm, and caused a sudden disturbance of the whole machinery of credit." [154] " There is much legitimate speculation," Clews continued with a masterly exhibit of equivocation, " the effect of which upon production is healthy and stimulating. It is surely a grave question for the consideration of a minister of finance, whether it is justifiable to embarrass and injure the whole commerce of the country, for the sake of dealing a blow at a few gambling speculators." [155] In conclusion, the private banker declared that " While all admit the gravity of the patient's disease, yet most have full confidence of his power of self-recovery, and seriously fear that official doctoring will aggravate the symptoms and protract the prostration." [156]

The financial opinions of Henry Clews are significant because they represent the viewpoint of a segment of banking which was at variance with the sentiments of a majority of the national bankers of the East. The close connection of the private bankers with the security markets developed a strong opposition on their part to the deflationary policy of contraction. Although the private bankers were not numerous, they were not loth to express their opinions and presented something of a counter-

---

[153] *Ibid.*, p. 823.
[154] *Ibid.*, pp. 823-824.

[155] *Ibid.*, p. 824.
[156] *Ibid.*, p. 825.

weight in capitalist circles to the deflationary views of national bankers such as Coe, Gallatin, and Spaulding.[157]

THE WESTERN VIEWPOINT

There is evidence that western bankers were largely opposed to McCulloch's efforts to contract the greenback currency, though the case is by no means clear-cut. Opposition to contraction, which was particularly strong among the small town bankers of the West, was largely a question of self-interest. It has been pointed out that the western and country banks were far more interested in the business of issuing currency than their colleagues in the great eastern cities. Demand deposits were of little importance in the rural areas of the West. Loans were commonly made and repaid in paper currency.[158] Though it can be argued that contraction of the greenbacks would put these banks in a stronger creditor position due to the increase in the value of money which would be the logical result of this policy, this advantage was outweighed in the minds of western bankers by other considerations. In the first place a rapid return to specie payments through contraction would mean that banks would be required to redeem their circulation in gold. This would mean that western banks would be forced to hoard in their vaults the gold interest received on their bonds deposited with the treasurer of the United States in order to build up a specie reserve. They would thus be deprived of the profitable business of selling gold for

---

[157] Senator John Sherman's correspondence with private bankers tends to support this. James P. Kilbreth, of Kilbreth, Smith and Company, private bankers and brokers of New York, wrote the Senator on February 7, 1867, expressing the view that contraction, if continued, "would break up almost all the business men of the country." He continued: "The people never had & never will have a currency they liked or will like so well as plain legal tender and nothing in the way of contraction would please the country so well as to see a contraction of several millions per month of its interest bearing obligations." E. B. Hale, a private banker of Cleveland, wrote Sherman on February 16, 1867, asserting, "The business of the country is *paralyzed* for needed Congressional action. The people *do not need expansion*—all they want is to *stop contraction* for the present. . . . The people would be glad to get greenbacks for their Compound int. notes but Uncle Sam is *so rich* and *so generous* that he *insists* on giving them a new obligation and *pay 4 per ct* for doing it. Magnificent infatuation!" Sherman Papers.

[158] Redlich, *The Molding of American Banking*, II, 119-120.

greenbacks at a premium. In the second place it must be remembered that the fortunes of these banks were largely bound up with the fortunes of their customers. Although from a purely monetary point of view it would seem that the banks would gain from an increase in the value of the monetary unit, it was nonetheless true that they could not prosper if the regions they served did not prosper. Contraction which was another name for deflation could by no stretch of the imagination benefit the credit starved economy of the West.

There is evidence to support this view. The Merchants' Union Law Company which fought central redemption on behalf of some of the country banks of the West also fought contraction of the currency. The petition which was circulated by this company asked that Congress " refrain from the passage of any act authorizing the curtailment of the national currency, or having in view the return, within a limited time, to specie payments. They [the petitioners] respectfully represent that the further reduction of the volume of the currency, at present, would prove highly injurious to the banking, manufacturing, and mercantile interests of the country, and would entail suffering upon nearly every member of the community." [159]

This attitude was further reflected in several articles which appeared in the *Bankers' Magazine*. Writing in the issue of March, 1866, a western banker answered the question of what should be done with the greenback currency. " The answer is short: *Let the currency alone!* Lay no violent hands upon it. Do not disturb its equilibrium by experiments. After such an unprecedented struggle the country needs all the rest it can obtain; and every facility for its recuperation should be resolutely preserved intact, until its prostrate energies are again brought into action, its immense resources developed, and its industry established upon a solid and permanent foundation. In order to establish these desirable and paramount objects, money is absolutely necessary. For these purposes we need all the currency we have; its diminution to any considerable extent would immediately put a stop to the recuperative efforts of the country to repair the damages inflicted by the war, and plunge it into a deeper abyss of financial calamity." [160]

[159] See the petition in the Sherman Papers referred to *supra*, p. 234.
[160] " New Views on the Currency Communicated to the Bankers' Magazine

Somewhat the same attitude was expressed by another western banker in an article which appeared in July, 1868. This writer felt there was no need for a contraction of the greenbacks, but he advocated specie convertibility at a gradually increasing rate beginning at 70 cents in gold for $1.00 in legal tender through January 1, 1869 and appreciating to par convertibility by January 1, 1875.[161] This plan was almost identical with the plan adopted by the British government in 1820 as a means for returning to specie payments.[162] Its weakness was the weakness of all plans for returning to specie without contraction, namely the necessity of accumulating a large gold reserve.

The author felt that this plan would place the responsibility for the amount of currency in the hands of the people, and it is obvious that he did not feel they would choose contraction voluntarily.[163]

If the amount of currency is excessive, it would be reduced under the operation of a self-regulating system, and if not excessive, contraction would cease. The power to contract would be intrusted to the people, and the nation would be relieved from the relentless application of an inflexible rule. It is believed that contraction would cease by choice of the people, and that it would be shown the business of the country needed all the currency in circulation. A better kind of currency, nearer related to real money, is desired, not a diminished amount of bad currency. Contraction, as practiced, has not improved the commercial value of the currency, as shown by the gold premium, nor has it made a resumption of specie payments more easy. By producing commercial distress and despondency it has impaired the ability of the people to pay taxes, and rendered uncertain the collection of the revenue, thus wounding the credit of the nation, and depressing the commercial value of the currency.

---

by a Western Banker," *Bankers' Magazine*, XX (Old Series) (March, 1866), 680-681. The author was probably Jonathan Binns, Cashier of the First National Bank of Mt. Pleasant, Ohio. In pointing out the differences between the eastern and western attitudes, it is significant to note that at the end of this article, the editor of the *Bankers' Magazine* appended a note, as follows: " We give place to the communication of our Western correspondent, in order that both sides may be heard on the currency question; but we do not adopt the views of the writer." *Ibid.*, p. 683.

[161] A Western Banker, " The Legal Tender Currency," The *Bankers' Magazine*, XXIII (Old Series) (July, 1868), 14-19. The article is signed " W. P. B.," but the identity of this individual is unknown.

[162] Feavearyear, *The Pound Sterling*, p. 206.

[163] A Western Banker, *op. cit.*, p. 18.

Letters received by John Sherman in this period also reflect an opposition to contraction and deflation on the part of small town western bankers. A. H. Moss, President of the First National Bank of Sandusky, Ohio, questioned the idea that there was an overabundance of currency. " ' Redundancy of currency ' is a favorite, constantly reiterated cry of the destructionists. Where is money too plenty? Where is this superabundance to be found?" [164] L. S. Hubbard, President of the Second National Bank of the same town, opined that only under an inflated paper currency could banks " make fair dividends & pay the taxes now assessed, but no longer than that inflation exists." [165]

It cannot, however, be maintained that opposition to contraction was universal among western bankers. As the Sandusky banker, A. H. Moss, pointed out to Senator Sherman, bankers in the larger western cities such as St. Louis, Chicago, and Cleveland tended to react somewhat the same as their colleagues in New York, Boston, and Philadelphia and for the same reason—their profits did not depend so much on circulation.[166] T. P. Handy, President of the Merchants' National Bank of Cleveland, reflected this metropolitan western attitude when he expressed the opinion to Sherman that contraction would not seriously disturb business. He asserted that he had great confidence in the Secretary of the Treasury. All that was needed was " time and patience to get back to a specie basis." [167] George W. Rathbone, President of the Evansville National Bank of Evansville, Indiana, also supported the policy of McCulloch. In a letter to the Secretary, this gentleman declared that he could not believe that " Congress will be so unwise, not to say insane, as to yield to this senseless outcry." [for expansion of the currency] " After all," the Indiana banker wrote, " the practical views presented in your report must . . . prevail. Otherwise we shall for a time go up, as we did during the war, like a baloon to come down next-time like a stick." [168] The fact

---

[164] A. H. Moss to John Sherman, January 28, 1867. Sherman Papers.
[165] L. S. Hubbard to John Sherman, May 7, 1866. *Ibid.*
[166] A. H. Moss to John Sherman, January 28, 1867. *Ibid.*
[167] T. P. Handy to John Sherman, February 5, 1867. *Ibid.*
[168] George W. Rathbone to Hugh McCulloch, December 11, 1867. McCulloch Papers.

that the issue of contraction was not discussed at the Chicago convention of western bankers in 1866 would seem remarkable except for the probability that agreement on the question of what to do with the greenbacks was precluded by a hopeless division of opinion.[169]

The preceding pages have been devoted to an exposition of banking opinion on the currency issue as well as to a presentation of the institutional rationale for that opinion. The attitudes of bankers on this issue are seen to be diverse and extremely complex, only to be understood in the light of pertinent economic factors. There is no doubt a certain unpleasant bluntness about the assumption of economic interest as a touchstone of historical interpretation. Nonetheless it is true that without this assumption that *ceteris paribus* men will tend to act and rationalize their thoughts in their own economic interest, the diversity of attitude within the American banking fraternity on the issue of contraction of the greenbacks would be completely bewildering. Given the touchstone of self-interest to guide our researches, the varying attitudes of the great New York bankers, the country bankers, the private bankers, of Jay Cooke and James Gallatin all become understandable.

In general it can be said that bankers provided Hugh McCulloch with his most important reservoir of support on the contraction issue. This support was strongest among the arch-conservative bankers of the eastern seaboard, though it was by no means exclusively confined to this area. Even the country bankers of the West who opposed contraction cannot accurately be described as inflationists. Their attitudes were simply a logical response to an actual dearth of currency. Though the bankers were not important numerically, they were important in terms of power and influence. The support which Hugh McCulloch derived from the general run of metropolitan bankers throughout the country provides us with a good part of the explanation of why the basically unpopular policy of contraction was inaugurated and why it was persisted in for nearly two years.

[169] See the proceedings of this convention in the *Bankers' Magazine*, XXI (Old Series) (November, 1866), 321-333.

Appendix III

RECONSTRUCTION ISSUES AND THE NEW YORK BUSINESS COMMUNITY

The friendly disposition of James Gallatin toward Andrew Johnson and his Reconstruction policy was by no means an isolated phenomenon among New York merchants and bankers. In fact, support of Johnson tended to be the rule rather than the exception. The political counterpart of the gold standard— free trade views of Wall Street was a general tendency to look with favor upon the moderate approach to the problems of Reconstruction. This attitude dated back at least to the spring of 1865 when the Chamber of Commerce of the State of New York, representing the banking and mercantile interests of the metropolis, resolved: " That while we would have nothing left undone that is essential to the complete and permanent restoration of the national authority, we yet trust and urge that such restoration may be everywhere signalized by magnanimity and clemency, and that it may nowhere be stained by a single act which will be condemned as needlessly harsh or revengeful by the cool judgment of the humane and liberty-loving in any part of the civilized world." [1]

That the economic policies of the Radicals were deemed injurious to the interests of New York is attested by a memorial adopted unanimously by the Chamber on July 5, 1866 protesting against the tariff bill then before the House of Representatives on the grounds that the duties proposed by the bill were " in many cases so high that they must prove prohibitive." The memorial asserted that " The proposed enhancement of duties is chiefly, if not altogether, on imported articles which come directly in competition with similar domestic products, such, for example, as iron, wool, woolens, worsteds, linens and cigars. These are all leading articles in our import trade; and no one familiar with that trade can doubt that the exorbitant duties

---

[1] *Eighth Annual Report of the Chamber of Commerce of the State of New York For the Year 1865-'66* (New York, 1866), p. 4.

which this bill proposes to subject them to would greatly diminish their import, and thereby lessen the revenue of the Government. . . . There is reason to apprehend that the joint effect of the two measures might so reduce the revenue of the Government as to leave the aggregate insufficient to meet its current expenses and maturing interest, and thus weaken the public credit." [2] The apparent concern for the revenue of the government may perhaps be discounted, but the interests of the business community of New York City which this memorial expressed were quite real.

Support for administration policies and for the President personally was dramatically demonstrated by the mercantile-financial interests of New York upon the occasion of Andrew Johnson's visit to that city late in August, 1866. This visit was a part of the famous " Swing Around the Circle " in which the President sought to defend his policies before the people. It followed his vetoes of the Freedman's Bureau and Civil Rights Bills which had brought the differences between Johnson and the Radicals in Congress to the boiling point.

The President's visit to the great American metropolis at this crucial point in his career was a gala occasion, and everywhere the support of the business community was made evident. When the chief executive arrived in the city, he was met by a committee which included the following: Moses Taylor, President of the City Bank and one of the half-dozen most important bankers in New York; William B. Astor, real estate tycoon and probably the richest man in the United States; William H. Vanderbilt, railroad king and son of the famous " Commodore "; Abiel Abbott Low, President of the Merchants' Bank; John Q. Jones, long-time President of the Chemical Bank and an important member of the Finance Committee of the Associated Banks in 1861; John J. Cisco, formerly Sub-Treasurer of the United States and now an important private banker; and Jonathan Sturges, one of the founders of the Bank of Commerce and one of New York's most successful importers. One of the chief organizers of the President's reception in the city was

[2] *Ninth Annual Report of the Chamber of Commerce of the State of New York for the Year 1866-'67* (New York, 1867), p. 29.

none other than the merchant-prince Alexander T. Stewart who rode with Johnson through the streets of New York in an open barouche, together with Secretary Seward and Mayor Hoffman. A Committee of Merchants two-hundred strong formed a significant part of the procession.[3]

The procession route had been laid out through the heart of the business and financial district. From the front of Messrs. Cochran & Co. was displayed a large banner which read: " WELCOME TO THE PRESIDENT OF OUR WHOLE COUNTRY! " Over the Ninth National Bank was the motto: " Welcome Andrew Johnson—Honor to the Chief Magistrate! " The Eighth National Bank prominently displayed a quotation from one of Johnson's latest speeches. Other business establishments similarly indicated support of the President and pleasure at his visit.[4]

A great banquet was held in honor of the President and his party at Delmonico's restaurant. All of the distinguished merchants and bankers listed above attended the affair. Other guests whose names loomed large in the commercial life of New York were Henry Grinnell, Augustus Schell, Abram S. Hewitt, H. C. Fahnestock, W. H. Vermilye, C. L. Tiffany, August Belmont, and Henry Clews.[5]

Johnson's speech on this occasion was greeted with enthusiasm. When he strongly defended his moderate Reconstruction policies, the audience interrupted several times with applause. Warming to his task, the President declared: " You have about three thousand millions of dollars in bonds. How are you going to preserve the credit of them? Will you tell me how the security, how the value, how the ultimate payment of the interest and principal of those bonds is to be secured? It is by continuing this Government, disrupted as it is, by crippling our energies, and dividing us up into half a dozen petty States? Let me tell you, and mark what I tell you, that there is no way by which those bonds can be ultimately paid, interest and principal than by the consolidation of our nationality, the per-

---

[3] New York *Times*, August 29, 1866.
[4] *Ibid*., August 30, 1866.
[5] *Ibid*.

petuity and completeness of the Union of the States." [6] The great applause which greeted this tying together of economic interest and political policy indicated that Andrew Johnson had a thorough understanding of the motivations of the New York business community. In light of this evidence there seems little doubt that the mercantile-financial interests of New York supported the political program of Andrew Johnson just as they supported the financial program of his Secretary of the Treasury.

[6] *Ibid.* For other accounts of Johnson's friendly reception in New York, see George Fort Milton, *The Age of Hate: Andrew Johnson and the Radicals* (New York, 1930), pp. 360-361; Lloyd Paul Stryker, *Andrew Johnson: A Study in Courage* (New York, 1929), pp. 341-348. Milton points out that after Johnson's veto of the Freedmen's Bureau bill, there was a great meeting of civic leaders in New York and that a committee including such business leaders as Moses Taylor and William B. Astor was appointed to go to Washington to confer with the President to see what the New Yorkers could do to effectively support Johnson's policies. Milton, pp. 289-290.

CHAPTER VII

CONCLUSION

The preceding pages have explored many different aspects of the financial history of the Civil War and Reconstruction. Attention has been given to the origin of the greenbacks in 1862, to the subsequent issues of paper money, and to the general importance of the legal tenders as an expedient of war finance. Considerable space has been devoted to an analysis of the political struggle over the issue of contraction which became important in the years following the war. In order to present a clearer picture of the forces behind this struggle, in order to understand the motives of politicians and the essential meaning of the various legislative enactments, it has been necessary to probe deeply into the economic rationale of four crucially important groups, manufacturers, farmers, laborers, and bankers. Only by achieving an understanding of the effects of the issue of the greenbacks on each of these groups as well as a comprehension of the philosophies which rationalized their interests is it possible to extract the full meaning from the bitter fight over the issue of contraction.

By using the tools of economic analysis to probe the problem of group motivation in its relation to the currency issue, it is hoped that some of the darker recesses of Reconstruction history have been illuminated. This presentation has involved the generous use of both fact and theory. We need not be told today that facts alone are meaningless, that the mind of man comprehends the concrete instance only within a conceptual framework. Whether the mind of the historian works from theory to fact or from fact to theory, whether it is inductive or deductive in its method—this is unimportant. The vitally important consideration is whether theory and fact are in harmony. If this condition is fulfilled, progress is possible in the field of historical interpretation. It is my feeling that the prevailing interpretation of the economic history of the Civil War and Reconstruction, particularly as it regards financial issues, is at fault. Misinterpretation has prevailed because theory and fact have not been in harmony. Where historians have begun their work with a preconceived theory of the economic basis of the Civil War and Reconstruction, there has been a tendency for troublesome inconsistencies to be ignored. In those cases where the perplexities have been pointed out, there has been a disinclination to strike out on new pathways of general interpretation. It is the purpose of this concluding chapter to consider the ways in which the general interpretation of the politico-economic history of the Civil War and Reconstruction contained in this study differs from the currently prevailing interpretation. In order that these differences may be brought into sharper focus, it will be helpful to consider briefly the major conclusions which have been reached in the preceding pages.

I. In treating the origin of the greenbacks it has been concluded that the issue of some form of paper currency by the government was almost inevitable during the Civil War. To this author the inevitability, we might even say the necessity of this expedient, arose from a number of circumstances. Among these circumstances was the clearly evident fact that the Congressional leaders of the Republican party were unwilling to have the bonds of the government sold for whatever they would bring in the financial centers. When E. G. Spaulding objected " to any and every form of ' shinning ' by Government through Wall or State streets to begin with: . . . to the knocking down of Government stocks to seventy-five or sixty cents on the dollar . . . ," he was merely voicing the views of a majority in Congress.[1] Having failed to adopt an adequate program of taxation and having demonstrated a decided unwillingness to throw bonds on the market for what they would bring in specie, the remaining alternative left to Congress was the issue of some form of fiat money. The attractiveness of this proposition was enhanced by the fact that most financial leaders including Spaulding realized that, after a sufficient degree of inflation had been achieved, it would be possible to market government bonds at par.[2]

In considering the question of the " necessity " of the green-

---

[1] *Supra,* p. 32.   [2] *Supra,* p. 47 n.

backs, we are reduced to speculation as to whether the war could possibly have been financed on a specie basis. Given the state of public confidence after the suspension of specie payments and after all the early Union reverses, it seems highly unlikely that sufficient gold could have been obtained by the government. Even should a large amount of gold have come out of hoards in payment for government bonds, it is clear that they would have been heavily discounted in the financial centers. To the question as to whether the war could possibly have been financed on a gold basis, an unequivocal answer cannot be given. The logical " necessity " of the greenbacks cannot be fully established, as Mitchell and others have pointed out. A very good case, however, can be made for the historical " necessity " of this expedient. This argument is based on the unwillingness of Congress to authorize the sale of government bonds at prices far below par. In such a situation the issue of United States notes became the only reasonable alternative, a fact which men such as Spaulding, Hooper, and Sherman were quick to grasp. It was within this framework of ideas that these men and others argued for the " necessity " of the Legal Tender Acts.

An important facet of the case for the " necessity " of the greenbacks was the argument that the country was in desperate need of an adequate medium of exchange. Samuel Hooper in the House and John Sherman in the Senate emphasized that neither gold nor state bank-notes could be depended upon for this purpose.[3] Here again, of course, the assumption was implicit that sufficient gold could not be tempted out of hoards to provide the nation with a means of payment. In the early months of 1862, however, such an assumption seemed completely reasonable. I must confess that from the vantage point provided by nearly a hundred years of history, the assumption still seems reasonable to me. Although it is a minority view, contrary to that expressed in virtually all of the older works on the subject, and shared, to my knowledge, only by Professor Redlich, I feel that a very good case can be made for the historical " necessity " of the greenbacks.

[3] *Supra*, pp. 38-39, 44.

II. Among the more important results of this study is the conclusion that among the so-called Radical Republicans there were serious cleavages on financial questions. The soft-money line was taken and maintained with vigor by a group of the most ultra-Radical of the Radical contingent in Congress. Those Congressmen whose votes and speeches reflected an unswerving opposition to contraction and hard-money policies generally included the Pennsylvania ultras, Thaddeus Stevens, William D. Kelley, and John Covode. Also in this group should be included the Massachusetts Radical, Benjamin F. Butler. In the Senate the crusade against hard-money and contraction enlisted the eminent Radical talents of the Ohio ultra, Benjamin F. Wade. In this cause he was joined by the phlegmatic and enigmatic Senator from Rhode Island, William Sprague.[4] This group formed the hard core of opposition to McCulloch's policy of contraction as well as to hard-money policies generally. It was the vote on the Public Credit Act of 1869 which separated the principled greenbackers from the politicians, providing an important index of sincerity on financial policy. It is significant, therefore, that not a single vote in favor of the Public Credit Act was cast by a member of this group, a fact the more remarkable when it is considered that General Grant had been overwhelmingly elected on a " sound money " platform and had expressed himself in his inaugural in favor of a return to specie payments.[5]

[4] Although he was not in Congress, Wendell Phillips shared the financial opinions of his fellow ultras, Wade, Stevens, and Butler.

[5] In February, 1869, Covode, Kelley, Butler, and Wade voted against the Public Credit Act. Stevens was dead, but there can be little doubt but that he would have voted against it also. Sprague was recorded as absent. *Congressional Globe*, 40th Congress, 3rd Session, pp. 1538-39; 1678. Two other Radicals also voted against the Act, Senator S. C. Pomeroy of Kansas and Ignatius Donnelly. In my opinion, however, Pomeroy and Donnelly should not be considered as principled greenbackers inasmuch as Pomeroy had voted for contraction in 1866 and Donnelly's opinions were too erratic to deserve much consideration. In the 41st Congress the principled greenbackers had been reduced to a corporal's guard. Wade had failed of reelection and Covode no longer sat in the House. On the vote of March 12, 1869, Kelley was recorded as absent, but Butler joined a number of Democrats to oppose final passage of the Public Credit Act. The loss of Wade meant the end of all effective opposition in the Senate, since on the vote of March 15, Sprague, once again exercising the prerogatives of eccentricity, was recorded as absent. *Congressional Globe*, 41st Congress, 1st Session, pp. 61, 70.

Leading the fight against soft-money heresies and in favor of contraction and a rapid return to specie payments was another small group of Republicans whose views on the political aspects of Reconstruction were, on balance, somewhat more moderate than those of the first group named above. In this group are found James G. Blaine and William P. Fessenden of Maine, Justin S. Morrill of Vermont, Roscoe Conkling of New York, and James A. Garfield and Elihu B. Washburne of Ohio. It was from this group, which stood stanchly in favor of contraction and a quick return to specie payments, that Hugh McCulloch drew consistent support for his financial policies.

Holding the balance of power between these two groups was another group of Radicals who vigorously opposed contraction, deflation, and Andrew Johnson's Secretary of the Treasury in the years 1866-1868 but who nonetheless rallied to the cause of the sanctity of the public debt in 1869. This group would include such leading Radicals as George W. Julian of Indiana, John A. Logan of Illinois, John Sherman, Robert Schenck, and John A. Bingham of Ohio, James F. Wilson of Iowa, Thomas Williams of Pennsylvania, and George S. Boutwell of Massachusetts.[6] It was this group which determined the course of Radical action. Holding neither to the soft-money line of the first group nor to the hard-money dogma of the second, this group was motivated primarily by political considerations. In the years of depression and falling prices which followed the war, it was politically smart to oppose the deflationary policies of Andrew Johnson's Secretary of the Treasury. What was good politics until the summer of 1868, however, did not fall into that category after a soft-money plank had been hammered into the Democratic platform of that year. The trend of business was upward in 1868 and 1869, and Ulysses Grant was swept into office on a platform which loftily proclaimed the sanctity of the public debt. Now that the soft-money label could safely be pinned on the Democracy, there could be little doubt but that the Republican road

---

[6] Radicals who do not fit so neatly into one of these three patterns include James M. Ashley of Ohio and Senator Henry Wilson of Massachusetts who voted for contraction in 1866, against it in 1868, and in favor of the Public Credit Act in 1869. The strange case of Senator Charles Sumner of Massachusetts has been discussed at length above, pp. 132-134.

lay in the direction of specie payments. Passage of the Public Credit Act in 1869 marked the end of the first battle in the great money war which was to convulse the nation until the end of the century. It had been won by the hard-money dogmatists such as Morrill, Fessenden, and Garfield in league with the political Radicals who had sensed the change in the wind in the summer of 1868. Nevertheless it is quite clear that the Republican party was by no means the party of " sound finance " from the end of the war until the summer of 1868. The Democrats would have a far sounder claim to such a title. If indeed it can be said that the period from the end of the war until the impeachment of Andrew Johnson represents the apogee of Radicalism, then it is clear that Radicalism must be fit into the soft-money mold. That thesis may not be invalid which would hold that true Radicalism, economic, social, and political, did not survive the failure to convict Andrew Johnson, the election of Grant, the death of Stevens, the eclipse of Wade.[7]

If indeed Radicalism can be said to have an economic as well as a political philosophy, it would seem that it must be the philosophy of the true ultras, of Stevens, of Butler, of Wade, of Wendell Phillips, not the philosophy of those who were at heart moderates, of the Garfields, the Fessendens and the Morrills. If then we look at the core of ideas which bound these ultras together, we find nationalism, egalitarianism, a belief in economic freedom. In the economic sphere these ideas were translated by the economist and philosopher Henry C. Carey into a positive program of action. The twin pillars of this program were protectionism and soft-money. According to Carey and his Radical followers, only a high protective tariff could shield American industry from the onslaughts of foreign monopolists. Only the adoption of an easy money policy by the federal government could protect the manufacturer, the

---

[7] The distinction made by Louis M. Hacker between the " New Radicals " and the " Old Radicals " is, I feel, essentially valid. It would correspond somewhat with the distinction made here between men like Stevens, Wade, and Butler and the political Radicals. The correspondence is only rough because Professor Hacker devotes little space to analyzing the facets of the money question. See Louis M. Hacker, *The Triumph of American Capitalism: The Development of Forces in American History to the End of the Nineteenth Century* (New York, 1940), pp. 341-342.

farmer, and the laborer from the encroachments and eventual control of the money power, the financial oligarchs of the eastern seaboard cities. Given this frame of reference, opposition to slavery and the slave power had been inevitable. Once the war was over the principled Radicals turned much of their holy wrath upon the plutocracy of the North and its spokesmen, the McCullochs, Morrills, and their banker friends who, they felt, would gladly place the country at the mercy of finance capital.

In these terms Radicalism has meaning. Indeed it emerges as a fairly consistent social philosophy and not one to be despised. The ideas which bound together such men as Thaddeus Stevens, Benjamin Wade, Ben Butler, " Pig Iron " Kelley, Peter Cooper, Wendell Phillips, Horace Greeley, and Henry C. Carey were not the unworthiest vision of the America which could have arisen after the convulsive spasm of civil war.[8]

III. Along with an analysis of the essential nature of Radicalism this study has been concerned with an explanation of the monetary opinions held by the different factions within the Democratic party. The shift by the western wing of the Democracy from the hard-money line of pre-Civil War years to the " Ohio rag-baby " banner of the Reconstruction period ranks among the more puzzling phenomena of American history. In 1862 the most substantial opposition to the issue of the greenbacks came from the Democrats, and that opposition included none other than George Hunt Pendleton himself. In 1866 contraction and a rapid return to specie payments was favored by twenty-seven out of twenty-eight Democrats in the House and by the unanimous vote of that party's seven representatives in the Senate. Less than two years later House Democrats opposed further contraction by a vote of twenty-three to thirteen, and the three Democratic Senators unanimously opposed the policy of the Secretary of the Treasury. In February, 1869 House Democrats opposed passage of the Public Credit Act by a vote of twenty-four to twelve, and their colleagues in the Senate cast a solid vote against the bill. The sectional characteristics of this change in front are revealing. Whereas

[8] *Supra*, Chapter IV.

eastern Democrats, on balance, continued to favor a "sound money" policy by substantial margins in 1868 and 1869, the western Democrats went over almost entirely to the soft-money camp. In 1868 House Democrats from the western and western border states opposed further contraction by a margin of sixteen to two, and in 1869 these same Democrats voted against passage of the Public Credit Bill by a margin of sixteen to one.

The Democratic voting record in 1868 and 1869 makes it apparent that, whereas hard-money attitudes exemplified by such leaders as Horatio Seymour, Samuel J. Tilden, and August Belmont still predominated in the eastern Democracy, the soft-money philosophy had almost completely captured the western wing of the party. In this study an interpretation has been advanced to explain this remarkable change of attitude. While political expediency offers a partial explanation for the ideological flip-flop which was performed by the western Democracy beginning in 1867, it does not really provide us with a fully convincing reason why essentially principled men such as George Pendleton, Francis Preston Blair, Jr., and William Allen abandoned their previously held hard-money convictions. Probing deeper it is seen that the thread of continuity which linked the old hard-money Democracy of the age of Jackson with the "Ohio rag-baby" champions of the late sixties was a continuing antagonism toward banks, bankers, and particularly bank-notes. Since a return to hard-money was obviously impossible without a drastic deflation, old-line Democrats would naturally turn to greenbacks, the money of the people, in preference to the national bank-note currency which was the money of the bankers. The old Democracy of Jackson's time had stood for the proposition that only gold and silver minted by the government should be allowed to perform the functions of money. Aware of the impracticalities of such a program in the post-war years, what could be more natural than that old-line Democrats of the western variety should propose that the government keep to itself the money-making prerogative even if it meant paper money instead of gold and silver. In this light a puzzling enigma can be explained, and the essential continuity of Democratic thought is maintained.

Among the eastern Democrats hard-money attitudes continued to predominate. The power of financiers and capitalists such as August Belmont in the councils of the eastern Democracy as well as the more adequate supply of currency and credit-facilities in the East provides a reasonable explanation for this. This split on the question of monetary policy between the eastern and western branches of the Democratic party was destined to be a landmark on the political scene for many years to come. Consequently in tracing the history of the Democratic party in the generation which followed the Civil War, 1867 is seen to be a year of decision, leading to consequences of tremendous magnitude.

IV. In describing the failure of the "Ohio idea" in the West in the election of 1868, the failure of the Democracy to enlist the active support of the agricultural population was found to be crucial. The key to farmer apathy to the "Pendleton Plan" was found in the high prices for corn and wheat, the great staple crops of the West, which prevailed in the years 1866-1868. Inasmuch as political agitation on the part of farmers is virtually always inversely proportional to the movement of prices for agricultural products, it is not surprising that the farmers failed to be deeply moved by the "injustice" of paying the 5-20 bonds in gold or by the Democratic proposal to pay them off in greenbacks. Likewise, so long as they were receiving good prices, farmers were not likely to become agitated over the mal-distribution of the national bank currency, the inadequacy of credit facilities, and other financial problems. Such agitation lay in a less happy, more troubled future.

Available evidence tends in a negative way to corroborate this point of view. A study of Oliver H. Kelley's work on the founding of the Patrons of Husbandry turns up no evidence that economic discontent played any part in the establishment of that influential order. Agricultural journals for this period reveal no feeling of hard times, but rather exactly the opposite, a feeling that agriculture can pay and does pay well. Also indicative that no definable group attitude on the currency question existed among farmers in this period is the fact that, when some agitation did begin to develop among agriculturalists in 1870, it was directed entirely against the railroads. No interest in the currency question or the National Banking System was even remotely intimated. An important bit of corroborating evidence for this position is the testimony of the labor leader George F. McNeill that the National Labor Union, which was almost completely concerned with currency reform, was unable to enlist the interest of the farmers in its program.[9] It is consequently the conclusion here that the farmers, the economic group traditionally most interested in fiat money schemes, was the least interested group in the fight over specie resumption from 1865 to 1870.

V. One of the more important conclusions of this study is bound up with the concept of the monetary rationale of high protectionism. While doing preliminary research for this study, the author was surprised to learn that the leaders of the high protectionist school in the United States, men such as Henry C. Carey, Thaddeus Stevens, William D. Kelley, and Peter Cooper, were also the most outspoken friends of the greenbacks and soft-money policies generally. At first glance this seemed an extremely strange and unaccountable phenomenon. As one writer would have it, it was ". . . hopeless to rear any enduring tariff wall upon the shifting sands of an inflated currency" and efforts to do so were simply attempts to "reconcile the irreconcilable."[10]

Further research and analysis led to the conviction that the soft-money views of Carey, Stevens, Kelley, Cooper and others were by no means inconsistent with their protectionist inclinations. Indeed, in view of the special conditions which obtained in the years 1862-1879 when specie payments were not maintained, it can be argued that soft-money and high protectionism were not only not "irreconcilable" but that they were two aspects of the same nationalist-protectionist philosophy. The key to this argument was found in the operation of the premium on gold which came into existence soon after the issue of the greenbacks in 1862. A rising premium on gold fostered by emissions of legal tender notes was the same as increased protection for American manufacturers. A falling premium fos-

[9] *Supra*, pp. 192-193 n.
[10] Eiselen, *The Rise of Pennsylvania Protectionism*, p. 269.

tered by McCulloch's policy of contraction represented decreased protection and an actual inducement to the importation of foreign goods.[11]

The evidence tends to substantiate this view. Letters written by manufacturers to their Congressmen and Senators in the years 1866-1868 show that many of them were vehemently opposed to the policy of contraction of the currency. Manufacturing publications, particularly those associated with the iron and steel trade (the heart of protectionist sentiment in the United States) demonstrated a violent aversion to the policy of diminishing the currency supply. The spokesmen for the high protectionist point of view in Congress were among the most consistent enemies of the Secretary of the Treasury and his policies. In corroborating the concept of the monetary rationale of high protectionism, it is significant to note that the effect of the falling gold premium on the manufacturer was understood by the editor of the *Iron Age*, by James M. Cooper in his pamphlet *The Government the Partner of the Manufacturer*, as well as by Jonathan Sturges, the correspondent of Senator John Sherman.[12]

Available evidence seems to suggest that not all segments of American industry were affected to the same extent by the post-war decline in the premium on gold. The concern of the New England textile manufacturers with this factor seems to have been negligible. The greatest anxiety over the falling gold premium as well as the greatest opposition to the policy of contraction came from the representatives of the iron and steel trade, manufacturers of goods made from iron and steel, and their spokesmen in Congress such as Thaddeus Stevens and " Pig Iron " Kelley. This industry made up the most effective core of opposition to Hugh McCulloch and his policy of contraction. It is significant also that this industry constituted the traditional citadel of high protectionism in the United States. A careful evaluation of the evidence leads to the conclusion that the opposition to contraction on the part of the iron and steel manufacturers of Pennsylvania, New York, and the western states, and their allies was the most important single factor leading to the abandonment of that policy in 1868.

[11] *Supra*, pp. 149-153.   [12] *Supra*, pp. 151, 172-173.

VI. Despite the apparent inconsistency of the pre-war and post-war positions of the labor movement on the questions of financial policy, a strong thread of continuity can be discerned which links the hard-money attitudes of the ante-bellum years with the soft-money program of the late sixties. This thread is seen to be a continuing distrust of bankers, bank-notes, and the "money power" generally. It was apparent in the years following the Civil War that a return to specie payments and pre-war hard-money policies was impracticable inasmuch as the limited supply of gold would make this possible only at the risk of severe deflation. It was in this context that the leaders of the National Labor Union came to prefer greenbacks, the money of the people, to national bank-notes, the money of the bankers.[18] In this situation the Kellogg-Campbell interconvertible bond-currency scheme was ideally adapted both to set forth a proposed solution to the problem of insufficient currency and also to express the general petty bourgeoise philosophy of the post-war labor movement.

An analysis of the position of the labor movement on financial issues during this period reveals startling similarities between the conclusions reached and the program advocated by the leaders of the National Labor Union and the ideas which motivated the high protectionists such as Carey, Cooper, Stevens, and Kelley. The leaders of the National Labor Union and the spokesmen for high protectionism both attempted analyses of the economic problems of the nation based upon the same essential set of premises. Both philosophies emerged during a period of industrial capitalism when the independent entrepreneur was still an important force in economic life. Both are philosophies of independent enterprise in which low interest rates are seen as a key tool with which to combat the growing

---

[18] It is significant to note that prior to the Civil War, Democratic administrations supported by labor and espousing hard-money doctrines had on several occasions issued treasury notes made receivable for public dues. Though these notes (issued between 1837 and 1843 and again during the Mexican War) bore interest and were not invested with the legal tender quality, they were used as currency and were opposed by Thomas Hart Benton on that ground. With this precedent in the background, the advocacy of the greenbacks in the post-Civil War period by both labor and segments of the Democratic party seems even less anomalous. Dewey, *Financial History*, pp. 231-235; 255.

power of finance capital. The most remarkable similarity emerges in the fact that the rationale of the nationalist soft-money position brought leaders like Sylvis, Cameron, and Trevellick into the protectionist camp.

As evidence of the primary place which the money question occupied in the minds of the leaders of the labor movement it is extremely significant to note that the real heroes of labor in the political arena were the extreme Radicals who were most " heretical " on the money issue. In light of present-day inter-pretations of Reconstruction history it is fascinating to find that labor numbered among its true friends none other than Thaddeus Stevens, Benjamin F. Butler, and Ben Wade.

VII. Of the four economic groups considered in this study it has been concluded that the banking fraternity was the only group which, on balance, supported the policy of contraction of the currency. The key to this attitude is found in economic interest. Where a vested interest in deflation was most pro-nounced in this group, namely among the metropolitan bankers of the northeastern seaboard, there Hugh McCulloch derived his most consistent support. Outside the eastern cities and in the West, consideration of the profits which would accrue to creditors through deflationary appreciation in the value of money tended to be outweighed among country bankers by the effects of the actual dearth of currency, a situation of great importance in rural areas where demand deposits were of little significance compared to the importance of the circulating medium. In the western cities where credit and currency were more plentiful and demand deposits were of growing impor-tance, bankers tended to go along with their New York, Boston, and Philadelphia colleagues in supporting the policy of con-traction. An interesting exception to the prevailing opinion among metropolitan bankers in favor of contraction has been noted in the case of the private bankers. Because their business was largely sustained by speculative trading in securities, private bankers were largely opposed to financial policies which would have a tendency to lower the general level of prices.

Among the great bankers, particularly those of the financial center of New York, there was little disposition to support either the economic or political policies of the Radical Republican element in Congress. The gold standard—free trade leaning of Wall Street had as its political counterpart a general tendency to look with favor upon the moderate approach to the problems of Reconstruction. This attitude was made manifest as early as the spring of 1865 when the Chamber of Commerce of the State of New York, representing the banking and mercantile interests of the metropolis, resolved that the restoration of national authority in the South " may be everywhere signalized by magnanimity and clemency, and that it may nowhere be stained by a single act which will be condemned as needlessly harsh or revengeful by the cool judgment of the humane and liberty-loving in any part of the civilized world." [14] Dramatic evidence of the support given to Andrew Johnson and his policies by the mercantile-financial community of New York was provided on the occasion of the President's visit to the metropolis in the summer of 1866. The honor done to Johnson at this time by such men as A. T. Stewart, Moses Taylor, A. A. Low, John Q. Jones, William H. Vanderbilt, William B. Astor and others made it quite clear that the monied interests of New York were in sympathy with the President.[15]

The high protection—soft-money predilections of the Radical Republicans elicited little support and sympathy in New York. The tariff bill of 1866 was deemed definitely injurious to the

[14] *Eighth Annual Report of the Chamber of Commerce of the State of New York for the Year 1865-'66* (New York, 1866), p. 4. See *supra*, p. 272.

[15] That the political predilections of the New York financial community were well understood among Republican politicians is apparent in a letter written by Schuyler Colfax to John Sherman, December 26, 1867. Colfax says: " I see Wall St. don't like yr bill. [The reference is to Sherman's refunding bill reported out of the Finance Committee on December 17.] I suppose these gent^m think that, while they are voting the Dem. ticket, we are to fight the battle for them agst the Dem. war cry of ' Tax the bonds.' Perhaps if they knew how much feeling has been created amongst the people the past two years by the Dem. arguments on the subject, they might see what they don't see now." Sherman Papers. The general tendency of substantial men of business to support moderate Reconstruction policies and to oppose Radical measures has been ably described in William B. Hesseltine, " Economic Factors in the Abandonment of Reconstruction," *Mississippi Valley Historical Review*, XXII (September, 1935), 191-210. In this article Grant's aide-de-camp, Adam Badeau is quoted as writing that " all the sober, substantial men " of New York, St. Louis, and Washington were in favor of Johnson's policy. *Ibid.*, p. 192.

city by the Chamber of Commerce which unanimously adopted a memorial opposing the bill on the grounds that the duties proposed were " in many cases so high that they must prove prohibitive." The sentiment of the Chamber with respect to monetary policy was clearly expressed in the resolution of 1867 that the Treasury " should cautiously, but steadfastly, adhere to the policy of contraction, in so far as it can be done without adversely affecting the business and industrial interests of the country." [16]

The politico-economic attitudes of the New York banking fraternity are quite explicit in James Gallatin's " Letter on the Financial Economy of the United States " published in 1868 and addressed to Andrew Johnson. In this article the powerful New York banker argued forcefully in favor of hard-money and free trade and what is more, he strongly endorsed the Reconstruction policies of the President. The evidence seems indisputable that banking-mercantile opinion in the great financial center of New York was not only not lined up on the side of the Radical Republicans but rather that the rationale of that opinion tended in the direction of the policies advocated by the Johnson administration. The fact that this essentially moderate opinion on the political issues of Reconstruction was not expressed so forcefully as opinion on monetary policy helps account for the fact that the Radicals were able to carry through their harsh Reconstruction measures in the South whereas they were unable to succeed in committing the nation to a policy of easy money.

In the preceding pages the most important conclusions reached in this study have been briefly summarized. The task which remains is that of demonstrating in what respects these conclusions differ from those contained in what may be considered the prevailing interpretation of the history of the Civil War and Reconstruction. This necessarily involves an excursion into the historiography of the eighteen sixties. Two demurrers must be entered at the outset. No attempt has been made to

----

[16] *Ninth Annual Report of the Chamber of Commerce of the State of New York for the Year 1866-'67* (New York, 1867), p. 76.

consider all the works in which the prevailing economic interpretation appears. Only the works in which this interpretation was originally developed as well as a few works which demonstrate its current acceptance have been treated. Secondly, it must be emphasized that I have tremendous respect for the scholars whose works are analyzed here. This analysis has been made purely in the interest of obtaining a better understanding of the real meaning of a most controversial and perplexing period of American history.

In the opinion of the present author basic responsibility for the prevailing view of the economic meaning of the Civil War and Reconstruction must be assigned to the great American historian, Charles A. Beard. Beard must be included along with J. Allen Smith and Vernon L. Parrington in that select group of American scholars who in the first quarter of the twentieth century first assaulted the almost exclusive preoccupation of American historians with political, military, and constitutional history. By placing great emphasis upon social, cultural, technological, and particularly economic forces in historical development, Beard lay bare for all to see the real red meat of history. After the publication of his works on the Constitution and Jeffersonian Democracy, historians would neglect only at their very great peril the vital importance of economic factors in historical interpretation.[17]

In 1927 with the publication of *The Rise of American Civilization* Charles and Mary Beard impressed their method and predilections upon the whole course of American history. Perhaps no other aspect of this path-breaking work was more startling or iconoclastic than the Beards' now famous interpretation of the Civil War and Reconstruction which they lumped together as the "Second American Revolution."[18] This inter-

---

[17] Charles A. Beard, *An Economic Interpretation of the Constitution of the United States* (New York, 1913) and *Economic Origins of Jeffersonian Democracy* (New York, 1915).

[18] Harold J. Laski asserted that *The Rise of American Civilization* is "certainly one of the half dozen most effective general narratives of a people's history that any nation possesses." He noted that the Beards' treatment of the Civil War was a "new conception" valuable in its "suggestiveness" to the specialist as well as to the general reader. Harold J. Laski, "Charles Beard: An English View," in *Charles A. Beard: An Appraisal*, ed. Howard K. Beale (Lexington, Ky., 1954), pp. 13-14.

pretation discounted the fondly held notion that the importance of the Civil War was to be sought in the movements of vast armies or in the interminable list of battles and skirmishes. " To be sure," wrote the Beards, " the battles and campaigns of the epoch are significant to the military strategist; the tragedy and heroism of the contest furnish inspiration to patriots and romance to the maker of epics. But the core of the vortex lay elsewhere. It was in the flowing substance of things limned by statistical reports on finance, commerce, capital, industry, railways, and agriculture, by provisions of constitutional law, and by the pages of statute books—prosaic muniments which show that the so-called civil war was in reality a Second American Revolution and in a strict sense, the First." The war was in essence " a social war, ending in the unquestioned establishment of a new power in the government, making vast changes in the arrangement of classes, in the accumulation and distribution of wealth, in the course of industrial development, and in the Constitution inherited from the Fathers." If indeed, " the operations by which the middle classes of England broke the power of the king and the aristocracy are to be known collectively as the Puritan Revolution, if the series of acts by which the bourgeois and peasants of France overthrew the king, nobility, and clergy is to be called the French Revolution, then accuracy compels us to characterize by the same term the social cataclysm in which the capitalists, laborers, and farmers of the North and West drove from power in the national government the planting aristocracy of the South. Viewed under the light of universal history, the fighting was a fleeting incident; the social revolution was the essential, portentous outcome." [19]

With the overall dimensions of this interpretation I have no quarrel. To the historian who considers essential meanings rather than the sound and fury of events, the ultimate significance of the Civil War and Reconstruction lies in the fundamental fact of social upheaval, the process by which the power of the planting aristocracy in the South was broken and the hegemony of other economic groups established.[20] The

---

[19] Charles A. Beard and Mary R. Beard, *The Rise of American Civilization*, rev. ed., 2 vols. in 1 (New York, 1934), II, 53-54.

[20] The point must be insisted upon that I do not dispute the general validity

core of my disagreement with Professor Beard lies not in the overwhelming emphasis which he placed upon economic forces but rather in the fact that he failed to disentangle the interests of the various triumphant economic groups and to show that they were frequently contradictory. It will be noted that Beard has the " capitalists, laborers, and farmers of the North and West " accomplishing the defeat of the planting aristocracy. The spoils of the victory which accrued to the laborers and farmers are hurriedly sketched. For the former the benefits were virtually non-existent and are consequently passed over with scarcely a comment.[21] For the latter the fruits of victory consisted essentially of the passage of the Homestead Act and the high farm prices which ensued because of inflation.[22] With these elements of the coalition Beard is actually concerned very little. It is the " capitalists " who really gain the choicest spoils of war, and it is with this group that Beard is primarily concerned. It is on the question of the meaning of the term " capitalists " and its use in the Beardian interpretation that this study takes issue with the concept of the " Second American Revolution."

In treating " capitalists " as the chief beneficiaries of the social upheaval of Civil War and Reconstruction, the Beards have created a conceptual monolith. They have failed to recognize the cleavages which existed within the capitalist group itself on various questions of economic policy. Fundamentally they have failed to consider the frequently divergent interests of industrial and financial capitalists, the entrepreneurs and the money-lenders. Let us analyze the interpretation as it emerges in the Beards' own words.[23]

While the planting class was being trampled in the dust—stripped of

---

of the concept of the " Second American Revolution " but only certain aspects of the Beardian construct of this phenomenon.

[21] In a later chapter on the labor movement the Beards admit that laborers were actually worse off during the war since wages failed to keep pace with rising prices. Beard and Beard, *The Rise of American Civilization*, II, 212-213.

[22] *Ibid.*, II, 114-115. The Beards are among the few historians who have realized that the farmers were prosperous not only during the Civil War but after it as well. To quote them briefly: " For many years a prosperous farming class, tasting the sweets of profit, could look upon the new course of politics and pronounce it good." *Ibid.*, II, 115.

[23] *Ibid.*, II, 105.

its wealth and political power—the capitalist class was marching onward in seven league boots. Under the feverish stimulus of war the timid army marshaled by Webster in support of the Constitution and Whig policies had been turned into a confident host, augmented in numbers by the thousands and tens of thousands who during the conflict made profits out of war contracts and out of the rising prices of manufactured goods. At last the economic structure of machine industry towered high above agriculture—a grim monument to the fallen captain, King Cotton. Moreover, the bonds and notes of the federal government, issued in its extremity, furnished the substance for still larger business enterprise. And the beneficent government, which had carefully avoided laying drastic imposts upon profits during the war, soon afterward crowned its generosity to the capitalists by abolishing the moderate tax on income and shifting the entire fiscal burden to goods consumed by the masses.

The benefits referred to here, the profits derived from war contracts and rising prices as well as the "substance for still larger business enterprise" provided by the bond and note issues of the government, accrued to the active entrepreneurs, particularly to the manufacturers. This fact is not in dispute. Evidence cited above supports the view that the manufacturers were the chief economic beneficiaries of the inflationary situation produced by the war.[24] But what of the money-lenders, the finance capitalists of the eastern seaboard cities? Here again let us turn to the text.[25]

Although the bonds issued from time to time varied greatly in their stipulations, according to the prospects of ultimate success which seemed to lie before the Union cause, their provisions were seldom ungenerous to the money lenders. Often the rate of interest ran to seven per cent, occasionally slightly higher. In some cases certain depreciated Greenbacks were received in exchange for bonds payable, interest and principal, in gold, thus giving the holder two or three times the rate of annual return nominally written in the contract. As always, necessity was the mother of policy: the exigencies of the federal government were great; the risks incurred by money-lenders were serious though time proved their faith well justified; and in its distress the federal treasury had to deal gently with its creditors. If the Union had been dissolved their losses would have been overwhelming; as things turned out, their earnings were immense.

In treating the National Banking System which the Beards refer to as the "other great requirement of business enterprise,"

[24] *Supra*, pp. 141-144.
[25] Beard and Beard, *The Rise of American Civilization*, II, 107-108.

it is maintained that " in those dark and trying days, the statesmen of sound money found a chance to return to the policies
which had been so ruthlessly discarded by Jacksonian Democracy." Preempting the field from state banks with their oftimes
questionable note issues, the legislation of 1863 and 1864 authorized the formation of national banks which could " buy federal
securities, receive interest from the government on its holdings,
and then issue on the strength of those securities paper bills
to be lent to borrowers at the current discount." The process
did not end here for " Having driven this wedge into the
system of local currency and having attracted the support of
powerful banks by favorable terms, the party of sound money
[the Republicans] completed its program in 1865 by carrying
through Congress an act which imposed a tax of ten per cent
on all state bank notes, absolutely wiping them out by a single
stroke. In this fashion sweeping designs which neither Clay
nor Webster had been able to accomplish by oratory in days
of peace, Republican leaders effected by arrangement during
the pressing time of war. When southern statesmen returned
to the Union after the curtain was rung down on the battlefield,
they found the national banking system intrenched in the
financial structure of the nation." [26]

These passages are such a curious blend of truth and misinterpretation that they are very difficult to criticize. Nevertheless, the net impression is, in my opinion, so erroneous that
the attempt must be made.

It is quite clear that what the Beards refer to as the " money-
lenders " did not fare at all well during the Civil War. Evidence
has been presented in Chapter VI which shows that the interest
rate on loans never rose sufficiently during the war period even
to compensate lenders for the losses sustained on principal
much less to permit any real gains. Wesley Mitchell concluded
that during the years of inflation the finance capitalists lost
even more relatively than the wage-earners.[27]

The interest rates of six and seven per cent on government
securities issued during the war were by no means so generous
as the Beards would have us believe. Such rates were not

[26] *Ibid.*, II, 108-110.
[27] Mitchell, *History of the Greenbacks*, p. 368.

unusual in the nineteenth century. During the Mexican War bonds were issued which bore negligible risks compared with the securities issued during the Civil War. Nonetheless these bonds were payable principal and interest in gold at six per cent. In 1861, before the inauguration of Lincoln, Secretary of the Treasury Dix had borrowed money at rates of ten and twelve per cent.[28] Indeed, considering the enormous risks involved, it seems almost incredible that Chase and Fessenden were able to obtain money at such moderate rates.

It is true of course that with respect to yield not all of the debt created during the Civil War can be considered on the same basis. A very large portion consisted of short-term issues payable principal and interest in paper currency at rates of anywhere from 3.65 to 7.3 per cent. It is evident that investors in these issues were adversely affected by the inflation of the war years and, on balance, probably lost rather than gained through lending their capital to the government. Another large portion of the debt consisted of long-term bonds payable principal and interest in gold. In this category were the so-called " 5-20's " bearing interest at 6 per cent and the " 10-40's " at 5 per cent. Inasmuch as the gold interest on these bonds could be converted into greenbacks at the high premiums which prevailed after 1862, holders of these securities were in a more favorable position than those who had invested in the various short-term issues.

The position of investors in " 5-20's " and " 10-40's " is, however, not so simple as it might appear on the surface, for, although gold interest could be converted into greenbacks at a nice premium, the windfall monetary gains accruing were almost totally nullified by the rising price level. Real interest in terms of purchasing power even on 5-20 bonds yielding 6 per cent in gold were consequently limited to an average of about 6.1 per cent for the years 1862-1865. It should be noted that in terms of real purchasing power the value of a bond bought in 1862 was actually considerably less in 1865 than it had been three years earlier. In other words the rise in the currency value of bonds was not nearly so great as the rise

[28] Dewey, *Financial History*, pp. 255-256; *supra*, p. 18.

in the general price level.[29] It thus seems apparent that even holders of gold interest bonds did not fare so well during the war years as might appear on the surface and that these very moderate gains by no means compensated the money-lending capitalist class for the great losses sustained on virtually all other classes of loans including the great volume of short-term government issues as well as the hundreds of millions of dollars loaned by banks and individuals to businessmen.[30]

Evidence which has been cited elsewhere in this study casts further doubt on the Beardian position that money-lenders had a vested interest in government financial operations. It will be remembered that the metropolitan bankers of the eastern seaboard came to a bitter *impasse* with the government in 1862 over the question of the real interest rates to be offered on goverment bonds (whether the bonds should be sold at or below par). This unresolved conflict of 1862 which involved a basic dispute over the price at which finance capitalists should lend their support to the government was the opening incident in a battle between the urban bankers of the East and the government which was to last until well after the guns of the opposing Union and Confederate armies had been silenced.[31] Despite what the Beards have written, it is inaccurate to imply that finance capital supported Chase's method of financing the war or that finance capitalists felt there was any profit to be derived from helping maintain the government's credit. In so far as the issue of the greenbacks was concerned, it was clear all along that this expedient was dreaded by finance capitalists above all else.[32] Once Chase and the Congressional leaders agreed on

[29] This analysis involves the use of Carl Snyder's general price index and Wesley Mitchell's computations of the average annual price of gold in greenbacks. For a comparison of the prices of bonds in 1862 and 1865, see Mitchell, *History of the Greenbacks*, p. 378.

[30] Of course, this type of analysis can also be employed to show that real profits accruing to active men of business were not so large as paper profits. The point is, however, that real profits during the war years were extremely large even computed on a gold basis. One of the reasons for this as Mitchell has pointed out is the fact that entrepreneurs made substantial gains at the expense of other groups, notably wage-earners and money-lending capitalists. For a treatment of this point, see *ibid.*, ch. VIII.

[31] For a discussion of this opposition, see Redlich, *The Molding of American Banking*, II, 92-95, 108-113. Redlich refers to the " unabated hostility of powerful bankers in the East " to the system in 1865.

[32] *Supra*, pp. 31-33.

the use of paper money to finance the war, all bridges between the associated bankers and the government had been cut. From this point on the attitude of the powerful eastern bankers was one of continuing hostility.[33]

The Treasury was successful in raising money essentially for two reasons: first because the issue of the greenbacks had created the purchasing power and the inflationary condition necessary to sell bonds at par, thus meeting Congressional demands on the question and second because Jay Cooke created a marketing organization which appealed to prospective purchasers, small town bankers and businessmen rather than metropolitan capitalists on grounds of patriotism rather than profit.[34]

To say that the *ultimate* profits of bondholders were large is to state a fact, but it was a fact that could not have easily been foretold in the years of Fredericksburg, Chancellorsville, and Chickamauga. It would be accurate to maintain that in the long run capitalists would have been well advised to support the government, but such a statement takes no account of the fact that the most powerful members of this class, piqued by Chase and his methods, did very little. Long run considerations have little weight in determining the economic actions of individuals, for, as Lord Keynes so aptly remarked, " In the long run, we are all dead." To compress this argument in a nutshell, finance capitalists did not support the policies of Secretary Chase and Congress because they did not feel it was to their economic advantage to do so.[35]

In their treatment of the establishment of the National Banking System the Beards have again, in my opinion, misinterpreted the situation. Here again it is implied that finance capitalists supported the policies of the Republican party. Rather than attracting " the support of powerful banks by favorable terms " the National Banking Acts of 1863 and 1864 only intensified

[33] Redlich, II, 94-95.

[34] Dewey, *Financial History*, pp. 310-311.

[35] Redlich, II, 108-109. In connection with this argument that finance capitalists did not actually gain from the Civil War, it is relevant to note a fact which has been mentioned earlier, namely, that the capital of the Associated Banks in New York actually decreased between 1860 and 1864, a clear indication that the business of banking was relatively unprofitable during these years. See *supra*, p. 238.

the already virulent opposition of eastern bankers to the policies of the government. This opposition was manifested in a most decisive fashion when in 1864 the New York Clearing House resolved " that all National Bank currency be treated as uncurrent money unless the bank [whose notes were in question] redeem at par through a member of this Association." [36] Strong opposition to the new system was also manifested in the financial centers of Boston, Philadelphia, and Baltimore.[37] As was the case with the failure of the associated bankers to support the credit of the government, the key to this opposition was self-interest. The large eastern banks which depended very little upon note issues for their profits simply had very little to gain and something to lose in joining the system. Professor Redlich has pointed out that " with profit as the flywheel of the economic system, the inherent logic of the latter forbade conversions and the establishment of National Banks in large parts of the country." There was simply " no incentive to convert unless there were reasons other than making money or profit chances from opportunities other than a regular banking business." Where motives of patriotism were absent, powerful state bankers " kept aloof or went on showing outright hostility." [38] Such facts can hardly be squared with the Beards' general thesis that all " capitalists " not only profited by the Civil War but that they labored to erect in this time of crisis social institutions such as the National Banking System which would ensure their dominance and profit for years to come.[39]

Essentially the Beards make the mistake of confusing the divergent interests of industrial and finance capitalists. Whereas the former group tended to profit from wartime inflation, the latter group tended to suffer.[40] Whereas industrialists generally favored high protective tariffs and a policy of easy money,

---

[36] *Supra,* p. 227.

[37] Redlich, II, 107-109.

[38] *Ibid.,* II, 108-109.

[39] Whether the Beards imply that the Republicans conspired to take advantage of the distractions of war to engraft their economic convictions on the body politic is a matter for subjective judgment. It cannot be proved from the text, but in the passages quoted above, particularly those dealing with the establishment of the National Banking System, it seems to me that the idea of conspiracy is implicit.

[40] For evidence on this point see *supra,* pp. 141-144, 238-240.

finance capitalists tended toward free trade and sound money.[41] The touchstone of self-interest was present in both cases, but the Beards have failed to understand that the interests of these two groups were entirely different. When the divergent interests of financial and industrial capitalists, of bankers and manufacturers are understood, the conceptual monolith of the interests of "capitalists" which the Beards have created falls to the ground, and it becomes apparent that the economic history of the Civil War and Reconstruction must be approached from the standpoint of the conflicting interests of various economic groups.[42]

It will be noted that in the passages quoted above the Beards refer twice to the Republicans as the party of sound money. In another place they are referred to as "the party of industrial progress and sound money." [43] Just what the Beards mean by "sound money" is difficult to elicit from the text, but to the present author it is impossible to imagine as the champion of "sound money" that party which passed the First Legal Tender Act against strong Democratic opposition in 1862, which supported the policy of contraction in the House by a bare margin of five votes in 1866 while the Democrats were supporting it twenty-seven to one, and which decisively opposed further contraction in 1868 by a vote of one-hundred and three to eighteen.[44] If the Beards mean to imply that the Republicans donned the mantle of "sound money" by their establishment of the National Banking System, it should be pointed out that the real "sound money" advocates of the time (including the New York Clearing House and the economist Amasa

[41] See the memorial against the tariff bill of 1866 adopted by the Chamber of Commerce of the State of New York, *supra*, pp. 272-273.

[42] It might be argued that the Beards' thesis is itself un-Beardian. In 1916 Charles A. Beard paraphrased James Madison before an audience of Amherst students: "A landed interest, a transport interest, a railway interest, a shipping interest, an engineering interest, a manufacturing interest, a public-official interest, with many lesser interests, grow up of necessity in all great societies and divide them into different classes actuated by different sentiments and views." Howard K. Beale, "Charles Beard: Historian," in *Charles A. Beard: An Appraisal*, p. 117. Had Beard analyzed the divergent interests involved, sounder results may well have ensued.

[43] Beard and Beard, *The Rise of American Civilization*, II, 111.

[44] *Supra*, pp. 36-46, 74-78, 111-113.

Walker) regarded the system, which placed its greatest emphasis on the note-issuing function, as little better than the "wildcat" banking of earlier years.[45] If indeed the national bank
currency can be regarded as an improvement over the old state
bank issues, it should be understood that the new system was
still a long way from fulfilling the demands of the most ardent
advocates of "sound money." In any event it is impossible to
see how the Republicans can be regarded in these years as the
patrons of "sound money." Until 1867 the Democrats would
have far sounder claim to this distinction.[46]

The Beards' concept of the "Second American Revolution"
has been of basic importance in recent American historiography.
The persuasiveness, (if not the logic), the panoramic scope,
as well as the general iconoclastic nature of the thesis have
recommended it to readers of history as well as to historians.[47]
The concept has been of such great significance that it has
formed the framework within which a whole school of historians has interpreted the economic meaning of the Civil War
and Reconstruction. From the standpoint of historiographical
influence perhaps the most influential member of this school
has been Professor Howard K. Beale whose scholarly work,
The Critical Year, has impressed the general Beardian frame
of reference upon the economic history of Reconstruction.[48]

Beale accepts the Beards' thesis that "capitalists" were the
chief beneficiaries of the economic *fait accompli* of the Civil
War and Reconstruction. Like the Beards he also fails to
distinguish between the divergent interests of industrial and
finance capitalists. Beale carries the conspiracy concept of the

---

[45] Redlich, II, 105-106, 150. James Gallatin expressed this point of view in
his "Letter on the Financial Economy of the United States" in 1868. *Supra*,
p. 252.

[46] By 1867, of course, the "Ohio idea" had created a cleavage between the
eastern and western branches of the Democratic party. *Supra*, pp. 101, 111.

[47] Professor Beale has written that in the Beards' *Basic History of the United
States* (Philadelphia, 1944), "the famous economic thesis about the Civil
War disappeared entirely." Howard K. Beale, "Charles Beard: Historian,"
in *Charles A. Beard: An Appraisal*, p. 124. I do not believe this to be the
case. A careful reading of chapter XX of the *Basic History* reveals that most
of the essential elements of the famous thesis are still present, though they have
been toned down. See particularly *Basic History*, p. 323.

[48] Howard K. Beale, *The Critical Year: A Study of Andrew Johnson and
Reconstruction* (New York, 1930).

Beards one step further, for he sees conspiracy on the part of the Radical Republicans, representing the interests of "big business," to keep Southern representatives from regaining their seats in Congress. The motive for this conspiracy was economic as he points out.[49]

If Southern economic interests had coincided with those of the rising industrial groups of the North, there would have been no Radical reconstruction. The real danger from 'a return of rebels to power' was not overthrow of the Union, but ousting of the new industrial forces from control in Washington through a renewed union of Southern planters and Western farmers. In an alignment on the new industrial questions, the Radicals would have been outnumbered even in the North. If Johnson had staked his fortunes on them instead of on the indeterminable condition of a remote South, his chances of success would have risen.

Again in another passage Beale gives his impression of the economic factors at work and the possible consequences of readmitting the South to the Union.[50]

Contraction of the currency was already a subject of heated controversy, though the opposition to it had not yet gained the momentum necessary to the launching of a political party. Still, most of the factors that in subsequent years underlay Greenbackism, the Granger movement, Populism, Progressivism, and the Farm Bloc were at work in 1866. It is significant that it was while in retirement on his farm from May of 1866 to the following May that Kelley in conversation with his Minnesota friends worked out the details of the Granger organization suggested to him by what he saw on a Southern trip early in 1866. Therefore, while the first Grange was not organized until 1867, its need was based on conditions of 1866. Had the South been back in the Union, similar economic conditions would have united the Northwest and the South in advocacy of an inflated currency. Realization of this fact was one of the reasons for Radical determinations to keep the South out of the Union.

Let us analyze these passages in light of the conclusions reached in the present study. In the first place Beale assumes that the farmer's discontent with his economic lot played an important part in Oliver Kelley's early attempts to organize the Grange. As has been pointed out above, this was simply not the case. Farmers were prosperous in the years following the

[49] *Ibid.*, p. 225.   [50] *Ibid.*, p. 236.

Civil War.[51] There is no evidence in Kelley's writings to support the notion that the discontent of farmers with their economic lot played a part in his organizational efforts.[52] The original objectives of the Grange were, as Solon Buck has written, " to advance agriculture and bind the farmers together." [53] Social and cultural betterment was the goal, not political agitation based on economic hardship. There is little evidence available to support the thesis that the farmers as a group favored expansion of the currency or even a halt to contraction.[54] Their prosperous condition until about 1869 left them relatively unconcerned with financial questions.

If we accept the premise that the farmers were as a group uninterested in the outcome of the contraction-expansion controversy, Beale's thesis is vulnerable. If agricultural opinion was apathetic on this issue then it is misleading and incorrect to assert that had the South been back in the Union " similar economic conditions would have united the Northwest and the South in advocacy of an inflated currency " through a " renewed union of Southern planters and Western farmers." But the thesis is not vulnerable on this ground alone, for Professor Beale assumes that " Realization of this fact was one of the reasons for Radical determination to keep the South out of the Union." In making this statement Beale is creating the same type of conceptual monolith that the Beards engendered in their use of the idea of the group interest of " capitalists." He is assuming that the Radical Republicans represented a cohesive group of politicians possessing well defined aims in the economic sphere on which there was essential agreement. A large part of this study has been devoted to disproving that

[51] *Supra*, pp. 102-104, 136-138.
[52] *Supra*, pp. 135-136.
[53] Buck, *The Granger Movement*, p. 41.
[54] To substantiate his thesis that farmers opposed contraction, Beale cites two letters, one from a New Englander to Senator Fessenden detailing opinions gathered during a trip through the West, one from a Philadelphian named Lewis directed to Thaddeus Stevens giving the writer's opinion of conditions among western farmers, and two clippings from the *Herald* of Norristown, Pennsylvania, opposing contraction. Beale, *The Critical Year*, pp. 237-238, 240-241, 245-246. None of this, in the opinion of the present author, can be regarded as legitimate farmer opinion on the issue. Not only is the evidence insufficient, but Beale's almost exclusive reliance on manuscript collections for evidence of group opinion is decidedly dangerous.

notion. There was actually no agreement whatsoever on financial policy between such Radicals such as Thaddeus Stevens, Benjamin F. Butler, William D. Kelley, and Ben Wade on the one hand and Radicals such as Roscoe Conkling, Justin Morrill, James A. Garfield, and William P. Fessenden on the other. As a matter of fact the most radical of the Radicals were the group which tended most definitely toward the soft-money philosophy. Those who held " sound money " views were often essentially moderates both on economic and political issues.[55] Beale's thesis is thus vulnerable on another count. Radicals could hardly have conspired to keep the South out of the Union because of fear that Southerners would unite with Westerners to inflate the currency, because there was absolutely no unity on this point among the Republicans themselves.

At various points Beale seems a little embarrassed by his own theory. He cites at least as much evidence that Radicals opposed contraction as that they favored it. For example, he says, " Even that inveterate Radical, George L. Stearns of Boston, feared a panic would result from contraction." [56] At another place he writes regarding the contraction bill that " so strong was the opposition even among Radicals, that they had to accept a compromise proviso. . . ." [57] Again he writes: " Even in the East the bill faced bitter opposition." [58]

Inasmuch as Beale accepts the proposition that the Radicals, on balance, favored contraction as well as the general thesis that they represented the " business " interest, he is led to declare that " Manufacturers generally sought contraction of the currency along with an increase of tariff rates." [59] So far as the present author has been able to determine, he cites not one jot of evidence to support this thesis.[60] Now the opinions of manufacturers on the contraction issue present a very complex problem as we have been at pains to point out, but it is

---

[55] *Supra*, pp. 130-132, 279-282.
[56] Beale, *The Critical Year*, p. 239.
[57] *Ibid.*, pp. 239-240.
[58] *Ibid.*, p. 240.
[59] *Ibid.*, p. 278.
[60] As a matter of fact he cites at least one letter to support the opposite conclusion, namely a letter from a Chicago manufacturer to Senator Trumbull opposing contraction. *Ibid.*, p. 241.

quite clear that manufacturers did not generally seek contraction of the currency. The most vocal of their number sought just the opposite, namely a cessation of contraction. The high protectionists, with which Beale is especially concerned, were the most powerful single element in opposition to Hugh McCulloch's policy of contraction of the currency.

In his treatment of the National Banking System Professor Beale once more assumes that the interests of "business" formed some sort of monolithic unity.[61]

Around the new national banks centered continual controversy. A strong tradition of opposition to the idea of a national bank remained from Jackson's day. The new banks were different, but they bore the onus of the popular distrust of the "monied monster" of the 'Thirties. In truth the new banks *were* a potent influence; they were intended to be. They aroused Western oppostition by intensifying the concentration of financial control in the Northeast—in New York, Philadelphia, and Boston. Endowed with greater resources than the old state banks, they wielded great power. "Business" stood solidly behind them as it had behind the Bank of Jackson's day, and urged their extension. These new national banks it was that later helped Big Business in the extraordinary financing of the last years of the century. Small banks, Western state banks, debtors, hated them as early as 1866 for their very stabilizing activity, and for their apparent favoring of Easterners and business men.

This treatment involves some oversimplifications. Like the Beards, Beale holds that "business" including finance as well as industrial capitalists presented a solid phalanx of mutual self-interest to the "Small banks, Western state banks, [and] debtors" who hated the National Banking System. Now this characterization may be accurate for a later period, but it is misleading for the year 1866. In that year "business" was by no means so greatly enamoured of national banking. It has been pointed out above that only in some states of the West where the excesses of "wildcat" banking were best remembered was there any real enthusiasm in banking circles for the legislation of 1863 and 1864.[62] Among the powerful bankers of the eastern seaboard cities, national banking continued to be suspect for years.[63] It was only the punitive act of March 3,

---

[61] *Ibid.*, pp. 247-248.   [62] *Supra*, p. 227.

[63] *Supra*, pp. 248-250. Note the opinion of Augustus Ely Silliman, President

1865, placing a ten per cent tax upon the note issues of state banks, which hastened the conversion of large eastern banks.[64] In October, 1865 the new system was described by James Gallatin as " an odious system of plundering the people by a double interest process." [65] Such a statement might well have been expected to come from a western agrarian. Actually, it came from one of the most powerful and conservative of New York bankers. The known hostility to the new system of the country's most powerful bankers leads the present author to seriously question Beale's statement that " Business' stood solidly behind them [the national banks] as it had behind the Bank of Jackson's day, and urged their extension." On balance, " business " (if such a conglomerate term has any meaning at all) may have stood behind the new banking system, but there were important elements within the realm of finance capital who distrusted and opposed it.

In their treatment of the interests of " capitalists " and of " business " the Beards and Professor Beale have created a conceptual monolith ill adapted to the purpose of explaining the real meaning of the economic history of the Civil War and Reconstruction. I have no quarrel with the Beard-Beale concept that the economic play within a play constitutes the hard core of meaning which can be elicited from the drama of Civil War and Reconstruction. For purposes of analysis, however, the Beard-Beale thesis has provided us with a meat cleaver instead of the more useful scalpel. Only by understanding the interplay and contest of forces within the " capitalist " or " business " group itself can the historian begin to arrive at a sound and comprehensive interpretation of this formative period of American history.

The Beard-Beale concept of the " Second American Revolution " has had an enormous impact upon the writing of history. The complete genealogy of the interpretation is beyond our purpose here, though it will be useful to deal briefly with a few works of recent years in order to demonstrate the pervasive-

---

of the Merchants Bank of New York that the new system would " flood the country with a currency essentially irredeemable." *Supra*, pp. 249-250.

[64] *Supra*, p. 229.

[65] Quoted in Redlich, II, 123.

ness of the general concept. In *The Triumph of American Capitalism* published in 1940, Professor Louis M. Hacker accepts the framework of the Beard-Beale thesis.[66] There are times when I find myself almost in agreement with Mr. Hacker in his treatment of the financial aspects of the Civil War and Reconstruction. Essentially Hacker finds that these years marked the victory of industrial capitalism in the political and economic arena. He points out quite correctly that the issue of the greenbacks was a boon to industrial capitalists.[67] He also is on sound ground when he asserts that the Radicals represented generally the interests of this economic group.[68] Hacker separates the Radicals into two types which he calls the "Old Radicals" and the "New Radicals."[69] Such a classification can validly be made, but Hacker does it for the wrong reasons. He assumes that both types represented the interests of industrial capitalists, but that the "Old Radicals" such as Stevens and Greeley differed from the "New Radicals" such as Conkling, Blaine, and Garfield in that the former were egalitarians who "labored heroically in the interests of the establishment of Negro rights" but that since the "New Radicals" "were too young themselves to have suffered in the Abolitionist struggle," "Negro emancipation, for them, was not a burning faith but a weapon."[70] Professor Hacker makes his dichotomy on the basis of attitudes toward Negro rights. There is considerable truth in this classification, but it would have been less obscured had Mr. Hacker realized that the "Old Radicals" were the faithful representatives of the entrepreneurial type of industrial capitalism whereas the so-called "New Radicals" such as James Garfield and Roscoe Conkling more often than not supported the interests of finance capital and the oligopolistic brand of industrial capitalism.

It is in his treatment of the money question that Hacker's failure to note the difference in economic rationale between the "Old Radicals" and the "New Radicals" is most apparent. For example, he holds that Johnson's heresies on financial issues

[66] Hacker, *The Triumph of American Capitalism*, p. 339.
[67] *Ibid.*, p. 340.
[68] *Ibid.*, p. 341.
[69] *Ibid.*, pp. 340-342.
[70] *Ibid.*, pp. 341-342.

demonstrate the reason why the "Old Radicals" had to oppose him.[71] Actually, as has been pointed out above, Johnson's position on these questions was far closer to that of Wade, Stevens, and Butler than it was to that of Conkling, Garfield, and Morrill.[72] Professor Hacker, in the tradition of the Beard-Beale thesis, fails to recognize the essential cleavages on financial issues which existed within the Radical camp itself. Again, using the traditional stereotype, Hacker asserts with regard to the contraction issue that "The inflationists were the debtors generally and the farmers in particular, who sought more money to maintain high crop prices and to make their debt burden as light as possible." [73] Here again he fails to recognize that the farmers were the least concerned of economic groups in the outcome of this controversy immediately after the war and that it was rather the triumphant entrepreneurial industrial capitalists which constituted the most powerful element opposed to the policy of contraction. Thus, although I find myself in agreement with Professor Hacker on certain points, his failure to recognize the divergencies on financial issues within the Republican party as well as his neglect of the cleavages within the capitalist group tend to mar the validity of his analysis.

One of the results of the Beard-Beale thesis has been the identification of the Radical Republicans with the interests of "business." The following excerpt from an article by James

[71] *Ibid.*, pp. 374-375.

[72] *Supra*, pp. 118, 122-123. Fortunately or unfortunately, depending upon the point of view, autonomous factors can never be eliminated from the study of historical causation. Thus the fortuitous advocacy of the essentials of what was later to become the "Ohio idea" by the Cincinnati *Enquirer* in 1867 may well have been of enormous consequence for the future. Had the western Democrats remained true to their pre-war hard-money proclivities, contractionist elements within the Republican Party would have been deprived of one of their most effective arguments (namely that the "party of treason" advocated "repudiation"), and the principled greenbackers within the Republican Party would have been hard to contain as they were effectively by the Public Credit Act of 1869. *Supra*, pp. 97-101, 120-130. Another autonomous element which is treated only lightly in this study is the pervasive influence of classical economic doctrine. Men like James Garfield and Charles Sumner did not support hard-money because they desired to ally themselves with the deflationary interests of finance capital but rather because they firmly believed in the validity of the principles of the Manchester school of political economy.

[73] Hacker, p. 386.

G. Randall illustrates how this concept has been engrafted upon the main stem of American historiography.[74]

Among the leaders of the Radicals may be mentioned Sumner, Wade, Stevens, Zachariah Chandler, Henry Winter Davis, J. A. Logan, James M. Ashley, Boutwell, and Julian. By 1866 these vindictives had made themselves masters of Congress through the Republican party (now no longer a Lincoln party) and the drastic Reconstruction regime was peculiarly their work. In this they encountered the determined resistance of President Johnson, and the height of Radical vengefulness was reached in the almost successful effort to remove him on impeachment. As used in this article, the term ' Radical " does not mean ' liberal.' The Radicals had small regard for civil rights, and some of their fiercest denunciations were hurled at the Supreme Court for upholding civil rights (in the North) in the Milligan case of 1866.

Historians now recognize that there was an economic motive in Radical policy, for their control of the National Government favored Northeastern manufacturing and financial interests against those of the West and South.

It will be noted that Professor Randall specifically disassociates the term " Radical " from the connotation " liberal." What Randall means by the word " liberal " cannot be determined with any degree of certainty. If he is using the word in its nineteenth century sense to imply the John Stuart Mill brand of " liberalism " with its peculiar interpretation of political and economic freedom, he is quite correct in his statement that " ' Radical ' does not mean ' liberal '." The Radical brand of economic nationalism was certainly not consonant with this type of " liberalism." If, on the other hand, by this disassociation Professor Randall means to imply that the Radicals represented the interests of " capitalists " or " business " and were opposed to the aspirations of other economic groups, then the present author must take exception to his interpretation. The second paragraph of the excerpt quoted above would tend to indicate that this was what he had in mind, although his mention of the Radical reaction to the Milligan case muddies the waters a bit.[75] If indeed Professor Randall means to imply

[74] James G. Randall, "Radical Republicans," in *Dictionary of American History*, ed. James Truslow Adams, 5 vols. (New York, 1940), IV, 395.

[75] If the Radicals are to be judged anti-" liberal " by their opposition to the decision in *Ex parte* Milligan, President Lincoln must be tarred with the same brush inasmuch as he established the military commission by which Milligan

that the Radicals served the interests of the economic royalists, it is difficult to square such an interpretation with the plain fact that the most ultra of the tribe were the political heroes of the American labor movement. Such a thesis would be hardly consonant with the indisputable evidence which exists that the labor movement of the sixties regarded such men as Thaddeus Stevens, Ben Wade, and Benjamin F. Butler as its champions in the struggle against the " money monopolists." [76] Professor Randall's interpretation of the economic role of Radicalism (if this is his interpretation) is a legitimate deduction from the Beard-Beale concept of the " Second American Revolution," but in my opinion, it is completely inaccurate.

The multiplex ramifications of the Beard-Beale concept of the " Second American Revolution" are beyond the scope of this study.[77] It must suffice to say that few theses in American historiography have had greater influence. Some years ago in his brilliant study of American radicalism, Chester M. Destler questioned the prevailing sectional interpretation of the politico-

was tried. It should also be pointed out that the outcry against the decision transcended the Radicals and included moderate and anti-Radical organs such as the New York *Times* and the New York *Herald*. Charles Warren, *The Supreme Court in United States History*, 3 vols. (Boston, 1923), III, 140-176. No less of an authority than Edward S. Corwin has held that the opinion of the minority justices in this case was far more " realistic " and that Lincoln's course in meeting a wartime emergency was " accordant with the most ancient traditions of Anglo-American law." Edward S. Corwin, *The President, Office and Powers, 1787-1948: History and Analysis of Practice and Opinion*, 3rd rev. ed. (New York, 1948), pp. 280, 369.

[76] The Radical Wendell Phillips was, of course, also a champion of labor. *Supra*, pp. 203-205. The egalitarian nature of such measures as the Homestead Act and the Morrill Land-Grant Act (originally introduced by the Radical Senator Ben Wade) as well as the egalitarian nature of Radical policy on the South provide other points of dissent from the concept that " Radicalism " and " liberalism ' are mutually exclusive terms.

[77] To cite a few works where the core of the Beard-Beale thesis can be found, see James G. Randall, *The Civil War and Reconstruction* (Boston, 1953), p. 748; Philip S. Foner, *History of the Labor Movement in the United States from Colonial Times to the Founding of the American Federation of Labor* (New York, 1947), p. 391; Matthew Josephson, *The Politicos, 1865-1896* (New York, 1938), pp. 38-60; Thomas C. Cochran and William Miller, *The Age of Enterprise: A Social History of Industrial America* (New York, 1943), ch. V. Elements of the interpretation can also be found in many of the standard texts on economic history. For example, Harold Underwood Faulkner, *American Economic History*, 7th ed. (New York, 1954), pp. 345, 379-380, 513-514.

economic history of the Reconstruction period. Destler suggested that the struggles over such issues as contraction of the currency, the tariff, the National Banking System, and the " Pendleton Plan " were intra-sectional rather than sectional in nature involving contests among " opposing banking, investing, mercantile, industrial, labor, and agricultural interests." [78] The results of this study tend to confirm Professor Destler's impressions. In concluding that the " Second American Revolution " can only be understood in the light of the divergent interests of various economic groups, it is hoped that something has been contributed toward a sounder understanding of the most formative years in the molding of the American nation.

FINIS

<hr>

[78] Destler, *American Radicalism*, p. 49.

BIBLIOGRAPHY

An attempt has been made in the following pages to evaluate the most important works used in the preparation of this study. Where the work has been factually useful in one or two specific instances but of little or no general importance to the development of the thesis, it has simply been listed. By and large only works referred to in the text have been included except in cases where a more general bibliographical discussion has seemed to be in order.

MANUSCRIPTS

Although manuscript materials have not constituted the *sine qua non* of sources for this study, they have been useful and extremely important. Two collections have been of special significance. These are the Hugh McCulloch papers and the John Sherman papers both in the Library of Congress. The McCulloch collection consists of four bound volumes of correspondence covering the Indianian's tenure as Secretary of the Treasury. These contain mostly letters written to McCulloch but also a few in the Secretary's own hand including several to his friend, John Forbes, the Boston capitalist. Correspondents of McCulloch from 1865 through 1869 included Elbridge G. Spaulding, Amasa Walker, Horace Greeley, Edward Atkinson, Henry J. Raymond, Francis Lieber, Francis Bowen, Arthur Latham Perry, and John Wentworth. The collection contains many letters from prominent and influential bankers which help demonstrate the proposition that the bulk of the eastern banking fraternity supported his policies. Particularly important are several letters from Edward Atkinson, the Boston industrialist, in which McCulloch is repeatedly advised to stand firm in his policies and to disassociate himself if possible personally and politically from Andrew Johnson.

The John Sherman papers in the Library of Congress have been of equal, if not greater importance in the preparation of this study. The Ohio Senator's incoming correspondence during the years 1865-1869 was quite considerable, and a good part of it has been preserved in some twenty-five bound volumes. Very few letters in the Senator's own hand are included in the collection, but this lack is more than compensated for by the great variety of opinion on financial topics expressed by Sherman's correspondents. The collection contains letters from many bankers both western and eastern which serve to illustrate subtle regional differences on the question of contraction as well as on other financial topics. The Senator's correspondence also includes letters from a number of manufacturers which tend to substantiate the thesis that this economic interest was bitterly opposed to the deflationary policy of contraction. The collection contains letters from a great variety of persons both prominent and obscure. It is precisely because the Ohioan attracted correspondence from run-of-the-mill bankers and manufacturers that the collection has been so important in this study. It has also been significant because of the light it casts on certain aspects of Ohio politics during these years and shows good political cause for Sherman's devious course on financial issues. Evidence of the differing interests and convictions operating on Sherman appear in letters from such personages as Jay Cooke and his brother Henry, Schuyler Colfax, Hugh McCulloch, Joseph Medill, H. R. Hulburd, and Henry C. Carey. A very important letter from the New York capitalist Jonathan Sturges demonstrates a very thorough contemporary understanding of the subtle effect of changes in the gold premium described in Chapter IV.

Other collections have been of some value in the writing of this study. The Thaddeus Stevens papers contain several letters demonstrating the opposition of the high protectionist manufacturing interest of Pennsylvania to the policy of currency contraction. Likewise the Lyman Trumbull papers contain evidence showing a similar attitude on the part of Illinois manufacturers. The Zachariah Chandler papers produced little that was germane to this study except a letter from Senator Benjamin Wade in which the effect of the "Ohio idea" on the Ohio elections of 1867 is discussed. The Wade papers were similarly barren from the point of view of the author except for an interesting letter written to the Ohio Senator by the "Moses" of the National Labor Union's currency reformers, Alexander Campbell, which demonstrates the high regard felt for the Radical Senator by an important member of the labor movement. The William Pitt Fessenden papers contain several letters of interest from bankers and businessmen. The John A. Logan papers were consulted but revealed nothing of interest. All of the collections cited in this study are deposited at the Library of Congress in Washington.

GOVERNMENT DOCUMENTS

Of crucial importance to this study has been the *Congressional Globe* for the 37th through the 41st Congresses, 1861-1869. The debates and votes on the Legal Tender Acts, the Contraction Bill of 1866, the Anti-contraction Bill of 1868, the Public Credit Act of 1869, and various other measures have been studied closely and form the basis for much of my analysis and conclusions. Also of great usefulness have been the annual *Reports of the Secretary of the Treasury* for the years 1860 through 1869. These contain an indispensable view of government finances at particular points in time and provide insight into the economic philosophies of the two principal incumbents of the Treasury during these years, Salmon P. Chase and Hugh McCulloch. Included in the Secretary's *Reports* for the years 1864-1869 are the annual " Reports of the Comptroller of the Currency." These contain useful statistical information on the National Banking System as well as the interesting recommendations and predilections of the various occupants of this office, Hugh McCulloch, Freeman Clarke, and H. R. Hulburd.

Several of the publications of the National Monetary Commission authorized by the 61st Congress have been helpful. Most of these are listed below under secondary sources (since this is their essential nature). In this category should be mentioned here 61st Congress, 2nd Session, Senate Document No. 580, A. T. Huntington and Robert J. Mawhinney, compilers, *Laws of the United States Concerning Money, Banking, and Loans, 1778-1909* (Washington, 1910). This compilation of statutes has been cited many times in the text. In ascertaining the official views of Presidents Lincoln, Johnson, and Grant on financial questions, the chief source has been James D. Richardson ed., *A Compilation of the Messages and Papers of the Presidents, 1789-1908* (Washington, 1909). This was published by the Bureau of National Literature and Art but appeared earlier as *House Miscellaneous Documents*, 53rd Congress, 2nd Session, ser. no. 3265, doc. no. 210. Correspondence of Secretary Chase with Congress which did not appear in the *Congressional Globe* during 1861 and 1862 can be found in 37th Congress, 1st Session, *Senate Executive Documents*, no. 2 and 37th Congress, 2nd Session, *House Miscellaneous Documents*, no. 81.

Of great importance in providing an empirical base for the analytical portions of this work have been relevant statistical data pertaining to the years 1860 through 1870. Much of this has been readily available in the United States Department of Commerce, Bureau of the Census, *Historical Statistics of the United States, 1789-1945: A Supplement to the Statistical Abstract of the United States* (Washington, 1949). This work contains the general price index of Carl Snyder and the wholesale price indexes of George F. Warren and Frank A. Pearson cited above.

NEWSPAPERS AND PERIODICALS

Newspapers and periodicals have constituted the single most important category of source materials for this study. The metropolitan press of the period, however, has been of slight importance. Scattered references are found in the text to the New York *Times*, the New York *Herald*, the Chicago *Republican*, and the Cincinnati *Daily Gazette*. The editorial strictures of these journals have been found useful on occasion to illustrate a point or typify a general reaction, but the author has never assigned to them any basic significance. This has been precluded by the general methodology of the work.

One of the most important tasks of this study has been to ascertain the economic interest of four specific groups, manufacturers, farmers, laborers, and bankers as they related to the problems presented by the currency situation after the Civil War. Necessarily the problem of determining what represents valid evidence of group opinion has been difficult. No solution within the bounds of finite research is likely to be completely adequate. My investigations, however, have convinced me that the most useful and complete evidence of group interest and opinion on the questions considered in this work is to be found in the pages of newspapers, magazines and other periodicals which *represent a specific interest*. Other evidence has, of course, been extremely significant, sometimes crucial, but without the demonstrations of group interest found in the pages of farming, manufacturing, banking, and labor journals and newspapers, this study could not have been written.

In treating the manufacturing interest two periodicals have been utilized which specifically represented the interests of that economic group. These are John Williams' weekly newspaper, *Iron Age* and the weekly *Bulletin* of the American Iron and Steel Association. A fairly complete file of the former has been perused for the years 1866-1868, and a complete file of the latter for the years 1865-1869. Both of these publications accurately reflect the high protectionist-soft-money point of view. The *Iron Age* which concerned itself with the problems of manufacturers in a very broad sense has been virtually indispensable. Other periodicals which proved helpful in dealing with the manufacturing interest were the *Commercial and Financial Chronicle* of New York, which, though not representative of the manufacturing group, contains much of interest about problems faced by producers, and *DeBow's Review* which published some interesting paragraphs illustrating one post-Civil War Southern reaction to the philosophy of high protectionism.

Inasmuch as the conclusion has been reached in this study that the farmers constituted the economic group least interested in the issue of contraction or expansion of the currency in the years 1865 through 1870, most of the farm journals consulted by the author have been useful in a purely negative way. This has been true of the *Prairie Farmer* of Chicago which was scanned for the years 1865-1869, the *Maryland Farmer* of Baltimore which was used for the period 1866-1869, and *Colman's Rural World and Valley Farmer* of St. Louis which was consulted for the years 1868-1869. The *American Agriculturist* of New York contained no evidence of farm opinion on questions of government financial policy, but a scanning of this journal did bring to light some interesting evidence of the prosperity of farmers in 1867 and the pain felt by that group when confronted with the fall of prices for agricultural commodities in 1869. This journal was available for the years 1866-1870. The *Kansas Farmer* of Leavenworth which was available for the years 1866-1869 also contained evidence of discontent among farmers in the year 1869. The *Minnesota Monthly* of St. Paul, which began publication in 1869, and was consulted by the present writer for the years 1869-1870, was the only one of these farm journals in which any evidence was uncovered of any real interest in the currency issue. It is questionable whether the article referred to, which was published late in 1869, reflected anything other than a personal interest in financial questions on the part of the author.

Periodicals have been of crucial importance in ascertaining the economic predilections of the American labor movement in years following the Civil War. By far the most important of the labor journals from the standpoint of this work is the Chicago *Workingman's Advocate* which was studied for the period 1865-1870. Edited by Andrew Cameron in its early years and later by Cameron and William Sylvis, this weekly newspaper was the official organ of the National Labor Union. Because both of its editors as well as most of the top leadership of the N. L. U. were tremendously interested in the question of currency reform, the pages of this journal present an ideal source from which the various shades and nuances of labor opinion on questions of financial policy can be elicited. Copies of the *Iron Molders' International Journal* have been utilized for the years 1866-1867. Proceedings of the Baltimore convention of the N. L. U. in 1866 are reported in this journal. Since it was published by the union of which William Sylvis was president, this periodical's comments on the protective tariff were of particular interest. *Fincher's Trades' Review* which was published in Philadelphia from 1863 through 1866 and its successor the *National Trades' Review* which appeared briefly in 1866 have been of limited use to the author since the period of its publication antedated the period when currency reform was the *cause celebre* of the labor movement. The Boston *Daily Evening Voice*, which was published in the years 1865-1867, has been of considerable importance in illuminating the point of view of New England labor leaders which in many cases differed significantly from that of the leaders of the N. L. U.

In ascertaining the rationale of banking opinion on the issues considered in this study, three contemporary periodicals have been of crucial importance. These publications are the *Bankers' Magazine*, *Hunt's Merchants' Magazine*, and the *Commercial and Financial Chronicle*. All three were published in New York City. The first two were utilized for the discussion of the war years as well as for the period 1865-1870. The *Commercial and Financial Chronicle* began publication in the summer of 1865 and was studied by the present author for the years 1865-1870. All three of these magazines project the gold standard-free-trade bias of the mercantile-banking interests of New York. From the standpoint of evidence of banker opinion on financial topics, the *Bankers' Magazine* was most helpful, for the pages of this journal contain many articles from bankers large and small, eastern and western. In its monthly issues there was also found a good deal of relevant statistical data. As its name implies, *Hunt's Merchants' Magazine* was directed at an audience larger than the banking fraternity. The issues of this monthly magazine, however, contain a number of expressions of opinion on financial questions by leading bankers including the very important *Letter* by James Gallatin referred to in chapter VI. Like the *Bankers' Magazine* this publication printed a large amount of statistical material as well as many articles illuminating the general economic condition of the country. Unlike the two monthly publications referred to above, the *Commercial and Financial Chronicle* has not been particularly useful from the standpoint of providing evidence of banker opinion. Its usefulness (and this has been great) has consisted in the fact that it provides an unrivaled reporting of economic events and comments thereon for the period 1865-1870. Its point of view is always that of the conservative business and financial interests of New York, but its reporting is not limited to any particular segment of economic subject matter. Articles and editorials roam freely over the gamut from foreign trade to monetary policy, from labor unions to the trends in the general price level. The usefulness, therefore, has been largely a function of the general comprehensiveness of its coverage. One other periodical which has been of use in pointing up the general conflict of ideas between free traders and protectionists is *The League*, organ of the American Free Trade League whose president was William Cullen Bryant. This monthly publication was consulted for the years 1867-1869. It should be noted that a number of articles from some of these periodicals, chiefly the *Bankers' Magazine* and *Hunt's Merchants' Magazine* have been cited in the text. A listing of these here would make this section even longer and more tedious to no very good purpose. They have consequently been omitted.

PAMPHLETS

Considering the volume of pamphlet literature which has been consulted, it is amazing how little of it has been germane to this study. No accurate count has been kept, but the author suspects that well over a hundred pamphlets relating to the financial controversies of the Civil War decade have been perused. The library of The Johns Hopkins University alone contains a marvelous collection of this literature. Many other such pamphlets were found at the Library of Congress, the Peabody Institute Library of Baltimore, and the Maryland Historical Society. In all honesty it must be stated that a high percentage of this material was of little or no real value. Had the author been interested in compiling a history of financial panaceas and nostrums for the period in question, pamphlet literature would have constituted the indispensable source, for apparently one of the chief hobbies of nineteenth century Americans, literate and illiterate, consisted in the devising of schemes for a better banking system, a more adequate currency medium, or a means of paying off the public debt. Such palliatives for the body politic usually first saw the light of day through the medium of a pamphlet. The trouble is that the vast majority of such efforts represented the inspiration of some obscure scribbler whose musings could by no means be connected with any of the specific economic interests considered in this study.

Among the specimens of pamphlet literature which have been useful must be included several writings of Henry C. Carey. Most of these are contained in the *Miscellaneous Works of Henry C. Carey with a Memoir by Dr. William Elder and a Portrait*, 2 Vols. (Philadelphia, 1883). They are cited separately here because the *Miscellaneous Works* actually consists of a collection of pamphlets, originally published over a long period of years, stitched together and issued in two volumes. They have been extremely useful inasmuch as they contain the pungent criticism of national financial policies during the Reconstruction period leveled at sundry objects of scorn by the leading exponent of high protectionism. Carey's pamphlets cited in the text include *Reconstruction: Industrial, Financial, and Political, Letters to the Hon. Henry Wilson, Senator from Massachusetts* (Philadelphia, 1867) ; *The Finance Minister, the Currency, and the Public Debt*, 2nd ed. (Washington,

1868) (this pamphlet is not included in the *Miscellaneous Works*);
*Currency Inflation: How It Has Been Produced, and How It May
Profitably Be Reduced, Letters to the Hon. B. H. Bristow, Secretary
of the Treasury* (Philadelphia, 1874); *Monetary Independence, Letter
of Mr. H. C. Carey to the Hon. Moses W. Field, Chairman of the
Committee of Invitations for the Detroit Convention* (Philadelphia,
1875), and *Commerce, Christianity, and Civilization Versus British
Free Trade. Letters in Reply to the London Times* (Philadelphia,
1876).

Samuel Wilkeson, *How Our National Debt May Be a National
Blessing. The Debt is Public Wealth, Political Union, Protection of
Industry, Secure Basis for National Currency* (Philadelphia, 1865), a
pamphlet issued by Jay Cooke, has been of interest, because a study
of the writings of his paid agent Wilkeson gives an indication of
how the great Philadelphia banker viewed certain financial questions
after the Civil War. James M. Cooper's pamphlet, *The Government
the Partner of the Manufacturer* (Pittsburgh, 1865) has been of
significance because it provides another piece of evidence that the
protective nature of a rising gold premium was well understood by
many manufacturers. The pamphlet by Alexander Campbell, *The
True American System of Finance; The Rights of Labor and Capital,
and the Common Sense Way of Doing Justice to the Soldiers and Their
Families. No Banks: Greenbacks the Exclusive Currency* (Chicago,
1864) has been of great importance, because the ideas of Campbell
expressed therein provide the link between the earlier proposals of
Edward Kellogg and the monetary reform program of the National
Labor Union. A pamphlet issued by the Milwaukee *News, Payment
of the Public Debt in Legal Tender Notes!! Speech of Hon. George H.
Pendleton* (Milwaukee, 1867), has been quite useful in tracing the
genesis of the " Pendleton Plan." It contains reports of two important
speeches delivered by Pendleton in Cleveland and Milwaukee in the
fall of 1867 and shows the emphasis placed by this leading Democrat
on questions of government financial policy.

PROCEEDINGS AND REPORTS

The proceedings of various meetings and conventions of bankers,
businessmen, laborers, and farmers have been extremely useful in
analyzing the differing economic interests involved. Many of these
meetings were reported in banking, manufacturing, or labor periodicals.
The proceedings of some have been gleaned from John R. Commons
et al., A Documentary History of American Industrial Society, 10 vols.
(Cleveland, 1911), IX and X. Others have been available in the form
of printed pamphlets or books.

In the latter category there have been cited three pamphlets relating to the manufacturing interest. These are: *Proceedings of the New England Manufacturers' Convention Held at Worcester, Mass., January 22, 1868* (Boston, 1868) : *Proceedings of a Convention Held in the City of New York, Wednesday, April 29, 1868, for the Purpose of Organizing The National Association of Cotton Manufacturers and Planters* (Boston 1868) ; and *Proceedings of the First Annual Meeting of the National Association of Cotton Manufacturers and Planters Held in the City of New York, Wednesday, June 30, 1869* (Boston, 1869). These have been useful in the rather negative sense that they point to a definitely minor degree of concern on the part of New England manufacturers with the currency issue, as compared with their protectionist colleagues of Pennsylvania and the West.

The *Proceedings of the National Bank Convention Held in New York City, Wednesday, June 23, 1869* (Syracuse, 1869) has been helpful in analyzing the rationale of banking opinion, particularly because it contains a report of the speech by Elbridge Gerry Spaulding which has been discussed in the text. Likewise the *Proceedings of the Second Annual Meeting of the National Board of Trade Held in Richmond, December, 1869* (Boston, 1870), published in hard covers, contains the interesting remarks of George Opdyke which have also been treated. Especially significant have been the *Annual Reports of the Chamber of Commerce of the State of New York* (New York, 1866-1870) for the years 1865-1869. These contain useful statistical information as well as crucial evidence bearing on the banking interests of New York City.

PRINTED WRITINGS OF CONTEMPORARIES

Evidence available in the works of contemporaries has been essential in the writing of this study. In this category fall memoirs, published diaries and correspondence, autobiographies, collections of speeches and lectures, histories, and various tracts for the times.

Of the published memoirs, three have been especially significant. Hugh McCulloch's *Men and Measures of Half a Century* (New York, 1889) has naturally been of great interest. In treating his tenure as Secretary of the Treasury under Lincoln and Johnson, McCulloch is very sketchy. More useful information can actually be gleaned from his annual *Reports* than from this autobiography. Nonetheless there are many pertinent comments on the financial issues of the day as well as justification for his particular economic point of view. John Sherman, *Recollections of Forty Years in the House, Senate and Cabinet*, 2 vols. (Chicago, 1895) and James G. Blaine, *Twenty Years of Congress:*

From Lincoln to Garfield with a Review of the Events Which Led to the Political Revolution of 1860, 2 vols. (Norwich, Conn., 1884) have been of tremendous importance. Both Blaine and Sherman were active participants in the drama of Civil War and Reconstruction. As testimony John Sherman's work is the more important, for the Ohio Senator exercised a tremendous influence on the financial legislation of the Civil War decade. Like most such works Sherman's *Recollections* is partially self-justifying in nature. Nonetheless the Senator had a keen appreciation for both the political and economic facets of various financial issues, and his writings are an important key to the understanding of the economic aspects of Reconstruction. Blaine's *Twenty Years of Congress* also demonstrates a keen appreciation of the importance of financial issues. This work was written by a very literate politician with a flair for good prose. Even today it is an extremely interesting, if partisan account, of politics during the age of conflict. Blaine's prejudices were in favor of hard-money, but he does not allow them to intrude upon a very useful account of the complexities involved in such issues as contraction of the currency.

George S. Boutwell, *Reminiscences of Sixty Years in Public Affairs*, 2 vols. (New York, 1902) has been of only limited usefulness inasmuch as Boutwell is little concerned with the crucial question of currency contraction during the Johnson administration. Benjamin F. Butler, *Autobiography and Personal Reminiscences of Major-General Benjamin F. Butler; Butler's Book* (Boston, 1892) contains useful testimony on this Radical's conversion to the greenback standard in 1866. George W. Julian, *Political Recollections, 1840-72* (Chicago, 1884) has proved barren from the point of view of this study.

The *Diary of Gideon Welles, Secretary of the Navy under Lincoln and Johnson*, ed. Edgar T. Welles, 3 vols. (Boston, 1911) has been useful in discerning the personal relationships which existed between members of Johnson's cabinet and refreshing for its trenchant comment on the political personalities of the time. *Inside Lincoln's Cabinet: The Civil War Diaries of Salmon P. Chase*, ed. David Donald (New York, 1954) has been of limited significance for this study. Chase was almost completely preoccupied with politics and personalities, and this published diary provides little useful information on the Ohian's motives and policies as Secretary of the Treasury. *Garfield-Hinsdale Letters: Correspondence between James Abram Garfield and Burke Aaron Hinsdale*, ed. Mary L. Hinsdale (Ann Arbor, 1949) provides interesting evidence on the impact of the Ohio state election of 1867 on Republicans along with some evidence as to the unpopularity of contraction with the manufacturing interest.

Several collections of speeches and writings have been quite useful. Peter Cooper, *Ideas for a Science of Good Government, in Addresses, Letters and Articles on a Strictly National Currency, Tariff and Civil Service* (New York, 1883) contains the thought of this grand old man of American industry on such questions as the tariff and the contraction of the currency. In similar vein is William D. Kelley, *Speeches, Addresses and Letters on Industrial and Financial Questions* (Philadelphia, 1872) which makes clear the soft-money predilections of that noted protectionist. Wendell Phillips, *Speeches, Lectures, and Letters*, Second Series (Boston, 1891) has been extremely helpful in tracing the evolution of the thought of this great Radical who combined in his person the ideals of abolitionism, labor reform, protectionism, and opposition to the "money monopolists."

A variety of contemporary works on subjects relating to this study have been helpful. Elbridge Gerry Spaulding's *History of the Legal-Tender Paper Money Issued During the Great Rebellion* (Buffalo, 1869) is an account of the passage of the Legal Tender Acts by the man who is regarded as the "father of the greenbacks." It contains evidence available in no other work regarding the motives which dominated the men who steered the legal tender legislation through Congress. Henry Adams and Francis A. Walker, "The Legal Tender Act" which originally appeared in the *North American Review* for April, 1870 and later in Henry Adams, *Historical Essays* (New York, 1891) is a contemporary analysis of the legislation of 1862 in which the role of Spaulding is assessed very critically. As has been indicated, I think none too highly of the Adams-Walker approach. An unsigned article, "The Great Gold Conspiracy," *Harper's Magazine*, XI (April, 1870) provides interesting evidence of the reaction of businessmen to the cessation of hostilities in 1865. Alexander Dana Noyes, *Forty Years of American Finance* (New York, 1909) is an interesting, if sketchy, account by a contemporary of American financial history in the years following the Civil War.

Several contemporary works dealing with politics have been cited. These are: Edward McPherson, *A Handbook of Politics for 1868* (Washington, 1868); Republican National Committee, *1868 Text Book for the Republican Campaign* (New York, 1868); and William H. Barnes, *History of the Thirty-ninth Congress of the United States* (New York, 1868). Though useful on occasion, these works have been of only minor importance.

In treating the labor movement of the Civil War decade several works by contemporaries have been useful. Terrence V. Powderly, *Thirty Years of Labor, 1859-1889* (Columbus, Ohio, 1890) includes some information about the labor movement of the sixties, though naturally the emphasis is on the later period. James Dawson Burn, *Three Years Among the Working Classes in the United States During the War* (London, 1865) provides some interesting vignettes of industrial life in the North. Of great importance has been George E. McNeill, *The Labor Movement: The Problem of Today* (Boston, 1887). This work by a leading New England labor leader of the sixties contains first-hand testimony on issues crucial to this study such as the lack of interest on the part of farmers in the program of the National Labor Union and the cleavage in the New England labor movement between the eight-hour advocates and the currency reformers. Oliver H. Kelley, *Origin and Progress of the Order of Patrons of Husbandry in the United States; a History from 1866 to 1873* (Philadelphia, 1875) is of considerable significance inasmuch as Kelley's account of the founding of the Grange makes it clear that economic discontent among farmers was not a root cause of his organizational efforts.

Contemporary works in the field of political economy referred to in the text include Edward Kellogg, *A New Monetary System: The Only Means of Securing the Respective Rights of Labor and Property, and of Protecting the Public from Financial Revulsions*, ed. Mary Kellogg Putnam, 6th ed. (Philadelphia, 1878). This was the revised version of Kellogg's earlier work, *Labor and Other Capital* (New York, 1849). Though diffuse and disjointed, this work was the Bible of the post-Civil War currency reformers and has been discussed at length in the text. Henry C. Carey, *The Harmony of Interests, Agricultural, Manufacturing, and Commercial* (Philadelphia, 1872) presents the economic *Weltanschauung* of the high priest of protectionism in the light of post-war developments. David A. Wells, *The Recent Financial, Industrial and Commercial Experiences of the United States: A Curious Chapter in Politico-Economic History* (New York, 1872) contains important evidence on the stimulating effect of the rising premium of gold on American exports during the Civil War.

ARTICLES

Two articles which have been published within the last year are highly recommended for those readers who may care to pursue further the subject matter of this study. These are Irwin Unger, "Business Men and Specie Resumption," *Political Science Quarterly*, LXXIV (March, 1959), 46-70 and Stanley Coben, "Northeastern Business and Radical Reconstruction: A Re-examination," *Mississippi Valley Historical Review*, XLVI (June, 1959), 67-90. Inasmuch as this study was completed long before I had had the benefit of reading these articles, they had no influence upon my work. It was nonetheless somewhat reassuring that the conclusions reached by Messrs. Unger, Coben and myself with respect to the attitudes of the buiness community are remarkably similar.

Articles which have been useful in the preparation of this work include Herbert S. Schell, " Hugh McCulloch and the Treasury Department, 1865-1869," *Mississippi Valley Historical Review*, XVII (1931). Though limited in scope, this article does an admirable job of presenting the problems faced by McCulloch, both financial and political, during his tenure as Secretary of the Treasury. Frank D. Graham, " International Trade Under Depreciated Paper: The United States, 1862-79," *Quarterly Journal of Economics*, XXXVI (1922) contains important evidence relating to the effect of changing gold premiums (largely induced by international borrowing) on the course of foreign trade. This evidence has been cited by Howard K. Beale, " The Tariff and Reconstruction," *American Historical Review*, XXXV (1929-30), though Professor Beale does not come to the conclusion which to me is unavoidable and sustained by the evidence; namely, that the declining gold premium was an important factor in causing many manufacturers to oppose contraction of the currency. I disagree with several statements in this article including one to the effect that factory owners usually favored contraction of the currency and the assertion that farmers were badly hurt by the fall in the general price level after the war.

William B. Hesseltine, " Economic Factors in the Abandonment of Reconstruction," *Mississippi Valley Historical Review*, XXI (1939) corroborates the general thesis presented here that conservative mercantile-financial interests supported a moderate program of Reconstruction and were by no means opposed to Andrew Johnson. John D. Hicks, " The Political Career of Ignatius Donnelly," *Mississippi Valley Historical Review*, VIII (1921) has been helpful in tracing the tergiversations of this flamboyant political figure on financial issues. John Lee Coulter, " Organization Among the Farmers of the United States," *Yale Review*, XVIII (1909) is a useful study of the factors which stimulated or retarded farmer organization in the post-Civil War generation. An old article by Thorstein Veblen, " The Price of Wheat Since 1867," *Journal of Political Economy*, I (December, 1892) has been helpful in documenting the generally prosperous economic condition of farmers after the Civil War. Rafael A. Bayley, " History of the National Loans of the United States," *International Review*, XII (1882) describes the economic conditions under which each loan was made through the year 1880 and the terms of the various issues. Williston H. Lofton, "Northern Labor and the Negro During the Civil War," *Journal of Negro History*, XXXIV (1949) and Albon P. Man, Jr., "Labor Competition and the New York Draft Riots of 1863," *Journal of Negro History*, XXXVI (1951) have been cited in the discussion of the anti-Negro bias of many Northern workingmen during the Civil War.

Articles cited from books include Oliver Mitchell Wentworth Sprague, "Loans and Taxes in War Finance" in Arthur Smithies and J. Keith Butters eds., *Readings in Fiscal Policy Selected by a Committee of the American Economic Association* (Homewood, Ill., 1955). This article lays emphasis on the importance of heavy and adequate taxation in the financing of wars. The article by James G. Randall, "Radical Republicans," in *Dictionary of American History*, ed. James Truslow Adams, 5 vols. (New York, 1940) has the merit of compressing the essentials of the conventional version of the Radical, a version with which I profoundly disagree. Harold J. Laski, "Charles Beard: An English View," and Howard K. Beale, "Charles Beard: Historian," in *Charles A. Beard: An Appraisal*, ed. Howard K. Beale (Lexington, Ky., 1954) as well as other articles from the same work have been extremely helpful in assessing the concept of the "Second American Revolution."

SECONDARY MATERIALS

Most general historians who have dealt with the Civil War and Reconstruction years have devoted only a few pages to financial history. All take the traditional point of view and demonstrate for the most part little sympathy for the anti-contractionist argument. A possible exception to this general statement is William A. Dunning, *Reconstruction, Political and Economic, 1865-1877* (New York, 1907) in Albert Bushnell Hart ed., *The American Nation: A History*, XXII. Dunning at least has the merit of recognizing that those who opposed contraction had a good argument and does not consign them to the outer limbo of heresy. He also realizes the political impracticability of the McCulloch program. James Ford Rhodes, *History of the United States from the Compromise of 1850*, 8 vols. (New York, 1899-1919), VI, devotes about ten pages to the currency issue. Rhodes treatment is competent though in the traditional vein. He feels that McCulloch was basically right and sees little merit in the arguments against contraction. James Schouler, *History of the United States under the Constitution*, 7 vols. (New York, 1894-1913), VII, is little concerned with the financial history of the early Reconstruction period. He is, however, a great personal admirer of Hugh McCulloch. Ellis Paxson Oberholtzer, *A History of the United States Since the Civil War*, 5 vols., (New York, 1922) is disappointing on financial questions. Although the author's knowledge of the subject was very great (this is obvious in the same author's biography of Jay Cooke), he allows his personal prejudice in favor of "sound money" too much weight. As a result Oberholtzer's treatment of the financial history of Reconstruction is not only traditional but obviously extremely biased. Allan Nevins, *The Emergence of Modern America, 1865-1878* (New York, 1927) in Arthur M. Schlesinger and Dixon R. Fox eds., *A History of American Life*, VIII, devotes little attention to financial history. As is the case in many other works, Professor Nevins assigns basic responsibility for the demand for more currency to the farmers of the West, a position which I do not find tenable. Charles A. Beard and Mary R. Beard, *The Rise of American Civilization*, 2 vols. (New York, 1927) has been discussed extensively in the text. This work, of course established the concept of the "Second American Revolution." James G. Randall, *The Civil War and Reconstruction* (Boston, 1953) is strictly in the Beard-Beale tradition so far as the interpretation of economic issues is concerned. It nonetheless remains the best and most useful contemporary treatment of the Civil War and Reconstruction. Claude G. Bowers, *The Tragic Era: The Revolution after Lincoln* (Cambridge, Mass., 1929) and George Fort Milton, *The Age of Hate: Andrew Johnson and the Radicals* (New York, 1930) are very readable political history but devote little space to economic issues.

Of the general economic histories of the United States Harold Underwood Faulkner, *American Economic History*, 7th ed. (New York, 1954), Edward C. Kirkland, *A History of American Economic Life*, 3rd ed. (New York, 1951), and Chester Whitney Wright, *Economic History of the United States*, 2nd ed. (New York, 1949) have been the most useful. Faulkner has been used most frequently here as a reference work, but from the standpoint of the treatment of the complexities of the money problem, Kirkland's work is undoubtedly the best.

Documentary histories and collections of documents have proved helpful to some extent. By far the most important has been John R. Commons *et al., A Documentary History of American Industrial Society*, 10 vols. (Cleveland, 1911), IX, X. The resolutions and proceedings of various farmer and labor conventions are contained in this work. In the case of the proceedings of the conventions of the National Labor Union, all could have been cited from labor periodicals of the period, but it would seem a needless exercise of pedantry to cite a virtually inaccessible source when one that is readily available can be referred to. Henry Steele Commager ed., *Documents of American History*, 4th ed. (New York, 1948) has been useful in several instances. Walter L. Fleming, *Documentary History of Reconstruction*, 2 vols. (Cleveland, 1906-07) contains nothing of relevance to this study.

Of the financial histories of the United States, Davis R. Dewey, *Financial History of the United States*, 12th ed. (New York, 1934) is still the most useful. Though wedded to the traditional " sound money " approach to monetary problems, it is thorough and contains excellent, if somewhat dated, bibliographical references. W. J. Shultz and M. R. Caine, *Financial Development of the United States* (New York, 1937) is more critical than Dewey and is written from a more modern point of view. It is not, however, so useful for reference purposes. Two older volumes by Albert S. Bolles, *The Financial History of the United States from 1789 to 1860* (New York, 1883) and *The Financial History of the United States from 1861 to 1885* (New York, 1886), though wandering and oftimes verbose, are helpful in understanding financial issues presented in the words of a contemporary.

There are a number of works which deal with the history and consequences of the greenbacks. The best works on the subject are Wesley Clair Mitchell, *A History of the Greenbacks with Special Reference to the Economic Consequences of Their Issue* (Chicago, 1903) and the same author's *Gold, Prices, and Wages under the Greenback Standard* (Berkeley, 1908). The former work covers the period from 1862 to 1865, and, though it is now well over fifty years old, it is still a model of dispassionate scholarship. Though the present author disagrees with Professor Mitchell on the question of the " necessity " of the greenbacks, he has found the *History of the Greenbacks* an extremely helpful and stimulating work. *Gold, Prices, and Wages* covers the period from 1862 to 1879 and is useful chiefly for the statistical material it contains. Don C. Barrett, *The Greenbacks and the Resumption of Specie Payments, 1862-1879* (Cambridge, Mass., 1931) is defective in several respects. Like Mitchell, Barrett argues against the " necessity " for the issue of the legal tenders. He also argues rather unconvincingly that specie payment could have been effected shortly after the end of hostilities. All in all Barrett's work shows a lack of comprehension of the political and economic necessities of the Civil War and Reconstruction periods. Alonzo Barton Hepburn, *History of Coinage and Currency in the United States and the Perennial Contest for Sound Money* (New York, 1903) and the same author's *A History of Currency in the United States with a Brief Description of the Currency Systems of All Commercial Nations* (New York, 1915) treat the currency issue of the Civil War decade from the point of view of a conservative banker and former Comptroller of the Currency. Other specialized works on the money problems of the Civil War and Reconstruction periods which have been cited or consulted include William Graham Sumner, *A History of American Currency* (New York, 1876) John Jay Knox, *United States Notes*, 3rd. ed. (New York, 1894); Jacob K. Upton, *Money in Politics* (Boston, 1884); M. S. Wildman, *Money Inflation in the United States* (New York, 1905); Henry R. Linderman, *Money and Legal Tender in the United States* (New York, 1877); and the *Report of the Monetary Commission of the Indianapolis Convention of Boards of Trade, Chambers of Commerce, Commercial Clubs, and Other Similar Bodies of the United States* (Chicago, 1898).

Works on a number of aspects of financial history have been useful in the preparation of this study. David Kinley, *The History, Organization and Influence of the Independent Treasury of the United States* (New York, 1893) traces the genesis and development of this uniquely American institution. Frederic C. Howe, *Taxation and Taxes in the United States under the Internal Revenue System, 1791-1895* (New York, 1896) and Herbert Ronald Ferleger, *David A. Wells and the American Reveue System, 1865-1870* (New York, 1942) are helpful in understanding the workings of the complex internal taxation system which evolved during the Civil War. Ernest Ludlow Bogart, *War Costs and Their Financing: A Study of the Financing of the War and the After-war Problems of Debt and Taxation* (New York, 1921) analyzes the methods adopted by the federal government to finance the Civil War. Albert Edgar Feavearyear, *The Pound Sterling: A History of English Money* (Oxford, 1931) has been useful in ascertaining the course of British financial history during the sixties.

The standard works on the tariff are Frank W. Taussig, *The Tariff History of the United States*, 5th ed. (New York, 1910) and Edward Stanwood, *American Tariff Controversies in the Nineteenth Century*, 2 vols. (Boston, 1903). The former is the sounder work from an economic point of view, but the latter is more useful in indicating the political background of tariff legislation. Malcolm Rogers Eiselen, *The Rise of Pennsylvania Protectionism* (Philadelphia, 1932) details the factors influencing the rise of protectionist sentiment in the Keystone state. Eiselen, however, fails to see the link between the ideas of protection and soft-money.

In the field of American industrial history Victor S. Clark, *History of Manufactures in the United States*, 3 vols. (New York, 1929) is the standard authority. Clark's work has been particularly useful, because it lays stress upon the particular economic climate which existed during a given period. Clark also recognizes, although he does not analyze and rationalize, the soft-money leanings of many American manufacturers of the post-bellum period. A large number of business histories have been consulted. Those which have been cited include George Sweet Gibb, *The Whitesmiths of Taunton: A History of Reed & Barton, 1824-1943* (Cambridge, Mass., 1943); Evelyn H. Knowlton, *Pepperell's Progress: History of a Cotton Textile Company, 1844-1945* (Cambridge, Mass., 1948); and Thomas R. Navin, *The Whitin Machine Works Since 1831: A Textile Machinery Company in an Industrial Village* (Cambridge, Mass., 1950). N. S. B. Gras and Henrietta M. Larson, *Casebook in American Business History* (New York, 1939) has been useful in assessing the general climate of business after the Civil War. Emerson David Fite, *Social and Industrial Conditions in the North during the Civil War* (New York, 1910) contains much useful information on business and industry in the North during the years of conflict. Though perhaps lacking in the quality of critical analysis, it is the only existing work which attempts a broad survey of all major segments of the economy during the Civil War.

In the area of banking history specifically and to this study generally Fritz Redlich, *The Molding of American Banking: Men and Ideas*, 2 vols. (New York, 1951) has been of preeminent importance. Professor Redlich probably knows more than any man has known before about the entire range of American monetary and banking history. His work has been an inspiration and a sustenance in times of trial. Since Professor Redlich eschews determinism in the field of economic history, he might well disapprove of certain somewhat deterministic elements in this study. Be that as it may, in questioning some of the traditional notions which have long been dominant in the interpretation of the financial, industrial, and social history of the Civil War and Reconstruction periods, I have derived considerable support, as much implicit as explicit, from Professor Redlich's great work.

Other works in this field have also proved useful. Leonard Helderman, *National and State Banks, A Study of Their Origins* (Boston, 1931) is a brief though critical and provocative survey of American banking through the early years of the National Banking System. Though meandering and incredibly disorganized, John Jay Knox, *A History of Banking in the United States*, Rev. ed (New York, 1903) contains much technical and factual information about the National Banking System by a man whose experience as Comptroller of the

Currency made him intimately familiar with its operations. Andrew McFarland Davis, *The Origin of the National Banking System* (Washington, 1910), though almost totally lacking in critical content, contains a helpful store of knowledge, particularly on the passage of the national banking legislation of 1863 and 1864. Though it deals mostly with a later period, Oliver Mitchell Wentworth Sprague, *History of Crises Under the National Banking System* (Washington, 1910) incorporates a good deal of analytical material regarding the basic weaknesses of the National Banking System. The sectional aspects of that system receive comprehensive treatment in George Laverne Anderson, *The National Banking System, 1865-1875: A Sectional Institution*. This is an unpublished doctoral dissertation in the library of the University of Illinois. N. S. B. Gras, *The Massachusetts First National Bank of Boston, 1794-1934* (Cambridge, Mass., 1937) has been consulted but contains little that is relevant to this study. Esther Rogoff Taus, *Central Banking Functions of the United States Treasury, 1789-1941* (New York, 1943) is an admirable treatment of the effects of Treasury operations on the money market, while Margaret G. Myers, *The New York Money Market: Origins and Development* (New York, 1931) includes useful material on the impact of the National Banking System on the nation's financial center. Charles A. Conant, *History of Modern Banks of Issue, With an Account of the Economic Crises of the Nineteenth Century and the Crisis of 1907*, 4th ed. (New York, 1909) has been of limited usefulness. William Graham Sumner, *History of Banking in the United States* (New York, 1896) contains very little on American banking after the Civil War.

Horace White, *Money and Banking Illustrated by American History*, 5th ed. (Boston, 1914), one of the first textbooks in the field of money and banking, includes a number of chapters on American financial history. Like most of the scholars who have worked in this field, White was opposed to the issue of the legal tender notes. He nonetheless ranks among the better of the older authorities on financial history. Considering that this work was used as a text, it is interesting to compare its almost completely historical treatment of money and banking with the more theoretical handling of the subject in contemporary texts. Harold L. Reed, *Money, Currency and Banking* (New York, 1942) and George N. Halm, *Monetary Theory: A Modern Treatment of the Essentials of Money and Banking*, 2nd ed. (Philadelphia, 1946), two modern works in the field, have proved helpful in the handling of various theoretical problems.

In dealing with the labor movement of the Civil War decade John R. Commons *et al., History of Labor in the United States*, 2 vols. (New

York, 1918) in addition to Commons *et. al., Documentary History of American Industrial Society* already listed have been the most useful published works. The *History of Labour* greatly emphasizes the philosophical and ideological aspects of the labor movement of the sixties, and this emphasis has been welcomed on more than one occasion. Norman J. Ware, *The Labor Movement in the United States, 1860-1895: A Study in Democracy* (New York, 1929) is not so helpful on the currency reform issue as it related to the labor movement of the sixties. Philip S. Foner, *History of the Labor Movement in the United States from Colonial Times to the Founding of the American Federation of Labor* (New York, 1947) has been a useful work from the standpoint of the present author despite the fact that Foner's Marxian bias makes it impossible for him to have anything other than contempt and scorn for what he regards as the petty bourgeoise doctrines of the currency reformers.

Jonathan P. Grossman, *William Sylvis, Pioneer of American Labor: A Study of the Labor Movement During the Era of the Civil War* (New York, 1945), a biographical treatment of the most important labor leader of the sixties, has been extremely helpful both for its general interpretation of the labor movement and Sylvis' crucially significant role and also for its excellent bibliography. Other useful monographs in the field of labor history include Edith Abbott, *The Wages of Unskilled Labor in the United States, 1850-1900* (Chicago, 1905); Frank T. Stockton, *The International Molders Union of North America* (Baltimore, 1921); and Edward A. Wieck, *The American Miners' Association: A Record of the Origin of Coal Miners' Unions in the United States* (New York, 1940).

The question of farmer interest in the currency issue of the sixties has never been adequately treated, possibly because evidence of a group attitude on the subject is impossible to find. Solon J. Buck, *The Granger Movement: A Study of Agricultural Organization and Its Political, Economic and Social Manifestations, 1870-1880* (Cambridge, Mass., 1913) includes information on the economic position of the farmer during the sixties as well as a description of the founding of the Grange. Lee Benson, *Merchants, Farmers, and Railroads: Railroad Regulation and New York Politics, 1850-1887* (Cambridge, Mass., 1955) contains significant corroborative evidence on the prosperity of the farmers after the Civil War and the debilitating effect this had on the movement for cheap transportation. Henrietta M. Larson, *The Wheat Market and the Farmer in Minnesota, 1858-1900* (New York, 1926) notes the lack of interest on the part of the farmers in the currency question and asserts that until 1875 their basic tendency was toward hard-money.

In treating the political aspects of the financial history of the Civil War decade, the works by Dewey, Mitchell, Redlich, Hepburn, Helderman, and Davis listed above have been quite helpful. Two works which have been criticised in chapter VII above but which have nonetheless been of significance from the standpoint of politico-economic interpretation are Howard K. Beale, *The Critical Year: A Study of Andrew Johnson and Reconstruction* (New York, 1930) and Louis M. Hacker, *The Triumph of American Capitalism: The Development of Forces in American History to the End of the Nineteenth Century* (New York, 1940). Charles H. Coleman, *The Election of 1868: The Democratic Effort to Regain Control* (New York, 1933) has been of great use in assessing the effects of the money issue on the Grant-Seymour Contest. In my opinion, Mr. Coleman's book is an admirable work of scholarship. Chester McArthur Destler, *American Radicalism, 1865-1901: Essays and Documents* (New London, Conn., 1946) has been a source of inspiration since this study was first begun. Professor Destler's essays on Edward Kellogg and on the "Pendleton Plan" have been pioneer efforts, and his great understanding of the political and economic implications of Kelloggism and the "Ohio rag baby" have given me aid and comfort on numerous occasions. Professor Destler has also, to the knowledge of this author, been the only scholar who has seriously questioned the prevailing monolithic economic interpretation of Reconstruction.

A word must be said here about Joseph Dorfman, *The Economic Mind in American Civilization*, 3 vols. (New York, 1949). This work has been cited infrequently in this study mainly because the point of view and the purpose here are so completely different from that of Professor Dorfman. In many cases Professor Dorfman and the present writer have come more or less to the same conclusions independently. Though the debt to this great work has not been adequately demonstrated in the text of this study, it is nonetheless real.

Of the biographies and biographical studies cited a few stand out from the standpoint of general utility. Grossman's study of William Sylvis is obviously in this category. Ellis Paxson Oberholtzer, *Jay Cooke, Financier of the Civil War*, 2 vols. (Philadelphia, 1907), though almost completely uncritical where Cooke's actions are concerned, is very useful for its detailed account of Cooke's financial activities, his relationships with the incumbents of the Treasury, and for Cooke correspondence with various important public figures. Henrietta M. Larson, *Jay Cooke, Private Banker* (Cambridge, Mass., 1936) is more critical and also contains a wealth of useful information. Theodore Clarke Smith, *The Life and Letters of James Abram Garfield,*

2 vols. (New Haven, 1925) is very good on the financial aspects of Reconstruction, though like his protagonist, Smith takes the gold standard—free trade point of view. Other biographical works which have been cited include Robert Bruce Warden, *An Account of the Private Life and Public Services of Salmon Portland Chase* (Cincinnati, 1874); Jacob W. Schuckers, *The Life and Public Services of Salmon Portland Chase* (New York, 1874); Thomas Graham Belden and Marva Robins Belden, *So Fell the Angels* (Boston, 1956); Francis Fessenden, *Life and Public Services of William Pitt Fessenden*, 2 vols. (Boston, 1907); William Belmont Parker, *The Life and Public Services of Justin Smith Morrill* (Boston, 1924); Charles Richard Williams, *The Life of Rutherford Birchard Hayes*, 2 vols. (Boston, 1914); Robert Stewart Mitchell, *Horatio Seymour of New York* (Cambridge, Mass., 1938); Moorfield Storey, *Charles Sumner* (Boston, 1900); George H. Haynes, *Charles Sumner* (Philadelphia, 1909); Lloyd Paul Stryker, *Andrew Johnson, A Study in Courage* (New York, 1929); Robert W. Winston, *Andrew Johnson, Plebeian and Patriot* (New York, 1928); George Lowell Austin, *The Life and Times of Wendell Phillips* (Boston, 1901); Ralph Korngold, *Two Friends of Man, The Story of William Lloyd Garrison and Wendell Phillips and Their Relationship with Abraham Lincoln* (Boston, 1950); Abraham D. H. Kaplan, *Henry Charles Carey, A Study in American Economic Thought* (Baltimore, 1931); Edward C. Mack, *Peter Cooper, Citizen of New York* (New York, 1949); Allan Nevins, *Abram S. Hewitt with Some Account of Peter Cooper* (New York, 1935); Harold Francis Williamson, *Edward Atkinson: The Biography of an American Liberal, 1827-1905* (Boston, 1934); Reginald Charles McGrane, *William Allen: A Study in Western Democracy* (Columbus, Ohio, 1925); Allan Nevins, *Study in Power: John D. Rockefeller, Industrialist and Philanthropist*, 2 vols. (New York, 1953); and James C. Sylvis, *The Life, Speeches, Labors, and Essays of William H. Sylvis, Late President of the Iron-Molders' International Union; and Also of the National Labor Union* (Philadelphia, 1872).

INDEX

Adams, Henry, 15, 33, 261
Agricultural greenbackism; as concept in historiography, 85–86
Allen, William, 174, 197, 283; becomes greenbacker, 104–106
Alley, John B., 39 n., 41; supports contraction, 66, 73
Allison, William B., 71, 162
American Agriculturist, 136
American Emigrant Company, 180
American Industrial League, 159
American Iron & Steel Association, 158–159
Anthony, Henry B., 225
Anthony, Susan B., 195
Anti-Contraction Act of 1868, bill reported in House, 110; passed in House, 111; party and sectional characteristics of vote on in House and Senate, 111–114; conference committee appointed, 115; not signed by President Johnson; significance of, 117; deplored by Spaulding, 263–264
Ashley, James M., 111, 280 n., 309
Assignats, 15, 38
Associated Banks, support government in 1861, 21; strong condition of in December, 1861, 24; insist on receiving bonds, 24; success of loans to government, 23–24; oppose Legal Tender Bill, 31
Astor, William B., 275 n., 289; supports Andrew Johnson, 273
Atkinson, Edward, advises McCulloch, 119; economic ideas of, 162

Badeau, Adam, 289 n.
Balance of trade, 1865–1869, 152
Bankers, economic position of, 102, 238–241, 244–245, 267–271, 288–290, 296–300; support contraction, 241–265, 270, 288–290; unenlightened financial ideas of, 221; favor expanded bank-note circulation, 231–232; private bankers oppose contraction, 266–267 n., hostility of to Chase, 297–298; oppose National Banking System, 226–227, 298–299; and Beardian interpretation of Civil War and Reconstruction, 295–300
Bankers' Magazine, supports McCulloch and contraction, 64–65, 242–243; publishes articles by western bankers, 268–269
Bates, Edward, 30–31
Bayard, James A., 44 n.
Beale, Howard K., on House vote on Loan Act of 1866, 74–76; adopts Beardian thesis, 301–302; vulnerability of thesis, 303–306; on motives of Radicals, 302–305; on National Banking System, 305–306
Beard, Charles A., responsibility of for prevailing interpretation of Civil War and Reconstruction, 291; and "Second American Revolution" thesis, 291–301
Belmont, August, 274, 283; opposes Pendleton Plan, 101; attacked by labor movement, 216, 218
Bennett, James G., 176
Benson, Lee, on prosperity of farmers after Civil War, 137–138
Bingham, John A., 39 n., 77, 111
Blaine, James G., 111, 280, 307; on failure to levy taxes in 1861, 19; on Chase's *Report* of 1861, 26; supports contraction, 77; on results of contraction, 86; attacks Butler, 109; on Hugh McCulloch, 118; on election of 1868, 122; denounced by labor movement, 212, 214–215
Blair, Francis P., Jr., 197, 219, 283; becomes greenbacker, 106–107
Blake, Harrison G., 39 n.
Boston *Daily Evening Voice*, supports eight-hour movement; opposes formation of labor party, 200–201; supports Wade, 213–214; gold standard—free trade bias of, 201
Boston Eight-Hour League, 206

gold sales, 90; criticizes method of contraction, 91, 242; attitude toward contraction in 1868, 116; praises censure of Johnson, 124; on effects of paper money, 154; opposes issue of more bank-notes, 169–170, 247–248

Comptroller of the Currency, and the National Banking System, 227–228

Conkling, Roscoe, 39 n., 114, 131, 280, 304, 307, 308; opposes Legal Tender Bill, 42; supports contraction, 67, 77

Contraction of the currency, advocated by McCulloch, 63–64; supported by Johnson, 64; carried out by McCulloch in 1865, 67; House resolution of 1865, 66; debate on and passage of the Act of April 12, 1866, 66–80; supported by financial press, 64–65; supported by metropolitan bankers, 241–265, 270–271, 288–290; opposition to, 65, 77–78, 86, 92–97, 155–158, 214, 259–260, 266–267 n., 267-271, 285–286, 304–305; complexity as issue, 81; economic effects, 82; psychological effects, 91–92; abandoned in 1868, 107–115; reasons for abandonment, 117–120; as political issue from 1865–1869, 130–134; effects of on manufacturers, 145–153; effect on gold premium, 153; supported by New York Chamber of Commerce, 260–261; Beale's interpretation of, 302, 304–305

Cooke, Henry D, 245, 250; congratulates Sherman, 94; comments on Ohio election, 95

Cooke, Jay, 54, 271; resents assault by Logan, 108; and National Banking System, 245–246; monetary ideas of, 245–248; opposes contraction after 1867, 248

Cooper, James M., 286

Cooper, Peter, 282, 285; opposes contraction and free trade, 159–160; President of American Industrial League, 159; as old Jacksonian, 159 n.; on labor agitation, 167 n.; as greenbacker, 168; and labor movement, 287

Cotton, fall in price, 86

Covode, John, 111, 126, 279

Cowan, Edgar, 44 n., 49, 79

Crisfield, J. W., 39 n.

Cummings, Samuel P., 205

Currency reform, as issue in post-war labor movement, 174, 186–199, 219–220; and congruity of high protectionism, 208–210; opposed by New England labor leaders, 199–202, 206; advocated by some New England labor leaders after 1867, 202–205

Davis, Garrett, 79, 129

Davis, Henry Winter, 309

Dean, Henry Clay, 97–98

Demand notes, authorized by Congress, 20; and suspension of specie payments, 27–28; opposed by bankers, 28; brought within scope of Legal Tender Bill, 31; as alternative to greenbacks, 34–35; greenbacks substituted for, 46

Democratic Party, supports contraction in 1866, 74; opposes financial policy of Republicans, 93; and Ohio election, 94; reasons for failure in 1868, 101–104; East-West split on monetary policy, 104–107, 111, 128, 282–284; adopts Pendletonite platform in 1868, 121–122; importance of in struggle over contraction, 130–131; and labor movement, 215–219; political rationale on economic issues, 282–284; and "sound money," 301

Destler, Chester M., on Pendleton Plan, 97–99; and interpretation of Reconstruction history, 310–311

Dix, John A., 17–18, 296

Donnelly, Ignatius, 126, 279 n.

Doolittle, James, 44 n., 45

Draft riots of 1863, 177–178

Edmunds, George F., 114

Edwards, Thomas N., 39 n., 41

Eight-hour movement, importance in post-war labor movement, 185–186, 200

Election of 1868, analyzed, 101–104;